LSAT®

READING COMPREHENSION

by

David Lynch
& the Examkrackers Staff

ISBN 10: 1-893858-52-9
ISBN 13: 978-1-893858-52-7

1st Edition

To purchase additional copies of this book or any other in the Examkrackers LSAT 3-volume set,
call 1-888-572-2536 or fax orders to 1-859-255-0109.

examkrackers.com
osote.com
audioosmosis.com

Printed and bound in China

Acknowledgements

This book is dedicated to my wife, Sophie. You are my best friend and my inspiration, and none of this could have been possible without your unwavering support.

The efforts of many others also made this book possible. Thanks to Steven Horowitz, Chris Barrett, Brendan Burke, Jonathan Gaynor, and Jenny Lazar for their written contributions. Thanks to my editor, Cullen Thomas. Thanks to my parents and family for their support and editing contributions. Thanks to Chris Thomas for a skilled production job and thanks, of course, to Jonathan and Silvia Orsay for creating, building, and fostering the Examkrackers organization.

Contents

CHAPTER 6: THE "USING THE EVIDENCE" QUESTION FAMILY

LECTURE ④ CHAPTER 7: CONTROVERSY PASSAGES

CHAPTER 8: THE "BEYOND THE PASSAGE" QUESTION FAMILY

LECTURE 5 CHAPTER 9: COMPARATIVE READING PASSAGES

CHAPTER 10: THE COMPARATIVE READING QUESTION FAMILY

IN-CLASS EXAMINATIONS

EXPLANATIONS TO THE IN-CLASS EXAMINATIONS

INTRODUCTION

i.1 THE LSAT

If you're reading this book, you're probably getting ready to take the LSAT. Although taking the LSAT is probably less fun than getting a root canal, it's a necessary step in getting into law school.

The LSAT is a hard test. Even though people who take the LSAT are a very intelligent group, 99% of them answer at least **ten** questions incorrectly, and most people miss many more than that.

The good news is that the LSAT is also a very predictable test. Certain patterns of reasoning appear over and over. These patterns of reasoning often trick people the first time—or even the tenth time. But this book will give you everything you need to be able to spot, understand, and master these patterns. If you're willing to put in a lot of hard work and many hours of practice, you *can* raise your LSAT score substantially.

i.1.1 The Structure of the Test

The LSAT has six sections:

2 Logical Reasoning sections—These are often called the "Arguments" sections.

1 Analytical Reasoning section—This is often called the "Games" section.

1 Reading Comprehension section

1 Unscored section

1 Writing Sample section

You are given thirty-five minutes to complete each section, and (except for the Writing Sample) each one contains 22–28 questions. The Writing Sample is always the final section of the test, but the other five sections may appear in any order.

LSAC uses the unscored section to analyze the questions they plan to use in future versions of the LSAT. You get to pay for the privilege of being their guinea pig! The unscored section is always one of the first three sections of the test.

The unscored section may consist of Logical Reasoning, Analytical Reasoning, or Reading Comprehension. Thus, your test may contain a total of three Logical Reasoning sections, two Analytical Reasoning sections, or two Reading Comprehension sections. The person sitting next to you will have a different unscored section from yours, and will see a different order of sections.

Your performance on the unscored section does not count toward your score. However, there is **absolutely no way** to tell which section is the unscored section, so you must treat each one as if it does count toward your score. While standing in line to take the LSAT, I overheard a person saying that, the last time he had taken the test, he "figured out" which section was unscored—so he *skipped* that section. He put his head down and rested his brain. I'll leave it to you to figure out why he was standing in line to take the test again.

Like the unscored section, the Writing Sample does not count toward your score. However, your essay is scanned and sent to the schools to which you apply. Some schools read them, while others don't.

The entire test-taking experience will last at least four hours, and could take much longer if there are a lot of people in your testing center.

i.1.2 Scoring

The four scored sections will contain 100 or 101 questions, and the number you answer correctly is called your Raw Score. Using a conversion chart, the Raw Score is then converted into a Scaled Score, which can range from 120–180. This is the score that gets reported to law schools.

Never, ever leave a question blank on the LSAT. Even if you don't have time to finish a section, pick a Guess Letter and fill in that bubble for all the remaining questions.

The LSAT does not differentiate between wrong answers and questions left blank, so you should never leave a question blank. Even if you don't have time to read a question, you still have a 20% chance of getting the question right by guessing randomly.

Similarly, the LSAT does not differentiate between hard questions and easy questions. No question is worth more than any other, so spending five minutes on a difficult question is a bad use of your time if you could use that same five minutes to answer three or more easier questions.

Different LSATs vary slightly in difficulty, so the same Raw Score does not always result in the same Scaled Score. For example, answering 70 questions correctly may yield a Scaled Score of 159 on some tests but only a 157 on other tests. The scoring scale is adjusted to compensate for any variations in difficulty, so there is no advantage to be gained by taking the test at one time of the year as opposed to another.

The LSAT is designed to produce a range of scores in the shape of a bell curve—lots of people score in the middle, while few people score very high or very low. Nearly 70% of LSAT test-takers score between 140 and 160, but only about 4% of people score below 130 or above 170.

i.1.3 Test Administration

The LSAT is administered four times every year by the Law School Admission Council (LSAC). The four administrations usually occur in early February, early June, early October, and early December. Many law schools require that the LSAT be taken by December for admission the following fall. However, taking the test earlier—in June or October—is often advised.

The registration fee for the LSAT is currently $123. If you meet certain criteria, you may qualify for an LSAC fee waiver. Late registrants must pay an additional $62.

If you haven't already registered for the test, we suggest that you do so as soon as possible. If you wait, the most convenient test center for you may fill up, forcing you to take the LSAT in a less convenient location. In addition, most people find that having a firm deadline for perfecting their LSAT skills helps to focus their studying and improve their motivation.

Go to **www.lsac.org** to find details about testing dates and locations and to register.

i.1.4 LSDAS

Almost all ABA-approved law schools require that you register for the Law School Data Assembly Service (LSDAS). The LSDAS prepares a report for each law school to which you apply. The report contains information that is important in the law school admission process, including an undergraduate academic summary, copies of all undergraduate, graduate, and law/professional school transcripts, LSAT scores and writing sample copies, and copies of letters of recommendation processed by LSAC.

The registration fee for the LSDAS is currently $113. To register for the LSDAS and learn more, visit **www.lsac.org**.

> You need to register well ahead of time for the test. Regular registration ends about a month before the test; there are only a few days after that deadline during which you can register late, and late registration comes with an additional fee.

i.2 THE READING COMPREHENSION SECTION

The Reading Comprehension section of the LSAT consists of 26 to 28 multiple choice questions, which you have 35 minutes to complete. Each question will be associated with a passage or pair of passages totaling approximately 465 words, and the section will contain a total of four question sets.

The passages are presented in a rough order of difficulty, so they tend to be more difficult as the section progresses. Likewise, the questions pertaining to a particular passage tend to increase in difficulty. However, passages and questions of all difficulty levels are sprinkled throughout the section. So you should expect to see more challenging passages as you move through the section, but you should not be surprised by difficult passages early on or easy passages toward the end. Furthermore, you should not be surprised by questions of varying degrees of difficulty following a particular passage.

i.2.1 What It Tests

The Reading Comprehension section of the LSAT tests three skills:

1. Reading

The passages you will see on the Reading Comprehension section are dense, complex, and (some would say) boring. Nevertheless, you are expected to absorb them quickly with understanding and insight. Although any part of a passage could be the subject of a question, you should take special notice of certain important features of each passage, which this book will cover.

> The writers of the LSAT work according to the Convoluted Credo: "Never say in one simple word what you can express in many more complicated words."

2. Reasoning

Just as in the Logical Reasoning section, you will also be asked to apply new information to chains of reasoning in the passage, or determine how the information in the passage would apply to new contexts. You must use many of the same reasoning techniques in the Reading Comprehension section as you do in the Logical Reasoning section.

3. Time Management

To complete a Reading Comprehension section, you need to spend an average of 8 minutes, 45 seconds on each passage. That means you need to read the passage, analyze the passage, understand 5–8 questions, go back to the passage to find additional information, go through every answer choice, and bubble in your answers—all in less than nine minutes!

Of course, you shouldn't budget a specific amount of time per passage, as not all of them are equally difficult. The 8:45 figure is just to show you how tight the time constraints are if you answer every question. Not everyone can get through all four question sets in the section, but this book can show you how to score well even if you don't finish.

i.2.2 Importance to Your Score

The Reading Comprehension section contains 26–28 of the 100–101 questions on the test. Thus, your performance on this section determines a little more than a quarter of your score.

Unfortunately, it is sometimes treated like the "forgotten" section. Students often spend nearly all their time studying for the other sections of the test, thinking they already know how to read. This is a mistake. The Reading Comprehension section has about 4 more questions than the Analytical Reasoning section, and it can be a tremendous source of additional points for students. Don't assume that you already know how the section works. Taking the time to learn a solid strategy for this section can be well worth it.

i.3 PASSAGES

i.3.1 The Pieces of a Passage

When you open your test booklet to the Reading Comprehension section, this is what you'll see:

Test 22, Section 1, Questions 22–26

What it means to "explain" something in science often comes down to the application of mathematics. Some thinkers hold that mathematics is a kind of language—a systematic contrivance of signs, the
(5) criteria for the authority of which are internal coherence, elegance, and depth. The application of such a highly artificial system to the physical world, they claim, results in the creation of a kind of statement about the world. Accordingly, what matters in the
(10) sciences is finding a mathematical concept that attempts, as other language does, to accurately describe the functioning of some aspect of the world.

At the center of the issue of scientific knowledge can thus be found questions about the relationship
(15) between language and what it refers to. A discussion about the role played by language in the pursuit of knowledge has been going on among linguists for several decades. The debate centers around whether language corresponds in some essential way to objects
(20) and behaviors, making knowledge a solid and reliable commodity; or, on the other hand, whether the relationship between language and things is purely a matter of agreed upon conventions, making knowledge tenuous, relative, and inexact.
(25) Lately the latter theory has been gaining wider acceptance. According to linguists who support this theory, the way language is used varies depending upon changes in accepted practices and theories among those who work in a particular discipline. These
(30) linguists argue that, in the pursuit of knowledge, a statement is true only when there are no promising alternatives that might lead one to question it. Certainly this characterization would seem to be applicable to the sciences. In science, a mathematical statement may be
(35) taken to account for every aspect of a phenomenon it is applied to, but, some would argue, there is nothing inherent in mathematical language that guarantees such a correspondence. Under this view, acceptance of a mathematical statement by the scientific community—
(40) by virtue of the statement's predictive power or methodological efficiency—transforms what is basically an analogy or metaphor into an explanation of the physical process in question, to be held as true until another, more compelling analogy takes its place.
(45) In pursuing the implications of this theory, linguists have reached the point at which they must ask: If words or sentences do not correspond in an essential way to life or to our ideas about life, then just what are they capable of telling us about the world? In science
(50) and mathematics, then, it would seem equally necessary to ask: If models of electrolytes or $E = mc^2$, say, do not correspond essentially to the physical

world, then just what functions do they perform in the acquisition of scientific knowledge? But this question
(55) has yet to be significantly addressed in the sciences.

1. Which one of the following statements most accurately expresses the passage's main point?

(A) Although scientists must rely on both language and mathematics in their pursuit of scientific knowledge, each is an imperfect tool for perceiving and interpreting aspects of the physical world.

(B) The acquisition of scientific knowledge depends on an agreement among scientists to accept some mathematical statements as more precise than others while acknowledging that all mathematics is inexact.

(C) If science is truly to progress, scientists must temporarily abandon the pursuit of new knowledge in favor of a systematic analysis of how the knowledge they already possess came to be accepted as true.

(D) In order to better understand the acquisition of scientific knowledge, scientists must investigate mathematical statements' relationship to the world just as linguists study language's relationship to the world.

(E) Without the debates among linguists that preceded them, it is unlikely that scientists would ever have begun to explore the essential role played by mathematics in the acquisition of scientific knowledge.

PASSAGE

QUESTION STEM

ANSWER CHOICES

Take a look at each part of the section in detail:

1. The Passage

Each passage is approximately 440–490 words. Passages on the LSAT come from a variety of sources, including academic journals, scholarly books, and periodicals such as *The New York Times* or *Scientific American*. The LSAT writers take longer works and distill them down into dense passages with absolutely no fluff or wasted words.

The passages are completely self-contained. You are not expected to bring in any outside knowledge of the topic. All the information you need in order to answer every question will be contained within the passage.

You will probably see one passage on each of these areas: law, social science, arts & humanities, and natural science. Although you probably have a favorite and least favorite category to read about, the topic of the passage has absolutely nothing to do with how the passage is structured or how you should approach it in your analysis.

One of the four passages on every test is a Comparative Reading set. This feature presents you with two shorter works that add up to the same length as one full-length passage. The two smaller passages are written by different authors on the same or related topics and are followed by a set of questions that asks you to compare the two.

> Comparative Reading is a new feature on the LSAT as of June 2007. LSAC justifies it by saying, "Comparative reading questions reflect the nature of some important tasks in law school work, such as understanding arguments from multiple texts by applying skills of comparison, contrast, generalization, and synthesis to the texts."

2. The Question Stem

The question stem tells you what you must do with the information from the passage. There are a small number of common tasks that question stems can ask you to perform, and each one can have several variations. Question stems may ask you to

- Determine the major structural elements of the passage
- Retrieve specific information from the passage
- Evaluate and interpret evidence from the passage
- Manipulate a chain of reasoning found in the passage

This book discusses in detail each variation on these tasks, but it's important to recognize that the different tasks are largely rearrangements of the same basic set of skills. We will point out the similarities between question stems throughout this book.

3. The Answer Choices

Every Reading Comprehension question is followed by five answer choices, labeled (A) through (E). Your job is to find the *best* answer.

The *best* answer is not always *perfect*, so you shouldn't be too aggressive as you go through the answer choices. At the same time, the *best* answer is definitely *better* than all of the other choices, so if you think two answer choices are equally good, then you need to reread them carefully. The four wrong answers are always wrong for concrete reasons.

i.4 GENERAL STRATEGY

i.4.1 The Six-Step Approach

The Examkrackers approach allows you to solve every single Reading Comprehension question using the same six-step approach.

The first two steps are concerned with the passage:

Some test prep companies advise you to choose your approach to each passage based on its topic. This is nonsense. The LSAT writers will ask you questions about the logical structure, not the topic.

1. Identify the Passage

First, *identify the passage* type. There are five types of passages that appear on the LSAT. The passage type has nothing to do with the topic; rather, it describes the purpose and structure of the passage. There are several clues to look for that can tell you relatively early on what type of passage you are reading. Your analysis will depend on what type of passage you are dealing with.

2. Analyze the Passage

Second, *analyze* the passage. Depending on the passage type, this could mean finding the major structural elements summarizing the author's primary thesis, or determining the core question that the passage is designed to answer.

A strong initial analysis of the passage will increase your accuracy on *all* the questions and allow you to answer many questions without having to refer back to the passage since you will anticipate many of the commonly asked question types.

The next four steps should be repeated for each question associated with a passage. They are identical to the four steps you should use for each question in the Logical Reasoning section.

The two most important skills you must develop for the Reading Comprehension section are:
- Strong passage analysis
- Accurate identification of the question types, including knowing how to approach each

3. Identify

Next, *identify* the question type by reading the question stem. This way, you know precisely what your task is and what to look for in the passage.

4. Analyze

After that, *analyze* the passage further based on the question stem. You will have already done some analysis when you first read the passage, but you will sometimes need to return to the passage and look more carefully based on the task you are given in the question stem.

5. Prephrase

Then, *Prephrase* an answer to the question based on your analysis. Prephrasing means having your own answer in mind *before* attacking the answer choices. This way, you can avoid some of the LSAT's traps and find the correct answer quickly.

Prephrasing—taking a moment to figure out what the correct answer should say or do before you read the answer choices—is an important habit to develop in order to increase your score.

Not all questions lend themselves to precise Prephrased answers. Sometimes, Prephrasing means knowing what you don't want in an answer choice rather than having a particular answer in mind.

6. Attack

Finally, *attack* the answer choices. Be aggressive and look for reasons to eliminate answer choices rather than simply searching for the right answer.

As you consider each answer choice, you have two options:

1. **Keep it** if you think it might be right, if you are not sure about it, or if you don't understand it.

2. **Cut it** if you're sure it's wrong.

Never select an answer choice without reading all five options, and never eliminate a choice simply because you don't understand it.

i.4.2 Pacing

Time is tight on the LSAT, so you need to have a pacing plan. There are some general pacing principles that you should follow:

1. **Work as quickly as you can *without sacrificing accuracy.*** You have limited time, so you need to work quickly, but it makes no sense to blaze through the section carelessly. You should find a pace at which you can work quickly but comfortably enough to remain accurate. Understand that you may not finish the entire section.

2. **Work the passages that will give you the most points in the shortest time first.** While there is no simple formula for what makes a passage difficult, you will develop a sense of what makes a passage time-consuming. In general, if the language or subject matter is very complex, then the passage might take a long time. If a time-consuming passage is accompanied by only a few questions, *skip it* and return to it later if you have time. There's no reason to spend twelve minutes answering five questions when you could spend that same time answering eight questions.

3. **Work each passage as a unit.** Skipping around between different passages is a bad idea. Each time you change passages, you have to re-familiarize yourself with the content and how the passage works. This can be a significant waste of time. When you begin a passage, keep working on it until you have finished all the questions associated with that passage. Only if a question has you completely stumped should you guess and move on to the next passage. Return to it if you have extra time remaining after answering everything else.

Pick a Guess Letter and use it for any question you don't have time to answer.

i.5 HOW THIS BOOK IS STRUCTURED

i.5.1 Lectures

This book is divided into six lectures. The lectures are the fundamental units of the text—you should study the lectures, one at a time and in order. After you finish each lecture, you should complete the corresponding exam in the back of the book.

i.5.2 Chapters

Each lecture contains two chapters. The first discusses a certain *passage type* in detail. The second discusses a certain *question family* in detail.

Any question type can be associated with any passage type, so don't assume that a certain question type will show up only with the passage type presented in that particular lecture. However, we have constructed the lectures so that they contain passage and question types that fit well together as a discussion.

Every lecture has the same structure, which is organized around the six-step approach. In the first chapter, there are three sections:

1. Identify the Passage
Learn what clues to look for to identify the chapter's passage type.

2. Analyze the Passage
Next, learn how to break down the content of the passage and prepare yourself for success on the questions.

3. Putting It All Together
After learning about the first two steps in detail, you get to put the steps together in this section. This section includes a complete passage, just like you will see on your LSAT, and you will practice identifying and analyzing it. Each practice passage is accompanied by complete explanations. You will use your analysis of each passage as you go on to study the question family in the next chapter.

In the second chapter of every lecture, there are four sections to accompany each question type:

1. Identify
In this section, you learn how to spot the chapter's question type, and you see examples of how that type has appeared on past tests.

2. Analyze

Next, you see how to use your analysis of the passage and perform new analysis to successfully deal with information in the passage. The examples will be taken from the passage that you analyzed in the "Putting It All Together" section earlier in the same lecture.

3. Prephrase

Here, you learn how to Prephrase an answer for the question type. For some question types, there are techniques to come up with a specific Prephrased answer. For other question types, it isn't useful to come up with a specific Prephrased answer, so on these you should focus on the more general characteristics of the kind of answer you are looking for.

4. Attack

In the attack section, you learn about the common distracters, which are wrong answers that the LSAT writers use to distract you from choosing the correct one.

Again, the questions will be based on the passage that you analyzed earlier in the lecture.

Within each of these sections, there are short drills to test your understanding of the specific topics covered. These drills isolate each of the skills necessary for success on the lecture's passage and question types. By working through the drills and their explanations, you are better prepared to put the entire technique together.

i.5.3 Exams

Every lecture has a corresponding exam in the back of the book. Each exam is like a miniature LSAT. It covers the passage and question types discussed within the lecture, and it allows you to test your skills while being exposed to many different questions. Each exam is followed by full explanations.

i.5.4 Extra Practice Suggestions

You can find practice and homework regimens tailored specifically to a variety of schedules and intensity levels at www.examkrackers.com.

This book contains hundreds of sample problems, but truly serious students will want to get as much practice as they can, including taking full-length, timed exams. LSAC has published over 5,000 official questions from past tests, which we did not include in this book in order to keep it under $200! You can purchase as many of these past tests as you wish from **www.lsac.org**, and we provide a full list of extra practice drills and ideas for ways to use this official material.

i.5.5 The Use of Color

Colorblind students need not worry. You can still get one hundred percent of the useful information from this book without the colors.

This book uses color to help make important concepts stand out. Of course, we don't expect you to take the LSAT with a fist full of colored pencils. In fact, everything in this book would still be valid and complete if converted into black and white. However, accentuating important categories of logic with different colors helps you understand them, keep them straight in your mind, and train yourself to recall important elements as you work passages.

Here is a key for the different colors used:

Green: Things that are definitely true. For example, since you must accept the premises in a chain of reasoning as true, they are written in green when they are listed as part of discussion.

Blue: Things that might be true. For example, hypotheses, when they are listed as part of discussion, are written in blue.

Red: Things that are wrong or forbidden. The names of common distracters are written in red.

Orange: Used for the names of important techniques (Tools) and for the list of steps that comprise the Tool.

LECTURE 1 CHAPTER 1

THESIS PASSAGES

1.1 IDENTIFYING THESIS PASSAGES

The first type of passage you'll study is called the Thesis passage. Over one third of all Reading Comprehension passages are Thesis passages, so you are very likely to see at least one of them on your official LSAT.

All Thesis passages follow the same pattern:

- **The passage argues for a single conclusion.** Each Thesis passage is essentially a long *argument* for a single conclusion. There isn't a clash of various perspectives, and the purpose of the passage is not merely to provide information. A Thesis passage aims to argue for a conclusion, and the entirety of the passage exists to support that conclusion.

- **The conclusion appears in a one-sentence thesis statement.** All Thesis passages present their primary claim in a single sentence, and this **thesis statement** is the main point of the passage.

- **The thesis statement always appears in the first paragraph of the passage.** The thesis statement is not developed over the course of the passage. Instead, it is always presented in the first paragraph. It is usually the last sentence of the first paragraph, but it can appear anywhere in the first paragraph.

The first paragraph also sometimes contains a feature commonly seen in Main Point questions in the Logical Reasoning section—a **counterargument**. These are easy to recognize. In a counterargument, the author of the passage introduces a viewpoint but quickly contradicts that viewpoint or says it is mistaken. The author's thesis is the negation of the so-called "wrong" viewpoint. Thesis passages do not spend much time illustrating the details of the "wrong" viewpoint; it is offered simply as a contrast to the author's main conclusion.

Since the first paragraph of the Thesis passage is so distinctive, you should be able to tell if you are reading a Thesis passage by the end of the first paragraph.

Be sure to read the introduction before you get started with Lecture 1.

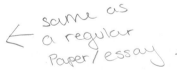
same as a regular paper/essay.

1.2   ANALYZING THESIS PASSAGES

To analyze a Thesis passage, look for:

1. **The main point**

2. **The purpose of each paragraph**

1.2.1.   The Main Point

You should always identify the main point of any passage, and you should mark it by placing it in brackets, just as you should do to the conclusion of a Logical Reasoning passage.

The main point of every Thesis passage appears in a **thesis statement**. Here are some tips that can help you find the thesis statement:

- The thesis statement always appears in the first paragraph. It is often, but not always, the final sentence of the first paragraph.

- The thesis statement sounds more like an opinion than a fact.

- The thesis statement tends to be one of the most specific statements in the first paragraph.

- The thesis statement is the negation of the so-called "wrong" viewpoint, if there is one.

In sum, what you're looking for is a single, specific statement that sounds like an opinion. Try to identify the thesis statement in the paragraph below, which is the first paragraph of a Thesis passage:

> Dependency theory holds that the wealthiest nations in the world depend for their prosperity on exploiting poorer countries. Most contemporary sociologists have abandoned or modified the theory because they believe that it does not hold up in light of globalization. However, this may reflect more on the sociologists than on the theory. For, despite its critics, dependency theory becomes an even more apt tool to describe modern economics as the world is increasingly affected by globalization.

This is a typical first paragraph of a Thesis passage. It starts very general, describing an issue, question, or problem. The second-to-last sentence implies that a certain viewpoint is "wrong," which sets up the thesis statement—the last sentence of the paragraph:

> [Dependency theory becomes an even more apt tool to describe modern economics as the world is increasingly affected by globalization.]

Note that this sentence is a single, specific statement, and it sounds like an opinion. This isn't a general description of what the theory *is*—it's a specific statement that makes a *judgment* about the theory. In addition, it is a counterargument against the sociologists who believe that dependency theory "does not hold up in light of globalization." This thesis statement is the main point of the passage. Since this is the main point, you should mark it with brackets. Compare the thesis statement to the first sentence:

> Dependency theory holds that the wealthiest nations in the world depend for their prosperity on exploiting poorer countries.

This is *not* a thesis statement. It is general and sounds more like a fact than an opinion. While this kind of sentence often appears in the first paragraph of a Thesis pas-

Be open to the possibility that the LSAT writers may play games with syntax—they could spread the thesis statement out over two consecutive sentences.

Being able to find (or express in your own words) the main point of *every* passage is the single most important skill you need in the Reading Comprehension section.

sage—usually as the first sentence—this kind of statement is *never* the main point of a Thesis passage.

1.2.2 Drill: The Main Point

Each of the following is the first paragraph of a Thesis passage. Mark the main point of each with brackets.

1.   The debate over the environmental crisis is not new; anxiety about industry's impact on the environment has existed for over a century. What is new is the extreme polarization of views. Mounting evidence of humanity's capacity to damage the environment irreversibly coupled with suspicions that government, industry, and even science might be impotent to prevent environmental destruction have provoked accusatory polemics on the part of environmentalists. In turn, these polemics have elicited a corresponding backlash from industry. The sad effect of this polarization is that it is now even more difficult for industry than it was a hundred years ago to respond appropriately to impact analyses that demand action.

Test 23, Section 4, Passage 3

2.   In spite of a shared language, Latin American poetry written in Spanish differs from Spanish poetry in many respects. The Spanish of Latin American poets is more open than that of Spanish poets, more exposed to outside influences—indigenous, English, French, and other languages. While some literary critics maintain that there is as much linguistic unity in Latin American poetry as there is in Spanish poetry, they base this claim on the fact that Castilian Spanish, the official and literary version of the Spanish language based largely on the dialect originally spoken in the Castile region of Spain, was transplanted to the Americas when it was already a relatively standardized idiom. Although such unity may have characterized the earliest Latin American poetry, after centuries in the Americas the language of Latin American poetry cannot help but reveal the influences of its unique cultural history.

Test 40, Section 4, Passage 2

Answers & Explanations

1. [The sad effect...that demand action.] The final sentence of the paragraph sounds like an opinion and is more specific than the rest of the paragraph.

2. [Although such unity...unique cultural history.] The clearest indicator that the last sentence in this paragraph is the main point is that it's a counterargument against those who believe "there is as much linguistic unity in Latin American poetry as there is in Spanish poetry."

1.2.3 THE PURPOSE OF EACH PARAGRAPH

By dividing passages into paragraphs, the writers of the test have provided you with a tremendously useful tool. If you determine the **purpose of each paragraph**, you will have collected just about all the information you need from a Thesis passage.

In a Thesis passage:

- **The purpose of the first paragraph is to assert the thesis.**

- **The purpose of each remaining paragraph is to support the thesis with a major premise.** Your job is to understand each major premise and how it works to strengthen the thesis.

Just as the passage as a whole has a main point, each individual paragraph has a main point—its major premise. The set of main points from all the paragraphs works as a collection of premises that support the thesis of the entire passage.

When you find the main point of a paragraph, you should place it in brackets, just as you do in the Logical Reasoning section.

Although understanding the examples and details in the paragraph is helpful, this is not your major concern. You do not need to process *every* piece of information for any Reading Comprehension passage on the LSAT. After all, your score comes from answering questions correctly, and if a specific piece of information does not help you answer a question, it isn't worth remembering.

Here are some tips that can help you find the main point of each paragraph:

1. **Pay attention to location.** The main point of most paragraphs is usually found in the first sentence. Sometimes, it's the second sentence, particularly when the sentence begins with a **turnaround word**. While the main point of a body paragraph can be located somewhere besides the first or second sentence, these are the first places you should expect to look.

2. **Find the most general statements in the paragraph.** Main points of body paragraphs tend to be expressed in very general terms.

3. **Look for statements that are either supported by evidence or elaborated upon.** If a statement is the main point of a paragraph, then it should have plenty of support or evidence.

> Turnaround words include *but, however, yet, although.*

There are two benefits to this approach. First, if you are only reading to determine the main point of each paragraph, then you can move more quickly through the passage. Second, any question that requires intricate knowledge of details will force you to revisit the evidence in the passage. This is a good thing. Test takers who don't refer back to the passage on such questions often get a false sense of security from relying on memory—and fall for trap answers.

Here's an example of a body paragraph. This comes from the Dependency Theory passage introduced on page 10.

> The nearly effortless transportation of money and goods permitted by globalization makes readily apparent the legislative framework found in many wealthy countries designed to protect their own multinational corporations' ability to exploit poorer countries. In 1960, the British government forced the government of the newly independent African nation of Nigeria to cede control of its major oil fields to a corporation jointly owned by British and Dutch interests. While the African nation found itself in the fortunate position of possessing tremendous natural resources, nearly all of the revenue generated by those assets flowed out of the country, leaving local residents destitute. When citizens of the area, hoping to regain control of the oil fields, moved to declare independence from Nigeria, the corporation lobbied the British government to prevent such a move, which initiated a series of events culminating in a destructive civil war.

There's a bunch of stuff in this paragraph that doesn't matter. You should only be concerned with one thing when reading this paragraph: what is the main point?

Since there is no quick turnaround after the first sentence of this paragraph, the first sentence is probably the main point. Furthermore, the first sentence is a general statement and is elaborated upon. So the main point of this paragraph is this: [The nearly effortless…exploit poorer countries.] Mark this with brackets.

> You have to strike a balance between reading so closely that you're memorizing (this clearly takes too long) and reading so quickly that you miss important ideas (this will not prepare you for success on the questions). This balance comes through practice.

You should not try to memorize all of the rest of the information in the paragraph. Just remember that it elaborates on the paragraph's main point, and come back to it if it's necessary to answer a question.

1.2.4 Drill: The Purpose of Each Paragraph

Each of the following is the second paragraph of a Thesis passage. Mark the main point of each paragraph with brackets.

1.　　Unlike today's adversaries, earlier ecological reformers shared with advocates of industrial growth a confidence in timely corrective action. George P. Marsh's pioneering conservation tract *Man and Nature* (1864) elicited wide acclaim without embittered denials. *Man and Nature* castigated Earth's despoilers for heedless greed, declaring that humanity "has brought the face of the Earth to a desolation almost as complete as that of the Moon." But no entrepreneur or industrialist sought to refute Marsh's accusation, to defend the gutting of forests or the slaughter of wildlife as economically essential, or to dismiss his ecological warnings as hysterical. To the contrary, they generally agreed with him.

Test 23, Section 4, Passage 3

2.　　The most distinctive note in Latin American poetry is its enthusiastic response to the modern world, while Spanish poetry displays a kind of cultural conservatism—the desire to return to an ideal culture of the distant past. Because no Spanish-language culture lies in the equally distant (i.e., pre-Columbian) past of the Americas, but has instead been invented by Latin Americans day by day, Latin American poetry has no such long-standing past to romanticize. Instead, Latin American poetry often displays a curiosity about the literature of other cultures, an interest in exploring poetic structures beyond those typical of Spanish poetry. For example, the first Spanish-language haiku—a Japanese poetic form—were written by José Juan Tablada, a Mexican. Another of the Latin American poets' responses to this absence is the search for a world before recorded history—not only that of Spain or the Americas, but in some cases of the planet; the Chilean poet Pablo Neruda's work, for example, is noteworthy for its development of an ahistorical mythology for the creation of the earth. For Latin American poets there is no such thing as the pristine cultural past affirmed in the poetry of Spain: there is only the fluid interaction of all world cultures, or else the extensive time before cultures began.

Test 40, Section 4, Passage 2

Answers & Explanations

1. [Unlike today's adversaries…corrective action.] The first sentence of this paragraph is the most general, and it is supported and elaborated upon by the rest of the paragraph.

2. [The most distinctive…the distant past.] Just as in question 1, the first sentence of this paragraph is among the most general, and it is supported and elaborated upon by the rest of the paragraph.

1.3 PUTTING IT ALL TOGETHER

1.3.1 Drill: Thesis Passages

Practice the Identify and Analyze steps on the following passage.

Leading questions—questions worded in such a way as to suggest a particular answer—can yield unreliable testimony either by design, as when a lawyer tries to trick a witness into affirming a particular
(5) version of the evidence of a case, or by accident, when a questioner unintentionally prejudices the witness's response. For this reason, a judge can disallow such questions in the courtroom interrogation of witnesses. But their exclusion from the courtroom by no means
(10) eliminates the remote effects of earlier leading questions on eyewitness testimony. Alarmingly, the beliefs about an event that a witness brings to the courtroom may often be adulterated by the effects of leading questions that were introduced intentionally or
(15) unintentionally by lawyers, police investigators, reporters, or others with whom the witness has already interacted.

Recent studies have confirmed the ability of leading questions to alter the details of our memories
(20) and have led to a better understanding of how this process occurs and, perhaps, of the conditions that make for greater risks that an eyewitness's memories have been tainted by leading questions. These studies suggest that not all details of our experiences become
(25) clearly or stably stored in memory—only those to which we give adequate attention. Moreover, experimental evidence indicates that if subtly introduced new data involving remembered events do not actively conflict with our stored memory data, we
(30) tend to process such new data similarly whether they correspond to details as we remember them, or to gaps in those details. In the former case, we often retain the new data as a reinforcement of the corresponding aspect of the memory, and in the latter case, we often
(35) retain them as a construction to fill the corresponding gap. An eyewitness who is asked, prior to courtroom testimony, "How fast was the car going when it passed the stop sign?" may respond to the query about speed without addressing the question of the stop sign. But
(40) the "stop sign" datum has now been introduced, and when later recalled, perhaps during courtroom testimony, it may be processed as belonging to the original memory even if the witness actually saw no stop sign.
(45) The farther removed from the event, the greater the chance of a vague or incomplete recollection and the greater the likelihood of newly suggested information blending with original memories. Since we can be more easily misled with respect to fainter and more
(50) uncertain memories, tangential details are more apt to become constructed out of subsequently introduced information than are more central details. But what is tangential to a witness's original experience of an event may nevertheless be crucial to the courtroom issues
(55) that the witness's memories are supposed to resolve.

For example, a perpetrator's shirt color or hairstyle might be tangential to one's shocked observance of an armed robbery, but later those factors might be crucial to establishing the identity of the perpetrator.

Test 40, Section 4, Passage 4

1. How can you identify what type of passage this is?

   _____

   _____

   _____

   _____

2a. What are the goals of your analysis of the passage?

   _____

   _____

   _____

   _____

2b. What are the results of your analysis of the passage?

   _____

   _____

   _____

   _____

Answers & Explanations

1. This passage contains all the features of a Thesis. It argues for a single conclusion, which is found in a one-sentence thesis statement in the first paragraph. The first paragraph also contains a counterargument. Therefore, this is a Thesis passage.

2a. Your goals in analyzing this Thesis passage are to identify the main point of the passage, then to identify the main point of each subsequent paragraph.

2b. This is the main point of the passage: [Alarmingly, the beliefs...has already interacted.]

You can identify this as the main point of the passage because it appears in the first paragraph, it sounds more like an opinion than a fact, it is one of the most specific statements in the first paragraph, and it is the negation of the viewpoint that their exclusion from the courtroom eliminates the effects of leading questions on eyewitness testimony.

Next, determine the purpose of each paragraph by identifying its main point. The main point of the second paragraph is this: [Recent studies...tainted by leading questions.]

You can identify this as the main point of the second paragraph because it appears as the first sentence of the paragraph, it is more general than most other sentences in the paragraph, and it is elaborated upon in the rest of the paragraph. Furthermore, it acts to support the thesis of the passage. The main thesis says that a witness's version of an event may be tainted by leading questions asked before the witness appears in a courtroom; this sentence says that leading questions has proven can alter our memories.

The main point of the third paragraph is this: [...tangential details are more apt...crucial to the courtroom...]

This is slightly trickier, since the main point is spread over a few sentences, but you can tell this is the main point of the third paragraph because it is more general than what follows and is supported by an example. Furthermore, it acts to support the thesis of the passage. The main thesis says that the effects of leading questions are alarming; this sentence says that the memories most likely to be constructed as a result of leading questions may also be the most crucial in the courtroom. Alarming indeed!

NOW MOVE ON TO THE SECOND CHAPTER OF LECTURE 1. WHEN YOU HAVE COMPLETED IT, YOU CAN GET FURTHER PRACTICE WITH THESIS PASSAGES IN THE CORRESPONDING EXAM AT THE END OF THE BOOK.

LECTURE ①　CHAPTER ②

THE STRUCTURAL QUESTION FAMILY

always look for the main point!

Structural questions ask you to understand the big picture of a passage. They ask you to understand the overall point of the passage and how each part of the passage functions to make it work as a whole. For Thesis and all other types of passages, you should be able to answer Structural questions simply by using the work you have done in your Analysis of the passage.

There are three basic types of Structural questions:

1. Main Point

2. Purpose

3. Organization

2.1 MAIN POINT QUESTIONS

Main Point questions ask you to choose the best expression of the passage's main point. As you read any passage, you will always identify the main point as part of your analysis. The only thing about Main Point questions that may present difficulty is the fact that the correct answer choice will be a *rewording* of the main point as it was stated in the passage. You must look for something that says the same thing in different words.

2.1.1 IDENTIFY

Main Point questions are easy to identify. Here are some keys to identifying them:

1. **Main Point questions are almost always the first question for each passage**, if they appear.

2. **Main Point questions always include the words** *main point* **or** *main idea*.

3. **Main Point questions always ask for the answer that** *most accurately* **states or expresses the Main Point.**

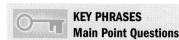

KEY PHRASES
Main Point Questions

Main point
Main idea
Central idea

Most accurately states
Most accurately expresses
Best summarizes

Here are some sample Main Point question stems:

> Which one of the following most accurately expresses the main point of the passage?

> Which one of the following most accurately states the main idea of the passage?

> Which one of the following best summarizes the central idea of the passage?

All of these ask you for the main point of the passage, and since they ask you for the answer that *most accurately* expresses the main point, they are really asking you for the best rewording of the main point.

2.1.2 ANALYZE

Because you always mark the main point of a passage during your initial analysis of it, there is very little you need to do for the analysis step on Main Point questions.

All you really need to do is remind yourself of the main point of the passage. For example, suppose you were asked for the main point of the Leading Questions passage in chapter 1. Here's the question:

> 1. Which one of the following most accurately states the main point of the passage?
>
> Test 40, Section 4, Question 20

When you initially read the passage, you marked the last sentence of the first paragraph as the main point: [Alarmingly, the beliefs…has already interacted.]

That's all you need to do to analyze Main Point questions. Revisit and reread the main point that you marked when you read the passage.

2.1.3 PREPHRASE

For other types of passages, you may have to express the main point in your own words. In such a case, revisit your notes instead of the bracketed sentence.

Prephrasing on a Main Point question requires nothing more than stating the conclusion. Fortunately, the conclusion is already stated for you in the passage, so you don't have to do anything for this step. Don't bother trying to reword, simplify, or paraphrase the main point; the correct answer choice will do that for you. However, make sure you have determined the passage's main point *before* you start looking at the answer choices.

2.1.4 ATTACK

Before you attack the answer choices, you should be aware of the most common distracters for Main Point questions:

Incomplete
Sometimes, an answer choice consists of ideas that were only a small part of the passage, such as a particular sentence or the main point of one of the paragraphs. Don't pick an answer choice that leaves out any major topic that was discussed in detail.

Out of Scope
If an answer choice mentions new information that never appeared in the passage, it can't be correct.

Extreme
Extreme answers use much stronger language than is warranted by the passage. For example, if the passage calls something an effective method, don't pick an answer choice that calls it the best method.

Opposite
Some answer choices say the *opposite* of the main point from the passage. This is one more reason to carefully read the answer choices.

It's time to attack the answer choices for this example. Look at each one and decide whether it matches what you determined to be the main point.

    (A)   The unreliability of memories about incidental aspects of observed events makes eyewitness testimony especially questionable in cases in which the witness was not directly involved.

Choice (A): This answer choice starts out looking good, but then it mentions "cases in which the witness was not directly involved." This idea never appeared in the passage, so the answer choice is **out of scope**. *Cut it.*

    (B)   Because of the nature of human memory storage and retrieval, the courtroom testimony of eyewitnesses may contain crucial inaccuracies due to leading questions asked prior to the courtroom appearance.

Choice (B): This answer choice contains almost exactly the same information as the thesis statement on lines 11–17. The only additional idea is the mention of "the nature of human memory storage and retrieval," but the passage discusses this topic in detail in the second and third paragraphs. *Keep it.*

    (C)   Researchers are surprised to find that courtroom testimony is often dependent on suggestion to fill gaps left by insufficient attention to detail at the time that the incident in question occurred.

Choice (C): The passage never mentions researchers being surprised to find anything, so that's **out of scope**. You are also told in lines 7–8 that a judge can prevent suggestive questions from being asked in the courtroom, so testimony is certainly not "dependent on suggestion." *Cut it.*

    (D)   Although judges can disallow leading questions from the courtroom, it is virtually impossible to prevent them from being used elsewhere, to the detriment of many cases.

Choice (D): This choice does contain a few details that were mentioned in the passage, but it fails to refer to the lengthy discussion of how leading questions work, so it's **incomplete**. It also contains an **extreme** claim: the passage said that leading questions are often introduced, but it never says they are "virtually impossible to prevent." *Cut it.*

    (E)   Stricter regulation should be placed on lawyers whose leading questions can corrupt witnesses' testimony by introducing inaccurate data prior to the witnesses' appearance in the courtroom.

Choice (E): For the most part, this choice looks good, but it has one fault. Although the author clearly thinks leading questions are a problem, the passage stops short of ever calling for stricter regulation. That idea is **out of scope**. *Cut it.*

Choice (B) is the correct answer.

2.1.5 VARIATION: TITLE QUESTIONS

There is an uncommon variation of Main Point questions called Title questions. These questions ask you for an appropriate title for the passage. A good title summarizes the contents of the passage, so you are, in essence, looking for an answer choice that contains the main point. Your approach to Title questions is identical in every way to your approach to Main Point questions, and you should eliminate precisely the same distracter answer choices. Even though they look a little different, you should consider Title questions to be exactly the same as Main Point questions.

Here's the sentence you bracketed as the main point:

["Alarmingly, the beliefs about an event that a witness brings to the courtroom may often be adulterated by the effects of leading questions that were introduced intentionally or unintentionally by lawyers, police investigators, reporters, or others with whom the witness has already interacted."]

Cut an answer choice when you are fairly certain that it is wrong. Keep an answer choice when you think it could be right, when you are not sure about it, or when you don't understand it.

2.2 PURPOSE QUESTIONS

Purpose questions ask you to describe the function of

1. A word or phrase,

2. An entire paragraph, or

3. The passage itself.

Although Purpose question stems never use the word "why," the best way to think about these questions is to consider them to be asking you *why* a certain word was used, *why* a certain paragraph was included, or *why* the passage was written.

2.2.1 PURPOSE OF A PHRASE

2.2.1.1 Identify

Here are some keys to identifying Purpose of a Phrase questions:

1. The question stem always directs your attention to a particular word, phrase, or sentence. It often does this by telling you the specific lines in which the phrase can be found.

2. The question stem usually uses the term *primary purpose, primary function,* or *primarily in order to.*

3. The question stem does *not* ask you what a word <u>means</u> or what the author is <u>referring to</u>. Instead, it asks you to determine *why* the phrase was used.

Here are some sample Purpose of a Phrase question stems:

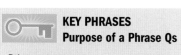

> Which one of the following most accurately expresses the primary purpose of the sentence in lines 27–30?

> The author mentions the relative difficulty of interpreting ice core samples primarily in order to

> The primary function of the reference to outdated schools of economic thought (lines 34–41) is to

All of these ask you to determine the reason a phrase was used in the passage. Note that Purpose of a Phrase questions are very similar to Role questions in the Logical Reasoning section. One recent official LSAT asked a Purpose of a Phrase question using a question stem that was identical to a Role question stem.

KEY PHRASES
Purpose of a Phrase Qs

Primary purpose
Primarily in order to
Primary function

Discusses
Mentions
References

Questions that ask you what a word means are Definition questions, which will be covered in chapter 4.

2.2.1.2 Drill: Identifying Purpose of a Phrase Question Stems

Determine whether each of the following is a Purpose of a Phrase question stem.

1. As it is used in the passage, "understudy" (line 19) refers most specifically to

   Purpose of a Phrase question? ☐ Yes ☑ No

2. Based on the passage, the term "irrevocable privilege" (line 35) most clearly refers to which one of the following?

   Purpose of a Phrase question? ☐ Yes ☑ No

3. The author refers to "some birds' navigational abilities" (lines 47–49) most probably in order to

   Purpose of a Phrase question? ☑ Yes ☐ No

4. The author most likely lists some of the everyday objects used as decorative pieces of art (lines 12–17) primarily to

   Purpose of a Phrase question? ☑ Yes ☐ No

5. Which one of the following most accurately describes the author's purpose in referring to the scientific method as being "willfully blind" (line 5) in some cases?

   Purpose of a Phrase question? ☑ Yes ☐ No

6. That some economists "never receive disproportional encouragement" (lines 27–33) most likely means that these economists

   Purpose of a Phrase question? ☐ Yes ☑ No

7. The phrase "uncommon perspective" (line 43) is used in the passage to refer to which one of the following?

   Purpose of a Phrase question? ☐ Yes ☑ No

8. The discussion of Echternach's compositions is intended primarily to

   Purpose of a Phrase question? ☑ Yes ☐ No

Answers & Explanations

1. **No.** The stem asks what the word refers to—a way of asking what it means.
2. **No.** The stem asks what the term refers to—a way of asking what it means.
3. **Yes.** The stem asks *why* the author refers to the birds' abilities.
4. **Yes.** The stem asks *why* the author lists the objects.
5. **Yes.** The stem asks for the author's purpose in using that phrase.
6. **No.** The stem asks you to provide the meaning of the phrase.
7. **No.** The stem asks what the phrase refers to—a way of asking what it means.
8. **Yes.** The stem asks what the discussion is intended to do, which is its purpose.

2.2.1.3 Analyze

Your analysis for Purpose of a Phrase questions requires a few steps:

1. Find the phrase in question in the passage.

2. Read the surrounding area to get the context.

3. Determine why the phrase was used or what role it plays.

Take a look at the following question, which also comes from the Leading Questions passage on page 14:

> 2. Which one of the following most accurately describes the author's main purpose in lines 36–44 of the passage?

This question asks about the author's purpose in writing certain lines, so it's a Purpose of a Phrase question.

The first step is to find the phrase in question in the passage. This is easy when there are line numbers, as in this case. Otherwise, you'd have to scan for the phrase or rely on your memory to find it.

Lines 32-48:

...details. In the former case, we often retain the new data as a reinforcement of the corresponding aspect of the memory, and in the latter case, we often retain them as a construction to fill the corresponding gap. An eyewitness who is asked, prior to courtroom testimony, "How fast was the car going when it passed the stop sign?" may respond to the query about speed without addressing the question of the stop sign. But the "stop sign" datum has now been introduced, and when later recalled, perhaps during courtroom testimony, it may be processed as belonging to the original memory even if the witness actually saw no stop sign.

The farther removed from the event, the greater the chance of a vague or incomplete recollection and the greater the likelihood of newly suggested information blending with original memories. Since we can be more...

Next, read the surrounding area to get the context. These lines come right after a discussion about how we process new data in two different cases, and right before a discussion about tangential details being important in the courtroom.

Finally, determine the role of the lines. They don't really fit so well into the discussion in the third paragraph, but they do relate to the preceding discussion—they refer to a case in which new data fill in a gap in memory.

2.2.1.4 Prephrase

On Purpose of a Phrase questions, you should **always** come up with an answer in your own words as to *why* the author used the phrase in question. Don't read the answer choices until you have done this.

Due to the nature of the question stems for Purpose of a Phrase questions, most answer choices will describe some sort of action. For example

- to prove that…
- to illustrate that…
- to criticize the fact that…
- to argue that…
- to underscore the fact that…
- to praise…

Because this is what the answer choices will look like, your Prephrased answer should also be centered around an action.

On this particular question, a good Prephrased answer looks something like this:

> Purpose: Lines 36–44 give an example of one of the two ways that new data can be processed in memory. In this case, the new "stop sign" datum did not exist in the witness's memory, so it functioned to fill in a gap in the witness's recollection.

2.2.1.5 Attack

Before you attack the answer choices, familiarize yourself with the most common distracters for Purpose of a Phrase questions.

Wrong Action

For example, if the purpose of a phrase was to raise a question, don't pick an answer choice that says "to prove…"

Wrong Part of the Passage

The phrase you are asked about fits into a certain place in the passage, but some answer choices refer to a completely unrelated part of the passage.

Contradicts the Passage

If an answer choice contradicts any information from the passage, it can't be correct.

Now go ahead and attack these answer choices.

> (A)   to suggest a way in which investigators may aid a witness in recalling certain details of an event when the witness has a vague or incomplete memory of the experience

Choice (A): This answer choice describes the **wrong action**. The author was *giving an example* in lines 36–44, not *suggesting* anything. And the author certainly does not approve of leading questions, which is what this example is all about. *Cut it.*

>   (B)   to show an example of a case in which new
>   data are integrated with current memories
>   as reinforcement of a witness's preexisting
>   recollection of an incident

Choice (B): This choice starts off well, but it has a problem. In the example, the "stop sign" was *not* part of the witness's preexisting recollection; the passage says that the witness "actually saw no stop sign." This choice **contradicts the passage.** *Cut it.*

>   (C)   to explain the mechanism by which new data are
>   processed by the human mind when those facts
>   actively conflict with memories a person already
>   has

Choice (C): The passage only talks about what happens when new data "do not actively conflict with stored memory data," but this answer choice talks about a situation in which there *is* a conflict. *Cut it.*

>   (D)   to provide an illustration of a situation in which
>   a novel component of a leading question may
>   be later recalled as belonging to the original
>   memory of an event

Choice (D) looks a lot like the Prephrased answer. Even though it uses different words, "provide an illustration" means the same thing as "give an example," and it talks about a new piece of information filling a gap in a person's memory. *Keep it.*

>   (E)   to argue that the reliance on details that a
>   witness may have considered tangential during
>   an experience plays too critical a role in the
>   courtroom, given the possibility of inaccuracy

Choice (E) starts out with the **wrong action**—the author is not arguing for anything here—and finishes off with a topic from the third paragraph, which is the **wrong part of the passage.** *Cut it.*

Choice (D) is the correct answer.

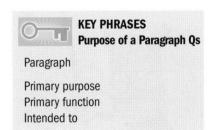

Just focusing on the action verb that begins most choices can do a lot of good and help you eliminate wrong answers quickly.

2.2.2 PURPOSE OF A PARAGRAPH

2.2.2.1 Identify

Identifying Purpose of a Paragraph questions is not hard. Here are some of their features:

1. The question stem always asks about a particular paragraph.

2. The question stem usually uses the term *primary purpose* or *primary function.*

Here are some sample Purpose of a Paragraph question stems:

>   The primary purpose of the second paragraph is to
>
>   The primary function of the third paragraph of the passage is to
>
>   The discussion in the second paragraph is intended primarily to
>
>   Which one of the following statements most accurately describes the function of the final paragraph?

KEY PHRASES
Purpose of a Paragraph Qs

Paragraph

Primary purpose
Primary function
Intended to

These question stems are quite similar to Purpose of a Phrase question stems, except that they refer to a larger chunk of text. They all ask the reason a certain paragraph was used in the passage. Your approach will also be very similar.

2.2.2.2 Analyze

Your analysis for Purpose of a Paragraph questions is actually done as you read the passage for the first time. For every passage that you encounter, you will always determine the purpose of each paragraph by deciding what role it plays in the passage as a whole. You just learned that in Thesis passages, the purpose of the first paragraph is to assert the thesis, and the purpose of each remaining paragraph is to support the thesis with a major premise. In other types of passages, paragraphs may have different functions, but you should develop the habit of always determining the purpose of each paragraph the first time you read the passage.

Take a look at the following question, which refers to the Leading Questions passage.

> 3. The second paragraph consists primarily of material that
>
> Test 40, Section 4, Question 25

In other types of passages, paragraphs can have other purposes, such as conveying historical information, answering a question, or countering an argument.

This question stem is slightly odd, but it does ask about a particular paragraph and the role played by the material in it, so it's a Purpose of a Paragraph question.

In your initial reading of the passage, you found that this paragraph acts to support the thesis of the passage—specifically, it explores how leading questions can alter memories.

2.2.2.3 Prephrase

On Purpose of a Paragraph questions, you should **always** come up with an answer in your own words as to *why* the author included the paragraph in question. Don't read the answer choices until you have done this.

Just like other Purpose questions, most Purpose of a Paragraph answer choices will describe some sort of action. Thus, your Prephrased answer should also be centered around an action. Your answer should also include an indication of how the particular paragraph relates to the other paragraphs and the main idea of the passage.

For this particular question, a good Prephrased answer looks something like this:

> Purpose: The second paragraph explores how leading questions can alter memories, a discussion that supports the main thesis from the first paragraph, which says that a witness's version of an event may be tainted by leading questions asked before the witness arrived in the courtroom.

2.2.2.4 Attack

Before you attack the answer choices, familiarize yourself with the most common distracters for Purpose of a Paragraph questions.

Wrong Action
Just like on Purpose of a Phrase questions, don't pick an answer choice that describes an action different from the one performed by the paragraph in question.

Incomplete
Just like on Main Point questions, don't pick an answer choice that leaves out a major part of the paragraph.

Wrong Part of the Passage
Some incorrect answer choices try to trick you by accurately describing the purpose of a different paragraph.

Contradicts the Passage
If an answer choice contradicts any information from the passage, it can't be correct.

Attack these answer choices.

> (A) corroborates and adds detail to a claim made in
> the first paragraph

Choice (A): This answer uses very general language—it doesn't mention leading questions at all. However, the Prephrased answer did say that the second paragraph supports the main thesis, which does happen to be "a claim made in the first paragraph." *Keep it.*

> (B) provides examples illustrating the applications of
> a theory discussed in the first paragraph

Choice (B): This answer is not bad either. Hold on to this one as well. *Keep it.*

> (C) forms an argument in support of a proposal that is
> made in the final paragraph

Choice (C): This answer choice goes way off track. The second paragraph doesn't "form an argument" (that's the **wrong action**), and there is no proposal in the third paragraph. That **contradicts the passage**. *Cut it.*

> (D) anticipates and provides grounds for the rejection
> of a theory alluded to by the author in the final
> paragraph

Choice (D) is also pretty far off the mark. There is no "rejection of a theory" anywhere in the passage. *Cut it.*

> (E) explains how newly obtained data favor one of
> two traditional theories mentioned elsewhere in
> the second paragraph

Choice (E): There is a theory in the second paragraph that addresses two different cases, but it's only one theory, not two, and there is no favoritism of one case over the other. *Cut it.*

At this point, you have narrowed your attack to two answer choices. How can you decide between the two? If you are stuck between two answer choices, it often helps to revisit the question stem. In this case, you are trying to decide what the second paragraph "primarily consists of." Choice (B) says that it consists of "examples." But there is only one example in the paragraph, and it fills only 8 lines out of 27. Choice (B) has other problems, too: the example does not show the "applications" of a theory, and it illustrates the research that was mentioned in the second paragraph, not the first. *Cut it.*

> When you are down to two answer choices, try to isolate differences between them, and then see which one matches the passage better. Every wrong answer is wrong for a concrete reason.

Choice (A) is the correct answer.

2.2.3 PURPOSE OF A PASSAGE

2.2.3.1 Identify

You can easily spot Purpose of a Passage questions. They are characterized by these features:

1. The question stem always asks about the passage as a whole.

2. The question stem uses the term *primary purpose* or asks what the author is *primarily concerned* with.

Here are some sample Purpose of a Passage question stems:

> The author's primary purpose in writing the passage
> is to
>
> Which one of the following best describes the
> primary purpose of the passage?
>
> The passage is primarily concerned with

These question stems are similar to other Purpose question stems, and your approach will also be very similar.

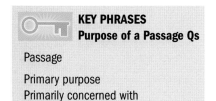

Passage

Primary purpose
Primarily concerned with

2.2.3.2 Analyze

Your analysis for Purpose of a Paragraph questions is also done as you read the passage for the first time. As you Identify and Analyze each passage, you will be doing all the work necessary to determine the purpose of the passage. You just learned in chapter 1 that the purpose of Thesis passages is to argue for a single conclusion. Common purposes of other types of passages include:

- to argue that a particular viewpoint is incorrect

- to describe a scientific or historical phenomenon

- to suggest a revision to the traditional understanding of something

- to show that one theory is better than another

- to examine the details of a problem

Take a look at the following question, which again refers to the Leading Questions passage.

4. The author's primary purpose in the passage is to

This question stem is concerned with the entire passage, and it asks about the author's primary purpose. Thus, it's a Purpose of a Passage question.

In your initial reading of the passage, you found that it is structured to argue in favor of the thesis statement found at the end of the first paragraph.

2.2.3.3 Prephrase

On Purpose of a Passage questions, you should **always** come up with an answer in your own words as to *why* the author wrote the passage. Don't read the answer choices until you have done this.

While Main Point questions and Purpose of a Passage questions are closely related, there are some important differences. First, Main Point questions are always specifically about the topic of the passage—they don't use general language. Purpose of a Passage questions, on the other hand, will use more general language, and may not even mention the specific topic at hand.

Second, Main Point answer choices are complete ideas, while Purpose of a Passage answer choices, like those of other Purpose questions, revolve around an action. Thus, your Prephrased answer should also be centered around an action. Compare these two answer choices:

Typical Answer Choice for a Main Point Question	Typical Answer Choice for a Purpose of a Passage Question
The actions of the Trankarnian government gave rise to a pair of conflicting movements in the popular sculpture of that country, neither of which was completely independent of the principles against which it attempted to revolt.	to discuss the roots and ramifications of two competing schools of artistic thought

For this particular question, a good Prephrased answer looks something like this:

Purpose: The passage argues in support of the thesis statement at the end of the first paragraph, which, in general terms, shows that there is a problem in the courtroom that is not completely solved by measures that judges can take.

2.2.3.4 Attack

The most common distracters for Purpose of a Passage questions should be familiar by now.

Wrong Action

Just like on other Purpose questions, don't pick an answer choice that describes an action different from the one performed by the passage.

Incomplete

Just like on Main Point questions, don't pick an answer choice that leaves out a major part of the passage.

Out of Scope

If an answer choice mentions new information that never appeared in the passage, it can't be correct.

Contradicts the Passage

If an answer choice contradicts any information from the passage, get rid of it.

Attack these answer choices.

> (A)   propose a solution to a problem inherent in the methods used by police interrogators

Choice (A): The passage spends a lot of time talking about the problem, but it never proposes a solution. This answer choice describes the **wrong action**. *Cut it.*

> Again, focusing on the first action verb in each choice can be very helpful.

> (B)   argue that eyewitnesses known to have been asked leading questions should not be allowed to testify in the courtroom

Choice (B): The idea that witnesses should be banned from the courtroom never appeared in the passage, so this answer choice is **out of scope**. *Cut it.*

> (C)   condemn judges who allow the testimony of eyewitnesses to be corrupted by leading questions

Choice (C): The author thinks leading questions are a problem, but never goes so far as to condemn judges. This is the **wrong action**. *Cut it.*

> (D)   summarize the results of recent research into how the human mind stores new data

Choice (D): Although the second paragraph does talk about this particular research, there is a lot more contained in the passage. This answer choice is **incomplete** because it does not mention anything about the courtroom. *Cut it.*

> (E)   illustrate how the prohibition of leading questions from the courtroom fails to eliminate their problematic effect on eyewitness testimony

Choice (E): This looks like the Prephrased answer. The author talks about the "effect" of leading questions and their "prohibition from the courtroom" in the first paragraph, he "illustrates" how they work in the second paragraph, and he discusses why they are "problematic" in the third paragraph. *Keep it.*

Choice (E) is the correct answer.

2.3   ORGANIZATION QUESTIONS

Organization questions are the final type of Structural questions. They simply ask you to describe the organization of the passage or a part of the passage.

2.3.1 IDENTIFY

Organization questions all share very similar question stems. They have one main characteristic:

1. The question stem always asks about the *organization* or the *presentation* of the material in the passage or a part of the passage.

Here are some sample Organization question stems:

> Which one of the following most accurately describes the organization of the passage?
>
> Which one of the following sequences most accurately and completely corresponds to the presentation of the material in the passage?
>
> Which one of the following most accurately describes the organization of the material presented in the first and second paragraphs of the passage?

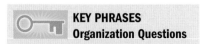

KEY PHRASES
Organization Questions

Describes the organization
Corresponds to the presentation of the material

2.3.2 ANALYZE

As with most other Structural questions, you should be well prepared to answer Organization questions after your initial analysis of the passage.

The answer choices to Organization questions are presented as lists, and the number of items on the lists usually corresponds to the number of paragraphs in the passage. Occasionally, if a paragraph serves two major purposes, it will correspond to two items on the list. Otherwise, each item on the list describes the purpose of one of the paragraphs.

Therefore, since you read each paragraph of every passage with the goal of determining its purpose, you will have done all the analysis you need before you encounter an Organization question.

Take a look at the following question, which is the last one pertaining to the Leading Questions passage.

> 5. Which one of the following most accurately describes the organization of the passage?

This the classic question stem of an Organization question.

In your initial reading of this example passage, you found the first paragraph introduced the author's thesis, the second paragraph discussed scientific research that supports the thesis, and the third paragraph showed why leading questions are a problem in the courtroom.

2.3.3 PREPHRASE

On Organization questions, you should **always** come up with an answer in your own words before you read the answer choices.

The method you use to come up with a Prephrased answer is the same one you use on Purpose of a Paragraph questions. The only difference is that you should articulate the purpose of *each* paragraph. Your Prephrased answer should be a list of actions and should include an indication of how each particular paragraph relates to the others.

2.3.4 ATTACK

Here are the most common distracters that you will see on Organization questions:

Out of Order

The different parts of the passage have to appear in the correct order in the answer choice. If something is mixed up, eliminate the answer choice.

The answer is...

(A) description of a problem in developmental psychology in relation to a historical source of the problem; a second example of such occurrence of the problem

(B) description of a problem; explanation of two theories about the problem; detailed delineation of one of those theories; call for an innovative solution to the problem

(C) description of a problem; presentation of scientific research related to the problem; illustration of that research with an example; mention of the implications of the problem

(D) description of a problem; demonstration of that problem by an example; discussion of the implications of the problem; reference to recent studies of the problem

(E) description of a problem; presentation of one understanding of the nature of the problem; refutation of that understanding; proposal of a different perception of the problem

Contradicts the Passage

If an answer choice contradicts any information from the passage, get rid of it.

Out of Scope

If an answer choice mentions new information that never appeared in the passage, it can't be correct.

The answer choices on Organization questions can often be intimidating because the long lists can be difficult to read. However, if you find even one item on the list that is incorrect, don't bother reading the rest of the list. Eliminate the answer choice and move on to the next one.

Attack these answer choices.

> (A)   description of a problem; demand for
>   psychological attention to the problem; relation
>   of a historical incidence of the problem; a
>   second example of an occurrence of the problem

Choice (A): The first item on the list looks right, but the second is **out of scope** because the author makes no demands. No need to read the rest of the choice. *Cut it.*

> (B)   description of a problem; explanation of two
>   theories about the problem; detailed delineation
>   of one of those theories; call for an innovative
>   solution to the problem

Choice (B): You should start to get skeptical when you see the phrase "two theories," and by the time you get to "call for an innovative solution," you should be sure that this choice is **out of scope** and incorrect. *Cut it.*

> (C)   description of a problem; presentation of
>   scientific research related to the problem;
>   illustration of that research with an example;
>   mention of the implications of the problem

Choice (C) looks good. The second and third items on the list accurately describe the purpose of the second paragraph, and the final item on the list matches the last paragraph. *Keep it.*

> (D)   description of a problem; demonstration of that
>   problem by an example; discussion of the
>   implications of the problem; reference to recent
>   studies of the problem

Choice (D): This answer choice contains good descriptions of the different parts of the passage, but they are **out of order**. The mention of recent studies came in the middle of the passage, not at the end. *Cut it.*

> (E)   description of a problem; presentation of one
>   understanding of the nature of the problem;
>   refutation of that understanding; proposal of a
>   different perception of the problem

Choice (E): As soon as you read "refutation," you can stop and eliminate this answer choice. That never happened, so it is **out of scope**. *Cut it.*

Choice (C) is the correct answer.

STOP. THIS IS THE END OF LECTURE 1. DO NOT PROCEED TO THE CORRESPONDING EXAM UNTIL INSTRUCTED TO DO SO IN CLASS.

INFORMATIONAL PASSAGES

3.1   IDENTIFYING INFORMATIONAL PASSAGES

All Informational Passages follow the same pattern:

- **The purpose of the passage is to convey information.** Unlike Thesis passages, Informational passages don't really argue for any particular point. Instead, they describe a series of events, a life story, or some other set of facts.

- **Accordingly, the main point of an Informational passage is always descriptive.** If you identify the main point of a passage and find it is a counterargument or calls for a certain course of action, then the main point isn't descriptive, and you aren't looking at an Informational passage. The purpose of an Informational passage is to describe, so its main point is merely descriptive.

- **The main point of an Informational passage is not really up for debate.** Thesis passages can also have descriptive main points, but they are always debatable. Compare the following sentences:

    1. Beethoven's lesser-known compositions are some of the best pieces he ever wrote.
    2. Beethoven is among the best-known composers of classical music.

    The first one is the sort of sentence that would appear in a Thesis passage, whereas the second is purely Informational.

If a passage reads like a life story, a recounting of a historical event, or a mere collection of information, then it's probably an Informational passage.

> All passages have a main point, even if they aren't arguing for a particular conclusion.

Blah blah blah blah blah blah blah blah blah blah blah blah blah blah blah blah blah blah blah blah blah blah blah blah blah blah. Blah blah blah blah blah blah blah blah. Blah blah blah blah blah blah blah blah blah. Blah blah blah blah. Blah blah blah blah blah blah blah blah blah blah. Blah blah blah blah blah blah blah blah blah blah.

There is always a MAIN POINT. Blah blah, blah blah blah blah blah blah blah blah blah blah blah blah blah blah.

3.2   ANALYZING INFORMATIONAL PASSAGES

To analyze an Informational Passage, look for:

1. **The main point**

2. **The purpose of each paragraph**

3. **Major structural elements** such as dichotomies, lists, or timelines.

3.2.1   THE MAIN POINT

Informational passages aren't based on an argument or a viewpoint, but they do have a main point. The purpose of an Informational passage is to convey a collection of information, and the main point is a sentence that captures all of the most important information in a single statement. Often, the main point is explicitly stated in the passage. Here are some tips to help you find the main point:

- The main point tends to appear in either the first or last paragraph of the passage.

- The main point is one of the most general statements in the passage.

- *All* of the paragraphs help to elaborate on the main point.

> If the main point is not expressed succinctly or in a single sentence, you have to synthesize it yourself.

Occasionally, there is no single sentence that captures all of the most important information. If you encounter this situation, you should express the main point in your own words—either in your head or in a quick note you jot on the page—before moving on to the questions.

To get a sense of what an Informational passage can look like, examine the following paragraph, which is the first paragraph from an Informational passage.

> Some Native American tribes have had difficulty establishing their land claims because the United States government did not recognize their status as tribes; therefore during the 1970s some Native Americans attempted to obtain such recognition through the medium of U.S. courts. In presenting these suits, Native Americans had to operate within a particular sphere of U.S. government procedure, that of its legal system, and their arguments were necessarily interpreted by the courts in terms the law could understand: e.g., through application of precedent or review of evidence. This process brought to light some of the differing perceptions and definitions that can exist between cultures whose systems of discourse are sometimes at variance.

Test 28, Section 4, Passage 1

If you try looking for a thesis in this paragraph, you won't find it. The last sentence says that some interesting issues came up. That's hardly a point worth arguing about, but it is the point the writer of the passage is interested in, and the rest of the passage elaborates on this sentence. The main point, expressed in slightly different words than those used in the passage, is this: [Court cases involving Native American land claims brought out the differences between cultures with different systems of discourse.]

This is what the passage is all about. It's a general, descriptive sentence that summarizes the most important information contained in the Informational passage.

3.2.2 DRILL: THE MAIN POINT

Directions: Each of the following is the first paragraph of a passage. Determine whether they are part of a Thesis passage or an Informational passage. In either case, mark the main point with brackets.

1.　　In April 1990 representatives of the Pico Korea Union of electronics workers in Buchon City, South Korea, traveled to the United States in order to demand just settlement of their claims from the parent company of their employer, who upon the formation of the union had shut down operations without paying the workers. From the beginning, the union cause was championed by an unprecedented coalition of Korean American groups and deeply affected the Korean American community on several levels.

Test 24, Section 1, Passage 2

Thesis or Informational? _____

2.　　In recent years, scholars have begun to use social science tools to analyze court opinions. These scholars have justifiably criticized traditional legal research for its focus on a few cases that may not be representative and its fascination with arcane matters that do not affect real people with real legal problems. Zirkel and Schoenfeld, for example, have championed the application of social science tools to the analysis of case law surrounding discrimination against women in higher education employment. Their studies have demonstrated how these social science tools may be used to serve the interests of scholars, lawyers, and prospective plaintiffs as well. However, their enthusiasm for the "outcomes analysis" technique seems misguided.

Test 24, Section 1, Passage 3

Thesis or Informational? _____

3.　　Medievalists usually distinguished medieval public law from private law: the former was concerned with government and military affairs and the latter with the family, social status, and land transactions. Examination of medieval women's lives shows this distinction to be overly simplistic. Although medieval women were legally excluded from roles thus categorized as public, such as soldier, justice, jury member, or professional administrative official, women's control of land—usually considered a private or domestic phenomenon—had important political implications in the feudal system of thirteenth-century England. Since land equaled wealth and wealth equaled power, certain women exercised influence by controlling land. Unlike unmarried women (who were legally subject to their guardians) or married women (who had no legal identity separate from their husbands), women who were widows had autonomy with respect to acquiring or disposing of certain property, suing in court, incurring liability for their own debts, and making wills.

Test 23, Section 4, Passage 2

Thesis or Informational? _____

4.　　James Porter (1905–1970) was the first scholar to identify the African influence on visual art in the Americas, and much of what is known about the cultural legacy that African American artists inherited from their African forebears has come to us by way of his work. Porter, a painter and art historian, began by studying African-American crafts of the eighteenth and nineteenth centuries. This research revealed that many of the household items created by African-American men and women—walking sticks, jugs, and textiles—displayed characteristics that linked them iconographically to artifacts of West Africa. Porter then went on to establish clearly the range of the cultural territory inherited by later African-American artists.

Test 26, Section 4, Passage 2

Thesis or Informational? _____

Answers & Explanations

1. **Informational.** This paragraph simply sets the scene for a description of an event, and it does not put forward anything that seems up for debate. The main point of the passage is introduced in the general last sentence. [From the beginning...on several levels.]. A better expression of the main point would include some mention of what those effects were, which you would know after reading the rest of the passage.

2. **Thesis.** This paragraph revolves around a counterargument. It describes a certain technique used by some scholars, but then advances the thesis that [their enthusiasm for "outcome analysis" seems misguided.]. A more specific expression of the main point would reference the author's suggestion for a better technique, which is described later in the passage.

3. **Thesis.** This paragraph also revolves around the opinion that many medievalists are wrong: [Examination of medieval...overly simplistic]. When a Thesis passage contains a statement that says one view is wrong, you should express the main point—the view the author feels is correct—yourself, if it is not explicitly stated. In this case, the main point is that medieval public law and private law were *not completely* distinct.

4. **Informational.** There are no opinions or arguments in this paragraph, and nothing in it is really up for debate. The main point is the very general and descriptive first sentence [James Porter...his work.].

3.2.3 THE PURPOSE OF EACH PARAGRAPH

In addition to determining the main point of the passage, you should look for the purpose of each paragraph. The purpose will ultimately be to convey some information, but you should be more specific—what kind of information is presented? In what way is the information presented? How does the information relate to the main point?

Determining the purpose of each paragraph involves much more than just determining the *topic* of each paragraph. Think about *why* the author included the paragraph in the passage.

There are various answers to these questions. For example, a paragraph could offer a chronological account of scientific processes, provide a description of an author's best-known work, or describe the reasons behind a particular occurrence. While reading a body paragraph, you should determine what the purpose is. When you have done so, make a mental note or jot a few words next to the paragraph to help you remember its purpose. This example of a body paragraph is the second paragraph in the passage about Native American land claims:

> In one instance, the entire legal dispute turned on whether the suing community—a group of Mashpee Wampanoag in the town of Mashpee, Massachusetts— constituted a tribe. The area had long been occupied by the Mashpee, who continued to have control over land use after the town's incorporation. But in the 1960s, after an influx of non-Mashpee people shifted the balance of political power in the town, the new residents were able to buy Mashpee-controlled land from the town and develop it for commercial or private use. The Mashpee's 1976 suit claimed that these lands were taken in violation of a statute prohibiting transfers of land from any tribe of Native Americans without federal approval. The town argued that the Mashpee were not a tribe in the sense intended by the statute and so were outside its protection. As a result, the Mashpee were required to demonstrate their status as a tribe according to a definition contained in an earlier ruling: a body of Native Americans "governing themselves under one leadership and inhabiting a particular territory."
>
> Test 28, Section 4, Passage 1

The first sentence provides a clue to the purpose of this paragraph: the phrase *in one instance* signals an *example*. The example here is the Mashpee people. What's the purpose of talking about them? The paragraph describes the reasons for their dispute. So the purpose of this paragraph is to introduce the example of the Mashpee people and to describe why they had a land-claim dispute.

3.2.4 MAJOR STRUCTURAL ELEMENTS

Informational passages contain a huge amount of data, but they often suggest a way to break down, organize, and understand that information. For example, a passage may say that an artistic movement experienced three separate phases, which the passage then goes on to describe in chronological order. Or a passage may say that a judge addressing a certain legal question had two important principles to consider, and the passage is organized around those two principles.

If you encounter a situation like this, take special note of the way the author organizes the information. Underline the different categories or phases and mark the passage with symbols such as ①, ②, and ③. In such passages, questions often revolve around the organization itself or require you to know the difference between the parts of the organization. Furthermore, your symbols can help you form a map of the passage that will save you time when you need to come back and search for a particular detail.

3.2.5 Drill: The Purpose of Each Paragraph and Major Structural Elements

Directions: Each of the following is the second paragraph from an Informational passage. Determine the purpose of each paragraph and mark any major structural elements.

1.   An example of this aspect of Porter's research occurs in his essay "Robert S. Duncanson, Midwestern Romantic-Realist." The work of Duncanson, a nineteenth-century painter of the Hudson River school, like that of his predecessor in the movement, Joshua Johnston, was commonly thought to have been created by a Euro-American artist. Porter proved definitively that both Duncanson and Johnston were of African ancestry. Porter published this finding and thousands of others in a comprehensive volume tracing the history of African-American art. At the time of its first printing in 1943, only two other books devoted exclusively to the accomplishments of African-American artists existed. Both of these books were written by Alain LeRoy Locke, a professor at the university where Porter also taught. While these earlier studies by Locke are interesting for being the first to survey the field, neither addressed the critical issue of African precursors; Porter's book addressed this issue, painstakingly integrating the history of African American art into the larger history of art in the Americas without separating it from those qualities that gave it its unique ties to African artisanship. Porter may have been especially attuned to these ties because of his conscious effort to maintain them in his own paintings, many of which combine the style of the genre portrait with evidence of an extensive knowledge of the cultural history of various African peoples.

Test 26, Section 4, Passage 2

Purpose: _____

_____

_____

_____

2.   First, it served as a rallying focus for a diverse community often divided by generation, class, and political ideologies. Most notably, the Pico cause mobilized many young second-generation Korean Americans, many of whom had never been part of a political campaign before, let alone one involving Korean issues. Members of this generation, unlike first-generation Korean Americans, generally fall within the more privileged sectors of the Korean American community and often feel alienated from their Korean roots. In addition to raising the political consciousness of young Korean Americans, the Pico struggle sparked among them new interest in their cultural identity. The Pico workers also suggested new roles that can be played by recent immigrants, particularly working-class immigrants. These immigrants' knowledge of working conditions overseas can help to globalize the perspective of their communities and can help to establish international ties on a more personal level, as witnessed in the especially warm exchange between the Pico workers and recent working-class immigrants from China. In addition to broadening the political base within the Korean American community, the Pico struggle also led to new alliances between the Korean American community and progressive labor and social justice groups within the larger society—as evidenced in the support received from the Coalition of Labor Union Women and leading African American unionists

Test 24, Section 1, Passage 2

Purpose: _____

_____

_____

_____

Answers & Explanations

1. This paragraph has two major purposes. The first is to *give an example* of how Porter identified the influence of African artists. The second is to *show how Porter's work was different from any work that came before it by comparing it to the work of Locke.*

2. The purpose of this paragraph is to *list the effects of the Pico union struggle.* Since the list forms the major structural organization of the paragraph, you should underline its elements and mark them with numbers:

    (1) served as a rallying focus

    (2) sparked new interest in cultural identity

    (3) suggested new roles for immigrants

    (4) led to new alliances

3.3 PUTTING IT ALL TOGETHER

3.3.1 Drill: Informational Passages

Directions: Practice the Identify and Analyze steps on the following passage.

Painter Frida Kahlo (1910–1954) often used harrowing images derived from her Mexican heritage to express suffering caused by a disabling accident and a stormy marriage. Suggesting much personal and
(5) emotional content, her works—many of them self-portraits—have been exhaustively psychoanalyzed, while their political content has been less studied. Yet Kahlo was an ardent political activist who in her art sought not only to explore her own roots, but also to
(10) champion Mexico's struggle for an independent political and cultural identity.

Kahlo was influenced by Marxism, which appealed to many intellectuals in the 1920s and 1930s, and by Mexican nationalism. Interest in Mexico's culture and
(15) history had revived in the nineteenth century, and by the early 1900s, Mexican *indigenista* tendencies ranged from a violently anti-Spanish idealization of Aztec Mexico to an emphasis on contemporary Mexican Indians as the key to authentic Mexican culture.
(20) Mexican nationalism, reacting against contemporary United States political intervention in labor disputes as well as against past domination by Spain, identified the Aztecs as the last independent rulers of an indigenous political unit. Kahlo's form of *Mexicanidad*, a romantic
(25) nationalism that focused upon traditional art uniting all *indigenistas*, revered the Aztecs as a powerful pre-Columbian society that had united a large area of the Middle Americas and that was thought to have been based on communal labor, the Marxist ideal.
(30) In her paintings, Kahlo repeatedly employed Aztec symbols, such as skeletons or bleeding hearts, that were traditionally related to the emanation of life from death and light from darkness. These images of destruction coupled with creation speak not only to
(35) Kahlo's personal battle for life, but also to the Mexican struggle to emerge as a nation—by implication, to emerge with the political and cultural strength admired in the Aztec civilization. Self-Portrait on the Border between Mexico and the United States (1932), for
(40) example, shows Kahlo wearing a bone necklace, holding a Mexican flag, and standing between a highly industrialized United States and an agricultural, preindustrial Mexico. On the United States side are mechanistic and modern images such as smokestacks,
(45) light bulbs, and robots. In contrast, the organic and ancient symbols on the Mexican side—a blood-drenched Sun, lush vegetation, an Aztec sculpture, a pre-Columbian temple, and a skull alluding to those that lined the walls of Aztec temples—emphasize the
(50) interrelation of life, death, the earth, and the cosmos. Kahlo portrayed Aztec images in the folkloric style of traditional Mexican paintings, thereby heightening the clash between modern materialism and indigenous tradition; similarly, she favored planned economic

(55) development, but not at the expense of cultural identity. Her use of familiar symbols in a readily accessible style also served her goal of being popularly understood; in turn, Kahlo is viewed by some Mexicans as a mythic figure representative of nationalism itself.

Test 22, Section 1, Passage 1

1. How can you identify what type of passage this is?

_____

_____

_____

_____

2a. What are the goals of your analysis of the passage?

_____

_____

_____

_____

2b. What are the results of your analysis of the passage?

_____

_____

_____

_____

Answers & Explanations

1. This passage has all the features of an informational passage. It doesn't argue for any particular viewpoint. Instead, it simply describes the political content of a painter's work. The main point of the passage is not really debatable.

2a. Your goal in analyzing this informational passage is to identify the main point of the passage, then to identify the main point of each paragraph and any major structural elements, if they exist.

2b. First, find the main point of the passage. In this case, it is found in lines 8–11: [Kahlo was an ardent...cultural identity.]

You can identify this as the main point of the passage because it appears in the first paragraph, it is one of the most general statements in the passage, and it is elaborated upon in each of the subsequent paragraphs.

Next, determine the purpose of each paragraph. The purpose of the second paragraph is described in its first sentence. It explores Kahlo's influences, which were Marxism and Mexican nationalism.

The purpose of the third paragraph is to describe features of her paintings, such as the use of symbols, through a specific example.

The purpose of the final paragraph is to discuss Kahlo's goals and show how her work was popularly received.

Finally, mark any major structural elements. The main point of the passage (the last sentence in the first paragraph) describes two goals: (1) to explore her own roots, and (2) to champion Mexico's struggle. It's a good idea to mark this like a list when it appears in the main point. You could reasonably expect that the rest of the passage is organized around this list, and if it is, you should mark the same (1) and (2) later in the rest of the passage. However, this passage is mostly concerned with the second topic, so looking for this dichotomy in later parts of the passage is not so productive in this case.

NOW MOVE ON TO THE SECOND CHAPTER OF LECTURE 2. WHEN YOU HAVE COMPLETED IT, YOU CAN GET FURTHER PRACTICE WITH INFORMATIONAL PASSAGES IN THE CORRESPONDING EXAM AT THE END OF THE BOOK.

LECTURE ② CHAPTER ④

THE RETRIEVAL QUESTION FAMILY

All **Retrieval** questions ask you to do the same thing: to go back to the passage and find a specific piece of information. You don't have to synthesize multiple statements, nor do you have to determine how or why the author conveyed any particular information.

There are three types of Retrieval questions:

1. Detail

2. Definition

3. Search

4.1   DETAIL QUESTIONS

Detail questions ask you a question that can be answered by retrieving a particular detail from the passage. The answer is explicitly stated in the passage, so if the question stem is specific enough, you should always determine the answer on your own before you look at the answer choices.

4.1.1   IDENTIFY

Here are some keys to identifying Detail questions:

1. **The question indicates that the answer is *directly stated* in the passage**. Some phrases that accomplish this include *the passage cites* and *according to the passage*.

2. **The question asks about a specific fact**, rather than about the implications or intentions of a statement.

3. **The question doesn't ask about anyone's *perspective* or *opinion*.**

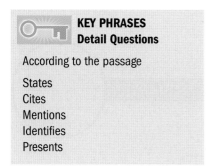

Here are some sample Detail question stems:

> The passage cites which one of the following as a value central to the treaty establishing a constitution for Europe?

> According to the passage, the elimination of which one of the following obstacles allowed researchers to determine the age of the Milky Way galaxy to within 800 million years?

> Which one of the following does the passage identify as being a result of physiological development?

> According to the passage, which one of the following is a goal of the conservation movement?

All of these ask you to retrieve a specific fact directly stated in the passage.

4.1.2 ANALYZE

Your analysis for Detail questions requires a few steps:

1. **Make sure you understand the specific question in the question stem.** Put it into simpler terms if you need to.

2. **Find the topic** of the question in the passage.

3. **Reread the surrounding area** to get the context.

4. **Locate the detail that answers the question.**

Detail questions almost never give you a line number to look at or even tell you which paragraph to look in. Thus, the first major challenge of any Detail question is to find the topic of the question.

If you can't remember where the topic of interest was discussed, your analysis of the passage should help. For every passage, no matter what type, you will have determined the purpose of each paragraph. Revisit the sentences you bracketed or your notes next to each paragraph to help you find where the topic would likely appear.

If you are still having trouble locating the topic, you will have to scan the entire passage to look for it. This is very time consuming, so it's a situation you want to avoid! The solution to this problem is careful reading the *first* time you look at a passage. Even if you don't absorb every detail or every nuance of every argument, you should certainly notice at least the topic of discussion in each part of the passage.

Take a look at the following Detail question, taken from the Frida Kahlo passage at the end of chapter 3:

> 1. Which one of the following stances toward the United States does the passage mention as characterizing Mexican nationalists in the early twentieth century?
>
> Test 22 Section 1, Question 3

This question asks about a specific fact that is directly mentioned in the passage, so it's a Detail question.

The first step is to understand the specific question in the question stem. A simpler way to ask the same question is, "How did Mexican nationalists feel about the U.S.?"

Next, find the topic of the question in the passage. In your analysis of the passage, you found that the second paragraph talked about Marxism and Mexican nationalism, so the answer is probably there. The United States is mentioned once in this paragraph, in line 21. This is where the answer is located.

Finally, reread this area and determine how the Mexican nationalists felt about the U.S. There is only one stated detail about this: they were "reacting against United States political intervention in labor disputes." That's all you know, but it's all you need to know to answer the question.

4.1.3 Prephrase

You should always Prephrase an answer to a Detail question. Fortunately, your Prephrased answer can usually be taken directly from the text. If the answer is spread out over a sentence or two, then you may have to rearrange the words to put together an answer that makes grammatical sense, but you don't have to do any reinterpretation. Just use the words that are already on the page.

The correct answer choice, however, will probably not use precisely the same words that are in the passage. You will usually have to search for a choice that *means* the same as the Prephrased answer, although stated in different words.

For this example, your Prephrased answer can be taken directly from lines 20–21.

> Prephrase: Mexican nationalists were reacting against United States political intervention in labor disputes.

4.1.4 Attack

These are the common distracters you will see on Detail questions:

Wrong Part of the Passage
Most wrong answers to Detail questions are about parts of the passage that have nothing to do with the question at hand.

Word Trap
The LSAT writers like to create distracters that contain certain words that are likely to be in your Prephrased answer but that don't *mean* the same thing.

Out of Scope
If an answer choice mentions new information that never appeared in the passage, it can't be correct.

Attack these answer choices.

(A)   opposition to United States involvement in
       internal Mexican affairs

Choice (A): This uses different words but means the same thing as the Prephrased answer. *Opposition* is the same as *reaction against*, *United States involvement* matches *Unites States intervention*, and *labor disputes* could certainly be considered *internal Mexican affairs. Keep it.*

(B)   desire to decrease emigration of the Mexican
       labor force to the United States

Choice (B): This is a **word trap**. It contains the word *labor*, just like the Prephrased answer, but the Prephrased answer said nothing about emigration. *Cut it.*

(C)   desire to improve Mexico's economic
       competitiveness with the United States

Choice (C): Economic competition with the U.S. is not mentioned anywhere in the passage. This is **out of scope**. *Cut it.*

(D)   reluctance to imitate the United States model of
       rapid industrialization

Choice (D) talks about the **wrong part of the passage**—a highly industrialized United States is mentioned way down in lines 41–42. *Cut it.*

(E)   advocacy of a government based upon that of
       the Marxist Soviet Union rather than that of the
       United States

Choice (E): This has nothing to do with the Prephrased answer, and the Soviet Union is never mentioned in the passage. *Cut it.*

Choice (A) is the correct answer.

4.2   DEFINITION QUESTIONS

Definition questions ask for the meaning of a particular word or statement from the passage. In English, most words can have several meanings, but your job is to find the meaning of the word *as it was used in the passage*. Thus, the LSAT writers have to give you other words in the surrounding context that tell you the definition of the word in that particular case. To answer a Definition question, you have to retrieve the contextual clues and match them to the answer choices.

4.2.1   IDENTIFY

Here are some keys to identifying Definition questions:

1. **The question stem always refers to a word or phrase, presented in quotation marks.**

2. **The question stem almost always refers to a specific line in the passage.**

3. **The question asks you what the word or phrase from the passage *means* in context or *refers to*.**

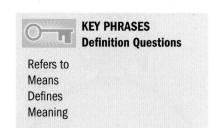

KEY PHRASES
Definition Questions

Refers to
Means
Defines
Meaning

Here are some sample Definition question stems:

> Based on the passage, the term "primary part" (line 34) most clearly refers to which one of the following?

> Which one of the following phrases could replace the word "compelling" in line 30 without substantively altering the author's meaning?

> Which one of the following most accurately expresses what the author means by "ambassadors of style" (line 27)?

All of these ask you to define a word or phrase from the passage. It's important to note that these questions do *not* ask for the most common dictionary definition of the word or phrase. They ask you for the meaning *in the context of the passage*.

4.2.2   ANALYZE

Your analysis of Definition questions is much like your analysis of Detail questions:

1. **Find the word or phrase** in question in the passage.

2. **Reread the surrounding area** to get the context.

3. **Locate the contextual clues** that indicate the meaning of the word or phrase.

Here's a sample Definition question:

> 2.   In the context of the passage, which one of the following phrases could best be substituted for the word "romantic" (line 24) without substantially changing the author's meaning?
> Test 22 Section 1, Question 4

This question asks about the meaning of "romantic" in line 24, so you need to go back to that line in the passage and read the surrounding area to get the context.

In this passage, "romantic" is used to describe Kahlo's brand of nationalism, which is explained in lines 25–29. The contextual clues found in these lines are all you need to answer the question.

4.2.3   PREPHRASE

To Prephrase for Definition questions, you should use the contextual clues to come up with a succinct definition (if possible), or a list of the important elements that the correct answer should contain. The correct answer choice will probably not use exactly the same words that you use in your definition, but it will *mean* the same thing. Establishing the definition of the word on your own *before* looking at the answer choices is essential to avoiding trap answer choices.

In this example, lines 25–29 contain the definition of "romantic" as used by the author. There is a lot of information in those lines, so it's hard to come up with a succinct definition. But you can list the important elements that the definition should contain. It should be compatible with

- focusing on traditional art
- revering a past culture
- valuing communal labor and the unification of a people

The correct answer will not use these exact words, but its meaning will fit with these ideas.

4.2.4 ATTACK

Here are the distracters commonly seen on Definition questions:

Most Common Definition
If the word in the passage functioned simply to denote its most common meaning, then the LSAT writers would not be asking you about it. Test takers would be able to get the question right without reading the passage, and the LSAT writers don't like to award points so easily. Don't be fooled by an answer choice that contains the most common definition of the word.

Out of Scope
If an answer choice includes new ideas that never appeared in the passage, it can't be correct.

Half Wrong
Many answer choices for Definition questions have several parts. Be sure to read all of the parts! Often, the test writers will create distracters that match the Prephrased answer perfectly in some parts, only to go wrong in other parts. If it's half wrong, it's all wrong.

Go ahead and attack the answers for this example.

    (A)   dreamy and escapist

Choice (A): Although Kahlo's nationalism focuses on the past, the Prephrased definition refers to several concrete concepts—they aren't dreamy—and the idea of escaping anything is not mentioned. *Cut it.*

    (B)   nostalgic and idealistic

Choice (B): Revering traditional art and a past culture is a good match for *nostalgic*, and respecting communal labor (the Marxist ideal) and the unification of a people is a good match for *idealistic*. *Keep it.*

    (C)   fanciful and imaginative

Choice (C) suggests that "romantic" has something to do with creating fictional fantasies. These ideas are never mentioned in lines 25–29, so this answer is **out of scope**. *Cut it.*

    (D)   transcendental and impractical

Choice (D): Although some people may consider communal labor to be impractical, the Prephrased answer from lines 25–29 doesn't contain this idea, and the concept of transcending anything is completely **out of scope**. *Cut it.*

> Lines 24–29:
>
> Kahlo's form of *Mexicanidad*, a romantic nationalism that focused upon traditional art uniting all *indigenistas*, revered the Aztecs as a powerful pre-Columbian society that had united a large area of the Middle Americas and that was thought to have been based on communal labor, the Marxist ideal.

> Purpose of a Phrase questions ask you *why* the author used a certain phrase. Definition questions ask you *what* a certain word *means*.

(E)   overwrought and sentimental

Choice (E): *Sentimental* is not a terrible match, since the Prephrased answer does mention revering a past culture, but *overwrought*—tense and overexcited—has nothing to do with the Prephrased answer. At best, this answer is **half wrong**, which means it's all wrong. *Cut it.*

Choice (B) is the correct answer.

4.3   SEARCH QUESTIONS

Search questions ask you whether or not a particular piece of information was contained in the passage. Sometimes the correct answer choice will be the one piece of information that *did* appear, but usually the question stem will ask you to find the one piece of information that *did not* appear in the passage.

4.3.1   IDENTIFY

Here are some characteristics to help you identify Search questions:

1. **The question stem refers to something *mentioned, cited, stated, affirmed,* etc. in the passage.**

2. **The question stem asks you to find the one answer choice that appeared in the passage or says that each answer choice appeared EXCEPT one.**

Here are some sample Search question stems:

Which one of the following does the author mention in the passage?

Each of the following statements is affirmed by the passage EXCEPT:

The passage offers information to help answer each of the following questions EXCEPT:

Which one of the following is NOT identified by the author of the passage as a characteristic of Anastasio's compositions?

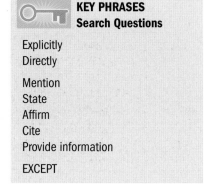

**KEY PHRASES
Search Questions**

Explicitly
Directly

Mention
State
Affirm
Cite
Provide information

EXCEPT

4.3.2   ANALYZE

Most Search question stems, like the first three examples above, do not specify what you need to look for. If you encounter such a question stem, there is no way to Analyze or Prephrase before you look at the answer choices. Instead you have to go directly to the answer choices and react to each one.

Some Search questions are more specific when it comes to the information they ask you to search for. In such cases, your analysis can be very similar to that of a Detail question.

1. **Make sure you understand the topic or specific question in the question stem.** Put it into simpler terms if you need to.

2. **Find the topic** of the question stem in the passage. The topic may be discussed in several places.

3. **Reread the surrounding area** to get the context.

4. **Locate as many instances as you can** of a detail that answers the question.

The only difference between this analysis and that of a Detail question is that, since the question stem usually includes *EXCEPT* or *NOT*, you must retrieve four details that answer the question instead of just one. To make things harder for you, the LSAT writers usually scatter those four details throughout the passage rather than put them all in one place. That's the main difficulty of Search questions: they can become very time-consuming if you have to reread the entire passage to find the information you are looking for.

Again, a good initial analysis of the passage is your best weapon against wasting time. By determining the purpose of each paragraph and noting the topic of discussion in each part of the passage the *first* time you read, you will arrive at the questions with a map of the passage. You can use this map to help you decide where to look for the information you need to answer the question.

Take a look at this question, the final one from the Frida Kahlo passage.

3. The passage mentions each of the following as an Aztec symbol or image found in Kahlo's paintings EXCEPT a

Test 22 Section 1, Question 5

This question stem says that "the passage mentions" four of the symbols and asks which one given as an answer choice was not mentioned. This is a Search question.

The question stem is also specific enough to allow for some analysis before looking at the answer choices.

To start, understand what you are looking for. In this case, you must search for Aztec symbols or images found in Kahlo's paintings.

Next, find the place in the passage that contains these details. From your initial analysis, you found that the third paragraph discussed features of her paintings using a specific example. This is a great place to start.

In lines 30–31, two Aztec symbols are mentioned—this is useful, but you need to find at least four in order to eliminate all the incorrect answer choices. Keep looking. In lines 40–45, there is a list of some non-Aztec images, and lines 46–49 contain five more ancient symbols. This should be enough to answer the question.

> From the passage:
>
> Kahlo repeatedly employed Aztec symbols, such as skeletons or bleeding hearts...Kahlo wearing a bone necklace, holding a Mexican flag...modern images such as smokestacks, light bulbs, and robots...a blood-drenched Sun, lush vegetation, an Aztec sculpture, a pre-Columbian temple, and a skull...

4.3.3 PREPHRASE

Just as on other types of questions in the Retrieval family, you don't have to reword or reinterpret the passage to come up with an answer. Since you are simply retrieving information that was already stated in the passage, you can leave the information in the same words that the passage uses, although you should be ready for answer choices that may use different words to mean the same thing. In addition, you don't have to make your own list of what the four incorrect answers might be—just be ready to refer back to the places you identified in the Analyze step, and cut the answer choices contained in the passage.

4.3.4 ATTACK AND THE EXCEPT TOOL

Regardless of whether or not the question stem gave you specific instructions as to what information to look for, your job is to decide whether each answer choice was contained in the passage. The only difference is that if the question stem was specific, you will have already located the important information in the passage. On the other hand, if the question stem is vague, you will have to search for it *after* reading each answer choice, using the same techniques discussed in the Analyze section (4.3.2).

Rather than a range of distracters, there are only two types of answer choices on Search questions: details or information that appeared in the passage and details or information that didn't. Differentiating between the two seems like an easy task, but test-takers get Search questions wrong all the time. Why? The main reason is that they rely on their memory instead of looking back at the passage. The test writers are good at creating answer choices that didn't appear in the passage but *sound like they could have*. If you go back and check, you won't fall for this trap.

The other reason test-takers make mistakes is that most Search questions are EXCEPT questions. EXCEPT questions can be confusing because they require an extra step of reversal that often leads people to forget what they are looking for and to pick the wrong answer. This confusion can be overcome with a tool that takes advantage of the simple fact that the correct answer will always be somehow different from the other four answers. The tool is called the EXCEPT Tool, and it works like this:

1. **Determine from the question stem what the four incorrect answers will do.** For Search questions, the four incorrect answer choices will appear in the passage. For other types of questions, the four incorrect answer choices may match your Prephrased answer or do something else.

2. **Instead of cutting or keeping each answer choice, make a mark next to it depending on what it does.** For example, on a Search question, write a Y if the piece of information did appear in the passage, and an N if it did not.

3. **The correct answer is the one that looks different from the rest.** For example, the correct answer choice on a Search question will have an N next to it, while the other four choices have a Y. Similarly, the correct answer choice on a Weaken EXCEPT question will be the one without a W next to it.

> You can use the EXCEPT Tool in the Reading Comprehension section exactly as you do in the Logical Reasoning sections.

This tool applies to any EXCEPT question, not only to those of the Search variety. You can treat EXCEPT questions like any other questions, but use the EXCEPT Tool to identify the correct answer.

Take a look at the answer choices for this example, and practice using the EXCEPT Tool.

> (A) skeleton

Choice (A): A skeleton was mentioned in line 31. Write a Y next to this choice.

> (B) sculpture

Choice (B): A sculpture was mentioned in line 47. Write a Y.

> (C) serpent

Choice (C): There is no mention of a serpent in the passage. Write an N.

> (D) skull

Choice (D): A skull was mentioned in line 48. Write a Y.

> (E) bleeding heart

Choice (E): a bleeding heart is mentioned in line 31. Write a Y.

So you should have:

> Y (A) skeleton
> Y (B) sculpture
> N (C) serpent
> Y (D) skull
> Y (E) bleeding heart

As you are looking for the one choice that is different from all the rest, pick **choice (C). This is the correct answer.**

STOP. THIS IS THE END OF LECTURE 2. DO NOT PROCEED TO THE CORRESPONDING EXAM UNTIL INSTRUCTED TO DO SO IN CLASS.

LECTURE ③ CHAPTER ⑤

ENLIGHTENMENT PASSAGES

5.1 IDENTIFYING ENLIGHTENMENT PASSAGES

Enlightenment passages take you on a journey from a point of confusion to a point of clarity. All Enlightenment passages share the following characteristics:

- **The purpose of the passage is to explore a core question**. This question is introduced at the beginning of the passage along with some background on the topic and an explanation as to why there is confusion or disagreement about the answer to the core question. The rest of the passage considers possible answers to the core question and usually presents one of them as the correct understanding.

- **The passage contains several hypotheses or viewpoints**. There are always several possible solutions to the core question presented in the passage. One of these viewpoints often belongs to the author, but sometimes they come only from experts in the field.

Although Enlightenment passages are not the only kind of passage that can contain several viewpoints, the core question is a feature found <u>only</u> in Enlightenment passages. Furthermore, the core question is usually presented in a manner that is easy to recognize. Thus, you should be able to identify Enlightenment passages as soon as you encounter the core question, which is typically in the first paragraph or the beginning of the second.

The **core** question can be introduced in several ways. The most common is a sentence that indicates that there is (or was) puzzlement over a certain phenomenon or the best way to understand something. For example:

> One of the most intriguing questions considered by geologists is how…

> Until recently, astronomers were unable to account for why…

> Historians have proposed two possible explanations for the unexpected rarity of…

Another common way that the core question is introduced is through a hypothetical question:

> Is string theory the best way to understand subatomic interactions?

> What is the purpose of philosophy?

If you see that the rest of the passage is concerned with answering that one hypothetical question, then you have found the core question.

Although many Enlightenment passages are about scientific topics, don't mistakenly assume that they all are. Enlightenment passages can also be about law, humanities, or sociology, for example. Passages about scientific topics can also be Thesis or Informational.

> Most tests include at least one Enlightenment passage.

5.2 ANALYZING ENLIGHTENMENT PASSAGES

To analyze an Enlightenment passage, look for:

1. **The core question**

2. **The various viewpoints**

3. **The main point**

4. **The purpose of each paragraph**

5.2.1 THE CORE QUESTION

As the primary purpose of an Enlightenment passage is to answer the core question, you should take special notice of it as soon as you find it. Put a circle around the core question, and if it is not expressed in the form of a question, or if it is expressed in a verbose or confusing way, write your own clear and compact version of it next to the passage. For example, "Why does El Niño occur?" or "How does capillary action work?"

5.2.2 Drill: The Core Question

Directions: Each of the following passage excerpts contains a core question. In each, circle the core question or write your own compact version of it under the paragraph.

1. At the center of the issue of scientific knowledge can thus be found questions about the relationship between language and what it refers to. A discussion about the role played by language in the pursuit of knowledge has been going on among linguists for several decades. The debate centers around whether language corresponds in some essential way to objects and behaviors, making knowledge a solid and reliable commodity; or, on the other hand, whether the relationship between language and things is purely a matter of agreed-upon conventions, making knowledge tenuous, relative, and inexact.

   Test 22, Section 1, Passage 4

   _____

   _____

   _____

2. What is dark matter? Numerous exotic entities have been postulated, but among the more attractive candidates—because they are known actually to exist—are neutrinos, elementary particles created as a by-product of nuclear fusion, radioactive decay, or catastrophic collisions between other particles. Neutrinos, which come in three types, are by far the most numerous kind of particle in the universe; however, they have long been assumed to have no mass. If so, that would disqualify them as dark matter. Without mass, matter cannot exert gravitational force; without such force, it cannot induce other matter to cohere.

   Test 40, Section 4, Passage 3

   _____

   _____

   _____

5.2.3 THE VARIOUS VIEWPOINTS

Enlightenment passages can be more complex than Thesis or Informational passages because, instead of expressing a single unified viewpoint, they usually discuss several different viewpoints, which may contradict each other. Your job is to look at each statement and determine which viewpoint it is associated with. Each statement in the passage will be part of either the **author's viewpoint**, **someone else's viewpoint**, or an **accepted fact**.

This process is basically the same as the process of finding the major structural elements of an Informational passage. In Enlightenment passages, the various viewpoints *are* the major structural elements around which the passage is organized.

As you identify the various viewpoints, mark the passage to remind yourself where the viewpoints are located.

The LSAT has several concrete and predictable ways of helping you figure out the various viewpoints.

> Passages that contain various viewpoints are often accompanied by questions that test your ability to remember which viewpoint belongs to whom and what the differences are between the viewpoints.

5.2.3.1 Accepted Facts

Some statements in the passage are not associated with any one particular viewpoint. Instead, they simply convey facts that are accepted by everyone and that act mainly to give you background information about the topic. These statements are much like the contents of Informational passages or premises in the Logical Reasoning section. They are:

- Descriptive
- Not really up for debate

Some examples include:

- The results of simple observation
- Matters of historical record
- Laws of nature
- Calculations
- Statistics

When you see accepted facts in an Enlightenment passage, you don't have to do much other than understand them and accept them yourself.

5.2.3.2 Someone Else's Viewpoint

Enlightenment passages generally spend a great deal of time describing the viewpoints of people other than the author. When the author wants to tell you about someone else's viewpoint he or she must always include an **indicator**. The indicator is a phrase that that tells you who the statement should be attributed to, and it appears in every statement that forms part of someone else's viewpoint, unless that statement is a clear continuation of the previous sentence. Here are some examples:

Some ethnomusicologists see this phenomenon as evidence that…

Interminable incarceration, they go on to reason, could lead to…

Many historiographers hypothesize that…

Some of Gordon's critics claim that…

Proponents of the hemispherical theory also point to recent experimental work that suggests that…

When you find a statement that introduces a new viewpoint, **underline the name of the theory or the name of the group that endorses the viewpoint.** Then, when you find a paragraph or isolated statement that supports the theory, mark the passage with a symbol that reminds you which viewpoint is being discussed. For example, Ⓒ could indicate critics, or Ⓗ could indicate the details of the hemispherical theory.

5.2.3.3 The Author's Viewpoint

The author usually goes beyond simply presenting someone else's viewpoint. Most Enlightenment passages spend time discussing the author's viewpoint as well. There are some simple clues that should alert you to the author's viewpoint.

- The author's viewpoint **does not have an indicator attributing it to someone else.**

- The author's viewpoint **sounds like an opinion, not an accepted fact**. Just as in passages in the Logical Reasoning section, opinions can take the form of a suggested course of action or a counterargument. Other clues that indicate opinions are opinionated words such as *clearly* or *obviously*.

- The author's viewpoint **cites evidence to support it.**

- The author's viewpoint **often includes judgments** that say something is

  · correct or incorrect

  · likely or unlikely

  · well or poorly reasoned

It's a good idea to circle these judgment words when you see them.

> Judgment words, no matter what kind of passage they appear in, are always important and can help you form a better picture of the author's viewpoint and the main point of the passage.

Here are some examples of sentences that would reveal the author's viewpoint:

The former explanation (seems unlikely.)

(It is reasonable to suppose) that punk music exercised no small degree of influence on pop music of the mid-1980s.

Such rigorous rules are (likely) to undermine the very goals of the movement.

To that end, future simulations (should) be designed to address the implications of the snowball earth hypothesis.

Stagflation has appeared in other countries under similar circumstances, (increasing the general plausibility) of such a theory.

The new evidence acts to disprove the earlier proposed mechanism without committing what Stewart (correctly) identifies as the unjustified assumption of interdependence.

Just as you do when you find statements that are part of someone else's viewpoint, mark the author's viewpoint with a symbol, such as Ⓐ, that reminds you where the author's viewpoint can be found.

You may have noticed that the last example on the previous page includes an **indicator** of someone else's viewpoint. This example actually includes two different but closely related viewpoints:

- **Stewart's viewpoint:** The assumption of interdependence is unjustified.

- **The author's viewpoint:** Stewart is correct. The assumption of interdependence is *indeed* unjustified. And the new evidence acts to disprove the earlier proposed mechanism without committing this mistake.

So if you ran across such a statement in a passage, you would mark it with both an Ⓢ and an Ⓐ.

5.2.4 Drill: The Various Viewpoints

Directions: Mark the various viewpoints in the following paragraphs.

1. Lately the latter theory has been gaining wider acceptance. According to linguists who support this theory, the way language is used varies depending upon changes in accepted practices and theories among those who work in a particular discipline. These linguists argue that, in the pursuit of knowledge, a statement is true only when there are no promising alternatives that might lead one to question it. Certainly this characterization would seem to be applicable to the sciences. In science, a mathematical statement may be taken to account for every aspect of a phenomenon it is applied to, but, some would argue, there is nothing inherent in mathematical language that guarantees such a correspondence. Under this view, acceptance of a mathematical statement by the scientific community— by virtue of the statement's predictive power or methodological efficiency—transforms what is basically an analogy or metaphor into an explanation of the physical process in question, to be held as true until another, more compelling analogy takes its place.

Test 22, Section 1, Passage 4

2. While slight, even the lowest estimate would yield a lot of mass given that neutrinos are so numerous, especially considering that neutrinos were previously assumed to have no mass. Still, even at the highest estimate, neutrinos could only account for about 20 percent of the universe's "missing" mass. Nevertheless, that is enough to alter our picture of the universe even if it does not account for all of dark matter. In fact, some cosmologists claim that this new evidence offers the best theoretical solution yet to the dark matter problem. If the evidence holds up, these cosmologists believe, it may add to our understanding of the role elementary particles play in holding the universe together.

Test 40, Section 4, Passage 3

Answers & Explanations

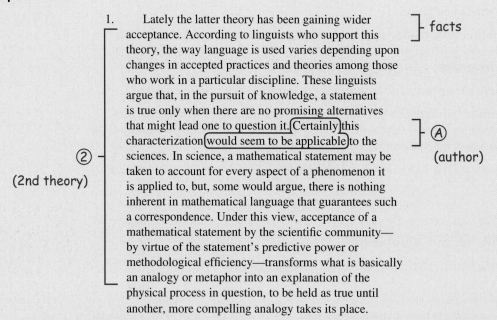

1. Lately the latter theory has been gaining wider acceptance. According to linguists who support this theory, the way language is used varies depending upon changes in accepted practices and theories among those who work in a particular discipline. These linguists argue that, in the pursuit of knowledge, a statement is true only when there are no promising alternatives that might lead one to question it. Certainly this characterization would seem to be applicable to the sciences. In science, a mathematical statement may be taken to account for every aspect of a phenomenon it is applied to, but, some would argue, there is nothing inherent in mathematical language that guarantees such a correspondence. Under this view, acceptance of a mathematical statement by the scientific community— by virtue of the statement's predictive power or methodological efficiency—transforms what is basically an analogy or metaphor into an explanation of the physical process in question, to be held as true until another, more compelling analogy takes its place.

② (2nd theory)

Ⓐ (author) — facts

The first sentence is a fact because it is a simple observation regarding which theory is more popular. The rest of the paragraph puts forth the viewpoint of the linguists who support the second theory. When the author uses opinion words to say that it "certainly seems applicable," he is exposing his own viewpoint, which, in this case, is in accord with the second theory.

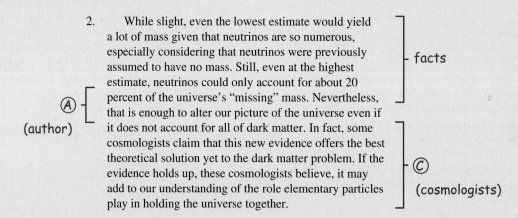

2. While slight, even the lowest estimate would yield a lot of mass given that neutrinos are so numerous, especially considering that neutrinos were previously assumed to have no mass. Still, even at the highest estimate, neutrinos could only account for about 20 percent of the universe's "missing" mass. Nevertheless, that is enough to alter our picture of the universe even if it does not account for all of dark matter. In fact, some cosmologists claim that this new evidence offers the best theoretical solution yet to the dark matter problem. If the evidence holds up, these cosmologists believe, it may add to our understanding of the role elementary particles play in holding the universe together.

Ⓐ (author)

facts

Ⓒ (cosmologists)

The first two sentences are facts because they are simple calculations. Saying something can "alter our picture of the universe" is more of an opinion. The last two sentences contain indicators that attribute them to a certain group of cosmologists.

5.2.5 The Main Point

You should always determine the main point of Enlightenment passages, and you should mark it with brackets or jot it down with a few of your own words next to the passage. The main point of Enlightenment passages can be more difficult to find than in some other types of passages because it is not always stated in a compact way or in a predictable place. However, you can still find it using these guidelines.

If the passage provides an <u>answer</u> to the core question, then the main point *is* that answer. The answer could come from someone else's viewpoint or from the author's. For example:

- The passage presents Theories 1 and 2. The author says that everyone now agrees that Theory 2 is correct.

  Main point: [The answer to the core question is Theory 2.]

- The passage presents Theories 1 and 2. The author says that Theory 2 is the best but creates her own viewpoint by pointing out some problems with Theory 2 and proposing some modifications to it.

  Main point: [The answer to the core question is close to Theory 2, but with the following modifications.]

- The passage presents Theories 1 and 2. The author counters these in his own viewpoint by proposing Theory 3.

  Main point: [The answer to the core question is the author's own viewpoint—Theory 3.]

On the other hand, some Enlightenment passages leave the core question unanswered. In such cases, the main point is more concerned with the *search* for the answer than with the answer itself. For example:

- The passage presents Theories 1 and 2. The author says that none of the theories is satisfactory and that there is still no agreement about the answer to the core question.

  Main point: [The answer to the core question is still unknown.]

- The passage presents Theories 1 and 2. The author discusses the details of the theories but does not offer any opinion about whether the theories are correct.

  Main point: [There are several competing schools of thought.]

As you can see, although the main point comes in several forms, it is always close to the author's viewpoint when there is one. The author's viewpoint usually comes at the end of the passage, but is sometimes alluded to in the first paragraph. However, there are no rules to prevent it from showing up anywhere in the passage.

5.2.6 THE PURPOSE OF EACH PARAGRAPH

In addition to determining the main point of the passage, you should look for the purpose of each paragraph. In Enlightenment passages, each paragraph is concerned with discussing either accepted facts, someone else's viewpoint, or the author's viewpoint, but you should be more specific. How does a particular viewpoint relate to the previous one? Do these accepted facts support one viewpoint better than another? Does this paragraph contain the main point?

There are various answers to these questions. For example, some paragraphs directly rebut previous paragraphs, while others introduce new sets of criteria to be considered. While reading each paragraph, you should determine what its purpose is. When you have done so, make a mental note or jot a few words next to the paragraph to help you remember its purpose.

Unlike in Thesis passages, the main point in Enlightenment passages may not be written concisely in a single sentence. It's up to you to synthesize it using all the major ideas from the passage.

5.3 PUTTING IT ALL TOGETHER

5.3.1 Drill: Enlightenment Passages

Directions: Practice the Identify and Analyze steps on the following passage.

Homing pigeons can be taken from their lofts and transported hundreds of kilometers in covered cages to unfamiliar sites and yet, when released, be able to choose fairly accurate homeward bearings within a
(5) minute and fly home. Aside from reading the minds of the experimenters (a possibility that has not escaped investigation), there are two basic explanations for the remarkable ability of pigeons to "home": the birds might keep track of their outward displacement (the
(10) system of many short-range species such as honeybees); or they might have some sense, known as a "map sense," that would permit them to construct an internal image of their environment and then "place" themselves with respect to home on some internalized
(15) coordinate system.

The first alternative seems unlikely. One possible model for such an inertial system might involve an internal magnetic compass to measure the directional leg of each journey. Birds transported to the release site
(20) wearing magnets or otherwise subjected to an artificial magnetic field, however, are only occasionally affected. Alternately, if pigeons measure their displacement by consciously keeping track of the direction and degree of acceleration and deceleration of
(25) the various turns, and timing the individual legs of the journey, simply transporting them in the dark, with constant rotations, or under complete anesthesia ought to impair or eliminate their ability to orient. These treatments, however, have no effect. Unfortunately, no
(30) one has yet performed the crucial experiment of transporting pigeons in total darkness, anesthetized, rotating, and with the magnetic field reversed all at the same time.

The other alternative, that pigeons have a "map
(35) sense," seems more promising, yet the nature of this sense remains mysterious. Papi has posited that the map sense is olfactory: that birds come to associate odors borne on the wind with the direction in which the wind is blowing, and so slowly build up an olfactory
(40) map of their surroundings. When transported to the release site, then, they only have to sniff the air en route and/or at the site to know the direction of home. Papi conducted a series of experiments showing that pigeons whose nostrils have been plugged are poorly
(45) oriented at release and home slowly.

One problem with the hypothesis is that Schmidt-Koenig and Phillips failed to detect any ability in pigeons to distinguish natural air (presumably laden with olfactory map information) from pure, filtered air.
(50) Papi's experimental results, moreover, admit of simpler, nonolfactory explanations. It seems likely that the behavior of nostril-plugged birds results from the distracting and traumatic nature of the experiment. When nasal tubes are used to bypass the olfactory
(55) chamber but allow for comfortable breathing, no disorientation is evident. Likewise, when the olfactory epithelium is sprayed with anesthetic to block smell-detection but not breathing, orientation is normal.

Test 27, Section 3, Passage 3

1. How can you identify what type of passage this is?

_____

_____

_____

_____

2a. What are the goals of your analysis of the passage?

_____

_____

_____

_____

2b. What are the results of your analysis of the passage?

_____

_____

_____

_____

Homing pigeons can be taken from their lofts and transported hundreds of kilometers in covered cages to unfamiliar sites and yet, when released, be able to choose fairly accurate homeward bearings within a minute and fly home. Aside from reading the minds of the experimenters (a possibility that has not escaped investigation) there are two basic explanations for the remarkable ability of pigeons to "home": the birds might keep track of their outward displacement (the system of many short-range species such as honeybees); or they might have some sense, known as a "map sense," that would permit them to construct an internal image of their environment and then "place" themselves with respect to home on some internalized coordinate system.

The first alternative seems unlikely. One possible model for such an inertial system might involve an internal magnetic compass to measure the directional leg of each journey. Birds transported to the release site wearing magnets or otherwise subjected to an artificial magnetic field, however, are only occasionally affected. Alternately, if pigeons measure their displacement by consciously keeping track of the direction and degree of acceleration and deceleration of the various turns, and timing the individual legs of the journey, simply transporting them in the dark, with constant rotations, or under complete anesthesia ought to impair or eliminate their ability to orient. These treatments, however, have no effect. Unfortunately, no one has yet performed the crucial experiment of transporting pigeons in total darkness, anesthetized, rotating, and with the magnetic field reversed all at the same time.

[The other alternative, that pigeons have a "map sense," seems more promising, yet the nature of this sense remains mysterious.] Papi has posited that the map sense is olfactory: that birds come to associate odors borne on the wind with the direction in which the wind is blowing, and so slowly build up an olfactory map of their surroundings. When transported to the release site, then, they only have to sniff the air at en route and/or at the site to know the direction of home. Papi conducted a series of experiments showing that pigeons whose nostrils have been plugged are poorly oriented at release and home slowly.

One problem with the hypothesis is that Schmidt-Koenig and Phillips failed to detect any ability in pigeons to distinguish natural air (presumably laden with olfactory map information) from pure, filtered air. Papi's experimental results, moreover, admit of simpler, nonolfactory explanations. It seems likely that the behavior of nostril-plugged birds results from the distracting and traumatic nature of the experiment. When nasal tubes are used to bypass the olfactory chamber but allow for comfortable breathing, no disorientation is evident. Likewise, when the olfactory epithelium is sprayed with anesthetic to block smell-detection but not breathing, orientation is normal.

Margin notes:

- ¶1: Purpose: intro topic & core Q — fact / core Q / OD / MS / A
- ¶2: discuss & disprove OD — A / OD
- ¶3: discuss MS & Papi (olfactory) — A
- *MP: map sense is probably correct, but still not understood
- ¶4: disprove Papi & olfactory — MS / (Papi) / A

Answers & Explanations

1. You can identify this as an Enlightenment passage because it has several viewpoints and explores a **core** question: How can we explain the ability of pigeons to home?

2a. The goals of your analysis are to find the **core question**, the various viewpoints, the main point, and the purpose of each paragraph.

2b. The **core question** (circled) is located in the first paragraph: How can we explain the ability of pigeons to home?

The various viewpoints are: the outward displacement (OD) hypothesis, the map sense (MS) hypothesis, Papi's theory (which is one possible explanation of the MS hypothesis), and the author's viewpoint. They are marked on the passage.

The main point is also marked as a brief note at the end of the passage. The author uses opinionated words (circled) to indicate that he believes the MS hypothesis but not Papi's specific version of it.

Finally, there are brief notes next to each paragraph to remind you of its purpose.

NOW MOVE ON TO THE SECOND CHAPTER OF LECTURE 3. WHEN YOU HAVE COMPLETED IT, YOU CAN GET FURTHER PRACTICE WITH ENLIGHTENMENT PASSAGES IN THE CORRESPONDING EXAM AT THE END OF THE BOOK.

LECTURE ③ CHAPTER

THE "USING THE EVIDENCE" QUESTION FAMILY

The most important characteristics of **Using the Evidence** questions are conveyed in the name of this question family. First, the questions are all based on **evidence** found in the passage. At first glance, some of the question stems may seem like they are asking you to guess, use outside knowledge, or just develop a gut feeling. However, this is not the case. The correct answer to every Using the Evidence question is correct because there is concrete evidence in the passage to support it.

The second important characteristic of this question family is described in the word **using**. These questions ask you to go beyond simple retrieval of information. You will have to synthesize multiple statements and use valid reasoning to determine the implications of the information in the passage.

> Using the Evidence questions can be harder than other question types because you have to *do something* with the evidence, rather than simply retrieve it.

There are four types of Using the Evidence questions:

1. Inference

2. Viewpoint

3. Attitude

4. Match

6.1 INFERENCE QUESTIONS

Inference questions ask you to make an inference based on the passage. An inference is something that is guaranteed to be true. An inference is not something that is likely or that might be true—it is something that the passage provides specific evidence for, and it must be true given the information in the passage.

Inference questions in the Reading Comprehension section follow exactly the same rules as Inference questions in the Logical Reasoning section. There are two types of inferences on the LSAT:

- Inferences formed by using valid logic to combine multiple statements from a passage
- Inferences that are mere restatements of part of a passage

Most inferences in the Reading Comprehension section fall into the first category.

6.1.1 IDENTIFY

There are a few phrases used on the LSAT to indicate Inference questions. All of them mean the same thing:

1. **The question stem asks you what you can *infer from* or what is *implied* or *suggested by* the passage.**

2. **The question stem asks you which answer choice is *supported by* information in the passage.**

Here are some sample Inference question stems:

> Which one of the following can most reasonably be inferred from the information in the passage?
>
> The passage implies that which one of the following is a reason that *E. Coli* bacteria are especially virulent?
>
> The passage suggests which one of the following about critics of postmodernism?
>
> The information in the passage provides the most support for which one of the following statements?

All of these ask you to make an inference in way or another.

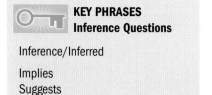

KEY PHRASES
Inference Questions

Inference/Inferred

Implies
Suggests

Passage provides the most support

6.1.2 ANALYZE

Your analysis of Inference questions depends on how specific the question stem is. Compare the following two question stems:

1. The information in the passage provides the most support for which one of the following statements?

2. Information in the passage most strongly supports which one of the following inferences about Gaussian transformations?

The difference between these questions is the amount of help they give you. The first question could be about any part of the passage—the stem provides no clue as to where in the passage the correct answer is likely to appear. The second gives you a little more help, since it at least tells you the topic that you should focus on.

For questions like the first one, your analysis is necessarily suspended until after you begin working with the answer choices.

For questions like the second one, your analysis has two steps:

1. **Find the topic** of the question in the passage.

2. **Reread the surrounding area** to locate any facts related to the topic.

Note that if the entire passage is about Gaussian transformations, then the second question is really no different from the first. But if Gaussian transformations were mentioned only in the second half of the third paragraph, then the correct answer would be concerned only with the information found in that location.

If you can't remember where the topic of interest was discussed, your analysis of the passage should help. For every passage, no matter what type, you will have determined the purpose of each paragraph. Revisit the sentences you bracketed or your notes next to each paragraph to help you find where the topic is likely to appear.

Try this Inference question, which comes from the Homing Pigeon passage at the end of chapter 5:

1. Information in the passage supports which one of the following statements regarding the "first alternative" (line 16) for explaining the ability of pigeons to "home"?

    Test 27, Section 3, Question 18

Since this question asks for a statement *supported by* information in the passage, it's an Inference question.

This question asks about the "first alternative," so you can at least narrow down the area of the passage in which you know the answer will be found. The first alternative was defined in lines 8–11: it's the "outward displacement" theory. In your analysis of the passage, you found that this hypothesis was discussed only in the second paragraph.

Any combination of information from the second paragraph could be the correct answer to this question. But anything that *isn't* related to this evidence is certainly wrong. After all, you can't infer something if the passage provides no evidence for it.

6.1.3 PREPHRASE

On Inference questions that do not point you to a specific place in the passage, Prephrasing just means reminding yourself of what the correct answer should look like: the correct answer must be true based on specific evidence from the passage.

On the other hand, if an Inference question does point you to a specific portion of the passage, you should Prephrase by determining the **scope** of what the correct answer will address.

In the current example, the second paragraph talks about

*   how the "outward displacement" theory could work
*   experiments that have been or could be performed to test it
*   the results of those experiments

Thus, the scope of the correct answer must be limited to these issues.

6.1.4 ATTACK

Regardless of whether or not the question stem gave you a specific topic to look for, your job is to decide whether each answer choice contains a valid inference. The only difference is that if the question stem was specific, you will have already located the important evidence in the passage. On the other hand, if the question stem is vague, you will have to search for the evidence *after* reading each answer choice, using the same techniques discussed in the Analyze section.

There are several common distracters that appear in Inference questions:

Out of Scope

For Inference questions, out of scope answer choices are those that are not related to specific evidence in the passage. Any answer that mentions new information that never appeared in the passage is wrong. Any answer choice that relies on evidence not related to the topic mentioned in the question stem is wrong.

Contradicts the Passage

If an answer choice contradicts any information from the passage, it can't be correct.

Word Trap

The LSAT writers like to create distracters that contain words that you recognize from the passage but that don't add up to something that is guaranteed to be true. Be suspicious of answer choices that repeat a part of the passage verbatim.

> The second paragraph:
>
> The first alternative seems unlikely. One possible model for such an inertial system might involve an internal magnetic compass to measure the directional leg of each journey. Birds transported to the release site wearing magnets or otherwise subjected to an artificial magnetic field, however, are only occasionally affected. Alternately, if pigeons measure their displacement by consciously keeping track of the direction and degree of acceleration and deceleration of the various turns, and timing the individual legs of the journey, simply transporting them in the dark, with constant rotations, or under complete anesthesia ought to impair or eliminate their ability to orient. These treatments, however, have no effect. Unfortunately, no one has yet performed the crucial experiment of transporting pigeons in total darkness, anesthetized, rotating, and with the magnetic field reversed all at the same time.

Extreme

Extreme answers use much stronger language than is warranted by the passage. If the passage says that something is a promising theory, don't choose an answer choice that says it's the *best* theory.

Go ahead and attack the answer choices for this example.

> (A)   It has been conclusively ruled out by the results
> of numerous experiments.

Choice (A): Line 16 says the first alternative is "unlikely," which is not nearly as strong as "conclusively ruled out." This answer choice is **extreme**. *Cut it.*

> (B)   It seems unlikely because there are no theoretical
> models that could explain how pigeons track
> displacement.

Choice (B) is a **word trap** because it repeats the word "unlikely" found in line 16. But keep reading: a theoretical model is found in lines 16–19, and another is mentioned in lines 22–26. This choice **contradicts the passage**. *Cut it.*

> (C)   It has not, to date, been supported by
> experimental data, but neither has it been
> definitively ruled out.

Choice (C) requires you to synthesize multiple statements in the second paragraph. The paragraph says the two experiments that were performed did not support the theory, but it mentions an additional "crucial experiment," not yet performed, that could test all the different parts of the theory. This matches well with saying the theory "has not yet been ruled out." *Keep it.*

> (D)   It seems unlikely in theory, but recent
> experimental results show that it may in fact be
> correct.

Choice (D) **contradicts the passage**. The results, discussed in lines 19–22 and 28–29, indicated that the various models were not correct. *Cut it.*

> (E)   It is not a useful theory because of the difficulty
> in designing experiments by which it might be
> tested.

Choice (E) **contradicts the passage** in a bad way. No fewer than three experiments to test the theory were mentioned in the second paragraph. *Cut it.*

Choice (C) is the correct answer.

6.2   VIEWPOINT QUESTIONS

Viewpoint questions ask you to pick a statement that corresponds to someone's viewpoint.

In your analysis of a passage, you always identify the author's main point, and in passages with more than one viewpoint, you always identify the various viewpoints. Accurate analysis of the passage is crucial when it comes to answering Viewpoint questions. The better you become at discerning the different voices within the passage, the more points you will earn on Viewpoint questions.

6.2.1   IDENTIFY

Viewpoint questions are easy to spot. Here are some keys to identifying them:

1.   **The question stem always asks about either the author or someone mentioned in the passage.**

2.   **The question stem always refers to a person's *view*, what they *believe*, or what they are *most likely to agree* with.**

Here are some sample Viewpoint question stems:

> With which one of the following statements would the author of the passage be most likely to agree?

> The passage suggests that the oenologists mentioned in line 17 would be most likely to agree with which one of the following statements?

> The passage most strongly supports the ascription of which one of the following views to ecologists who support controlled burns?

> According to the author, most early Greek philosophers believed that

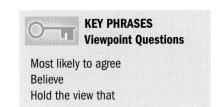

KEY PHRASES
Viewpoint Questions

Most likely to agree
Believe
Hold the view that

All of these ask you to choose the statement that corresponds to someone's viewpoint.

These question stems can be deceptive. It might seem as if these questions require creative thinking on your part—perhaps you should put yourself in the author's position? This is not the case. These questions are just as concrete as any other question type. There is evidence in the passage that makes one answer correct and the others wrong, and your job is to find that evidence.

6.2.2 ANALYZE

Your first analysis step was done when you analyzed the passage and determined the various viewpoints.

After that, Viewpoint questions are a lot like Inference questions: your analysis depends on how specific the question is. If the question is so general that the necessary evidence could come from anywhere in the passage, then you need to go straight to the answer choices.

If, on the other hand, it asks about a specific topic, then you should use your analysis of the passage to find the topic and do a little bit of rereading in that area, just as you do on several other question types. Likewise, if the question stem asks about a specific person's viewpoint, and that viewpoint is discussed only in a limited area, you should revisit that area and refresh your memory.

Try the following Viewpoint question, which refers to the Homing Pigeon passage:

> 2. Given the information in the passage, it is most likely that Papi and the author of the passage would both agree with which one of the following statements regarding the homing ability of pigeons?
>
> Test 27, Section 3, Question 21

This is a very interesting Viewpoint question because it requires you to think about *two* viewpoints and to find a point of agreement between them. You will definitely have to <u>use</u> the evidence you find in the passage.

In your analysis of the passage, you found that Papi was discussed in the third and fourth paragraphs. The author's viewpoint is found throughout the passage (which you should *not* reread in its entirety). So, while it's possible that the evidence you need could be anywhere, it's probably going to be found in the third and fourth paragraphs.

6.2.3 PREPHRASE

Prephrasing on Viewpoint questions can be challenging. Most of the time, you will not be able to predict what the correct answer will say. But you should at least know what correct answers to Viewpoint questions look like. Correct answers to Viewpoint questions are statements that have specific evidence from the passage to support them. You shouldn't rely on a gut feeling for Viewpoint questions: there is a reason why the correct answer is correct. You need to be able to point to the evidence.

Occasionally, you will be able to predict the answer to a Viewpoint question. If the question stem is specific enough, this question type can start to resemble Detail questions. For example, if a question stem asks "Based on the passage, the author would most probably agree with which one of the following statements about cognitive dissonance?" and cognitive dissonance was mentioned only *once* in the passage, then the correct answer will have to basically restate that one mention. In such a case, you could take your Prephrased answer directly from the text. Just use the words that are already on the page.

You won't be able to Prephrase anything too specific on most Viewpoint questions, especially when the question stems are vague.

This example presents the typical difficulty with Prephrasing. The author spends a lot of time disagreeing with Papi, so it's hard to Prephrase something they would agree on. If you can't think of anything, just move on to the answer choices.

6.2.4 ATTACK

Just like on Search and Inference questions, you may arrive at the answer choices without having already located the evidence. If that's the case, you will have to look for the supporting evidence after you read each answer choice.

In any case, you are looking for the answer choice that corresponds to the right viewpoint and that has evidence for it in the passage.

Before you attack the answer choices, you should be aware of the most common distracters for Viewpoint questions:

Wrong Viewpoint
It can be hard to remember who believes what, especially in passages that contain several viewpoints. The LSAT writers will create trap answers that correctly state *someone's* viewpoint—just make sure it belongs to the right person.

Out of Scope
Out of scope answers have no specific evidence in the passage. Even if you think it's likely that the author would agree with a given statement in an answer choice, it is out of scope unless you can point to specific evidence to support it.

Contradicts the Passage
If an answer choice contradicts any information from the passage, it can't be correct.

Extreme
Extreme answers use much stronger language than is warranted by the passage.

Attack the answer choices for this example.

> (A)   The map sense of pigeons is most probably
>   related to their olfactory sense.

Choice (A): This corresponds with Papi's viewpoint, which is introduced in lines 36–37. But the author cites several facts in the fourth paragraph that suggest the olfactory sense is *not* the best explanation. *Cut it.*

> (B)   The mechanism regulating the homing ability of
>   pigeons is most probably similar to that utilized
>   by honeybees.

Choice (B): Honeybees are mentioned way back in line 11 as an example of an animal that uses the "outward displacement" mechanism, but Papi's experiment is all about verifying the "map sense" mechanism. This choice corresponds to the **wrong viewpoint.** *Cut it.*

> (C)   The homing ability of pigeons is most probably
>   based on a map sense.

Choice (C): In line 35, the author says the map sense theory is the "more promising" of the two, so this choice corresponds to the author's viewpoint. Papi implicitly endorses the map sense theory by trying to figure out how it works, so this choice also corresponds to Papi's viewpoint. *Keep it.*

> (D)   The experiments conducted by Papi himself have provided the most valuable evidence yet collected regarding the homing ability of pigeons.

Choice (D): "The most valuable evidence yet collected" is an **extreme** characterization not supported by the passage. *Cut it.*

> (E)   The experiments conducted by Schmidt-Koenig and Phillips have not substantially lessened the probability that Papi's own theory is correct.

Choice (E): You aren't told anything at all about how Papi would view these experiments. The author calls their results a "problem" for Papi's hypothesis, so this certainly contradicts the author's viewpoint. *Cut it.*

Choice (C) is the correct answer.

6.2.5   PAN-INDIAN PASSAGE

Before you move on to the next two question types, please take a moment to read and analyze the following text. This excerpt is the first two paragraphs from a passage that explores the question of whether the "Pan-Indian" theory correctly describes the current state of Native American culture.

> Even in the midst of its resurgence as a vital tradition, many sociologists have viewed the current form of the powwow, a ceremonial gathering of native Americans, as a sign that tribal culture is in decline. Focusing on
> (5)   the dances and rituals that have recently come to be shared by most tribes, they suggest that an intertribal movement is now in ascension and claim the inevitable outcome of this tendency is the eventual dissolution of tribes and the complete assimilation of native Americans
> (10)   into Euroamerican society. Proponents of this "Pan-Indian" theory point to the greater frequency of travel and communication between reservations, the greater urbanization of native Americans, and, most recently, their increasing politicization in response to common
> (15)   grievances as the chief causes of the shift toward intertribalism.
>   Indeed, the rapid diffusion of dance styles, outfits, and songs from one reservation to another offers compelling evidence that intertribalism has been
> (20)   increasing. However, these sociologists have failed to note the concurrent revitalization of many traditions unique to individual tribes. Among the Lakota, for instance, the Sun Dance was revived, after a forty-year hiatus, during the 1950's. Similarly, the Black Legging
> (25)   Society of the Kiowa and the Hethuska Society of the Ponca—both traditional groups within their respective tribes—have gained new popularity. Obviously, a more complex societal shift is taking place than the theory of Pan-Indianism can account for.
>
> Test 25, Section 1, Passage 3

6.3   ATTITUDE QUESTIONS

Attitude questions ask you to identify how the author *feels* about a certain phenomenon or someone else's viewpoint. As on all Using the Evidence questions, you will not have to guess how the author feels. There will be specific words in the passage that tell you exactly what the author's attitude is on the topic.

Attitude questions are similar to Viewpoint questions in that your analysis of the author's viewpoint when your first read the passage is crucial, and you will use similar evidence to identify the correct answer. The difference is that, instead of looking for the *statement* the author would agree with, you are looking for the *feeling* that the author has for a particular statement or situation.

6.3.1   IDENTIFY

Attitude question stems are usually quite predictable.

> 1. **Most Attitude question stems contain the word** *attitude.*
>
> 2. **Other Attitude questions ask about** *how the author views something* **or** *what the author appears to value.*

Here are some sample Attitude question stems:

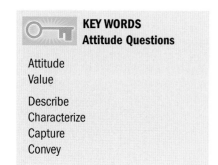

**KEY WORDS
Attitude Questions**

Attitude
Value

Describe
Characterize
Capture
Convey

> Which one of the following most accurately characterizes the author's attitude toward Silnesra's theory?
>
> Based on the passage, the author's attitude toward the school of thought presented in the third paragraph is most accurately described as
>
> It can be most reasonably inferred from the passage that the author views the double-blind strategy developed by Parrack as
>
> Based on the passage, which one of the following aspects of Overbeck's work does the author of the passage appear to value most highly?

The vast majority of Attitude questions look like the first example.

The third example contains the word *inferred*, which may lead you to think it's an Inference question. Treating it like an Inference question is not a problem, since doing so would simply mean that you'd look for supporting evidence in the text. However, you can get more specific—since the answer choices will all be *feelings* that the author may have toward Parrack's strategy, you can work more efficiently by limiting your search for evidence to places where the author conveys her attitude.

The fourth example is a more complicated Attitude question, since you'd first have to figure out the author's feelings for several different aspects of Overbeck's work, then determine which one the author feels best about.

6.3.2   ANALYZE

The first step in your analysis for Attitude questions was done when you first read the passage. Attitude questions always ask about the author's attitude toward a particular topic, so your search for evidence can be narrowed down to the part of the passage where that topic was discussed. Furthermore, in your analysis of the passage, you identified statements that conveyed the author's viewpoint and the main point. The evidence you need can be found in these statements.

To complete your analysis, identify opinionated words, such as

- clearly, obviously, by no means
- likely, probable, unlikely, improbable
- correct, incorrect

- appropriate, inappropriate
- well reasoned, reasonable, unreasonable
- supported, unsupported
- will, should, must

These words are the evidence you will use to answer the question.

Take a look at this question, which references the Pan-Indian passage on page 63.

> 3. Which one of the following most accurately describes the author's attitude toward the theory of Pan-Indianism?
>
> Test 25, Section 1, Question 18

Since this question stem asks about the author's attitude, it's an Attitude question.

In your analysis of the passage, you should have discovered that the first paragraph deals with the sociologists' viewpoint, and that the second paragraph describes the author's. Look more closely at the second paragraph. There are a few key phrases that convey the author's opinion:

- "offers compelling evidence" (lines 18–19)
- "failed to note" (lines 20–21)
- "obviously" (line 27)

These are the phrases that will allow you to determine the author's attitude.

6.3.3 PREPHRASE

You should always Prephrase an answer to Attitude questions. Use the evidence you found to complete this sentence:

> Prephrase: Regarding this topic, the author feels _____.

Remember, this is the LSAT. The answer choices will be complicated and nuanced. If your Prephrased answer is something as simple as "good" or "negative," you will probably have difficulty finding the correct answer. Make your Prephrased answer as specific and complete as you can.

In this example, you are trying to figure out how the author feels about the Pan-Indian theory. On one hand, the author says there is some "compelling evidence" to support it. But later, the author states, "Obviously, a more complex societal shift is taking place than Pan-Indianism can account for."

One way to Prephrase an answer would be, "Regarding the theory of Pan-Indianism, the author feels ambivalent." But this is probably too simplistic.

A better Prephrased answer would be:

> Attitude: Regarding the theory of Pan-Indianism, the author feels that it has some validity but does not tell the whole story.

6.3.4 ATTACK

Authors care about what they write about, and they usually approve or disapprove of things in a measured, academic way. Thus, they rarely have an attitude of unadulterated joy, crushing despondency, or indifferent apathy.

Attitude questions have some predictable distracters:

Extreme
If you determine that the author feels "hesitant approval" for something, don't pick an answer choice that contains "unmitigated enthusiasm."

Opposite
When an author feels positive about something, there will usually be trap answer choices that convey negative feelings, and vice versa.

Word Trap
The LSAT writers like to create distracters that contain words that you will recognize from the passage but that don't add up to the author's attitude. Be suspicious of answer choices that repeat a part of the passage verbatim.

Out of Scope

Some answer choices offer new information that was never mentioned in the passage. Get rid of these.

Take a look at the answer choices for this example.

> (A)   critical of its tendency to attribute political
>   motives to cultural practices

Choice (A): Even though the word *politicization* appeared in line 14, this answer choice has nothing to do with the Prephrased answer. It's a **word trap**. *Cut it.*

> (B)   discomfort at its negative characterization of
>   cultural borrowing by native Americans

Choice (B): The problem the author has with the theory is that it doesn't tell the whole story, not that it characterizes cultural borrowing negatively. *Cut it.*

> (C)   hopeful about its chances for preserving tribal
>   culture

Choice (C): The author had both good and bad things to say about the theory, but this answer choice is all positive, and thus **extreme**. *Cut it.*

> (D)   offended by its claim that assimilation is a
>   desirable consequence of cultural contact

Choice (D) is also **extreme**. It neglects to mention the positive things that the author said about the theory, and there is no evidence in the passage to indicate that the author was offended. *Cut it.*

> (E)   skeptical that it is a complete explanation of
>   recent changes in native American society

Choice (E) is a good match for the Prephrased answer. It's not completely dismissive nor completely accepting. The Prephrased answer said the theory doesn't tell the whole story; this choice says it isn't a complete explanation. *Keep it.*

Choice (E) is the correct answer.

6.4   MATCH QUESTIONS

Some passages contain a set of rules, a definition of a new term, or a list of something's defining characteristics. **Match** questions ask you to provide an example that matches the description or definition.

6.4.1   IDENTIFY

Since all Match questions revolve around finding an example of something that matches a certain definition or set of rules, they usually use the word *example* or *exemplify*.

Other Match questions find another way of asking for an example, such as asking which answer choice *illustrates the concept*.

Here are some sample Match question stems:

> Which one of the following examples best illustrates the type of legislative approach recommended by the academics mentioned in the fourth paragraph?

> Given the information in the passage, which one of the following most closely exemplifies Kamala's understanding of impressionism?

> Based on the passage, which one of the following is best explained as non-Newtonian fluid behavior?

> Which one of the following epidemiological studies would NOT be covered by the threefold categorization scheme proposed by Knechtley?

In the last example, four of the answer choices would match the scheme, while the correct answer choice would not. The EXCEPT Tool would be appropriate for this question.

6.4.2 ANALYZE

Your analysis for Match questions has two steps:

1. **Find the definition or set of rules** that you must provide an example of.

2. **Determine the major components** of that set of rules.

All Match question stems specifically mention the definition or set of rules that you must find an example of, but they usually don't tell you the line number. Use your analysis of the passage to find the right place.

Once you have found the definition, determine the major characteristics that would make something match the definition or rules. Usually these will be explicitly listed, but sometimes the author, instead of giving you a definition, gives you a list of examples. In such a case, you have to do some thinking to figure out what the examples all have in common and what the definition really is.

Take a look at this question, from the Pan-Indian passage.

> 4. Which one of the following situations most clearly illustrates the phenomenon of intertribalism, as that phenomenon is described in the passage?
>
> Test 25, Section 1, Question 20

The question stem asks for a situation that *illustrates the phenomenon* of intertribalism. That's the same as asking for an example, so this is a Match question.

Your first step is to find the place in the passage where intertribalism is defined. Unfortunately, intertribalism is discussed throughout the passage, not just in one place. Worse, there doesn't appear to be a spot in which the author gives a concrete definition of the concept. In this case, you'll have to find some examples of it and determine for yourself what the definition is.

One "suggestion" of an intertribal movement is in lines 4–6:

> Focusing on the dances and rituals that have recently come to be shared by most tribes

Lines 17–18 also provide "evidence" of intertribalism:

> the rapid diffusion of dance styles, outfits, and songs from one reservation to another

Although it's not the same as an *example*, the author also points out some potential "causes" of intertribalism in lines 11–15:

> the greater frequency of travel and communication between reservations, the greater urbanization of native Americans, and, most recently, their increasing politicization in response to common grievances

Your second step is to figure out what the important characteristics of intertribalism are. The one thing that all these makings of a definition have in common is the sharing of customs or communication between different tribes.

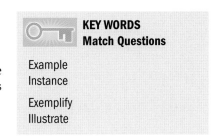

KEY WORDS
Match Questions

Example
Instance

Exemplify
Illustrate

Match questions are related to Logical Reasoning's Conform questions, specifically those that ask you to **apply** the principle.

6.4.3 PREPHRASE

Since there are many potential examples that could match a certain set of rules, you will not be able to predict the particular example that the correct answer will use. Don't bother trying. As long as you know the important features that the correct answer will have, you are ready to move on to the answer choices.

In this example a good Prephrased answer would be:

> Prephrase: The correct answer choice should illustrate the sharing of customs or communication between different tribes.

Don't try to get too specific with your Prephrased answer on Match questions.

6.4.4 ATTACK

Every incorrect answer choice will simply fail to match the definition. The LSAT writers create tempting distracters for Match questions in the usual ways.

Word Trap

These distracters use familiar words from the passage but don't correctly capture the important parts of the definition you're looking for.

Out of Scope

Be careful here. The correct answer choice will contain an example that *was not* mentioned in the passage, but it will conform to the rules that *were* specified or illustrated. If an answer choice has characteristics that were not contained in the relevant rules, then it's out of scope.

Take a look at the answer choices for this example.

> (A)   a native American tribe in which a number of powerful societies attempt to prevent the revival of a traditional dance

Choice (A): This has nothing to do with the sharing of customs or communication between different tribes. *Cut it.*

> (B)   a native American tribe whose members attempt to learn the native languages of several other tribes

Choice (B): This sounds like a good example of communication between different tribes. *Keep it.*

> (C)   a native American tribe whose members attempt to form a political organization in order to redress several grievances important to that tribe

Choice (C): This **word trap** may remind you of line 14, but it lacks the important feature of communication between different tribes. *Cut it.*

> (D)   a native American tribe in which a significant percentage of the members have forsaken their tribal identity and become assimilated into Euroamerican society

Choice (D): The sociologists mention this as an *outcome* of intertribalism, not an *example* of it. This is **out of scope**. *Cut it.*

> (E)   a native American tribe whose members often travel to other parts of the reservation in order to visit friends and relatives

Choice (E) also lacks the important feature of communication between different tribes. *Cut it.*

Choice (B) is the correct answer.

STOP. THIS IS THE END OF LECTURE 3. DO NOT PROCEED TO THE CORRESPONDING EXAM UNTIL INSTRUCTED TO DO SO IN CLASS.

LECTURE 4 | CHAPTER 7

CONTROVERSY PASSAGES

7.1 IDENTIFYING CONTROVERSY PASSAGES

Controversy passages are primarily about a conflict of views. For example, a Controversy passage may say that an expert thinks one thing, the critics think another, but the author thinks the critics are wrong—a total of three views. Within a section, a Controversy passage is often the hardest passage. They certainly present some interesting reading challenges.

Controversy passages are defined by the following characteristics:

- **The passage contains several viewpoints.** These viewpoints are well-developed and are not simply a single sentence that the author immediately refutes. In addition, the various viewpoints all concern the same topic, and each responds to points made in the others.

- **The passage is not designed to answer a core question.** The passage will of course address a particular topic, and the author may even advocate a certain "answer" or understanding, but there is no core question and no journey from confusion to clarity.

Controversy passages often appear in one of two major forms. The first is one in which the topic is introduced and then the various viewpoints of several different parties are presented. This form is rather straightforward.

The second can be a little more interesting. This form looks a little like a **book report** that you might have written in the third grade. The author spends a great deal of time, often the majority of the passage, fully reporting on and exploring a certain expert's thesis. At the end of the passage, the author steps in and delivers his or her own opinion of the expert's thesis. The author's opinion may be that the expert is largely correct, or the author may disagree.

The reason that this **book report** form is noteworthy is that, occasionally, the author *never* steps in with an opinion. The passage simply says, "Expert Q thinks X, Y, and Z," and nothing more. Such a passage does *not* contain several viewpoints, and thus is *not* a Controversy passage. If you see such a passage, you should treat it as a Thesis passage. Although the thesis in most Thesis passages comes from the author's point of view, it can come from a third party, as illustrated here.

> Don't waste time or energy stressing out about proper identification of passages. Instead, just be aware of what your analysis should be in each type of passage, and keep an eye out for the most important features.

Alert readers may have noticed that whether a **book report**–style passage is a Thesis or Controversy passage is determined by whether the author steps in and delivers his own opinion, which is unlikely to occur until the end of the passage. Therefore, sometimes you won't know what type of passage you are looking at until you reach the end of it. This isn't a problem. After all, in a Thesis passage, your analysis calls for finding the main point and the purpose of each paragraph. Your analysis of a Controversy passage calls for the same thing, plus a little more. As you read, simply watch carefully for a switch to another viewpoint. If it comes, note the various viewpoints. If it doesn't, then you have already completed your full analysis of a Thesis passage.

7.2 ANALYZING CONTROVERSY PASSAGES

To analyze a Controversy Passage, look for:

1. **The various viewpoints**

2. **The main point**

3. **The purpose of each paragraph**

7.2.1 THE VARIOUS VIEWPOINTS

The process of finding the various viewpoints in a Controversy passage is identical to that of finding them in an Enlightenment passage. Each statement in the passage will be part of the author's viewpoint, someone else's viewpoint, or an accepted fact.

As you identify the various viewpoints, mark the passage to remind yourself where the viewpoints are located.

Chapter 5 discussed the details of finding the various viewpoints. Here's a reminder:

Accepted Facts

Accepted facts look like the contents of Informational passages or premises in the Logical Reasoning section, since they are:

- Descriptive

- Not really up for debate

Some examples include:

- The results of simple observation

- Matters of historical record

- Laws of nature

- Calculations

- Statistics

Someone Else's Viewpoint

- These will appear with a viewpoint **indicator**—a phrase that that tells you who the statement should be attributed to.

- You should underline the name of the theory or the name of the group that endorses a particular viewpoint.

- Mark later occurrences of that viewpoint with a mnemonic symbol.

The Author's Viewpoint

- These statements do not have a viewpoint **indicator** attributing them to someone else.

- They sound like opinions, not accepted facts, and often use opinionated words.

- They often pass judgment, stating whether something is correct or incorrect, likely or unlikely, etc.

- You should also mark an author's viewpoint with a mnemonic symbol.

When the passage switches from discussing one viewpoint to another, it often uses a **turnaround word** such as *however*. Underline these and use them to help you separate the various viewpoints.

7.2.2 THE MAIN POINT

You should always determine the main point of Controversy passages, and you should mark it with brackets or jot it down in a few of your own words next to the passage.

The main point may be explicitly stated, or you may have to synthesize it yourself from several statements, but just as in Enlightenment passages, the main point will always be very closely related to the author's own viewpoint.

As in **all** passage types, the main point is one of the author's most general statements, it counters any so-called "wrong" viewpoints, and its supporting evidence is found throughout the passage.

7.2.3 THE PURPOSE OF EACH PARAGRAPH

In addition to determining the main point of the passage, you should look for the purpose of each paragraph. Most paragraphs have one of several common purposes.

1. **To introduce the topic.** The first paragraph of some Controversy passages contains only accepted facts and serves simply to familiarize you with the topic.

2. **To present a single viewpoint.** Controversy passages consist of conflicting viewpoints, and each of those viewpoints is presented just like an argument in the Logical Reasoning section—it is made up of a conclusion and supporting premises. When a paragraph contains only a single viewpoint, you should analyze it just like you analyze a passage in the Logical Reasoning section. Identify the premises and conclusion using the same tools:

   - **Conclusion and premise indicators** such as *so*, *given that*, *since* and *because*

   - **Facts and opinions**

   - **Suggestions**

   - The Why Tool, in which you ask, "Why [potential conclusion] ?" and look for supporting evidence in the rest of the paragraph.

   Just as in Logical Reasoning passages, mark the conclusion with brackets. The conclusion will represent the heart of one of the various viewpoints, so you may have marked it already. That's good.

3. **To counter a previous paragraph with a conflicting viewpoint.** Later paragraphs often go one step further: in addition to presenting a conclusion and premises, they serve to counter a previous paragraph. So, in addition to finding the premises and conclusion, you should determine **how** one viewpoint counters the other. Does it attack one of the premises? Does it bring in additional evidence? Does it point out a flaw in the reasoning? Does it show a necessary assumption to be false?

The main point is one of the most general statements in the passage, but it may be preceded by one or two even more general sentences that introduce the topic and set the stage for the passage. In this way the thesis statement can be more specific than the other sentences in the first paragraph.

See chapter 2 in the Examkrackers Logical Reasoning textbook for more information on these tools.

This can be one of the most challenging steps in your analysis. It means bringing together all the skills you use in the Logical Reasoning section—it's a lot like a Method, Point at Issue, Necessary Assumption, Flaw, and Weaken question, all in one. Difficult? Of course. But a strong analysis of the passage will greatly increase the number of points you can get from the questions, so start practicing!

4. **To present a viewpoint and counter it in the same paragraph.** This kind of paragraph accomplishes the same thing as the two previously discussed kinds, but all wrapped up in a single paragraph. Your analysis has the same components.

As you determine the purpose of each paragraph, you should mark the passage appropriately. This may be as simple as putting the main point of the paragraph in brackets. It may mean jotting down a few words to summarize **how** that paragraph accomplishes its purpose. Or it might even include drawing lines that point from one paragraph to another to indicate specific points that counter others made in different parts of the passage.

7.3 PUTTING IT ALL TOGETHER

7.3.1 Drill: Controversy Passages

Directions: Practice the Identify and Analyze steps on the following passage. Answer the questions that follow the passage.

Scientists typically advocate the analytic method of studying complex systems: systems are divided into component parts that are investigated separately. But nineteenth-century critics of this method claimed that
(5) when a system's parts are isolated its complexity tends to be lost. To address the perceived weaknesses of the analytic method these critics put forward a concept called organicism, which posited that the whole determines the nature of its parts and that the parts of a
(10) whole are interdependent.

Organicism depended upon the theory of internal relations, which states that relations between entities are possible only within some whole that embraces them, and that entities are altered by the relationships
(15) into which they enter. If an entity stands in a relationship with another entity, it has some property as a consequence. Without this relationship, and hence without the property, the entity would be different—and so would be another entity. Thus, the property is
(20) one of the entity's defining characteristics. Each of an entity's relationships likewise determines a defining characteristic of the entity.

One problem with the theory of internal relations is that not all properties of an entity are defining
(25) characteristics: numerous properties are accompanying characteristics—even if they are always present, their presence does not influence the entity's identity. Thus, even if it is admitted that every relationship into which an entity enters determines some characteristic of the
(30) entity, it is not necessarily true that such characteristics will define the entity; it is possible for the entity to enter into a relationship yet remain essentially unchanged.

The ultimate difficulty with the theory of internal
(35) relations is that it renders the acquisition of knowledge impossible. To truly know an entity, we must know all of its relationships; but because the entity is related to everything in each whole of which it is a part, these wholes must be known completely before the entity
(40) can be known. This seems to be a prerequisite impossible to satisfy.

Organicists' criticism of the analytic method arose from their failure to fully comprehend the method. In rejecting the analytic method, organicists overlooked
(45) the fact that before the proponents of the method analyzed the component parts of a system, they first determined both the laws applicable to the whole system and the initial conditions of the system; proponents of the method thus did not study parts of a
(50) system in full isolation from the system as a whole. Since organicists failed to recognize this, they never advanced any argument to show that laws and initial conditions of complex systems cannot be discovered. Hence, organicists offered no valid reason for rejecting
(55) the analytic method or for adopting organicism as a replacement for it.

Test 25, Section 1, Passage 4

1. How can you identify what type of passage this is?

_____

_____

_____

_____

2a. What are the goals of your analysis of the passage?

_____

_____

_____

_____

2b. What are the results of your analysis of the passage?

_____

_____

_____

_____

3. Which one of the following most completely and accurately summarizes the argument of the passage?

(A) By calling into question the possibility that complex systems can be studied in their entirety, organicists offered an alternative to the analytic method favored by nineteenth-century scientists.

(B) Organicists did not offer a useful method of studying complex systems because they did not acknowledge that there are relationships into which an entity may enter that do not alter the entity's identity.

(C) Organicism is flawed because it relies on a theory that both ignores the fact that not all characteristics of entities are defining and ultimately makes the acquisition of knowledge impossible.

(D) Organicism does not offer a valid challenge to the analytic method both because it relies on faulty theory and because it is based on a misrepresentation of the analytic method.

(E) In criticizing the analytic method, organicists neglected to disprove that scientists who employ the method are able to discover the laws and initial conditions of the systems they study.

Test 25, Section 1, Question 22

4. According to the passage, organicists' chief objection to the analytic method was that the method

(A) oversimplified systems by isolating their components

(B) assumed that a system can be divided into component parts

(C) ignored the laws applicable to the system as a whole

(D) claimed that the parts of a system are more important than the system as a whole

(E) denied the claim that entities enter into relationships

Test 25, Section 1, Question 23

5. The passage most strongly supports the ascription of which one of the following views to scientists who use the analytic method?

(A) A complex system is best understood by studying its component parts in full isolation from the system as a whole.

(B) The parts of a system should be studied with an awareness of the laws and initial conditions that govern the system.

(C) It is not possible to determine the laws governing a system until the system's parts are separated from one another.

(D) Because the parts of a system are interdependent, they cannot be studied separately without destroying the system's complexity.

(E) Studying the parts of a system individually eliminates the need to determine which characteristics of the parts are defining characteristics.

Test 25, Section 1, Question 25

Answers & Explanations

AM — Scientists typically advocate the analytic method of studying complex systems: systems are divided into component parts that are investigated separately. But nineteenth-century critics of this method claimed that when a system's parts are isolated its complexity tends to be lost. To address the (perceived weaknesses) of the analytic method these critics put forward a concept called organicism, which posited that the whole determines the nature of its parts and that the parts of a whole are interdependent.

¶1: two methods

O — Organicism depended upon the theory of internal relations, which states that relations between entities are possible only within some whole that embraces them, and that entities are altered by the relationships into which they enter. If an entity stands in a relationship with another entity, it has some property as a consequence. Without this relationship, and hence without the property, the entity would be different—and so would be another entity. Thus, the property is one of the entity's defining characteristics. Each of an entity's relationships likewise determines a defining characteristic of the entity.

¶2: TOIR (part of O)

¶3: problem with TOIR — [One (problem) with the theory of internal relations is that not all properties of an entity are defining characteristics:] numerous properties are accompanying characteristics—even if they are always present, their presence does not influence the entity's identity. Thus, even if it is admitted that every relationship into which an entity enters determines some characteristic of the entity, it is not necessarily true that such characteristics will define the entity; it is possible for the entity to enter into a relationship yet remain essentially unchanged.

¶4: 2nd problem with TOIR — [The (ultimate difficulty) with the theory of internal relations is that it renders the acquisition of knowledge impossible.] To truly know an entity, we must know all of its relationships; but because the entity is related to everything in each whole of which it is a part, these wholes must be known completely before the entity can be known. This seems to be a prerequisite impossible to satisfy.

A

¶5: The source of O's problem is misunderstanding of AM — [Organicists' criticism of the analytic method arose from their (failure) to fully comprehend the method.] In rejecting the analytic method, organicists overlooked the fact that before the proponents of the method analyzed the component parts of a system, they first determined both the laws applicable to the whole system and the initial conditions of the system; proponents of the method thus did not study parts of a system in full isolation from the system as a whole. Since organicists failed to recognize this, they never advanced any argument to show that laws and initial conditions of complex systems cannot be discovered. Hence, organicists offered (no valid reason) for rejecting the analytic method or for adopting organicism as a replacement for it.

AM

*MP: O flawed b/c it misunderstood AM and used faulty TOIR

1. You can identify this as a Controversy passage because it explores several opposing viewpoints in detail.

2a. The goals of your analysis are to find the various viewpoints, the main point, and the purpose of each paragraph.

2b. The various viewpoints are: the viewpoint of scientists who advocate the analytical method (AM), the organicists' (O), and the author's (A). They are marked on the passage.

The main point is also marked as a brief note at the end of the passage. The author uses opinionated words (circled) to indicate that he rejects organicism for several reasons.

Finally, there are brief notes next to each paragraph to remind you of the purpose of each paragraph.

3. Choice (D) is the correct answer.

This is a Main Point question, which you should have Prephrased an answer to in your analysis of the passage. The Prephrased main point was: [Organicism was flawed because it misunderstood the analytic method and used the faulty theory of internal relations.]

(A)   By calling into question the possibility that complex systems can be studied in their entirety, organicists offered an alternative to the analytic method favored by nineteenth-century scientists.

No. This **contradicts the passage** because organicists advocated studying a system in its entirety. Furthermore, this answer choice is **incomplete** because it makes no mention of organicism's problems.

(B)   Organicists did not offer a useful method of studying complex systems because they did not acknowledge that there are relationships into which an entity may enter that do not alter the entity's identity.

No. This is **incomplete** because it mentions only one of the major problems with organicism.

(C)   Organicism is flawed because it relies on a theory that both ignores the fact that not all characteristics of entities are defining and ultimately makes the acquisition of knowledge impossible.

No. This answer choice is better than choice (B) because it mentions two of the major problems with organicism, but it lacks any mention of the material in the last paragraph.

(D)   Organicism does not offer a valid challenge to the analytic method both because it relies on faulty theory and because it is based on a misrepresentation of the analytic method.

Yes. This choice is a good match for the Prephrased answer. It correctly points to all the problems with organicism discussed by the author.

(E)   In criticizing the analytic method, organicists neglected to disprove that scientists who employ the method are able to discover the laws and initial conditions of the systems they study.

No. This answer choice is **incomplete** because it cites only a single sentence from the last paragraph and neglects to mention the other major problems that the author pointed out.

4. Choice (A) is the correct answer.

This Viewpoint question asks about the organicists' viewpoint, so the answer will be found in the first two paragraphs. Specifically, the stem asks for their problem with the analytic method, which is revealed in lines 4–6: "critics of this method claimed that when a system's parts are isolated its complexity tends to be lost."

(A)   oversimplified systems by isolating their components

Yes. Although it uses different words, this choice means exactly the same thing as the Prephrased answer.

(B)   assumed that a system can be divided into component parts

No. Although the analytic method does assume that a system can be divided into component parts, the passage doesn't identify this as the reason organicists had a problem with it.

(C)   ignored the laws applicable to the system as a whole

No. This **contradicts** the information in lines 46–48.

(D)   claimed that the parts of a system are more important than the system as a whole

No. There is no information in the passage to say that scientists claimed one thing was more important than another. This is **out of scope**.

(E)   denied the claim that entities enter into relationships

No. This has nothing to do with the Prephrased answer and is not supported by the passage.

5. Choice (B) is the correct answer.

This Viewpoint question asks about the stance of the supporters of the analytic method. In your analysis of the passage, you found that their viewpoint was discussed in the first sentence of the passage and in the middle of the final paragraph. Look for an answer supported by the information in these places.

(A)   A complex system is best understood by studying its component parts in full isolation from the system as a whole.

No. This **contradicts the passage**, specifically lines 49–50.

(B)   The parts of a system should be studied with an awareness of the laws and initial conditions that govern the system.

Yes. This matches what was said in lines 45–48.

(C)   It is not possible to determine the laws governing a system until the system's parts are separated from one another.

No. This **contradicts the passage**, which says the laws governing the system were determined *before* its parts were studied.

(D)   Because the parts of a system are interdependent, they cannot be studied separately without destroying the system's complexity.

No. This is the **wrong viewpoint**. This is what the organicists believed.

(E)   Studying the parts of a system individually eliminates the need to determine which characteristics of the parts are defining characteristics.

No. The passage gives no information about how the supporters of the analytic method feel about defining characteristics. The passage contains only the author's viewpoint on that matter.

NOW MOVE ON TO THE SECOND CHAPTER OF LECTURE 4. WHEN YOU HAVE COMPLETED IT, YOU CAN GET FURTHER PRACTICE WITH CONTROVERSY PASSAGES IN THE CORRESPONDING EXAM AT THE END OF THE BOOK.

LECTURE **4** CHAPTER **8**

THE "BEYOND THE PASSAGE" QUESTION FAMILY

Questions in the **Beyond the Passage** family ask you to combine information in a passage with new information in order to arrive at the correct answer. All the questions in this family are similar to questions in the Logical Reasoning section of the test, and you will often use the same tactics to answer these questions when they appear in the Reading Comprehension section.

There are four types of Beyond the Passage questions:

1. Weaken/Strengthen
2. Analogy
3. Principle
4. Complete

8.1 WEAKEN / STRENGTHEN QUESTIONS

Weaken and **Strengthen** questions in the Reading Comprehension section work identically to those in the Logical Reasoning section. A conclusion is drawn in the passage, but the evidence used to support that conclusion is not enough to completely prove its validity. You are asked to choose a piece of new information that makes the conclusion less likely or more likely to be true.

8.1.1 IDENTIFY

All Weaken and Strengthen questions share the following characteristics:

1. **The question stem directs your attention to a particular claim.** In the Logical Reasoning section, a Weaken question stem may simply ask you to weaken "the argument," but in the Reading Comprehension section, the question stem will tell you exactly which claim to focus on.

2. **The question stem tells you to accept the answer choices as true.** This is significant—as you must accept the truth of the answer choices, you should never eliminate an answer choice simply because it seems implausible.

3. **The question stem asks you to find the answer choice that most weakens or strengthens the claim.** Some words that mean the same thing as *weaken* are:

   • Challenge

   • Call into question

   • Cast doubt on

Some words that mean the same thing as *strengthen* are:

   • Support

   • Lend credence to

Here are some sample Weaken question stems:

> Which one of the following, if true, most weakens the author's argument concerning imaginary number theory?

> Which one of the following, if true, most weakens the author's criticism of the assumption that secondary education invariably engenders increased empathy?

> Which one of the following, if true, would most seriously challenge the position of the legal theorists mentioned in line 22?

Here are some sample Strengthen question stems:

> Which one of the following, if true, most supports the author's claim about the relationship between broker recommendations and the stock market (lines 20–25)?

> Which one of the following, if true, would most help to strengthen the author's primary conclusion in the last sentence of the passage?

> Which one of the following, if true, would have lent the most credence to the manufacturers' position in the lawsuit?

8.1.2 ANALYZE

Your analysis for Weaken and Strengthen question has several steps:

1. **Find the relevant claim.** The question stem will tell you what to focus on, and it may even tell you the location of the claim. If it doesn't tell you the location, use your analysis of the passage to find the claim in question. Revisit the sentences you bracketed or your notes next to each paragraph to help you find where the topic is likely to appear.

2. **Identify the supporting premises for the claim and any weakness in the argument.** You should be able to express the weakness as a Concept Shift, an unsupported assumption, or a flaw. Occasionally, a claim will not have much supporting evidence at all, and you won't be able to identify the weakness. If that's the case, move on to the next step.

> To learn more about Concept Shifts, unsupported assumptions, and flaws, see chapter 4 in the Examkrackers Logical Reasoning textbook.

Take a look at this question (it's not associated with the Organicism passage):

1. Which one of the following, if true, would most undermine the author's explanation for the way Miles Davis is regarded by jazz critics?
   Test 20, Section 2, Question 6

This question directs your attention to a particular claim (the explanation for the way Miles Davis is regarded by jazz critics), tells you to accept the answer choices as true, and asks which answer choice would most undermine (weaken) the claim. Thus, it's a Weaken question.

First, find the relevant claim in the passage. In this case, it came in the first paragraph:

> The career of trumpeter Miles Davis was one of the most astonishingly productive that jazz music has ever seen. Yet his genius has never received its due. The impatience and artistic restlessness that characterized his work spawned one stylistic turn after another and made Davis anathema to many critics, who deplored his abandonment first of bebop and then of "cool" acoustic jazz for ever more innovative sounds.
>
> Test 20, Section 2, Passage 1

You haven't see this passage before, but we've provided all the relevant parts you need to answer this question.

Next, identify the supporting premises for the claim and any weakness in the argument. In this case, as is often the case in the Reading Comprehension section, the supporting evidence is rather weak. You know that Davis abandoned certain sounds and turned to different styles. Then the author concludes that this caused critics to despise him and not give him his due. The argument looks at two things that happened (*correlation*) and concludes that one caused the other (*causation*). That's a common flaw that you should recognize from the Logical Reasoning section.

8.1.3 Prephrase

To Prephrase for a Strengthen or Weaken question, first remember what the correct answer will do. The correct answer to a Weaken question will suggest (not prove) that the claim is *untrue*. The correct answer to a Strengthen question will suggest (not prove) that the claim is *indeed true*.

The next step in your Prephrasing is to decide **how** the correct answer will accomplish one of these two things. The correct answer to a Weaken question attacks a weakness already present in the argument. You don't need to Prephrase a specific attack on the argument. Instead, you should Prephrase what kind of attack the answer is likely to make. Sometimes, the correct answer takes the most obvious route and attacks a linking assumption or a flaw.

Other times, the correct answer weakens the argument by making the premises irrelevant to the conclusion. The premises are supposed to be the evidence for the conclusion, but an answer choice can make the premises irrelevant so that the conclusion no longer has any evidence to support it.

Finally, some correct answers weaken by introducing entirely new considerations that have little to do with any linking assumptions. If the new consideration gives you reason to think the conclusion might be false, then it weakens the argument.

For Strengthen questions, you should still focus on the weaknesses in the argument, but this time, determine how an answer choice could defend against the weakness. For example, the correct answer choice could provide explicit proof that the necessary assumption is true, or it could explicitly connect the two sides of the Concept Shift.

In the Miles Davis passage, the weakness in the argument is the causal flaw, which, as you should know, always allows the argument to be weakened in a few predictable ways. To weaken this conclusion,

Prephrase: The correct answer choice will probably show that the critics' disapproval was due to another cause, or show that Davis's artistic restlessness and the critics' opinions of him were not related—it was merely a coincidence that they both occurred.

8.1.4 ATTACK

Here are the common distracters on Weaken and Strengthen questions.

Opposite

On Weaken questions, don't pick an answer choice that strengthens the claim. On Strengthen questions, don't pick an answer choice that weakens the claim.

Out of Scope

Be *extremely* careful here. The correct answer choice will almost *certainly* introduce new information that did not appear anywhere in the passage. If you dismiss answers too quickly because they seem irrelevant, you may end up eliminating the correct answer. A true **out of scope** answer choice fails to address the weakness that exists between the claim and its evidence.

Take a look at the answer choices for this example:

> (A)   Many jazz musicians who specialize in improvisational playing are greatly admired by jazz critics.

Choice (A): The weakness in this argument is the connection between his artistic restlessness and the critics' frosty reception. Improvisational playing really is **out of scope**. *Cut it.*

> (B)   Many jazz musicians whose careers have been characterized by several radical changes in style are greatly admired by jazz critics.

Choice (B): This answer choice successfully addresses the weakness that exists between the claim and its evidence. If many other artistically restless musicians do *not* meet with critics' disapproval, that suggests it was merely a coincidence when it happened in Davis's case. *Keep it.*

> (C)   Several jazz musicians who perform exclusively on electronic instruments are very highly regarded by jazz critics.

Choice (C): Again, the weakness in this argument is the connection between his artistic restlessness and the critics' censure. Electronic instruments are **out of scope**. *Cut it.*

> (D)   The jazz innovators who are held in the highest regard by jazz critics had brief yet brilliant careers.

Choice (D): The mention of a "brief yet brilliant career" does not address the issue of whether these innovators underwent frequent stylistic turns, and so does not address the weakness in the argument. *Cut it.*

> (E)   Jazz critics are known to have a higher regard for musicality than for mere technical virtuosity.

Choice (E): The contrast between musicality and technical virtuosity is unimportant in this argument. *Cut it.*

Choice (B) is the correct answer.

Both Weaken and Strengthen answer choices introduce new information. As long as this new information has an impact on the reasoning or conclusion, it's not out of scope.

8.2 ANALOGY QUESTIONS

Analogy questions describe a situation or entity in the passage and ask you to find a different situation or entity that is analogous.

You can think of Analogy questions as similar to Parallel questions in the Logical Reasoning section.

8.2.1 IDENTIFY

Analogy questions are defined by the following characteristics:

1. **The question stem directs your attention to a particular situation, entity, or relationship.** Something in the passage has to act as one half of the analogy, and the question stem will tell you what it is and (sometimes) where to find it.

2. **The question stem asks you to find the answer choice that is most closely** *analogous to* **or most** *similar to* the first half of the analogy.

Here are some sample Analogy question stems:

> Which one of the following is a questionable moral guideline most similar to that discussed in the third paragraph?

> Based on the passage, which one of the following relationships is most analogous to that between a naturalist and a previously undiscovered species?

> As described in the passage, knowingly omitting certain truths in a courtroom is most closely analogous to which one of the following?

Analogy questions are related to Match questions, but the major difference is that the answer choices for Analogy questions address completely different topics than the one in the passage. Don't let this throw you off.

 **KEY PHRASES
Analogy Questions**

Most analogous
Most similar
Most like

8.2.2 ANALYZE

Of course, the first step in your analysis is to find the situation in question. Use the question stem (if it provides help), your memory, and your notes.

The most important step in your analysis is to **determine the major characteristics of the original situation or phenomenon** in the passage. This is the same thing that you do on Parallel questions in the Logical Reasoning section—there, you describe how many premises there are, their type, and the conclusion.

For Analogy questions, you must do the same kind of work. You won't always be examining premises and conclusions, but you'll still have to determine the major characteristics of the original situation. To do this, **describe the situation in general terms that are not related to the topic of the passage**.

For example, perhaps the original situation described a government that passed a law banning a certain pesticide in order to protect citizens' health, only to experience a sharp increase in an insect-borne disease that had previously been rare. A general description of the major components of that situation would be, "a problem-solving attempt aimed at a particular goal created a different problem that undermined the same goal." This general description doesn't mention pesticides, insects, diseases, or health, but it gives a broad description of the situation in general terms.

Take a look at the following question, which comes from the Leading Questions passage back in Chapter 1:

> 2. In discussing the tangential details of events, the passage contrasts their original significance to witnesses with their possible significance in the courtroom (lines 52–59). That contrast is most closely analogous to which one of the following?
>
> Test 40, Section 4, Question 23

This question stem directs your attention to a particular contrast in the passage and asks you to find an analogous one. It's an Analogy question.

The question stem gives you some help in finding the first half of the analogy. It's in lines 52–59:

> But what is tangential to a witness's original experience of an event may nevertheless be crucial to the courtroom issues that the witness's memories are supposed to resolve. For example, a perpetrator's shirt color or hairstyle might be tangential to one's shocked observance of an armed robbery, but later those factors might be crucial to establishing the identity of the perpetrator.
>
> Test 40, Section 4, Passage 4

To complete your analysis, recast the contrast in general terms that aren't explicitly related to the courtroom or a witness's memory. Here's one good way to do it: "a thing that is unimportant in one context may be essential in a different context."

8.2.3 PREPHRASE

You will certainly *not* be able to predict the details or the topic of the second half of the analogy. The topic could be anything at all, and it probably won't be related to the topic of the passage.

You *will* be able to predict one thing about the correct answer: when you recast it in general terms, it should be identical to the general terms you used to describe the original first half of the analogy in the passage. Simply put, its major characteristics will match.

8.2.4 ATTACK

When you attack the answer choices on a Analogy question, you are looking for an answer choice that has the same major characteristics as the first half of the analogy. That means you will have to put each answer choice in general terms as well and look for a match. It can be a lot of work, but it's the only way to be completely accurate. Fortunately, Analogy questions are relatively uncommon.

Watch out for these common distracters:

Topic Trap
Some answer choices will have a topic similar to the one in the passage. The writers of the LSAT hope you will be distracted by the similarities in topics and overlook the differences in reasoning. Never choose an answer based on topic.

Word Trap
Some answer choices will use identical words and phrases from the passage. Again, the LSAT writers hope that they can distract you with identical words and force you to ignore the differences in reasoning. Don't choose an answer choice based on identical wording.

Take a look at the answer choices for this example. Remember, you are trying to match the generalization of "a thing that is unimportant in one context may be essential in a different context."

(A) For purposes of flavor and preservation, salt and vinegar are important additions to cucumbers during the process of pickling, but these purposes could be attained by adding other ingredients instead.

Choice (A): A generalization of this choice would be "a thing (salt and vinegar) that is important in one context (pickling) could be replaced by a different thing (other ingredients) in the same context." This is a bad match. *Cut it.*

> (B) For the purpose of adding a mild stimulant effect, caffeine is included in some types of carbonated drinks, but for the purposes of appealing to health-conscious consumers, some types of carbonated drinks are advertised as being caffeine-free.

Choice (B): A generalization of this choice could be "a thing (caffeine) that is desirable in one context (stimulation) is undesirable in another context (health)." This is not a bad match. *Keep it.*

> (C) For purposes of flavor and tenderness, the skins of apples and some other fruits are removed during preparation for drying, but grape skins are an essential part of raisins, and thus grape skins are not removed.

Notice that these answer choices have nothing to do with the courtroom. That's typical of Analogy questions.

Choice (C): A generalization of this choice would be "a certain action (removing the skin) is beneficial when performed on some things (apples and other fruits), but not when performed on others (raisins)." This is a bad match. *Cut it.*

> (D) For purposes of flavor and appearance, wheat germ is not needed in flour and is usually removed during milling, but for purposes of nutrition, the germ is an important part of the grain.

Choice (D): A generalization of this choice would be "a thing (wheat germ) that is unimportant in one context (flavor and appearance) is important in a different context (health)." This is a good match. *Keep it.*

> (E) For purposes of texture and appearance, some fat may be removed from meat when it is ground into sausage, but the removal of fat is also important for purposes of health.

Choice (E): A generalization of this choice would be "a thing (fat) that is undesirable in one context (texture and appearance) is also undesirable in another context (health)." This is a bad match. *Cut it.*

At this point, two answer choices remain, and they are pretty similar. To find the correct answer, look at the differences between the choices. In choice (B), there is a contrast between *desirable* and *undesirable*. In choice (D), there is a contrast between *unimportant* and *important*. Which one matches the passage better? In the passage, noticing a perpetrator's shirt color or hairstyle wasn't *undesirable*—the witness wasn't actively trying to *block* that observation—it was just unimportant. The witness had other things on his mind. Thus, choice (D) is a better match.

Choice (D) is the correct answer.

8.3 PRINCIPLE QUESTIONS

Principle questions in the Reading Comprehension section are much like Conform questions in the Logical Reasoning section. Although in the Logical Reasoning section Principle questions can show up in a variety of different forms, the good news is that they are usually more predictable in the Reading Comprehension section.

On the LSAT, a "principle" is a general rule. For example, "people should treat others the way they themselves want to be treated" is a principle.

Principle questions in the Reading Comprehension section ask you to identify the general rule that underlies someone's line of reasoning.

Principle questions have become much less common than they used to be. The Principle question on the June 2007 LSAT was the first one to appear on the test since 2002.

8.3.1 IDENTIFY

All Principle questions share the following characteristics:

1. **The question stem uses the word *principle*.** On rare occasions, the word *principle* shows up in other types of question stems, so keep the second characteristic in mind as well.

2. **The question stem asks you to find the principle that *underlies* a claim or the principle that an argument is *based on*.**

Here are some examples of Principle question stems:

> Which one of the following principles is most in keeping with the passage's argument?

> Based on the passage, a post-modernist film critic is most likely to claim that a successful film is one that is based on which one of the following principles?

> Which one of the following principles most likely underlies the author's characterization of astronomical modeling?

Each of these asks you to find the principle that corresponds to the argument in the passage.

8.3.2 ANALYZE

The majority of your analysis for a Principle question was done in your initial analysis of the passage. Since these questions ask you about a particular argument in the passage, you need to identify and understand the premises and conclusion of that argument. Fortunately, you will have taken care of this step when you first read the passage. If you need to, look back at your notes to remind yourself of the main point of the viewpoint in question and its supporting premises. Most of your work comes when you attack the answers.

Take a look at this question. It comes from the Organicism passage at the end of chapter 7.

> 3. Which one of the following is a principle upon which the author bases an argument against the theory of internal relations?
>
> Test 25, Section 1, Question 26

This is a Principle question. It asks you to find the principle that the author's argument is based on.

In your initial analysis of the passage, you found that the author argued against the theory of internal relations in the third and fourth paragraphs. In those paragraphs, the author's conclusion was that the theory was faulty. The supporting premises were (1) that it didn't differentiate between defining characteristics and accompanying characteristics, and (2) that its prerequisite for acquiring knowledge was impossible to satisfy.

8.3.3 PREPHRASE

To Prephrase for a Principle question, remember what the correct answer will do. Since you are looking for a general rule that <u>underlies someone's argument</u>, the general rule must do two things:

1. **Match the circumstances.** A general rule that tells you what to do when life gives you lemons is not very useful in a situation in which no one has been given any lemons. If an answer choice applies to different circumstances than the ones in the passage, it can't be correct.

2. **Match the outcome.** In an argument, the outcome is the conclusion or the suggested course of action. No one trying to make an argument would cite a rule that reaches a conclusion different than the one he or she is arguing for.

Principle questions are related to Logical Reasoning's Conform questions, specifically those that ask you to state the principle.

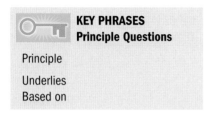

KEY PHRASES
Principle Questions

Principle

Underlies

Based on

To Prephrase on Principle questions, describe the argument in general terms, much as you do on Analogy questions. You don't have to totally avoid the topic of the passage, but you should include a mention of both the circumstances and the outcome, since those are the important features you are looking to match in the correct answer choice.

For this example, a good Prephrased answer might look like this:

> Principle: If a theory fails to make an important distinction or proposes unattainable prerequisites, it is faulty.

8.3.4 ATTACK

On Principle questions, you are ultimately looking for an answer that matches the passage. If an answer choice looks like your Prephrased answer, then definitely keep it, but be aware that the correct answer can look strange sometimes. It may use general language that does not match your Prephrased answer. Before eliminating any answer choice, determine whether it matches both the circumstances and the outcome in the passage, and be ready to match generalized terms in the answer choices to specific components of the passage.

Take a look at the answer choices for this example.

> (A)   An adequate theory of complex systems must define the entities of which the system is composed.

Choice (A): Was the problem with the theory its failure to define the system's entities? No. The problem was the failure to make an important distinction. This doesn't match the passage. *Cut it.*

> (B)   An acceptable theory cannot have consequences that contradict its basic purpose.

Choice (B): This is pretty abstract, but does it match the passage? First decide what the "basic purpose" of the theory is. The passage says that the whole debate is over the best way to study complex systems. Next, are there any "consequences that contradict" this purpose? Well, the author says that the theory "renders the acquisition of knowledge impossible." That sounds like it contradicts the idea of studying something. Finally, the outcome in the passage is that the author described the theory as faulty. The answer choice says that an adequate theory cannot do this. Looks like a good match. *Keep it.*

> (C)   An adequate method of study of complex systems should reveal the actual complexity of the systems it studies.

Choice (C): Nothing in the third or fourth paragraphs has anything to do with failing to reveal the actual complexity of the system. This doesn't match the passage. *Cut it.*

> (D)   An acceptable theory must describe the laws and initial conditions of a complex system.

Choice (D): The author says that the analytic method does indeed describe the laws and initial conditions. Furthermore, the author seems to think that the analytical method is an acceptable theory. The problem here is that the question stem is concerned with the argument *against* the theory of internal relations, not the argument *for* the analytic method. This choice is concerned with the wrong theory. *Cut it.*

> (E)   An acceptable method of studying complex systems should not study parts of the system in isolation from the system as a whole.

Choice (E): The author states that proponents of the analytic method did not study parts of a system in isolation from the system as a whole. But this has nothing to do with the theory of internal relations, which is the focus of the question. *Cut it.*

Choice (B) is the correct answer.

8.4 COMPLETE QUESTIONS

Complete questions ask you to add another sentence on to the end of the passage. Complete questions are rare.

8.4.1 IDENTIFY

Complete questions all find some way to ask you to choose an appropriate sentence to add to the end of the passage. Here are some examples:

> Given the passage's argument, which one of the following sentences most logically completes the last paragraph?

> Based on information in the passage, it can be inferred that which one of the following sentences could most logically be added to the passage as a concluding sentence?

> Which one of the following sentences could most logically be appended to the end of the last paragraph of the passage?

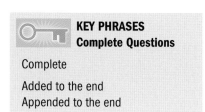

KEY PHRASES
Complete Questions

Complete

Added to the end

Appended to the end

8.4.2 ANALYZE

In your analysis for a Complete question, try to determine where the last paragraph is leading. Often, the author will be arguing for a certain viewpoint and will have presented his supporting evidence, but the passage will not explicitly state the conclusion. In such a case, the best sentence to add to the end of the passage would be the author's conclusion.

If the final paragraph is concerned with presenting a counterargument, then a good final sentence to add would be a statement that presents a conclusion that acts as an alternative to the viewpoint being argued against.

Take a look at this question:

> 4. Which one of the following could most logically be appended to the end of the final paragraph?

Because it asks for a sentence to be added to the end of the passage, it's a Complete question. Here's the last paragraph of the passage:

> Adherents to the Hubbert Peak theory point to the failure of geologists to discover any new major oil fields in the last 40 years as evidence that world oil production will begin an inexorable decline within the next decade. While their evidence is indisputable, proponents of the Hubbert Peak theory fail to see that the reason behind the paucity of such discoveries is economic, not geological. New exploration is not in the current best interest of oil-producing nations because they fear that new discoveries will lead to excess capacity, which would drive down oil prices. Additionally, major oil corporations have little interest in exploration due to its high cost and the pressure that investors place on them to provide short-term financial returns.

Here, the author is arguing against one idea in particular: the idea that new oil fields haven't been discovered for geological reasons—that is, that there are no more major oil fields left.

By extension, the author could also be seen to be arguing against the proponents' conclusion that world oil production will start to decline in the next decade.

8.4.3 PREPHRASE

In your Prephrasing step, remember what the correct answer will do. It must

1. **Be supported by evidence in the passage**. Anything that contradicts the author's viewpoint is incorrect.

2. **Flow logically with the text**. If an answer choice is concerned with something only mentioned in the beginning of the passage, it doesn't make a good addition to the end of the passage.

For this example, a good concluding sentence would complete the author's counter-argument. It could argue that there *are* more major oil fields left to be discovered. Or it could argue that world oil production will *not* begin to decline in the next decade.

8.4.4 ATTACK

As you attack the answers, eliminate any choice that contradicts the author's viewpoint, isn't supported by evidence in the passage, or does not flow logically with the text.

Take a look at the answer choices for this example:

> (A) If major oil companies and oil-producing countries were to seriously explore for new oil formations, they would likely not find any.

Choice (A): Although the proponents of the Hubbert Peak Theory might agree with this, it contradicts the author's viewpoint. *Cut it.*

> (B) Once it becomes in the best interest of both oil companies and oil-producing nations to seek out new oil formations, they will likely find them.

Choice (B): This concurs with the author's viewpoint that there *are* more major oil fields left to be discovered. It also flows well with the two preceding sentences, which discuss the best interests of oil-producing nations and companies. *Keep it.*

> (C) This concentration on short-term financial returns has forced major oil companies to act in a manner that is not in the best interest of consumers.

Choice (C): There is no evidence in the passage to support any statement about the best interest of consumers. *Cut it.*

> (D) Only when oil exploration becomes in the best interest of oil-producing countries and oil companies will accurate predictions regarding global oil production be possible using the Hubbert Peak theory.

Choice (D): Although the author argues that world oil production will *not* begin to decline in the next decade, there is no evidence in the passage to support any statement about when accurate predictions will become possible. *Cut it.*

> (E) Because it is likely that market pressure on short-term financial returns will never go away, it will never be in the interest of oil companies to explore for new oil formations.

Choice (E): There is no evidence in the passage to support the extreme statement that "market pressure on short-term financial returns will *never* go away." *Cut it.*

Choice (B) is the correct answer.

STOP. THIS IS THE END OF LECTURE 4. DO NOT PROCEED TO THE CORRESPONDING EXAM UNTIL INSTRUCTED TO DO SO IN CLASS.

LECTURE **5** CHAPTER **9**

COMPARATIVE READING
PASSAGES

9.1 IDENTIFYING COMPARATIVE READING PASSAGES

Comparative Reading is a new feature on the LSAT (as of June 2007) that looks slightly different from other parts of the Reading Comprehension section. The Comparative Reading part of the test presents you with **a set of two passages** that add up to about the same length as one normal Reading Comprehension passage. One of the passages is labeled **Passage A** and the other **Passage B**. The questions following the pair relate to *both* passages. Because of this unique format, you should be able to identify a Comparative Reading set as soon as you see it.

The two passages are written about the same or related topics and are distilled from longer works by two different authors. Thus, you know for certain that the set contains at least two distinct viewpoints. Just as with Controversy passages, identifying and understanding the different viewpoints is critical.

The two passages can fall into any of the four passage types you have already learned about. They usually involve argumentation, but since they are short, it is unlikely that either of them will have enough space to contain multiple viewpoints. Thus, most of the short passages can be categorized as miniature Thesis passages, but the set of two passages can be considered to be acting like a single Controversy passage because of the interaction between the viewpoints of the two authors.

Although the two passages address similar topics, they are independent. That is, the two authors present their viewpoints without any reference to each other. Neither author is writing as a direct response to the other, although they may in some cases address the same point.

Some of the questions associated with Comparative Reading sets are concerned with only one of the passages. For example, you may see a question asking you to determine the main point of passage A. Questions about only one of the passages are identical to the Reading Comprehension questions you have already studied.

Since this is a new feature on the LSAT, you won't be able to find any Comparative Reading sets in old LSATs. In addition to the ones in this book, you can find more practice sets at www.lsac.org and www.examkrackers.com.

However, the great majority of the questions are concerned with both passages and their relationship to each other. These questions are sometimes similar to question types you have already seen, but there are also some unique types of questions that appear only on Comparative Reading sets, as you will see.

In your Reading Comprehension section, you will see three "normal" full-length passages, and one set of Comparative Reading passages.

9.2 ANALYZING COMPARATIVE READING PASSAGES

Your analysis of the Comparative Reading passages should begin much like your analysis of other types of passages. Just as for every Reading Comprehension passage, look for:

1. **The main point**

2. **The purpose of each paragraph**

As each individual passage may be any one of the four types, keep an eye out for these additional features that either of the passages may have:

3. **The various viewpoints,** especially the author's

4. **Major structural elements,** like lists or timelines

5. **The core question,** if there is one

All of these tasks should be familiar by now, since you have seen and practiced them on other types of passages. However, when it comes to Comparative Reading, you should look for some additional things as part of your analysis:

6. **The relationship between the passages**

7. **The response each author would have to the other passage**

9.2.1 THE RELATIONSHIP BETWEEN THE PASSAGES

You are very likely to see a question that asks you about the relationship between the passages, so you should determine this as part of your initial analysis. There are a number of relationships the two passages are likely to have.

In some cases, **the two passages argue for directly opposing conclusions**. For example, one passage may advocate an increased use of educational television in classrooms, while the other passage may say that educational television in classrooms, even if it's commercial-free, is harmful to children and should be avoided. In such a case, you should take note of the premises each author uses to support his or her conclusion. Do the authors mention the same issues? Does one author bring up points that the other fails to consider? Do they agree on anything?

In some cases, **the two passages are in general agreement**. For example, both passages may argue for the cancellation of debts owed by impoverished countries to wealthier nations. But the two passages won't be identical, so look for differences. Perhaps one passage makes an appeal to basic principles of morality, while the other argues that debt cancellation will eventually benefit the economies of the wealthier nations. It's possible to reach the same conclusion by using different premises, so take note of the underlying reasoning in each passage.

In other cases, the **two passages have different scopes**. For example, one passage may discuss the general principles that make architectural structures aesthetically pleasing, while the other passage has a much more specific focus on the artistic merits of particular kinds of architecture. Again, note the relationship. Does the second passage implement the same principles outlined in the first? Does the second make judgments that conflict with those that would be reached by using the principles in the first passage?

Because of their uniqueness and the complexity of the required analysis, it may be best to save the Comparative Reading set for last.

9.2.2 EACH AUTHOR'S RESPONSE TO THE OTHER

Neither author has seen the other's passage. Regardless, the LSAT is likely to ask you how one of the authors would respond to either a point made in the other passage or to the other passage as a whole.

In order for you to be able to answer such a question, the passage has to provide you with some evidence. The only way you'd be able to say without guessing what someone's response would be to a certain idea or topic is if the passage already addressed the same idea or topic and passed some sort of judgment on it. Thus, a crucial part of you analysis is to look for places in which the same topic or idea is discussed in both passages.

When you see the same topic or idea discussed in both passages, draw a line showing the connection. You need to use some discretion when doing this. For example, if both passages are about the Amazon rain forest, then it's not helpful to draw lines connecting the entirety of passage A to the entirety of passage B.

However, if one sentence in passage A mentions a possible reason for the great diversity of species there, and one paragraph in passage B discusses a competing explanation for the same phenomenon, then you should definitely draw a connecting line between those two parts of the passages. You would be very likely to see a question regarding these competing viewpoints, and the question would likely come in the form of asking about one author's reaction to the material presented on the same topic by the other author.

9.3 PUTTING IT ALL TOGETHER

9.3.1 Drill: Comparative Reading Passages

Directions: Practice the Identify and Analyze steps on the following passage.

Passage A

In the 1930s and 40s, Theodore Adorno predicted that the culture industry—the production of songs, art, movies, books, and television programs—would mature and effectively cripple the critical capacities of
(5) the general public. His predictions have largely come true, a consequence of the nature of mass production and consumption.

The current industry relies on proven formulas and commonly accepted archetypes and dialectics to
(10) efficiently mass-produce cultural commodities. Challenging engagement of important values such as freedom or beauty is not possible in this industry because of the significant risk and effort involved in the production of goods that significantly deviate from
(15) established norms. The culture industry must continually produce new ideas, but this production is carefully executed and is constantly monitored for predictability and ease of consumer acceptance through focus groups and public opinion polls.
(20) People consume significant quantities of these pseudo-individuated works of culture, which are in reality isomorphic to one another, differing only in minor ways from a formulated archetype. Deep analysis would unveil this fact and make mass
(25) consumption unappealing. As a result, people spend time and effort repeatedly analyzing superficial differences—calling the aim of their attention deep understanding—while in the process uncritically accepting the underlying common structures and
(30) assumptions used in mass-produced culture. They neglect their capacity to deeply evaluate cultural commodities, and that ability atrophies.

Passage B

Popular culture is becoming a more complex and expressive medium. While there will always be
(35) demand among consumers for low-brow entertainment, the landscape of media production is becoming a more intellectually stimulating environment as producers of culture respond to a rising demand for more nuanced presentations.
(40) Good evidence of this claim can be found by analyzing television programs over the last 60 years. It is true that popular programs across this period address many common themes and formulas, but the important issue is that treatment of these themes has intentionally
(45) evolved, gaining greater informational content and complexity. For example, a comparison of police dramas such as *Dragnet* from the 1950s, *21 Jump Street* from the late 80s, and *NYPD Blue* from the 90s reveals a dramatic increase over time in the number of
(50) plot and subplot threads, the number of characters presented, character interrelation, and non-linear story progression. This effect is not limited to the police drama; every other major genre of television programming has seen a similar effect.

(55) A recent trend in programming, so-called "reality television," can also be understood as the result of an increased demand for nuanced presentation. These programs involve a large cast of characters, with complicated social interactions, and they are successful because they entertain people by encouraging a new
(60) level of active engagement in the featured situations, both through vote-in mechanisms, and community discussion.

1. How can you identify what type of passage this is?

_____

_____

2a. What are the goals of your analysis of the passage?

_____

_____

_____

_____

2b. What are the results of your analysis of the passage?

_____

_____

_____

_____

Answers & Explanations

Passage A

In the 1930s and 40s, Theodore Adorno predicted that the culture industry—the production of songs, art, movies, books, and television programs—would mature and effectively (cripple) the critical capacities of the general public. [His predictions have largely come true, a consequence of the nature of mass production and consumption.]*

The current industry relies on proven formulas and commonly accepted archetypes and dialectics to efficiently mass-produce cultural commodities. Challenging engagement of important values such as freedom or beauty is not possible in this industry because of the significant risk and effort involved in the production of goods that significantly deviate from established norms. The culture industry must continually produce new ideas, but this production is carefully executed and is constantly monitored for predictability and ease of consumer acceptance through focus groups and public opinion polls.

People consume significant quantities of these pseudo-individuated works of culture, which are in reality isomorphic to one another, differing only in minor ways from a formulated archetype. Deep analysis would unveil this fact and make mass consumption (unappealing.) As a result, people spend time and effort repeatedly analyzing (superficial) differences—calling the aim of their attention deep understanding—while in the process uncritically accepting the underlying common structures and assumptions used in mass-produced culture. They neglect their capacity to deeply evaluate cultural commodities, and that ability atrophies.

Passage B

Popular culture is becoming a more complex and expressive medium. [While there will always be demand among consumers for low-brow entertainment, the landscape of media production is becoming a more (intellectually stimulating) environment as producers of culture respond to a rising demand for more nuanced presentations.]*

Good evidence of this claim can be found by analyzing television programs over the last 60 years. It is true that popular programs across this period address many common themes and formulas, but the (important) issue is that treatment of these themes has intentionally evolved, gaining greater informational content and complexity. For example, a comparison of police dramas such as *Dragnet* from the 1950s, *21 Jump Street* from the late 80s, and *NYPD Blue* from the 90s reveals a dramatic increase over time in the number of plot and subplot threads, the number of characters presented, character interrelation, and non-linear story progression. This effect is not limited to the police drama; every other major genre of television programming has seen a similar effect.

¶3: Another example—reality TV

¶1: Introduce MP [Culture ind. crippled critical capacities, due to its nature]

¶2: Nature of culture production

¶3: How it affects critical capacities

¶1: Introduce MP [Culture now more intellectual, due to demand]

¶2: Themes get more evolved treatment, e.g. police dramas

¶3: A recent trend in programming, so-called "reality television," can also be understood as the result of an increased demand for nuanced presentation. These programs involve a large cast of characters, with complicated social interactions, and they are successful because they entertain people by encouraging a new level of active engagement in the featured situations, both through vote-in mechanisms, and community discussion.

1. You can identify this as a Comparative Reading set because there are two passages.

2a. The goals of your analysis are to find the main point of each passage and the purpose of each paragraph. Additionally, you should look for whether the passages contain various viewpoints, major structural elements, or a core question. Finally, look for the relationship between the passages and the response each author would have to the other passage.

2b. The main point of each passage is found in a one-sentence thesis statement at the end of the first paragraph. This suggests that each passage is a miniature Thesis passage, and this is confirmed by the lack of various viewpoints or a core question in either passage. There are no major structural elements to take note of.

The note next to the first passage clarifies the main point, since it's important to understand what "his predictions" are exactly. It's helpful to write your own notes like this when you need to clarify important parts of the passage

There are brief notes next to each paragraph to remind you of its purpose, and opinionated words are circled.

You should determine the relationship between the passages. They both address popular culture. Passage A is very critical of it, while passage B has good things to say, so there is some definite **disagreement**. More specifically, though, the main focus of passage A is Adorno's theories and what pop culture has done to people's critical capacities, while passage B has a different focus—the content of the media itself and how it's changing. So there is a slightly **different scope**.

Finally, think about the authors' likely response to each other. There are a few places where both authors address the same point. These are pointed out with lines drawn between the passages: both authors address how producers respond to the demand for new ideas; both authors address whether new works are the same or different from other works; and both authors discuss "analysis" of pop culture. Keep these connections in mind when it comes time to answer Response questions.

NOW MOVE ON TO THE SECOND CHAPTER OF LECTURE 5. WHEN YOU HAVE COMPLETED IT, YOU CAN GET FURTHER PRACTICE WITH COMPARATIVE READING PASSAGES IN THE CORRESPONDING EXAM AT THE END OF THE BOOK.

LECTURE (5) CHAPTER (10)

THE COMPARATIVE READING QUESTION FAMILY

Questions on Comparative Reading sets come in several varieties. Some concern only *one* of the passages, and these questions are essentially identical to the types you have already studied. For example, you may be asked about the main point or the primary purpose of one of the passages.

In contrast, there are several types of questions that appear only on Comparative Reading sets. These make up the **Comparative Reading question family**:

1. Relationship questions

2. Response questions

3. Dual questions

The category of Dual questions is actually made up of a large number of question types that are similar to one you have already seen but adapted so that they relate to both passages. Dual questions include:

- Dual Purpose

- Dual Definition

- Dual Search

- Dual Viewpoint

- Dual Attitude

- Dual Match

- Dual Analogy

10.1 RELATIONSHIP QUESTIONS

Relationship questions ask you about the relationship between the two passages. These ask you to explain how the arguments in the two passages unfold and how they compare to one another.

10.1.1 IDENTIFY

You can identify Relationship questions because:

> 1. **The question stem uses the word *relate* or *relationship*.** The question stem also concerns both passages.

Here are some sample Relationship question stems:

> Which one of the following most accurately describes the relationship between the argument made in passage A and the argument made in passage B?

> Which one of the following most accurately describes a way in which the two passages are related to each other?

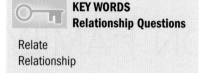
KEY WORDS
Relationship Questions

Relate
Relationship

10.1.2 ANALYZE

The analysis you need for Relationship questions is actually part of your analysis of the passages themselves. When you read a Comparative Reading set, you should note whether the passages reach similar or opposing conclusions or whether they have a more complex relationship, such as a different scope.

Take a look at this question, which comes from the Culture Industry passage in chapter 9:

> 1. Which one of the following most accurately describes the relationship between the argument made in passage A and the argument made in passage B?

You can identify this as a Relationship question because it asks about both passages and uses the word *relationship*.

In your initial analysis of the passages, you found that passage A is about Adorno's theories and what pop culture has done to people's critical capacities. You also saw that passage B, while still addressing the same general topic, uses examples and focuses on the content of media itself and how it's changing to argue for an opposing conclusion.

10.1.3 PREPHRASE

On Relationship questions, you should always come up with an answer in your own words before you read the answer choices.

This Prephrased answer is simply an articulation of what you determined in your initial analysis of the passages. In your Prephrased answer, make sure to go beyond simply describing each passage independently. Your answer should include some indication of the ways in which the passages are the same or different.

In this case, a good Prephrased answer would be:

> Relationship: Passage A is about Adorno's theories and what pop culture has done to people's critical capacities. Passage B addresses the same general topic, uses more concrete examples, and focuses on the content of media itself to argue for an indirectly opposing conclusion.

10.1.4 ATTACK

Here are the distracters commonly seen on Relationship questions:

Misrepresents a Passage

The answer choices make assertions about both passages, and everything they say about each one has to match what really happened in the passage. If a choice says anything extreme, out of scope, or contradictory to what happened in one of the passages, get rid of it.

Misrepresents the Relationship

The answer choices also make assertions about the relationship between the passages, and these too must match. For example, if an answer choice says the passages used the same evidence to reach opposite conclusions, you must consider whether their evidence really was the same and whether their conclusions really were opposite. This requires thinking about both passages at the same time, but your Prephrased answer should help.

Take a look at the answer choices for this example:

> (A)   Passage A weighs two positions, while passage B
>   analyzes the positions' historical development.

Choice (A): This choice goes bad right away when it says passage A weighs two positions. There are no two positions in passage A, so this **misrepresents a passage**. *Cut it.*

> (B)   Passage A makes an academic argument, while
>   passage B presents a direct rebuttal of that
>   argument.

Choice (B): This answer choice does a good job describing passage A, and passage B could be seen as a rebuttal of the argument that popular culture is becoming less complex and expressive. However, that's not the argument passage A is trying to make. Passage A's main point is about people's critical capacities, and passage B doesn't even mention that argument, let alone directly rebut it. This choice **misrepresents the relationship**. *Cut it.*

> (C)   Passage A contains a theoretical critique, while
>   passage B presents an analysis of trends related
>   to that critique.

Choice (C): Passage A is theoretical, and it does critique the culture industry. Passage B indeed presents an analysis of trends. So far, so good. Finally, are the trends in passage B related to the critique in passage A? Yes. They are both about the content of popular culture. This choice correctly describes both passages *and* their relationship. *Keep it.*

> (D)   Passage A questions the veracity of the purported
>   facts of an issue, while passage B responds in
>   support of those facts.

Choice (D): Like choice (A), this choice goes wrong quickly when it describes passage A, which contains no questioning of purported facts. This choice **misrepresents a passage**. *Cut it.*

> (E)   Passage A makes an argument supporting
>   another's claim, while passage B puts forward a
>   list of reasons to doubt that claim.

Choice (E): This choice has a good description of passage A, since the author indeed supports another's claim (Adorno's). Passage B has a lot of facts that may lead you to doubt that claim, but, like choice (B), this choice **misrepresents the relationship** because the "claim" in passage A (that the critical capacities of the general public have been effectively crippled) is not addressed in passage B. *Cut it.*

Choice (C) is the correct answer.

10.2 RESPONSE QUESTIONS

Response questions ask you to infer how one of the authors would respond to a view expressed in the other passage.

10.2.1 IDENTIFY

Response questions are defined by the following characteristics:

1. **The question stem mentions the author of one of the passages.**

2. **The question stem asks you to find the** *feeling, judgment,* **or** *conclusion* **the author would reach regarding something in the other passage.**

Here are some sample Response question stems:

> If the author of passage B were to read passage A, he or she would be most likely to draw which one of the following conclusions regarding matters addressed in passage A?

> The author of passage B would be most likely to make which one of the following criticisms about the predictions cited in passage A concerning a rise in interest rates?

10.2.2 ANALYZE

When you first read the passages, you did most of the analysis you need in order to answer a Response question.

The most important thing to take note of is when the two authors discuss the same topic or when one author mentions something that could be directly applicable to a topic in the other passage. In order to be able to say how one author would respond to something mentioned by the other, there must be some evidence regarding the author's feelings on the topic.

Some Response question stems are specific—they mention exactly the topic or statement that you must determine the response to. In these cases, revisit both passages in the areas you marked and re-familiarize yourself with the evidence you'll need to answer the question.

If, on the other hand, the question stem is vague—it just asks for one author's response to the entire other passage—then you have to do a little more work. First, determine which issues are fair game for a response—the responder's passage has to provide enough evidence to support drawing a conclusion as to the author's feeling. Then try to determine what that response would be.

Take a look at the following question, which also comes from the Culture Industry passage (as do the rest of the questions in this chapter):

> 2. If the author of Passage A were to read passage B, he or she would be most likely to reach which one of the following conclusions about the "good evidence" mentioned in the second paragraph of passage B (line 40)?

This question stem asks for author A's response to something mentioned in passage B. It's a Response question.

To complete your analysis, you have to find the evidence in passage A that will allow you to answer this question. The "good evidence" in passage B comes from "analyzing television shows over the last 60 years." Where in passage A does the author mention anything about this? In your initial reading of the passages, you found that the same topic (analyzing television shows) was discussed in broader terms in lines 25–30:

As a result, people spend time and effort repeatedly analyzing superficial differences—calling the aim of their attention deep understanding—while in the process uncritically accepting the underlying common structures and assumptions used in mass-produced culture.

This is the evidence you need in order to answer the question.

10.2.3 PREPHRASE

You should always Prephrase an answer to Response questions using the evidence you found in the responder's passage. You should leave your answer in the same words the author uses if you can. However, keep in mind that the correct answer choice is likely to rearrange the words or concepts. As long as a choice *means* the same as what you predicted or is *well supported* by the evidence, keep it.

In this example, the "good evidence" came from "analysis" of television programs, but author A says people only analyze superficial differences while in the process uncritically accepting the underlying common structures and assumptions used in mass-produced culture. This is a good Prephrased answer:

> Response: Author A would say the "good evidence" comes from analyzing superficial differences while in the process uncritically accepting the underlying common structures and assumptions used in mass-produced culture.

It's a mouthful, but look for something that captures this meaning.

10.2.4 ATTACK

When you attack the answer choices on a Response question, you should be in the same frame of mind as when you are dealing with an Inference question. The correct answer has to be supported by specific evidence you can point to in the responder's passage.

Watch out for these common distracters:

Wrong Viewpoint

Some answer choices may try to trick you by presenting the wrong author's response to the information. You have to keep the different authors' viewpoints straight.

Out of Scope

For Response questions, out of scope answer choices are those that do not have specific evidence in the responder's passage. Any answer that mentions new information that never appeared in the passage is wrong. Any answer choice that relies on evidence not related to the topic mentioned in the question stem is wrong.

Contradicts the Passage

If an answer choice contradicts any information from the responder's passage, it can't be correct.

Word Trap

Extreme

Take a look at these answer choices:

> (A)   It increases understanding of social interactions but does not contribute to a person's critical capacity.

Choice (A): This is a **word trap**. The choice looks familiar because it repeats the phrases "critical capacity" from passage A and "social interactions" from passage B, but it has nothing to do with the Prephrased answer and has no support in the passage. *Cut it.*

> (B)   It is superficial in that it accepts without question
>   the structures and assumptions commonly
>   employed in mass-produced culture.

Choice (B): This changes the wording up a little bit, but it is very close to the Prephrased answer and is well supported by lines 25–30. *Keep it.*

> (C)   It is useful only in the evaluation of police
>   dramas, since other genres do not display this
>   trend.

Choice (C): Passage A contains no discussion of which genres display which trends, so this is **out of scope**. *Cut it.*

> (D)   It suggests that television is becoming a more
>   intellectually stimulating medium and casts
>   doubt upon Theodore Adorno's argument.

Choice (D): This is what author B might have to say about the "evidence," but there is no support in passage A to indicate that its author thinks anything would cast doubt upon Adorno's argument. At best, this is the **wrong viewpoint**. *Cut it.*

> (E)   Its significance cannot be evaluated until the
>   analysis is expanded to include the treatment of
>   important values such as freedom and beauty.

Choice (E): This choice also uses a lot of phrases found in passage A, but its meaning is nowhere close to the Prephrased answer. This is a **word trap**. Author A criticizes *culture*, not analysis, for being unable to deeply address freedom and beauty. *Cut it.*

Choice (B) is the correct answer.

10.3 DUAL QUESTIONS

Dual questions are similar to the question types you have already seen. They are adapted so that they refer to both passages, but your approach to them is essentially the same as when they refer to just one passage.

Here's a brief review of these question types and a discussion of how they differ when they appear as Dual questions.

10.3.1 DUAL PURPOSE

Dual Purpose questions ask you to find a major theme, a core question, a main point, or a purpose that is common to both passages. Just as on regular Purpose of a Passage questions, a strong Prephrased answer should be possible. Your primary task is to find something common to both passages.

Here's a typical dual Purpose question stem:

> Which one of the following questions is central to
> both passages?

Try this example:

> 3. A discussion of which one of the following is central to
>   both passages?

You have to find something that's central to both passages. While passage A discusses people's critical capacities, passage B does not. And though passage B talks about specific examples of media, passage A does not. However, you know that both authors address how producers respond to the demand for new ideas, both authors address whether new works are more complex or the same as older works, and both authors discuss analysis of pop culture. Of these, the discussion of the complexity of new works seems most central, so look for something along these lines.

      (A)   the decay of the critical capacities of the common
               person

Choice (A): **No.** Passage B mentions a demand for more nuanced material, but the passage stops well short of talking about consumers' critical capacities.

      (B)   the rise in the quality of content in television
               police dramas

Choice (B): **No.** Passage A never talks about specific genres.

      (C)   the change in demand for interactive
               entertainment materials

Choice (C): **No.** Passage A never mentions interactive anything.

      (D)   the degree to which media is intellectually
               challenging

Choice (D): **Yes.** Passage A says media is so unchallenging that it causes intellectual atrophy, and it creates an argument as to why. Passage B say the media is a more intellectually stimulating environment than ever, and discusses how so.

      (E)   the inculcation of such values as freedom and
               beauty

Choice (E): **No.** Passage B never mentions freedom and beauty.

Choice (D) is the correct answer.

10.3.2 DUAL DEFINITION

In regular Definition questions, you have to find contextual clues in the passage to tell you what the author means by a certain word.

In dual Definition questions, the two authors use the same word, in the same way or perhaps in two different ways. Each answer choice contains one or two definitions, and you have to find the one that matches the right definition with the right passage.

Here's a typical dual Definition question stem:

      Which one of the following most accurately
      characterizes how the use of the word "structures"
      in passage A (line 12) relates to the use of the word
      "structures" in passage B (line 54)?

Try this example:

    4.   Which one of the following most accurately
        characterizes how the use of the word "engagement"
        in passage A (line 11) relates to the use of the word
        "engagement" in passage B (line 60)?

In passage A, *engagement* is used in a discussion of the production of goods and whether their content deviates from norms. So in this passage, the word refers to the treatment of values during the production of goods.

In passage B, *engagement* is exemplified by vote-in mechanisms and community discussion. So in this passage, the word refers to consumer participation in media.

      (A)   In passage A it refers to the way in which a critic
               articulates a situation's problems, whereas in
               passage B it refers to an object of attention.

Choice (A): **No.** The first half of this answer choice is way **out of scope**.

> (B)   In passage A it refers to the treatment of ideas in the creation of a work, whereas in passage B it refers to personal involvement by the consumer of a cultural phenomenon.

Choice (B): **Yes.** This is a great match for the Prephrased answer.

> (C)   In passage A it refers to how someone intends others to view an issue, whereas in passage B it refers to how people understand the intentions of someone who presents an issue.

Choice (C): **No.** The definition given for passage B is particularly bad, since there is nothing to support the idea of people understanding someone's intentions.

> (D)   In both passage A and passage B it refers to how the creator of something addresses its intricacies.

Choice (D): **No.** While in some Comparative Reading sets, the word may be used to mean the same thing in both passages, that is not the case here.

> (E)   In both passage A and passage B it refers to the commitment of individuals to their ideals.

Choice (E): **No.** Again, the word has different meanings in these two passages.

Choice (B) is the correct answer.

10.3.3 DUAL SEARCH

In regular Search questions, you are asked to react to each answer choice and determine whether or not the thing it mentions appeared in the passage.

In dual Search questions, you have to perform the same task, but you have to pay attention not only to *whether* something was mentioned, but also to *where* (in which passage) it was mentioned.

Most dual Search questions ask you to find something mentioned in one passage but not the other, although it is possible to see one that asks for something mentioned in both passages.

Here's a typical dual Search question stem:

> Which one of the following is identified in passage B but not in passage A as a possible consequence of lifetime judicial appointments?

Try this example:

> 5.   Which one of the following is identified in passage A but not passage B as a component of the production of works of culture?

You cannot Prephrase an answer to this question. You have to look at the answer choices and decide whether and where each one appeared. Incorrect choices will name things that appeared in the wrong passage, appeared in both passages, or didn't appear in either passage.

> (A)   response to an increased market for nuanced cultural commodities

Choice (A): **No.** This was mentioned in passage B (lines 38–39) but not in passage A.

> (B)   variation on established themes

Choice (B): **No.** This was actually mentioned in both passages, in lines 22–23 and lines 42–43.

Don't mix up passage A and passage B!

(C)   an increasing number of plot and subplot threads

Choice (C): **No**. This was mentioned in passage B only, in lines 49–50.

(D)   careful monitoring of the acceptability of new
        ideas

Choice (D): **Yes**. This was mentioned in lines 16–19 in passage A, but not at all in passage B.

(E)   deep understanding of important values

Choice (E): **No**. Only passage A mentions important values, but the passage says deep understanding is *impossible*. The question stem asks for something that *is* a component of the production of works of culture.

Choice (D) is the correct answer.

10.3.4 DUAL VIEWPOINT

In regular Viewpoint questions, you have to first identify the material in the passage that encompasses a certain person's viewpoint, using indicator words and statements that sound like opinions. Then you have to find the answer choice that matches the correct viewpoint without being out of scope, extreme, or contradictory to the passage.

In dual Viewpoint questions, you have to do the same thing, but you have the additional step of having to think about how *both* authors would view each answer choice. Sometimes you are looking for the choice that both would agree with, for example:

> It can be inferred from the passages that both authors
> hold which one of the following views?

While other times you have to find the choice that one would agree with but the other would disagree with, such as:

> The authors of the two passages would be most likely
> to disagree over

The second example is identical to a Point at Issue question in the Logical Reasoning section of the test, so you can use identical strategies. Look for an explicit disagreement in the two passages, and use the Survey Tool on any challenging answer choices.

> See chapter 3 in the Examkrackers Logical Reasoning textbook for more information on this tool.

Try this example:

> 6. The authors of the two passages would be most likely to
>   disagree over

This is essentially a Point at Issue question. First identify where the two authors' opinions are found. In this case, that's easy, since the two opinions are separated into the two passages, and each passage contains only one viewpoint.

Next look for any explicit disagreements. There are a few potential candidates. Author A says producers try to keep material predictable and formulaic, while author B says producers respond to demand with increasingly complex material. Another disagreement comes when author A says that works of culture are essentially all the same, while author B points out how they are changing in "important" ways. Finally, author A asserts that the typical analysis of works of culture is "superficial," while author B describes analysis as "good evidence" of noteworthy trends.

Keep these disagreements in mind as you look at the answer choices:

(A)   whether media affects the public's ability to
        deeply evaluate cultural commodities

Choice (A): **No**. This is **one-sided**, since author B never addresses the evaluative abilities of the public. Because you don't have any evidence as to how author B would feel about this statement, you cannot say that they would disagree over this choice.

> (B) whether police dramas are more able than other genres to explore important values

Choice (B): **No.** Passage A never talks about specific genres, so this is also **one-sided**.

> (C) whether modern television programs display substantive differences from the ones produced twenty years ago

Choice (C): **Yes.** Passage A says works of culture differ "only in minor ways," while passage B says popular culture is becoming a "more complex and expressive medium."

> (D) whether television should be considered popular culture

Choice (D): **No.** Both authors would **agree** that television is part of popular culture.

> (E) whether reality television programs feature characters with complex social interactions

Choice (E): **No.** You know author B would agree with this, but author A doesn't mention reality TV or complex social interactions. Perhaps author A considers them part of the formulaic archetypes, but you simply don't have enough evidence to support saying the authors would disagree over this choice.

Choice (C) is the correct answer.

10.3.5 DUAL ATTITUDE

In regular Attitude questions, you have to find the opinionated words in the passage that convey the author's attitude toward something.

In dual Attitude questions, you have to perform this task on both passages, then take the extra step of comparing the two.

Here's a typical dual Attitude question stem:

> Passage A differs from passage B in that passage A displays an attitude that is more

Try this example:

> 7. Passage A differs from passage B in that passage A employs a tone that is more

In this case, you circled some of the opinionated words in your initial analysis of the passages. In passage A, the author uses words like "cripple," "superficial," and "unappealing" to describe pop culture and various aspects of its production and effects. Author B, on the other hand, uses words like "intellectually stimulating" and "important," and seems to feel that recent developments in television programming are encouraging.

So you can Prephrase an answer that passage A certainly employs a more negative tone. See if this is specific enough to find the right answer:

> (A) disapproving

Choice (A): **Yes.** This is a good match for the Prephrased answer.

> (B) ambivalent

Choice (B): **No.** *Ambivalent* means undecided or having mixed feelings, but passage A presents only one view and does so forcefully.

         (C)   deferential

Choice (C): **No.** It's hard to describe passage A as being more respectful or polite than passage B.

         (D)   laudatory

Choice (D): **No.** If anything, this is backwards, since passage B seems to have a lot more praise for popular culture than passage A does.

         (E)   circumspect

Choice (E): **No.** Nothing about passage A seems any more cautious than passage B. Passage A seems pretty forceful in its opinions.

Choice (A) is the correct answer.

10.3.6 DUAL MATCH

In regular Match questions, the passage provides a definition or set of rules, and you have to find the example in the answer choices that matches the definition or follows the set of rules.

In dual Match questions, the matching example is actually found in the other passage. However, since the examples are then repeated for you in the answer choices, these questions are essentially identical to regular Match questions.

Here's a sample dual Match question stem:

> Which one of the phenomena cited in passage B is an instance of the kind of "situation" referred to in the second paragraph of passage A (line 16)?

Try this example:

> 8. Which one of the following pairs cited in passage B most closely exemplifies the term "isomorphic" as referred to in passage A (line 22)?

Your first step is to decide what isomorphic means in passage A. The author provides you a definition in lines 21–23: "works of culture…differing only in minor ways from a formulated archetype."

In the answer choices, you are looking for an example of this. Normally, you wouldn't be able to predict the example, but in dual Match questions, the question stem tells you that you already saw the example appear in the other passage. In this case, the only specific examples of works of culture in passage B are the police dramas named in lines 47–48. This is the most likely correct answer.

         (A)   consumers' demand for more nuanced presentation of material and producers' response to that demand

Choice (A): **No.** You're looking for works of culture, which these are not.

         (B)   vote-in mechanisms and community discussion

Choice (B): **No.** Again, these are not works of culture.

         (C)   police dramas and reality television

Choice (C): **No.** This choice is dubious since the question stem asks you for examples, but these are entire genres. It's also likely that, while author A may consider them formulaic, they may conform to *different* formulas since they are in different genres, so they wouldn't be isomorphic. Look for a better choice.

         (D)   character interrelation and non-linear story progression

Choice (D): **No.** These are features of works of culture, not works themselves.

> (E)   *21 Jump Street* and *NYPD Blue*

Choice (E): **Yes.** These are examples of works of culture, and author A would likely consider them isomorphic, since even author B acknowledges that they address many common themes and formulas.

Choice (E) is the correct answer.

10.3.7 Dual Analogy

In regular Analogy questions, you have to determine the major characteristics of the first half of the analogy (the part that appeared in the passage), describe them in general terms, and match these general terms to the second half of the analogy (the part that appears in the answer choices).

In dual Analogy questions, the first half of the analogy is always the relationship between the two passages. Thus, this type of question starts off essentially the same as a Relationship question, and asks you to take it one step further by finding another pair of documents with the same general relationship.

Here's an example of a dual Analogy question stem:

> Based on what can be inferred from their titles, the relationship between which one of the following pairs of documents is most analogous to the relationship between passage A and passage B?

Try this example:

> 9.   The relationship between passage A and passage B is most analogous to the relationship between the documents described in which one of the following?

> It's best to save dual Analogy questions until after you have completed any Relationship questions on the same set of passages.

It's best to save dual Analogy questions until after you have completed any Relationship questions associated with the set of passages. That way, you can use the correct answer to the Relationship question to help you define the characteristics that the documents in the correct answer to the dual Analogy question should have.

In this case, the LSAT writers described passages A and B as having this relationship: "Passage A contains a theoretical critique, while passage B presents an analysis of trends related to that critique." (This was the correct answer to question 1, the Relationship question for this same set of passages.)

Thus, you should look for an answer choice in which the documents have that same relationship.

> (A)   an article in a scholarly journal arguing about the dangers of Internet addiction; a magazine article chronicling some positive developments in the quality of Internet content

Choice (A): **Yes.** This looks good because there is both a critique and an analysis of related trends.

> (B)   a letter to the editor denouncing apparent partisanship in the content of a newspaper; an editorial responding with a justification of that paper's position

Choice (B): **No.** Passage B does not try to *justify* what passage A is critiquing. If anything, passage B contradicts the validity of passage A's complaint.

> (C)   a court decision aimed at reducing the recurrence of domestic violence; a research report on the harm of domestic violence to children

Choice (C): **No.** Passage A provides a critique of something but doesn't really aim to reduce anything or cause any particular outcome.

(D)   a magazine article listing accepted methods of
           cancer treatment; a journal article detailing new
           methods of treating cancer that are still under
           medical investigation

Choice (D): **No.** Passage A doesn't really have anything to do with a list of accepted methods.

(E)   a written history of the development of a
           scholar's ideas; a rebuttal of some of her claims
           in particular

Choice (E): **No.** Passage B is closer to being a "history of the development" of television, and neither passage is a direct rebuttal of particular claims in the other.

Choice (A) is the correct answer.

STOP. THIS IS THE END OF LECTURE 5. DO NOT PROCEED TO THE CORRESPONDING EXAM UNTIL INSTRUCTED TO DO SO IN CLASS.

LECTURE (11) CHAPTER (6)

READING COMPREHENSION REVIEW

11.1 THE FIVE PASSAGE TYPES

By now you have seen everything that the LSAT writers can throw at you in the Reading Comprehension section. You have seen that there are five types of passages and five major families of questions.

The passage type has nothing to do with the topic; rather, it describes the purpose and structure of a passage. There are several clues to look for to determine relatively early in a passage what type it is. Your analysis will depend somewhat on what type of passage you are dealing with.

However, you should have noticed one thing as you read the previous chapters: the analysis of every passage type contains the same key ingredients, and there is no way that you can mistakenly analyze a passage in the wrong way. That's because your analysis of every passage is rooted primarily in determining the **main point of the passage** and the **purpose of each paragraph**. If you finish reading every passage with a strong understanding of those two things, then you will be in good shape to answer the questions.

Where your analysis of the different passage types differs is when it comes to dealing with their specific features. But as long as you're on the lookout for things like the core question, major structural elements, the thesis statement, and the various viewpoints, then you can deal with them when and if they appear. If, for example, you get to the end of a passage and there was no core question, then you don't have to worry about having wasted your time, because you still focused on the main point, the purpose of each paragraph, and any important features that *did* appear.

Therefore, you don't have to spend any time deliberating on what type of passage you're looking at.

That being said, you should still be aware that the LSAT writers present passages that fall into five common patterns.

11.1.1 THESIS PASSAGES

1. Identify

All Thesis passages follow the same pattern:

- **The passage argues for a single conclusion**. Thesis passages are essentially a long argument for a single conclusion.

- **The conclusion appears in a one-sentence thesis statement**. All Thesis passages present their primary claim in a single sentence, and this thesis statement is the main point of the passage.

- **The thesis statement always appears in the first paragraph of the passage**. It is usually the last sentence of the first paragraph, but it can appear anywhere in the first paragraph.

The first paragraph sometimes contains a counterargument. In a counterargument, the author of the passage introduces a viewpoint but quickly contradicts it or says it is mistaken. The author's thesis is the negation of the so-called "wrong" viewpoint.

2. Analyze

To analyze a Thesis passage, look for:

1. **The main point**

    You should always identify the main point of any passage, and you should mark it by placing it in brackets, just as you do to the conclusion of a Logical Reasoning passage. The main point of every Thesis passage appears in a thesis statement. To help you find the thesis statement, remember:

    - The thesis statement always appears in the first paragraph. It is often, but not always, the final sentence of the first paragraph.

    - The thesis statement sounds more like an opinion than a fact.

    - The thesis statement tends to be one of the most specific statements in the first paragraph.

    - The thesis statement is the negation of any so-called "wrong" viewpoint, if there is one.

2. **The purpose of each paragraph**

    In a Thesis passage:

    - The purpose of the first paragraph is to assert the thesis.

    - The purpose of each remaining paragraph is to support the thesis with a major premise. Your job is to understand the major premise and how it works to strengthen the thesis.

11.1.2 INFORMATIONAL PASSAGES

1. Identify

All Informational passages follow the same pattern:

- **The purpose of the passage is to convey information**. Unlike Thesis passages, Informational passages don't really argue for any particular point. Instead, they describe a series of events, a life story, or some other set of facts.

- **The main point of an Informational passage is always descriptive**. If you identify the main point of a passage and find it is a counterargument or calls for a certain course of action, then the main point isn't descriptive, and you aren't looking at an Informational passage. The purpose of an Informational passage is to describe, so its main point is merely descriptive.

- **The main point of an Informational passage is not really up for debate.** Thesis passages can also have descriptive main points, but they are always debatable.

2. Analyze

To analyze an Informational passage, look for:

1. **The main point**

   The main point is a sentence that captures all of the most important information in a single statement. Often, the main point is explicitly stated in the passage.

   - The main point tends to appear in either the first or last paragraph of the passage.

   - The main point is one of the most general statements in the passage.

   - All of the paragraphs help to elaborate on the main point.

2. **The purpose of each paragraph**

   What kind of information is presented? In what way is the information presented? How does the information relate to the main point? While reading a body paragraph, you should determine what its purpose is. When you have done so, make a mental note or jot a few words next to each paragraph to help you remember its purpose.

3. **Major structural elements such as dichotomies, lists, or timelines.**

   Underline the different categories or phases and mark the passage with symbols such as ①, ②, and ③. In such passages, questions often revolve around the organization itself or require you to know the difference between the parts of the organization. Furthermore, your symbols can help you form a map of the passage that will save you time when you need to come back and search for a particular detail.

11.1.3 ENLIGHTENMENT PASSAGES

1. Identify

Enlightenment passages take you on a journey from a point of confusion to a point of clarity. All Enlightenment passages share the following characteristics:

- **The purpose of the passage is to explore a core question.** This question is introduced at the beginning of the passage along with some background on the topic and an explanation of why there is confusion or disagreement on the answer to the core question. The rest of the passage considers possible answers to the core question and usually decides on one as the correct understanding.

- **The passage contains several hypotheses or viewpoints.** There are always several possible responses to the core question presented in a passage. One of these viewpoints often belongs to the author, but sometimes they come only from experts in the field.

2. Analyze

To analyze an Enlightenment passage, look for:

1. **The core question**
   The core question can be introduced in several ways. The most common is a sentence that indicates that there is (or was) confusion over a certain phenomenon or the best way to understand something. Another common way to introduce the core question is through a hypothetical question.

2. The various viewpoints

As you identify the various viewpoints, mark the passage to remind yourself where they are located. The various viewpoints can come in several different forms:

- Accepted facts, which are descriptive and not really up for debate.

- Someone else's viewpoint, which always includes an indicator that tells you who the statement should be attributed to. When you find a statement that introduces a new viewpoint, underline the name of the theory that informs it or the name of the group that endorses the viewpoint. Then, when you find a paragraph or isolated statement that supports the theory, mark the passage with a symbol that reminds you which viewpoint is being discussed.

- The author's viewpoint, which does not have an indicator attributing it to someone else and which sounds like an opinion, not an accepted fact.

3. The main point

The main point of Enlightenment passages can be more difficult to find than in some other types of passages because it is not always stated in a compact way or in a predictable place. If a passage provides an answer to the core question, then the main point is that answer. The answer could come from someone else's viewpoint or from the author's.

4. The purpose of each paragraph

11.1.4 Controversy Passages

1. Identify

A Controversy passage is any passage primarily about a conflict of views. Controversy passages are defined by the following characteristics:

- **The passage contains several viewpoints.** These viewpoints are well-developed and are not simply a single sentence that that author immediately refutes. In addition, the various viewpoints all concern the same topic, and each responds to points made in the others.

- **The passage is not designed to answer a core question.** The passage will of course address a particular topic, and the author may even advocate a certain "answer" or understanding, but there is no core question and no journey from confusion to clarity.

2. Analyze

To analyze a Controversy passage, look for:

1. The various viewpoints

The process of finding the various viewpoints in a Controversy passage is identical to that of finding them in an Enlightenment passage. Each statement in the passage will be part of the author's viewpoint, someone else's viewpoint, or an accepted fact.

2. The main point

The main point may be explicitly stated, or you may have to synthesize it yourself using several statements, but just as in Enlightenment passages, the main point will always be very closely related to the author's own viewpoint.

3. The purpose of each paragraph

Most paragraphs have one of several common purposes:

- To introduce the topic—The first paragraph of some Controversy passages contains only accepted facts and serves simply to familiarize you with the topic.

- To present a single viewpoint—When a paragraph contains only a single viewpoint, you should analyze it just as you analyze a passage in the Logical Reasoning section. Identify the premises and conclusion using the same tools.

- To counter a previous paragraph with a conflicting viewpoint— In addition to finding the premises and conclusion, you should determine how one viewpoint counters the other. Does it attack one of the premises? Does it bring in additional evidence? Does it point out a flaw in the reasoning? Does is show a necessary assumption to be false?

- To present a viewpoint and counter it in the same paragraph—This kind of paragraph accomplishes the same thing as the two types previously discussed kinds, but all wrapped up in a single paragraph. Your analysis has the same components.

11.1.5 COMPARATIVE READING

1. Identify

Comparative Reading presents you with a set of two passages, labeled Passage A and Passage B. The questions that follow this set are largely concerned with both passages and how they compare to one another.

The two passages are written by different authors regarding the same or similar topics, but they are independent. That is, the authors present their viewpoints without any reference to the other passage. Neither author is writing as a direct response to the other, although they may in some cases address the same point.

The two miniature passages could themselves be any of the four "full-length" passage types, so look for the same features as you do when identifying longer passages.

As a whole, the set of two passages always contains at least two viewpoints (those of the two authors), so the set essentially functions as a single Controversy passage.

2. Analyze

To analyze a Comparative Reading set, first look for the same things you look for in every passage:

1. **The main point**

2. **The purpose of each paragraph**

As each individual passage may be any one of the four types, keep an eye out for these additional features that either of the passages may or may not have:

3. **The various viewpoints**, especially the author's

4. **Major structural elements**, like lists or timelines

5. **The core question**, if there is one

Finally, look for some additional things that are unique to your analysis of Comparative Reading sets:

6. **The relationship between the passages**

You are very likely to see a question that asks you about the relationship between the passages, so you should determine this as part of your initial analysis. There are a number of relationships the two passages are likely to have. For example, they could

- Argue for opposing conclusions

- Be in general agreement

- Have different scopes

7. The response each author would have to the other passage

The LSAT is likely to ask you how one of the authors would respond to either a point made in the other passage or the other passage as a whole. To be able to answer such a question without guessing, the set has to provide you with some evidence—both passages must address the same idea or topic and pass some sort of judgment on it. A crucial part of you analysis is to look for places in which the same topic or idea is discussed in both passages. When you see this, draw a line between the passages showing the connection.

11.2 THE STRUCTURAL QUESTION FAMILY

Structural Questions all ask you to understand the big picture of the passage. You are asked to understand the overall point of the passage and how each part of the passage functions to make it work as a whole. For all types of passages, you should be able to answer Structural questions simply by using the work you did in your analysis.

There are three basic types of Structural questions:

- Main Point

- Purpose

- Organization

11.2.1 MAIN POINT QUESTIONS

Main Point questions ask you to choose the best expression of the passage's main point. The correct answer choice will be a rewording of the main point as it was stated in the passage.

1. Identify

Main Point questions are easy to identify. Here are some keys to identifying them:

- Main Point questions are almost always the first question for each passage, if they appear.

- Main Point questions always include the words *main point* or *main idea*.

- Main Point questions always ask for the answer that most accurately states or expresses the main point.

Here are some sample Main Point question stems:

> Which one of the following most accurately expresses the main point of the passage?

> Which one of the following most accurately states the main point of the passage?

> Which one of the following most accurately summarizes the main idea of the passage?

2. Analyze

Because you always mark the main point of a passage during your initial analysis of it, there is very little you need to do for the analysis step on Main Point questions. Just revisit and reread the main point that you marked when you initially read the passage.

3. Prephrase

The conclusion is already stated for you in the passage, so you don't have to do anything for this step. Don't bother trying to reword, simplify, or paraphrase the main point; the correct answer choice will do that for you. However, make sure you have determined the passage's main point before you start looking at the answer choices.

4. Attack

Here are the most common distracters for Main Point questions:

- **Wrong action**—Sometimes, an answer choice consists of something that was only a small part of the passage, such as a particular sentence or the main point of one of the paragraphs. Don't pick an answer choice that leaves out any major topic that was discussed in detail.

- **Out of scope**—If an answer choice mentions new information that never appeared in the passage, it can't be correct.

- **Extreme**—Extreme answers use much stronger language than is warranted by the passage.

- **Opposite**—Some answer choices state the opposite of the main point of the passage.

11.2.1.1 Variation: Title Questions

There is an uncommon variation of Main Point questions called Title questions. These questions ask you for an appropriate title for the passage. A good title summarizes the contents of the passage, so you are in essence looking for an answer choice that contains the main point. Your approach to Title questions is identical in every way to your approach to Main Point questions, and you should eliminate precisely the same distracter answer choices. Even though they look a little different, you should consider Title questions to be exactly the same as Main Point questions.

11.2.2 PURPOSE QUESTIONS

Purpose questions ask you to describe the function of

- A word or phrase,

- An entire paragraph, or

- The passage itself.

Although the question stem will never use the word "why," the best way to think about these questions is to consider them to be asking *why* a certain word was used, *why* a certain paragraph was included, or *why* the passage was written.

11.2.2.1 Purpose of a Phrase

1. Identify

Here are some keys to identifying Purpose of a Phrase questions:

- The question stem always directs your attention to a particular word, phrase, or sentence. It often does this by telling you the specific lines in which the phrase can be found.

- The question stem usually uses the term *primary purpose*, *primary function*, or *primarily in order to*.

- The question stem **does not** ask you what a word means or what the author is referring to. Instead, it asks you to determine **why** the phrase was used.

Here are some sample Purpose of a Phrase question stems:

Which one of the following most accurately expresses the primary purpose of the sentence in lines 27–30?

The author mentions the relative difficulty in interpretation of ice core samples primarily in order to

The primary function of the reference to outdated schools of economic thought (lines 34–41) is to

2. Analyze

Your analysis for Purpose of a Phrase questions has a few steps:

- Find the phrase in question in the passage.

- Read the surrounding area to get the context.

- Determine why the phrase was used or what role it plays.

3. Prephrase

On Purpose of a Phrase questions, you should always come up with an answer in your own words as to why the author used the phrase in question. Don't read the answer choices until you have done this. Due to the nature of the question stems for Purpose of a Phrase questions, most answer choices will describe some sort of action, so your Prephrased answer should also be centered around an action.

4. Attack

Here are the most common distracters for Purpose of a Phrase questions.

- **Wrong action**—For example, if the purpose of a phrase was to raise a question, don't pick an answer choice that says "to prove…"

- **Wrong part of the passage**—The phrase you are asked about fits into a certain place in the passage, but some answer choices refer to a completely unrelated part of the passage.

- **Contradicts the passage**—If an answer choice contradicts any information from the passage, it can't be correct.

11.2.2.2 Purpose of a Paragraph

1. Identify

Here are some of the features of Purpose of a Paragraph questions:

- The question stem always asks about a particular paragraph.

- The question stem usually uses the term *primary purpose* or *primary function*.

Here are some sample Purpose of a Paragraph question stems:

The primary function of the third paragraph of the passage is to

Which one of the following statements most accurately describes the function of the final paragraph?

The primary purpose of the second paragraph is to

2. Analyze

Your analysis for Purpose of a Paragraph questions is actually done as you read the passage for the first time. For every passage that you encounter, you will always determine the purpose of each paragraph by deciding what role it plays in the passage as a whole.

3. Prephrase

On Purpose of a Paragraph questions, you should always come up with an answer in your own words as to why the author included the paragraph in question. Don't read the answer choices until you have done this. Most Purpose of a Paragraph answer choices describe some sort of action, and your answer should also include an indication of how the particular paragraph relates to the other paragraphs and the main idea of the passage.

4. Attack

These are the most common distracters for Purpose of a Paragraph questions:

- **Wrong action**—Just like on Purpose of a Phrase questions, don't pick an answer choice that describes an action different from the one performed by the paragraph in question.

- **Incomplete**—Just like on Main Point questions, don't pick an answer choice that leaves out a major part of the paragraph.

- **Wrong part of the passage**—Some incorrect answer choices will try to trick you by accurately describing the purpose of a different paragraph.

- **Contradicts the passage**—If an answer choice contradicts any information from the passage, it can't be correct.

11.2.2.3   Purpose of a Passage

1. Identify

Purpose of a Passage questions are characterized by these features:

- The question stem always asks about the passage as a whole.

- The question stem uses the term *primary purpose* or asks what the author is *primarily concerned with*.

Here are some sample Purpose of a Paragraph question stems:

> The author's primary purpose in writing the passage is to

> Which one of the following best describes the primary purpose of the passage?

> The passage is primarily concerned with

2. Analyze

Your analysis for Purpose of a Paragraph questions is also done as you read the passage for the first time. As you identify and analyze each passage, you are doing all the work necessary to determine its purpose. Thesis passages argue for a single conclusion. Other common purposes of passages include:

- to argue that a particular viewpoint is incorrect

- to describe a scientific or historical phenomenon

- to suggest a revision to the traditional understanding of something

- to show that one theory is better than another

- to examine the details of a problem and its solution

3. Prephrase

On Purpose of a Passage questions, you should always come up with an answer in your own words as to why the author wrote the passage. Don't read the answer choices until you have done this.

While Main Point questions and Purpose of a Passage questions are closely related, there are some important differences. First, Main Point answer choices are always specifically about the topic of the passage—they don't use general language. Purpose of a Passage questions, on the other hand, will use more general language and may not even mention the specific topic at hand.

Second, Main Point answer choices are complete ideas, while Purpose of a Passage answer choices, like those of other Purpose questions, revolve around an action. Thus, your Prephrased answer should also be centered around an action.

4. Attack

Here are the most common distracters for Purpose of a Passage questions:

- **Wrong Action.** Just like on other Purpose questions, don't pick an answer choice that describes an action different from the one performed by the passage.

- **Incomplete.** Just like on Main Point questions, don't pick an answer choice that leaves out a major part of the passage.

- **Out of scope.** If an answer choice mentions new information that never appeared in the passage, it can't be correct.

- **Contradicts the passage.** If an answer choice contradicts any information from the passage, get rid of it.

11.2.3 ORGANIZATION QUESTIONS

Organization questions ask you to describe the organization of a passage or one of its parts.

1. Identify

Organization questions all share very similar question stems. They have one main characteristic:

- The question stem always asks about the *organization* or the *presentation* of the material in the passage or a part of the passage.

Here are some sample Organization question stems:

> Which one of the following most accurately describes the organization of the passage?

> Which one of the following sequences most accurately and completely corresponds to the presentation of the material in the passage?

> Which one of the following most accurately describes the organization of the material presented in the first and second paragraphs of the passage?

2. Analyze

As with most other Structural questions, you should be well prepared to answer Organization questions after you have analyzed the passage.

The answer choices to Organization questions are presented as lists, and the number of items on the lists usually corresponds to the number of paragraphs in each passage. Occasionally, if a paragraph serves two major purposes, it will correspond to two items on a list. Otherwise, each item on a list describes the purpose of one paragraph. Therefore, since you read each paragraph of every passage with the goal of determining its purpose, you will have done all the analysis you need before you encounter an Organization question.

3. Prephrase

On Organization questions, you should always come up with an answer in your own words before you read the answer choices. The method you use to come up with a

Prephrased answer is the same one you use on Purpose of a Paragraph questions. The only difference is that you should articulate the purpose of *each* paragraph. Your Prephrased answer should be a list of actions and should include an indication of how the particular paragraph relates to the others.

4. Attack

Here are the most common distracters that you will see on Organization questions:

- **Out of order**—The different parts of the passage have to appear in the correct order in the answer choice. If something is mixed up, eliminate the answer choice.

- **Contradicts the passage**—If an answer choice contradicts any information from the passage, get rid of it.

- **Out of scope**—If an answer choice mentions new information that never appeared in the passage, it can't be correct.

The answer choices on Organization questions can often be intimidating because the long lists can be difficult to read. However, if you find one item on the list that is incorrect, don't bother reading the rest of the list. Eliminate the answer choice and move on to the next one.

11.3 THE RETRIEVAL QUESTION FAMILY

Retrieval questions all ask you to do the same thing: to go back to the passage and find a specific piece of information. You don't have to synthesize multiple statements, nor do you have to determine how or why the author conveyed any particular information.

There are three types of Retrieval questions:

- Detail
- Definition
- Search

11.3.1 DETAIL QUESTIONS

Detail questions ask you a question that can be answered by retrieving a particular detail from the passage. The answer is explicitly stated in the passage, so if the question stem is specific enough, you should always determine the answer on your own before you look at the answer choices.

1. Identify

Here are some keys to identifying Detail questions:

- The question indicates that the answer is directly stated in the passage. Some phrases that accomplish this include *the passage cites* and *according to the passage*.

- The question asks about a specific fact, rather than about the implications or intentions of a statement.

- The question doesn't ask about anyone's *perspective* or *opinion*.

Here are some sample Detail question stems:

> The passage cites which one of the following as a value central to the treaty establishing a constitution for Europe?

> According to the passage, the elimination of which one of the following obstacles allowed researchers to determine the age of the Milky Way galaxy to within 800 million years?

> According to the passage, the prevailing view of dynamic systems theory is that, in general,

2. Analyze

Your analysis for Detail questions has a few steps:

- Make sure you understand the specific question in the question stem. Put it into simpler terms if you need to.

- Find the topic of the question in the passage. If you can't remember where the topic of interest was discussed, revisit the sentences you bracketed or your notes next to each paragraph to help you find where the topic would likely appear.

- Reread the surrounding area to get the context.

- Locate the detail that answers the question.

3. Prephrase

You should always Prephrase an answer to a Detail question. Your Prephrased answer can usually be taken directly from the text.

4. Attack

These are the common distracters you will see on Detail questions:

- **Wrong part of the passage**—Most wrong answers to Detail questions are about parts of the passage that have nothing to do with the question at hand.

- **Word trap**—The LSAT writers like to create distracters that contain certain words from the Prephrased answer but that don't mean the same thing.

- **Out of scope**—If an answer choice mentions new information that never appeared in the passage, it can't be correct.

11.3.2 DEFINITION QUESTIONS

Definition questions ask for the meaning of a particular word or statement from the passage. In English, most words can have several meanings, but your job is to find the meaning of the word *as it was used in the passage*. Thus, the LSAT writers have to give you other words in the surrounding context that tell you the definition of the word in that particular case. To answer a Definition question, you have to retrieve the contextual clues and match them to the answer choices.

1. Identify

Here are some keys to identifying Definition questions:

- The question stem always refers to a word or phrase, presented in quotation marks.

- The question stem almost always refers to a specific line in the passage.

- The question stem asks you what the word or phrase *means in context* or *refers to*.

Here are some sample Definition question stems:

> Based on the passage, the term "primary part" (line 34) most clearly refers to which one of the following?

> Which one of the following phrases could replace the word "compelling" in line 30 without substantively altering the author's meaning?

> Which one of the following most accurately expresses what the author means by "ambassadors of style" (line 27)?

2. Analyze

Your analysis of Definition questions is much like your analysis of Detail questions:

- Find the word or phrase in question in the passage.
- Reread the surrounding area to get the context.
- Locate the contextual clues that indicate the meaning of the word or phrase.

3. Prephrase

To Prephrase for Definition questions, you should use the contextual clues to come up with a succinct definition (if possible), or a list of the important elements that the correct answer should contain.

4. Attack

Here are the distracters commonly seen on Definition questions:

- **Most common definition.**
- **Out of scope**—If an answer choice includes new ideas that never appeared in the passage, it can't be correct.
- **Half wrong**—Often, the test writers will create distracters that have some parts that match the Prephrased answer perfectly, but that go wrong in other parts. If it's half wrong, it's all wrong.

11.3.3 SEARCH QUESTIONS

Search questions ask you whether or not a particular piece of information was contained in the passage. Sometimes the correct answer choice will be the one piece of information that *did* appear, but usually the question stem will ask you to find the one piece of information that *did not* appear in the passage.

1. Identify

Here are some characteristics for identifying Search questions:

- The question stem refers to something *mentioned, cited, stated, affirmed,* etc. in the passage.
- The question stem asks you to find the one answer choice that appeared in the passage or says that each answer choice appeared EXCEPT one.

Here are some sample Search question stems:

> Which one of the following does the author mention in the passage?

> Each of the following statements is affirmed by the passage EXCEPT:

> The passage offers information to help answer each of the following questions EXCEPT:

> Which one of the following is NOT identified by the author of the passage as a characteristic of Anastasio's compositions?

2. Analyze

Most Search question stems do not specify what you need to look for. If you encounter such a question stem, there is no way to Analyze or Prephrase before you look at the answer choices. Instead you have to go directly to the answer choices and react to each one in turn.

Some Search questions are more specific when it comes to the information they ask you to search for. In such cases, your analysis can be very similar to that of a Detail question:

- Make sure you understand the topic or specific question in the question stem. Put it into simpler terms if you need to.

- Find the topic of the question stem in the passage. The topic may be discussed in several places.

- Reread the surrounding area to get the context.

- Locate as many instances as you can of a detail that answers the question.

By determining the purpose of each paragraph and noting the topic of discussion in each part of the passage the first time you read, you will arrive at the questions with a map of the passage. You can use this map to help you decide where to look for the information you need to answer the question.

3. Prephrase

Just as on other types of questions in the Retrieval family, you don't have to reword or reinterpret the passage to come up with an answer. You can leave the information in the same words that the passage uses, although you should be ready for answer choices that may use different words to mean the same thing.

4. Attack

Regardless of whether or not the question stem gave you specific instructions as to what information to look for, your job is to decide whether each answer choice was contained in the passage. If an answer choice appeared, then you should pick it or eliminate it appropriately, depending on whether the question stem contains an EXCEPT. The EXCEPT Tool is particularly useful on Search questions.

11.4 THE "USING THE EVIDENCE" QUESTION FAMILY

Using the Evidence questions are all based on evidence found in the passage. The questions in this family ask you to go beyond simple retrieval of information. You will have to synthesize multiple statements and use valid reasoning to determine the implications of the information in the passage.

There are four types of Using the Evidence questions:

- Inference

- Viewpoint

- Attitude

- Match

11.4.1 INFERENCE QUESTIONS

Inference questions ask you to make an inference based on the passage. An inference is something that the passage provides specific evidence for, and it **must** be true based on the evidence in the passage.

Inference questions in the Reading Comprehension section follow exactly the same rules as Inference questions in the Logical Reasoning section. There are two types of inferences on the LSAT:

- Inferences formed by using valid logic to combine multiple statements from the passage
- Inferences that are mere restatements of part of the passage

Most inferences in the Reading Comprehension section fall into the first category.

1. Identify

There are a few phrases used on the LSAT to indicate Inference questions. All of these mean the same thing:

- The question stem asks you about what you can *infer* or what is *implied* or *suggested* by the passage.
- The question stem asks you which answer choice is *supported by* information in the passage.

Here are some sample Inference question stems:

> Which one of the following can most reasonably be inferred from the information in the passage?
>
> The passage implies that which one of the following is a reason that *E. Coli* bacteria are especially virulent?
>
> The passage suggests which one of the following about critics of postmodernism?
>
> The information in the passage provides the most support for which one of the following statements?

2. Analyze

Your analysis of Inference questions depends on how specific the question stem is. For questions that don't point you in any specific direction in the question stem, your analysis is necessarily suspended until after you begin working with the answer choices.

For questions that tell you what you should be making an inference about, your analysis has two steps:

- Find the topic of the question in the passage.
- Reread the surrounding area to locate any facts related to the topic.

3. Prephrase

If an Inference question points you to a specific portion of the passage, you should Prephrase by determining the scope of what the correct answer can address. If you can Prephrase a specific inference, do so, but be ready to choose any answer choice that must be true, even if it doesn't match your Prephrased inference.

4. Attack

Regardless of whether or not the question stem gave you a specific topic to look for, your job is to decide whether each answer choice contains a valid inference. The only difference is that if the question stem was specific, you will have already located the important evidence in the passage. On the other hand, if the question stem is vague, you will have to search for the evidence after reading each answer choice, using the same techniques discussed in the Analyze section.

There are several common distracters that appear on Inference questions:

- **Out of scope**—For Inference questions, out of scope answer choices are those that do not have specific evidence in the passage. Any answer that mentions new information that never appeared in the passage is wrong. Any answer choice that relies on evidence not related to the topic mentioned in the question stem is also wrong.

- **Contradicts the passage**

- **Word trap**

- **Extreme**—Extreme answers use much stronger language than is warranted by the passage. If the passage says that something is a promising theory, don't choose an answer choice that says it's the best theory.

11.4.2 VIEWPOINT QUESTIONS

Viewpoint questions ask you to pick a statement that corresponds to someone's viewpoint.

In your analysis of the passage, you always identify the author's main point, and in passages with more than one viewpoint, you always identify the various viewpoints. Accurate analysis of the passage is crucial when it comes to answering Viewpoint questions.

1. Identify

Here are some keys to identifying Viewpoint questions:

- The question stem always asks about either the author or someone mentioned in the passage.

- The question stems always ask about a person's *view*, what they *believe*, or what they are *most likely to agree* with.

Here are some sample Viewpoint question stems:

> With which one of the following statements would the author of the passage be most likely to agree?
>
> The passage suggests that the oenologists mentioned in line 17 would be most likely to agree with which one of the following statements?
>
> The passage most strongly supports the ascription of which one of the following views to ecologists who support controlled burns?
>
> According to the author, most early Greek philosophers believed that

2. Analyze

Your first analysis step was done when you analyzed the passage and determined the various viewpoints.

After that, Viewpoint questions are a lot like Inference questions: your analysis depends on how specific the question is. If the question is so general that the necessary evidence could come from anywhere in the passage, then you need to go straight to the answer choices.

If, on the other hand, it asks about a specific topic, then you should use your analysis of the passage to find the topic and do a little bit of rereading in that area, just as you do on several other question types. Likewise, if the question stem asks about a specific person's viewpoint, and that viewpoint is discussed only in a limited area, you should revisit that area and refresh your memory of that person.

3. Prephrase

Most of the time, you will not be able to predict what the correct answer will say. But correct answers to Viewpoint questions are statements that have specific evidence in the passage to support them. You need to be able to point to the evidence.

4. Attack

Look for the answer that corresponds to the right viewpoint and has evidence for it in the passage.

Here are the most common distracters for Viewpoint questions:

- **Wrong viewpoint**—It can be hard to remember who believes what, especially in passages that contain several viewpoints. The LSAT writers love to create trap answers that correctly state *someone's* viewpoint—just make sure it belongs to the right person.

- **Out of scope**—Out of scope answers choices are those that are not related to specific evidence in the passage. Even if you think it's likely that the author would agree with a given statement, if you cannot point to specific evidence to support it, it is out of scope.

- **Contradicts the passage**

- **Extreme**—Extreme answers use much stronger language than is warranted by the passage.

11.4.3 ATTITUDE QUESTIONS

Attitude questions ask you to identify how the author feels about a certain phenomenon or about someone else's viewpoint. There must be specific words in the passage that tell you exactly what the author's attitude is on the topic.

1. Identify

Attitude question stems are usually quite predictable.

- Most Attitude question stems contain the word *attitude*.

- Other Attitude questions ask about how the author views something or what the author appears to value.

Here are some sample Attitude question stems:

> Based on the passage, the author's attitude toward the school of thought presented in the third paragraph is most accurately described as

> It can be most reasonably inferred from the passage that the author views the double-blind strategy developed by Parrack as

> Based on the passage, which one of the following aspects of Overbeck's work does the author of the passage appear to value most highly?

2. Analyze

First, narrow down your search for evidence to the part of the passage where the topic was discussed. Then, identify opinionated words, which are the evidence you will use to answer the question.

3. Prephrase

You should always Prephrase an answer to Attitude questions. Use the evidence you find to complete this sentence:

> Attitude: Regarding this topic, the author feels _____.

Make your Prephrased answer as specific and complete as you can.

4. Attack

Attitude questions have some predictable distracters:

- **Extreme**—If you determined that the author feels "hesitant approval" for something, don't pick an answer choice that contains "unmitigated enthusiasm."

- **Opposite**—When an author feels positively about something, there are usually trap answer choices that convey negative feelings, and vice versa.

- **Word trap**—The LSAT writers like to create distracters that contain words that you recognize from the passage but that don't add up to the author's attitude.

- **Out of scope**

11.4.4 MATCH QUESTIONS

Some passages contain a set of rules, a definition of a new term, or a list of something's defining characteristics. Match questions ask you to provide an example that matches a description or definition.

1. Identify

Since all Match questions revolve around finding an example of something that matches a certain definition or set of rules, they usually use the word *example* or *exemplify*.

Other Match questions find another way of asking for an example, such as asking which answer choice *illustrates the concept*.

Here are some sample Match question stems:

> Which one of the following examples best illustrates the type of legislative approach recommended by the academics mentioned in the fourth paragraph?

> Given the information in the passage, which one of the following most closely exemplifies Kamala's understanding of impressionism?

> Based on the passage, which one of the following is best explained as non-Newtonian fluid behavior?

> Which one of the following epidemiological studies would NOT be covered by the threefold categorization scheme proposed by Knechtley?

2. Analyze

Your analysis for Match questions has two steps:

- Find the definition or set of rules that you must provide an example of.

- Determine the major components of that set of rules.

3. Prephrase

You will not be able to predict the particular example that the correct answer will use. Don't bother trying. As long as you know the important features that the correct answer will have, you are ready to move on to the answer choices.

4. Attack

Every incorrect answer choice simply fails to match the definition. Look out for these distracters:

- **Word trap**—These distracters use familiar words from the passage but don't correctly capture the important parts of the definition you're looking for.

- **Out of scope**—Be careful here. The correct answer choice will contain an example that was not mentioned in the passage, but it will conform to the rules that were specified or illustrated. If an answer choice has characteristics that were not contained in the relevant rules, then it's out of scope.

11.5 THE "BEYOND THE PASSAGE" QUESTION FAMILY

Questions in the Beyond the Passage family ask you to combine the information in the passage with new information to arrive at the correct answer. All the questions in this family are directly comparable to questions in the Logical Reasoning section of the test, and you can often use the same tactics to answer these questions when they appear in the Reading Comprehension section.

There are four types of Beyond the Passage questions:

- Weaken/Strengthen
- Analogy
- Principle
- Complete

11.5.1 WEAKEN / STRENGTHEN QUESTIONS

Weaken and Strengthen questions in the Reading Comprehension section work identically to those in the Logical Reasoning section. A conclusion is drawn in the passage, but the evidence used to support that conclusion is not enough to completely prove its validity. You are asked to choose a piece of new information that makes the conclusion less likely or more likely to be true.

1. Identify

All Weaken and Strengthen questions share the following characteristics:

- The question stem directs your attention to a particular claim. In the Logical Reasoning section, a Weaken question stem may simply ask you to weaken "the argument," but in the Reading Comprehension section, the question stem tells you exactly which claim to focus on.

- The question stem tells you to accept the answer choices as true. This is significant—since you must accept the truth of the answer choices, you should never eliminate an answer choice simply because it seems implausible.

- The question stem asks you to find the answer choice that most *weakens* or *strengthens* the claim. Some words that mean the same thing as weaken are *challenge*, *call into question*, and *cast doubt on*. Some words that mean the same thing as strengthen are *support* and *lend credence to*.

Here are some sample Weaken question stems:

> Which one of the following, if true, most weakens the author's argument concerning imaginary number theory?

> Which one of the following, if true, most weakens the author's criticism of the assumption that secondary education invariably engenders increased empathy?

> Which one of the following, if true, would most seriously challenge the position of the legal theorists mentioned in line 22?

Here are some sample Strengthen question stems:

> Which one of the following, if true, most supports the author's claim about the relationship between broker recommendations and the stock market (lines 20–25)?

Which one of the following, if true, would most help to strengthen the author's primary conclusion in the last sentence of the passage?

Which one of the following, if true, would have lent the most credence to the manufacturers' position in the lawsuit?

2. Analyze

Your analysis for Weaken and Strengthen questions has several steps:

- Find the relevant claim. The question stem will tell you what to focus on, and it may even tell you the location of the claim. If it doesn't tell you the location, use your analysis of the passage to find it. Revisit the sentences you bracketed and/or your notes next to each paragraph to help you find where the topic is likely to appear.

- Identify the supporting premises for the claim and any weakness in the argument. You should be able to express the weakness as a Concept Shift, an unsupported assumption, or a flaw.

3. Prephrase

The correct answer to a Weaken question will *suggest* (not prove) that the claim is untrue. The correct answer to a Strengthen question will *suggest* (not prove) that the claim is indeed true. You should also decide how the correct answer will do it.

The correct answer to a Weaken question attacks a weakness already present in the argument.

The correct answer to a Strengthen question defends the argument against a potential attack upon a weakness already present in the argument.

4. Attack

Here are the common distracters on Weaken and Strengthen questions:

- Opposite—On Weaken questions, don't pick an answer choice that strengthens the claim. On Strengthen questions, don't pick an answer choice that weakens the claim.

- Out of scope—Be extremely careful here. The correct answer choice will almost certainly introduce new information that did not appear anywhere in the passage. If you dismiss answers too quickly because they seem irrelevant, you may end up eliminating the correct answer. A true out of scope answer choice fails to address the weakness that exists between the claim and its evidence.

11.5.2 ANALOGY QUESTIONS

Analogy questions describe a situation or entity in the passage and ask you to find a different situation or entity that is analogous. You can think of Analogy questions as being similar to Parallel questions in the Logical Reasoning section.

1. Identify

Analogy questions are defined by the following characteristics:

- The question stem directs your attention to a particular situation, entity, or relationship. Something in the passage has to act as one half of the analogy, and the question stem tells you what it is and (sometimes) where to find it.

- The question stem asks you to find the answer choice that is *most closely analogous to* or *most similar* to the first half of the analogy.

Here are some sample Analogy question stems:

> Which one of the following is a questionable moral guideline most similar to that discussed in the third paragraph?

> Based on the passage, which one of the following relationships is most analogous to that between a naturalist and a previously undiscovered species?

> As described in the passage, knowingly omitting certain truths in a courtroom is most closely analogous to which one of the following?

2. Analyze

The most important step in your analysis is to determine the major characteristics of the original situation or phenomenon in the passage. To do this, describe the situation in general terms that are not related to the topic of the passage.

3. Prephrase

You will certainly not be able to predict the details or the topic of the second half of the analogy. The topic can be anything at all, and it probably won't be related to the topic of the passage.

You will be able to predict one thing about the correct answer: when you recast it in general terms, it will be identical to the general terms that described the first half of the analogy in the passage. Simply put, its major characteristics will match.

4. Attack

When you attack the answer choices on a Analogy question, look for an answer choice that has the same major characteristics as the first half of the analogy. That means you will have to put each answer choice in general terms as well and look for a match. Watch out for these common distracters:

- Topic trap
- Word trap

11.5.3 PRINCIPLE QUESTIONS

On the LSAT, a "principle" is a general rule. For example, "people should treat others the way they want to be treated themselves" is a principle.

Principle questions in the Reading Comprehension section are much like Conform questions in the Logical Reasoning section. In the Reading Comprehension section, they ask you to identify the general rule that underlies someone's line of reasoning.

1. Identify

All Principle questions share the following characteristics:

- The question stem uses the word *principle*. On rare occasions, the word principle shows up in other types of question stems, so keep the second characteristic in mind as well.

- The question stem asks you to find the principle that underlies a claim or the principle that an argument is based on.

Here are some examples of Principle question stems:

> Which one of the following principles is most in keeping with the passage's argument?

> Based on the passage, a post-modernist film critic is most likely to claim that a successful film is one that satisfies which one of the following principles?

> Which one of the following principles most
> likely underlies the author's characterization of
> astronomical modeling?

Each of these asks you to find the principle that corresponds to the argument in the passage.

2. Analyze

Because these questions ask you about a particular argument in the passage, you need to identify and understand the premises and conclusion of that argument.

3. Prephrase

Since you are looking for a general rule that underlies someone's argument, the general rule must do two things:

- Match the circumstances
- Match the outcome

To Prephrase on Principle questions, describe the argument in general terms, much as you do on Analogy questions. You don't have to totally avoid the topic of the passage; you should include a mention of both the circumstances and the outcome, since those are the important features you are looking to match in the correct answer choice.

4. Attack

On Principle questions, you are ultimately looking for an answer that matches the passage. Before eliminating any answer choice, determine whether it matches both the circumstances and the outcome, and be ready to match generalized terms in the answer choice to specific components of the passage.

11.5.4 COMPLETE QUESTIONS

Complete questions ask you to add another sentence onto the end of the passage. Complete questions are rare.

1. Identify

All Complete questions find some way to ask you to choose an appropriate sentence to add to the end of the passage.

Here are some examples:

> Given the passage's argument, which one of the
> following sentences most logically completes the last
> paragraph?

> Based on information in the passage, it can be
> inferred that which one of the following sentences
> could most logically be added to the passage as a
> concluding sentence?

2. Analyze

In your analysis for a Complete question, try to determine where the last paragraph is leading.

3. Prephrase

In your Prephrasing step, remember what the correct answer will do. It must

- Be supported by evidence in the passage—Anything that contradicts the author's viewpoint is incorrect.

- Flow logically with the text—If an answer choice is concerned with something mentioned only in the beginning of the passage, it doesn't make a good addition to the end of the passage.

4. Attack

As you attack the answer choices, eliminate any choice that contradicts the author's viewpoint, isn't supported by evidence in the passage, or does not flow logically with the text.

11.6 THE COMPARATIVE READING QUESTION FAMILY

Questions associated with Comparative Reading sets come in several varieties. Some of them concern only one of the passages, and these questions are essentially identical to those that follow full-length passages.

In contrast, there are several types of questions that appear only on Comparative Reading sets. These make up the Comparative Reading question family:

- Relationship questions
- Response questions
- Dual questions

The category of Dual questions is actually made up of a large number of questions that are similar to question types in the other families, but adapted so that they relate to both passages.

11.6.1 RELATIONSHIP QUESTIONS

Relationship questions ask you about the relationship between the two passages. They ask you to explain how the arguments in the two passages unfold and how they compare to one another.

1. Identify

You can identify Relationship questions because:

- The question stem uses the word relate or relationship. The question stem also concerns both passages.

Here are some sample Relationship question stems:

> Which one of the following most accurately describes the relationship between the argument made in passage A and the argument made in passage B?

> Which one of the following most accurately describes a way in which the two passages are related to each other?

2. Analyze

The analysis you need for Relationship questions is actually part of your analysis of the passages themselves. When you read a Comparative Reading set, you should notice whether the passages reach similar or opposing conclusions, or whether they have a more complex relationship, such as a different scope.

3. Prephrase

On Relationship questions, you should always come up with an answer in your own words before you read the answer choices.

This Prephrased answer is simply an articulation of what you determined in your initial analysis of the passages. In your Prephrased answer, make sure to go beyond simply describing each passage independently. Your answer should include some indication of the ways in which passages are the same or different.

4. Attack

Here are the distracters commonly seen on Relationship questions:

- **Misrepresents a passage**—The answer choices make assertions about both passages, and everything they say about each one has to match what the passages actually contain. If a choice says anything extreme, out of scope, or contradictory to what happened in one of the passages, get rid of it.

- **Misrepresents the relationship**—The answer choices also make assertions about the relationship between the passages, and this too must match. For example, if an answer choice says the passages used the same evidence to reach opposite conclusions, you must consider whether their evidence really was the same and whether their conclusions really were opposite. This requires thinking about both passages at the same time, but your Prephrased answer should help.

11.6.2 RESPONSE QUESTIONS

Response questions ask you to infer how one of the authors would respond to a view expressed in the other passage.

1. Identify

Response questions are defined by the following characteristics:

- The question stem mentions the author of one of the passages.

- The question stem asks you to determine the feeling, judgment, or conclusion the author would reach regarding something in the other passage.

Here are some sample Response question stems:

> If the author of passage B were to read passage A, he or she would be most likely to draw which one of the following conclusions regarding matters addressed in passage A?

> The author of passage B would be most likely to make which one of the following criticisms about the predictions cited in passage A concerning a rise in interest rates?

2. Analyze

When you first read the passages, you did most of the analysis you need in order to answer a Response question.

The most important thing to take note of is when the two authors discuss the same topic or when one author mentions something that could be directly applicable to a topic in the other passage. In order to be able to say how one author would respond to something mentioned by the other, there must be some evidence regarding the author's feelings on the topic.

Some Response question stems are specific—they mention exactly the topic or statement that you must determine the response to. In these cases, revisit both passages in the areas you marked and re-familiarize yourself with the evidence you'll need to answer the question.

If, on the other hand, the question stem is vague—it just asks for one author's response to the entire other passage—then you have to do a little more work. First, determine which issues are fair game for a response—the responder's passage has to provide enough evidence to support drawing a conclusion in regard to the author's feeling. Then try to determine what that response would be.

3. Prephrase

You should always Prephrase an answer to Response questions using the evidence you found in the responder's passage. You should leave your answer in the same words the author uses if you can. However, keep in mind that the correct answer choice is likely to rearrange the words or concepts. As long as a choice *means* the same as what you predicted or is *well supported* by the evidence, keep it.

4. Attack

When you attack the answer choices on a Response question, you should be in the same frame of mind as you are when you attack an Inference question. The correct answer has to be supported by specific evidence you can point to in the responder's passage.

Watch out for these common distracters:

- **Wrong viewpoint**—Some answer choices may try to trick you by presenting the wrong author's response to the information. You have to keep the different authors' viewpoints straight.

- **Out of scope**—For Response questions, out of scope answer choices are those that are not related to specific evidence in the responder's passage. Any answer that mentions new information that never appeared in the passage is wrong. Any answer choice that relies on evidence not related to the topic mentioned in the question stem is wrong.

- **Contradicts the passage**—If an answer choice contradicts any information from the responder's passage, it can't be correct.

- **Word trap**

- **Extreme**

11.6.3 DUAL QUESTIONS

Dual questions are similar to the question types in the other four question families. They are adapted so that they refer to both passages, but your approach to them is essentially the same as when they refer to just one passage. The only added step is that you may be asked to perform the same task twice or make a comparison of material in the two passages.

Dual questions include:

- Dual Purpose
- Dual Definition
- Dual Search
- Dual Viewpoint
- Dual Attitude
- Dual Match
- Dual Analogy

11.7 THE EXCEPT TOOL

One area in which many test-takers make mistakes is EXCEPT questions. EXCEPT questions can be confusing because they require an extra step of reversal that often leads people to forget what they are looking for and to pick the wrong answer. This confusion can be overcome with a tool that takes advantage of the simple fact that the correct answer will always be different from the other four answer choices. The tool is called the EXCEPT Tool, and it works like this:

1. **Determine from the question stem what the four incorrect answer choices will do.** For Search questions, the four incorrect answers will appear in the passage. For other types of questions, the four incorrect answers may match your Prephrased answer or do something else.

2. **Instead of cutting or keeping each answer choice, make a mark next to it depending on what it does.** For example, on a Search question, write a Y if the piece of information did appear in the passage, and an N if it did not.

3. **The correct answer is the one that looks different from the rest.** For example, on a Search question it will have an N next to it, while the other four choices have a Y.

This tool applies to any EXCEPT question, not just to those of the Search variety. You can treat EXCEPT questions like any other questions, but use the EXCEPT Tool to identify the correct answer.

11.8 PACING

You need to have a pacing plan on the LSAT. As you saw in the introduction, there are some general pacing principles that you should follow:

1. **Work as quickly as you can** *without sacrificing accuracy.* You have limited time, so you need to work quickly, but it makes no sense to blaze through the section carelessly. You should find a pace at which you can work quickly but comfortably enough to remain accurate. Understand that you may not finish the entire section.

2. **Work the passages that will give you the most points in the shortest time first.** While there is no simple formula for what makes a passage difficult, you should develop a sense of what makes a passage take a long time. In general, if language or the subject matter is very complex, then the passage might take a long time. If a time-consuming passage is accompanied by only a few questions, skip it and return to it if you have time later. There's no reason to spend twelve minutes answering five questions when you could spend that same time answering eight questions.

3. **Work each passage as a unit.** Skipping around between different passages is a bad idea. Each time you change passages, you have to re-familiarize yourself with the content and how the passage works. This can be a significant waste of time. When you begin a passage, keep working until you have finished all the questions associated with it. Only if a question has you completely stumped should you guess and move on to the next passage. Return to it if you have extra time remaining after answering everything else.

If you are getting more than one question wrong per passage, then you're not working accurately. You can improve your accuracy by going back and reviewing techniques, reworking old passages, slowing down, and doing as many homework passages as possible.

STOP. THIS IS THE END OF LECTURE 6. DO NOT PROCEED TO THE CORRESPONDING EXAM UNTIL INSTRUCTED TO DO SO IN CLASS.

IN-CLASS EXAM ICE LECTURE 1

EXAMINATION

LECTURE 1 EXAM
Time—25 minutes
15 Questions

<u>Directions</u>: Each passage in this section is followed by a group of questions to be answered on the basis of what is <u>stated</u> or <u>implied</u> in the passage. For some of the questions, more than one of the choices could conceivably answer the question. However, you are to choose the <u>best</u> answer; that is, the response that most accurately and completely answers the question, and circle the corresponding answer choice.

Approximately only one out of every twenty individuals accused of a crime in the United States exercises the constitutional right to be tried by a jury of peers. Instead of going to trial, the vast majority of
(5) criminal cases within the nation's legal systems are resolved via the defendant entering a guilty plea or a plea of *nolo contendere*. Legal scholar John Langbein sees this situation as intolerable and believes it to be the direct result of the use of coercive measures that
(10) force defendants to give up their constitutional rights, and of a system in which prosecutors are given vastly too much power in deciding who is guilty and how the guilty are punished.

Most individuals charged with a crime in the
(15) United States are offered a plea bargain—a deal in which the prosecutor pledges that the defendant will receive a lighter sentence in exchange for admitting guilt to the levied charges or to a lesser offense. If this deal is not accepted, the defendant is told that a much
(20) harsher sentence will be forthcoming if a guilty verdict is returned by a jury. Langbein feels such deals are coercive and closely parallel the tortuous methods employed by medieval jurists to extract confessions from criminal defendants. In both cases, according to
(25) Langbein, defendants are given the choice between being punished twice or punished only once for a crime. In medieval Europe, the choice was to either admit guilt and be punished for the alleged crime, or submit to torture—a punishment itself—and then be
(30) punished for the offense. In the U.S., the choice is to admit guilt and receive a prison sentence or fine in accordance with the gravity of the offense, or to exercise constitutional rights by going to a trial and possibly receiving a sentence disproportionate to the
(35) alleged offense. According to Langbein, even in cases in which defendants are innocent of the levied charges, only fools, those with nothing to lose, and defendants with very good defense attorneys exercise their rights and refuse to accept prosecutors' deals.
(40) Additionally, Langbein says, the current system's heavy reliance on plea bargaining has handed nearly all judicial power to prosecutors and stripped defendants, judges, and juries of the legal power given to them by the framers of the constitution. Because prosecutors are
(45) given the power to decide who should be prosecuted, who is offered plea agreements, and what sentences are contained in these agreements, they effectively act not only as prosecutor, but also as jury and judge in cases in which defendants enter the pleas specified in the
(50) agreements—something that happens in 95 percent of criminal cases in the U.S.

Although Langbein does concede that the expediency of the plea bargaining system is useful in cases in which the criminal defendant is truly guilty, he
(55) feels the gains in efficiency justify neither the coercion of people out of their constitutional rights nor the unconstitutional transformation of prosecutors into supreme judicial magistrates.

1. Which one of the following most accurately expresses the main point of the passage?

    (A)   Langbein believes that plea bargain agreements place more power in the hands of prosecutors than was intended by the constitutional framers and that all criminal justice systems that use plea bargain agreements are unsound.

    (B)   According to Langbein, plea bargaining is expedient, and the underuse of the practice leads to constitutional problems parallel to those faced by prosecutors in medieval Europe.

    (C)   Langbein argues that criminal courts in the U.S. currently place too much emphasis on plea bargaining and calls for more legislative oversight to restrict its use.

    (D)   Langbein believes that the heavy reliance on plea bargaining in U.S. criminal courts is unjustifiable because the disproportionate influence given to prosecutors compels defendants to surrender their constitutional rights.

    (E)   According to Langbein, the whole of the U.S. legal system is deeply flawed because defendants, judges, and juries have been stripped of nearly all the power delegated to them by the constitution.

GO ON TO THE NEXT PAGE.

2. The primary function of the second paragraph of the passage is to

    (A)   demonstrate that plea bargaining was a form of torture used in medieval Europe
    (B)   suggest that the heavy reliance by U.S. criminal courts on plea bargaining is unconstitutional because it gives prosecutors too much power
    (C)   argue that plea bargaining is unjustly coercive by comparing it to torturous methods used in the past
    (D)   concede that plea bargaining can be effective in cases in which defendants are innocent of the levied charges
    (E)   show that some coercive measures, such as plea bargaining, are acceptable while others, such as torture, are not

3. Which one of the following most accurately describes the organization of the passage?

    (A)   Two criticisms are levied against a system; the first is supported with an analogy; the second is reasserted with a brief explanation; a concession of one advantage of the system is made while the overall criticisms are reconfirmed.
    (B)   Two criticisms are levied against a system; the first is supported with an analogy; the second is reasserted with a brief explanation; a concession is made that the advantages of the system outweigh the disadvantages.
    (C)   Two criticisms are levied against a system; the first is supported with several examples; the second is restated without support; a third criticism regarding the system is introduced.
    (D)   Two criticisms are levied against a system; the first is reasserted with a brief explanation; the second is supported with an extended analogy; a concession of one advantage of the system is made while the overall criticisms are reconfirmed.
    (E)   Two criticisms are levied against a system; the first is supported with an analogy; the second is reasserted with a brief explanation; a third criticism regarding the system is introduced.

4. In lines 45–47, the author lists the powers given to prosecutors primarily in order to

    (A)   strengthen Langbein's argument that the use of plea bargaining is analogous to the practice of torture
    (B)   illustrate how the system of plea bargaining can be expedient in cases in which the defendant is truly guilty
    (C)   provide a counterexample to weaken Langbein's argument that the system of plea bargaining is unconstitutional
    (D)   demonstrate that prosecutors are currently given powers parallel to those afforded to prosecutors in medieval Europe
    (E)   support Langbein's claim that the system of plea bargaining has deprived defendants, judges, and juries of deserved legal rights

5. The author's primary purpose in the passage is to

    (A)   encourage judges to find new ways to limit the use of plea bargain agreements
    (B)   call attention to flaws in the U.S. criminal court system, as viewed by one legal scholar
    (C)   explore the historical roots of one of the most prevalent elements of the legal system
    (D)   articulate one legal expert's theory of how the use of plea bargaining will eventually corrupt prosecutors
    (E)   reveal the unsupported assumptions made by those who compare plea bargaining to torture

GO ON TO THE NEXT PAGE.

It was the apolitical nature of Zora Neale Hurston's writings that kept her on the fringes of the Harlem Renaissance and out of the canon of African-American literature during her lifetime. Since then, however, her
(5) anthropological and literary works have produced attempts by several distinct movements to claim her as an archetypal member. More of an ethnographer than a polemicist, Hurston wrote a unique blend of literature and anthropology that stood outside of the accepted
(10) frames of literary and political movements, and her life's work continues to defy such classification.

Whereas the male writers of the Harlem Renaissance—Richard Wright, Langston Hughes and later Ralph Ellison—wrote consciously political texts,
(15) Hurston was first and foremost an ethnographer, recording the vernacular of the American South and documenting rural life. Political engagement was one of the dominant themes of African-American culture between the World Wars, but Hurston's work is
(20) remarkably removed from this trend. Her training with anthropologists such as Franz Boas and Margaret Mead required her to be more objective than authors without such training. Although her choice to focus on underrepresented African-American communities was
(25) eventually seen as a political statement tying her to the Harlem Renaissance, there is nothing in her autobiographical writing to suggest that the decision was anything but a natural desire to capture the sights and sounds of the world in which she had been raised.

(30) Recently, conservative libertarians have tried to reframe Hurston's longer texts as presentations of their own doctrine, pointing to journalistic articles she wrote opposing school desegregation and liberal politics in general. While it is true that she opposed government
(35) intervention in social issues, her stories and recorded folktales reveal a more complete picture of her political beliefs, one that does not fit neatly into the confines of the libertarian dogma. Feminist scholars, partly because the Harlem Renaissance was a male-dominated
(40) movement, have also claimed Hurston as the model of feminist contribution to the period. Feminist literary critics, led by Alice Walker, revived interest in her work, and Hurston is now firmly established as a canonical author. Many feminist arguments rely on
(45) subtextual clues taken from Hurston's literary works. But the resurrection of her status by feminist writers in the 1970s and 1980s says more about contemporary political thought then it does about Hurston's motives.

Her novel *Seraph on the Suwannee* exemplifies the
(50) divergence of her work from the themes and style embodied in the Harlem Renaissance and other movements. Focusing on a poor white community in the South, this work deals with universal themes of love, trust, and betrayal. Because it lacks any overt
(55) racial consciousness or strong feminist polemics, it is usually left out of reading lists by modern feminist advocates of her work and is also ignored by contemporary proponents of African-American literature. The strong objectivity of her work suggests
(60) that she was recording a historical milieu rather than

commenting upon it. Ignoring parts of her oeuvre diminishes the universality of her writing and misrepresents her intentions as an author.

6. Which one of the following best expresses the main idea of the passage?

(A) The works of Zora Neale Hurston have been claimed by diverse groups as representative of their own agendas, but the apolitical nature of her writing has belied these assertions.

(B) Feminist literary theorists, Harlem Renaissance historians, and libertarian social critics have all found elements of their own philosophies in the writing of Zora Neale Hurston.

(C) The work of Zora Neale Hurston has been misunderstood for many years and should be reexamined in the context of her political writings, which are opposed to common interpretations of her work.

(D) Although the literary and anthropological works of Zora Neale Hurston are apolitical, the fact that she wrote several political articles has allowed her work to be used by literary critics to make contradictory claims.

(E) Zora Neale Hurston had to create meaning through subtext because she was not encouraged to state her views explicitly by the male-dominated literary movements of her lifetime.

7. The function of the second paragraph is to

(A) argue that Hurston's work has incorrectly been classified as unrelated to the Harlem Renaissance

(B) reveal the connections between the Harlem Renaissance, libertarianism, and feminism

(C) identify the disparate elements that came together to create the Harlem Renaissance

(D) contrast the work of Hurston with that of the defining figures of the Harlem Renaissance

(E) describe the effect of the Harlem Renaissance on the work of Hurston

GO ON TO THE NEXT PAGE.

8. The author discusses Hurston's *Seraph on the Suwannee* in lines 49–61 primarily to

(A) demonstrate that she often disagrees with more well-known male writers of the Harlem Renaissance

(B) argue that the attempt to categorize her as a feminist writer applies to only some of her novels

(C) counter the claim that her works strove to raise opposition to government intervention in social issues

(D) explain why many critics and theorists find contradictory views in her work, even though such views do not exist

(E) suggest that classifying her as belonging to certain literary or political movements necessitates disregarding some parts of her work

9. Which one of the following most accurately describes the organization of the material presented in the passage?

(A) biographical information about Hurston; illustrations of how her work belongs to several literary movements; modifications to each of those illustrations; an example of her work that shows her independence from those movements

(B) a presentation of Hurston's approach to literature and how it has been received; several illustrations of attempts to classify her as belonging to a certain movement, each one disproved in turn; an example of her work that shows her independence from those movements

(C) an explanation of why Hurston's literature was historically ignored; several illustrations of attempts by certain movements to revive her works; a call for better understanding of the universality of her writing and her intentions as an author

(D) an argument regarding how Hurston's approach to literature should have been received; an illustration of attempts to classify her as a feminist; counterexamples discrediting those attempts; a conclusion that she is best regarded as a canonical member of the Harlem Renaissance

(E) praise for Hurston's unique blend of literature and anthropology; several examples of how she supported several political and literary movements during her lifetime; a discussion of one of her novels that unites these movements

10. The passage is primarily concerned with

(A) making the case that it is incorrect to view Hurston as simply a feminist or libertarian, since she also supported the ideals of the Harlem Renaissance

(B) discussing how some of Hurston's lesser-known novels compare to her journalistic articles

(C) arguing that, despite multiple attempts to classify it, Hurston's work falls outside the boundaries of literary and political movements

(D) dismissing critics who feel that Hurston's unique writing style lacks any overt racial consciousness or strong feminist arguments

(E) examining the role that Hurston's work played in revealing connections between several distinct political movements

GO ON TO THE NEXT PAGE.

Many kinds of gazelles, when confronted by their natural predators, revert to an unusual behavior known as stotting. Before fleeing, adult gazelles begin to run very slowly and make several precision leaps in the air,
(5) achieving heights of over 12 feet. This behavior has traditionally been seen as a signaling system, warning herd members of approaching danger. However, a recent theory, known as the handicap principle, asserts that stotting and other traits and behaviors that appear
(10) to reduce evolutionary fitness and endanger the individual are actually secondary sexual characteristics. Such traits and behaviors, referred to by biologists as handicaps, exhibit to others the true strength of the individual that possesses them.

(15) The peacock possesses a handicap in its prodigious tail, which is conspicuously used to impress peahens during mating rituals but is an encumbrance to the individual. An animal capable of surviving predation and other hazards with such an encumbrance openly
(20) reveals its fitness to prospective sexual partners. Potential sexual partners, furthermore, do not need to see other costly displays, as the handicap alone is indicative of a high quality genotype. A peacock's tail is known as an honest signal because, unlike species
(25) that display colorations that mimic those of other, more dangerous species, a peacock cannot falsely advertise the size of its tail. When individuals compete rigorously for reproductive dominance, the ability to support a handicap may have less of an impact than the
(30) failure to do so. Honest signaling is dangerous if the handicap is displayed inefficiently, since it communicates vulnerability.

Previously, the idea that a specific trait could harm an individual's chances of survival and still be
(35) developed in individual members of a group was explained through a theory of altruism. Stotting, construed as a warning signal to the herd, would improve the survival rates of close relatives with genes nearly identical to the individual's even if the
(40) individual perished. The handicap principle is superior in that it provides a more immediate justification for the behavior, one that allows for self-interest to replace altruism as a rationale. The gazelle who stots prior to the herd fleeing communicates information on several
(45) levels. Intuitively, the expenditure of so much energy before a life-threatening chase would seem to decrease the individual's chance of survival. The stotting gazelle, however, has honestly informed the predator, perhaps a swift cheetah, that it is a powerful member of
(50) the herd. The predator, in its own struggle against starvation, reflexively chases weak or debilitated creatures. The risk involved in expending energy on stotting may save a gazelle the massive energy output of a hard chase. In addition, the increased survival rate
(55) is accompanied by an increased reproductive rate spurred by females' observation of the display, so the stotting individual is benefited twice over.

11. Which one of the following most accurately states the main point of the passage?

(A) A peacock's tail or a gazelle's stotting encumber the animal with an awkward handicap, but such handicaps are necessary to separate weak members from the group.

(B) Predators and potential mates benefit equally from honest signaling, while individuals are impaired by inefficient signaling.

(C) Handicaps, such as a peacock's tail or a gazelle's stotting, are actually signals to prospective mates that the individual with the handicap is both healthy and altruistic.

(D) The handicap principle provides an explanation for how the presence of apparently harmful traits and behaviors can coexist with a theory of self-interested individuals.

(E) A recent theory, the handicap principle, successfully explains how secondary sexual characteristics can also be used by members of a group to warn others of approaching predators.

12. Which one of the following best describes the organization of the passage?

(A) A long-standing problem is identified. Two possible solutions to the problem are posed.

(B) A natural phenomenon is explored. One hypothesis to explain the phenomenon is advocated, while another is rejected.

(C) Two traits are described. A principle is proposed to account for the two traits. Further exploration of the principle shows it to be flawed.

(D) A scientific debate is introduced. Several issues contributing to the debate are summarized.

(E) An unusual behavior is illustrated. A second unusual behavior is shown to have more in common with the first than previously believed.

GO ON TO THE NEXT PAGE.

13. The primary purpose of the passage is to

(A) suggest that altruism plays a less significant role in evolution than previously believed

(B) evaluate the relative merits and flaws in two theories regarding the origin of stotting

(C) demonstrate that the handicap principle provides a better justification for certain behaviors than did a previous theory

(D) contrast the phenomenon of honest signaling with that of dishonest signaling, while noting that neither represents altruistic behavior

(E) argue that handicaps serve mainly to inform potential predators of an individual's health

14. The discussion in the second paragraph is intended primarily to

(A) provide several examples of honest signaling benefiting a self-interested individual

(B) explain how a handicap can act as a secondary sexual characteristic

(C) assert that a peacock's tail displays colorations that mimic those of more dangerous species

(D) show that the handicap principle is superior to the theory of altruism

(E) warn against the dangers of the inefficient display of a handicap

15. Which one of the following most accurately describes the author's main purpose in lines 36–40 of the passage?

(A) to explain how altruism was theorized to be able to propagate the genes of even those individuals that died

(B) to describe why many biologists still believe stotting can be understood as a warning signal to the herd

(C) to illustrate how stotting serves as a signal to dissuade predators from expending energy on a chase

(D) to defend the theory of altruism by asserting that it explains how information can be communicated on several levels

(E) to provide an example of a behavior that the author believes would harm an individual's chances of survival

STOP

IF YOU FINISH BEFORE TIME IS CALLED, YOU MAY CHECK YOUR WORK ON THIS EXAM ONLY.
DO NOT WORK ON ANY EXAM IN THE BOOK.

Answers

1. D
2. C
3. A
4. E
5. B
6. A
7. D
8. E
9. B
10. C
11. D
12. B
13. C
14. B
15. A

IN-CLASS EXAM · ICE · LECTURE 2

EXAMINATION

LECTURE 2 EXAM

Time—25 minutes

15 Questions

<u>Directions:</u> Each passage in this section is followed by a group of questions to be answered on the basis of what is <u>stated</u> or <u>implied</u> in the passage. For some of the questions, more than one of the choices could conceivably answer the question. However, you are to choose the <u>best</u> answer; that is, the response that most accurately and completely answers the question, and circle the corresponding answer choice.

Since it was first proposed, people have attempted to employ biology's theory of natural selection to explain systems as diverse as stock market fluctuations and political schemes of representation. The effort to
(5) apply the theory more rigorously to the examination of cultural phenomena has resulted in a new field of study called memetics. Memetics, consciously modeled after genetics, focuses on the meme as the unit of information that evolves rather than the gene. The field
(10) reveals that the manner in which cultural entities change and spread displays some similarities to genetic evolution, as well as some important differences.

Memeticists define a meme as any cultural entity that can be replicated, such as a song, an image, or an
(15) idea that can be repeated and passed on to new people. Memes are often assembled into meme complexes—combinations of ideas, habits, and moods that form recognized systems of thought, such as religious doctrines or political ideologies. Memes can change as
(20) they are passed from individual to individual, much as genes can change as they are passed from parent to offspring. For example, the body of thought known as Christianity has evolved as it spread, to the point where its original form no longer exists, and its current
(25) regional manifestations vary widely. The process is analogous to the genetic changes of an ancestral species that becomes extinct while its descendents differentiate into separate species. Memetics' central principle is that natural selection is a theory that
(30) describes all forms of change and that genes evolve not because there is a chemical basis for evolution, but because its processes are a universal truth.

Genetic theory dictates that the genetic variants that proliferate are those that confer an advantage for sexual
(35) reproduction. Since the methods of memetic propagation are different than those of genetic transmission, a different determinant must be proposed to explain why some memes spread while others disappear. One hypothesis suggests that altruism is the
(40) driving force. In the mid-1990s, a meme that warned people about something known as the Good Times computer virus quickly spread throughout the world, disseminated by newspapers, television, and internet communities. The warning contained a description of
(45) drastic damage that would result from opening any electronic mail labeled with the subject "Good Times," thereby unleashing the virus. Some memeticists theorize that the warning spread so quickly because people believed they were helping others by passing it
(50) on. However, the warning was a hoax; there was no such virus. When the invalidity of its information

became widely known, the meme became extinct. While the proposed altruism mechanism has gained some acceptance, some feel that the most important
(55) factor in determining whether a meme complex will spread is whether it contains an instruction to spread it. The Good Times virus hoax urged people to tell their friends about the virus, and some of the most widespread ideologies include as one of their pillars the
(60) directive to disseminate that very set of beliefs.

1. The "mechanism" mentioned in line 53 refers to

   (A)   the manner in which memes are replicated
   (B)   the type of machine thought to be endangered by the Good Times virus
   (C)   the basis for why only some memes proliferate
   (D)   the driving force behind the theory of natural selection
   (E)   the cause of the frequent mutation of memes

GO ON TO THE NEXT PAGE.

2. The passage mentions each of the following cultural entities as an example of a meme or meme complex EXCEPT:

   (A) a song
   (B) an image
   (C) a rumor
   (D) a religious doctrine
   (E) a hoax

3. The passage offers information to help answer which one of the following questions?

   (A) How can the theory of natural selection be used to explain stock market fluctuations?
   (B) What causes people to combine ideas and habits into meme complexes?
   (C) Which genetic variations are most likely to proliferate?
   (D) How did the Good Times virus hoax begin?
   (E) Why are some widespread ideologies built upon the instruction to spread the ideology?

4. According to the passage, which one of the following was true of the Good Times virus hoax?

   (A) It no longer exists in its original form, but rather in a variety of regional manifestations.
   (B) It caused widespread fear of the virus, costing companies millions of dollars.
   (C) It spread more quickly than any previous meme.
   (D) It contained an instruction to disseminate the meme.
   (E) Study of the hoax provided a major breakthrough in memetic theory.

5. According to the author, memes and genes are analogous in the sense that both

   (A) physically exist
   (B) are informational units capable of evolving
   (C) are used to explain cultural change
   (D) can be consciously manipulated in order to speed the process of evolution
   (E) employ similar methods of propagation

GO ON TO THE NEXT PAGE.

Trepanation has been called the world's oldest surgical technique. The process consists of opening a hole in the skull, known as a burr hole, using a drill or a process of scraping away at the skull until the dura
(5) mater—the outer layer of the brain—is exposed. Neurosurgeons still perform the operation to relieve pressure on the brain caused by a depressive fracture or to remove blood clots, but only rarely. An understanding of its long history is useful in examining
(10) the relation between medicine and spirituality, since the operation has been used as a cure for a variety of ailments as well as a pathway to spiritual enlightenment.

Historically, the operation was performed on a
(15) much broader scale. Trepanation holes were found in healthy craniums of prehistoric cadavers found near the cave paintings of Lascaux, France. The earliest extant written explanation of trepanning is from Hippocrates. Writing in 400 B.C., he advocated trepanation for
(20) fracture or contusion of the cranium caused by a blow. Barbers in Europe, who performed the work of modern surgeons during the Middle Ages, performed trepanation for a variety of maladies ranging from epilepsy and migraines to mental illness in general.
(25) Their purpose was often to allow the 'evil' that was thought to be causing the illness to exit through the burr hole. The relation between this surgery and the maladies it was believed to relieve shows a history of medicine closely related to doctrines of the soul, in
(30) which symptoms of madness were thought to be caused by evil. The essential spiritual nature of medicine, which strove to heal the body and spirit simultaneously, led to a further blurring of lines between surgery and spirituality.
(35) Excavations in Peru and Bolivia uncovered a ritual use of trepanation, based on the regularity of burr holes in a wide spectrum of the population, from women and children to grown men and the elderly. The commonality of the trepanned holes, as well as the
(40) incidence of multiple burr holes, suggests a non-therapeutic function for pre-Columbian trepanation. The precision and prevalence of the technique around the world suggests that other societies employed this ritual use as well. Non-therapeutic trepanation is also
(45) practiced in contemporary cultures worldwide, particularly in rural Kenya.

There has begun in the United States and Europe a movement to revive trepanation as a spiritual practice. Members of the movement postulate that by releasing
(50) pressure on the brain and allowing blood to move freely, patients can rediscover the awareness of their infant selves and expand their consciousness. Proponents argue that this motivation was the reason behind the wide-scale practice of trepanation in ancient
(55) times. However, modern advocates of non-therapeutic trepanation in Western countries must perform the surgery themselves, as it is illegal in many countries for doctors to participate in the operation due to the dangers associated with infection.

6. The passage states which one of the following about the use of trepanation in pre-Columbian Peru and Bolivia?

(A) It was used to allow the elderly to rediscover their infant selves.

(B) It was used to treat epilepsy and mental illness.

(C) The surgery was central to the religious beliefs of most pre-Columbian inhabitants of Peru and Bolivia.

(D) The surgery was sometimes performed multiple times on a single person.

(E) Historical accounts state that the surgery was performed on children, adults, and the elderly.

7. According to the passage, which one of the following is true of the modern residents of Europe and the U.S. who want to revive trepanation as a spiritual practice?

(A) They think that ancient peoples sought to become aware of their infant selves and expand consciousness.

(B) Some have become seriously ill due to infections caused by voluntary trepanation procedures.

(C) They believe that awareness of the infant self can lead to expanded consciousness.

(D) Many of them have undergone surgical procedures that were performed by non-licensed physicians.

(E) They share many of Hippocrates's beliefs pertaining to trepanation.

GO ON TO THE NEXT PAGE.

8. The passage states that each of the following performed or still performs trepanation procedures EXCEPT:

(A)   some contemporary rural Kenyans
(B)   Europeans of the middle ages
(C)   present-day spiritualists of Peru and Bolivia
(D)   prehistoric peoples of France
(E)   modern medical professionals

9. Which one of the following most accurately expresses the meaning of the phrase "non-therapeutic function" as used by the author in line 40–41?

(A)   trepanation to relieve pressure on the brain
(B)   trepanation for ritual purposes
(C)   trepanation performed by someone other than a doctor
(D)   trepanation practiced by a whole society
(E)   trepanation performed on people without a malady

10. The passage mentions each of the following reasons for the historical use of trepanation EXCEPT:

(A)   to relieve pressure on the brain caused by skull fracture
(B)   to allow blood and fluids to circulate more freely around the brain
(C)   to allow evil to escape from the cranium in order to cure migraines
(D)   to decrease the dangers associated with infection
(E)   to allow the patient to achieve an expanded consciousness

GO ON TO THE NEXT PAGE.

Judicial review has become such an integral function of the Supreme Court that it is easy to forget that the Constitution did not explicitly guarantee this power. Not until the case of Marbury v. Madison in
(5) 1803 did the Supreme Court declare an act of Congress unconstitutional. It took another fifty years until it would do so again, but the 1803 interpretation of the Court's jurisdiction would help define the form of the United States' government in terms of different
(10) branches holding checks and balances over their coequal partners. The Supreme Court has struck down over 150 acts of Congress in the last century, and Marbury is the case that allows the Court to do so.

The irony of the case is that the law that Chief
(15) Justice John Marshall and the other justices invalidated sought to give the Supreme Court more power. Section 13 of the Judiciary Act of 1789 granted the Court the power to issue writs compelling government officials to perform their duties if they were negligent. William
(20) Marbury and 41 others had been given appointments as district judges by the outgoing president, John Adams. The incoming president, Thomas Jefferson, and his secretary of state, James Madison, refused to seat the new judges on technical grounds. Marbury petitioned
(25) the court to issue a writ compelling the government to recognize their appointments.

Article III of the Constitution clearly states that the Supreme Court's review of appellate decisions may be addressed by acts of Congress. Marshall went on to
(30) conclude, however, that this explicit statement of jurisdiction also made an implicit statement about the Supreme Court's original jurisdiction. Since Marbury v. Madison was originally filed in the Supreme Court, it was within the Court's original jurisdiction and not
(35) an appellate review of a lower court's decision. Marshall ruled that the Constitution implied that Congress had no authority to modify the Court's original jurisdiction, only its appellate function. A 4–0 vote by the justices found that Section 13 was at cross-
(40) purposes with the Constitution, and judicial review of Congressional law was born.

Legal scholars critical of the decision argue that it implies that justices must try to find some underlying meaning to the Constitution beyond what is expressly
(45) stated. They argue that this gives the Court too much power and that justices should abide only by the text of the Constitution. Indeed, the intent of the framers of the Constitution is often invoked as a rationale in cases on the margins of constitutional language. However,
(50) the Judiciary Act of 1789 was written concurrently with the Constitution, and by the same individuals, so the Court was invalidating a law written by the framers themselves. In this case, the framers' intent was clear but ignored by the Court. The Court, by unanimously
(55) deciding to deny itself the power to issue the writ, consciously claimed for itself a far greater and lasting power. Judicial review is now seen as the primary function of the Supreme Court and Marbury v. Madison, not the Constitution itself, is the source of
(60) that power.

11. The passage states which one of the following about William Marbury?

(A) Marbury was a political ally of John Adams.
(B) Marbury sought to challenge Section 13 of the Judiciary Act of 1789.
(C) Marbury petitioned the court to issue a writ compelling the government to recognize Jefferson's decision.
(D) Marbury never had the opportunity to serve as a district judge.
(E) Marbury was one of 42 men appointed to district judge positions by President John Adams shortly before he left office.

12. According to the passage, the legal scholars mentioned in line 42 have criticized the Marbury v. Madison decision because

(A) they believe judicial review grants the Supreme Court too much power
(B) they think implicit powers should not be derived from the Constitution's text
(C) they think the court should have compelled Jefferson to allow Adams's judicial appointments to serve
(D) they feel judicial review should not be the primary role of the court
(E) they feel justices should rule according to only the text of the Constitution and legal precedent

GO ON TO THE NEXT PAGE.

13. The "irony of the case" (line 14) refers to the fact that

   (A) the Supreme Court created its own power of judicial review, which was accepted by Congress
   (B) the Court overturned a law that would have given it extended powers in order to create judicial review
   (C) the justices were, in fact, opposed to the Jefferson administration's attempt to withhold the commissions
   (D) the Court set the precedent of judicial review by denying itself the power to overturn decisions made by the lower courts
   (E) the history of the Court has been written without a full explanation of the effects of *Marbury v. Madison*

14. The passage provides explicit information about each of the following EXCEPT

   (A) the background of the *Marbury v. Madison* case decided by the Supreme Court
   (B) the reasoning of the Supreme Court in the *Marbury v. Madison* case
   (C) the importance of *Marbury v. Madison* in Supreme Court history
   (D) the political affiliations of Marshall and the other justices
   (E) the historical importance of the intent of the framers of the Constitution

15. According to the passage, the Judiciary Act of 1789

   (A) was written by the framers of the Constitution
   (B) contained several sections that were ruled unconstitutional
   (C) provided Thomas Jefferson with a reason to deny Marbury his judgeship
   (D) granted the Supreme Court the power to issue writs compelling government officials to abstain from performing certain duties
   (E) granted the Supreme Court the power of judicial review

STOP

IF YOU FINISH BEFORE TIME IS CALLED, YOU MAY CHECK YOUR WORK ON THIS EXAM ONLY.
DO NOT WORK ON ANY OTHER EXAM IN THE BOOK.

Answers

1. C
2. C
3. C
4. D
5. B
6. D
7. A
8. C
9. B
10. D
11. E
12. B
13. B
14. D
15. A

EXAMINATION

LECTURE 3 EXAM
Time—25 minutes
15 Questions

Directions: Each passage in this section is followed by a group of questions to be answered on the basis of what is <u>stated</u> or <u>implied</u> in the passage. For some of the questions, more than one of the choices could conceivably answer the question. However, you are to choose the <u>best</u> answer; that is, the response that most accurately and completely answers the question, and circle the corresponding answer choice.

For over one thousand years, the tusk that grows from the upper left jaw of the narwhal has inspired curiosity and speculation. When it was first brought to the medieval courts of western and central Europe by
(5) Viking and other northern traders, the tusk was thought to be the horn of the mythical unicorn, an object said to possess unique and magical powers. Once the supernatural speculation upon origins of narwhal tusks ceased in the mid-seventeenth century, scientific
(10) curiosity regarding the strange protrusions began to grow as naturalists of the age were baffled as to why a 14-foot, 3,000 pound whale would need an 8-foot-long tusk protruding from its upper left jaw. Hundreds of years later, when scientists did discern the function of
(15) the narwhal's tusk, it became clear that, while the horns are certainly not magical, they are unique in the animal kingdom.

When they first began speculating upon the natural purpose of the narwhal tusk, scientists suggested that
(20) the tusk, which is actually a spiraling elongated tooth, was used by the cetacean as a way to break through the ice of its Arctic Ocean domain. Later, some scientists theorized that the strange tusk was used as a sensory organ for echolocation. Other scientists postulated that
(25) bull narwhals used their tusks to display dominance in order to attract a mate, since females with developed tusks are exceedingly rare. This theory was further supported by observations of an activity called tusking, in which two males rub their tusks together, a behavior
(30) that scientists took to be a kind of rutting ritual.

New research conducted by Martin Nweeia, however, has concluded that all three of these speculations are incorrect, although the scientists who supported the echolocation hypothesis were not far off
(35) the mark. By examining electron micrographs of narwhal tusks, Nweeia discovered that they possess hydrodynamic sensory capabilities due to the 10 million or so nerve tubules that line the surface of each narwhal tusk. According to Nweeia's definitive work
(40) these incredibly sensitive nerve tubules are capable of detecting changes in water temperature, water pressure, and particle gradients. The ability to detect particulates in oceanic waters allows the narwhal to perceive the salinity levels of its oceanic environs, to navigate
(45) within its environment, and to sense particulates indicating the presence of squid, halibut, redfish, and shrimp, upon which the whale feeds. It is likely that the sheer uniqueness of the tusk and its hydrodynamic sensory abilities delayed its scientific explanation by
(50) decades. Furthermore, it was only by skillfully applying technology not available to earlier scientists

that Nweeia was able to make his important discovery. Scientists now speculate that the narwhal's observed tusking behavior might enable the narwhal to clean
(55) encrustations off the sensitive nerve tubules, or it might produce a unique and desirable sensation due to the tusk's sensory capabilities. Although the exact reason for the tusking behavior is not yet fully understood, it is likely that its purpose is not analogous to any other
(60) mammalian behavior, since the nature of the narwhal's sensory organ is itself unparalleled.

1. It can be inferred from the passage that the author would most probably agree with which one of the following statements?

   (A) The study of sensory organs in other animals will likely shed little light on why narwhals engage in tusking behavior because the tusks are so unique.

   (B) The prevalence of the hypothesis that narwhal tusks were horns of unicorns delayed the true scientific explanation by decades.

   (C) Narwhals are able to navigate the waters of the Arctic using mechanisms similar to those employed by other cetaceans.

   (D) Nweeia's contributions to the study of narwhals are relatively insignificant.

   (E) Bull narwhals exhibit the behavior of tusking in order to remove particulates and display dominance to potential mates.

GO ON TO THE NEXT PAGE.

2. The passage suggests that Nweeia would be most likely to agree with which one of the following statements?

(A) The narwhal tusk is a sensory organ used for echolocation.

(B) The narwhal tusk assists the animal in breaking through the ice of the Arctic Ocean.

(C) It is likely science will never find an adequate explanation as to why the narwhal has a tusk.

(D) The narwhal's tusk assists the animal in its search for squid.

(E) People were foolish to once think the narwhal's tusk was the horn of the unicorn.

3. The passage suggests which one of the following about the scientific hypotheses pertaining to the narwhal's tusk discussed in the second paragraph?

(A) One of them proved that the tusk was used to establish male dominance and attract a mate.

(B) All of them resorted to supernatural explanations to account for the purpose of the tusk.

(C) Some of them were able to correctly identify the nature of the tusk's sensory capabilities, but none could explain tusking behavior.

(D) None of them came anywhere close to identifying the natural purpose of the narwhal tusk.

(E) At least one of them was lent credence by examinations of narwhal actions in the wild.

4. Based on the passage, which one of the following most accurately characterizes the author's attitude toward Nweeia's research?

(A) interest in Nweeia's results but skepticism regarding their accuracy

(B) support for Nweeia's conclusion that the narwhal tusk is used for mating purposes

(C) criticism of Nweeia's methods as inhumane

(D) doubt that Nweeia's research will continue

(E) admiration for Nweeia's results and the manner in which he attained them

5. The passage provides the most support for which one of the following statements?

(A) Nweeia's conclusions have been lauded as a major breakthrough by the majority of the scientific community.

(B) Due to its high concentration of nerve tubules, the tusk is the narwhal's primary sensory organ.

(C) Electron micrographs have proven to be a useful tool for research on the narwhal.

(D) The ability to perceive salinity gradients is crucial to the survival of the narwhal.

(E) Female narwhals that lack developed tusks are unable to detect changes in water pressure.

GO ON TO THE NEXT PAGE.

From the beginning of the twentieth century until approximately 1965, the western was by far the most popular genre of American film. During that time period, studios produced thousands of highly profitable
(5) films set in the nineteenth-century American West. By the late twentieth century, however, the western was a nearly extinct film genre, as studios rarely, if ever, released films set in the nineteenth-century American West.

(10) Some film critics cite the deaths and retirements of stars such as John Wayne and Roy Rogers, and of filmmakers such as John Ford and Howard Hawks, as the principal cause of the western's decline in popularity. Without these icons and artists, they say,
(15) the western lost much of its vitality as a genre. However, this explanation insufficiently accounts for the near total collapse of the genre, as the western lost none of its popularity when the first generation of western idols, a group that included Tom Mix and
(20) William Hart, passed away or retired in the 1930s.

Other critics cite the changed attitudes of filmmakers as the cause for the western's demise. These critics correctly point out that the popularity of the traditional western was contingent upon the
(25) audience's belief in a mythologized version of the nineteenth-century American West, a place where absolutely moral cowboys tamed an unforgiving land and subdued the native "savages" who dwelled there. The western myth exalted in most westerns made
(30) before 1960 gave these films their drawing power, not the personality of Wayne or the direction of Ford. The American film industry's acceptance of the western myth began to wane after 1960 when filmmakers began to be influenced by the work of revisionist historians,
(35) who characterized the conquest of the West as the subjugation of a land and a people by an often racist nation through methods wrought with moral ambiguity. Soon screenwriters, directors, and producers could no longer make traditional westerns in good conscience,
(40) and they began making westerns that portrayed revisionist attitudes and values. These revisionist westerns often exposed the unacceptable racism toward Native Americans inherent in many traditional westerns. They also showed either that the puerile
(45) values behind the western myth were hopelessly antiquated, as in Sam Peckinpah's *The Wild Bunch*, or that the myth of the nineteenth-century American West was completely fallacious, as in Arthur Penn's *Little Big Man*.

(50) Although the arrival of revisionist ideas explains the downfall of the traditional western, the American film industry's rejection of the western myth does not sufficiently explain the complete downfall of the western as a cinematic genre. If revisionist westerns
(55) had been popular with audiences, the American film industry would have made many of those films. However, audiences disdained most revisionist westerns and showed little interest in films focused on discrediting the western myth. Instead, the public
(60) sought out mythic stories in other cinematic genres. It

is no accident that the ascent in popularity of film's science fiction genre coincides with the decline of the western.

6. With which one of the following statements would the author be most likely to agree?

(A) Revisionist westerns were better made than the more traditional western films that preceded them.

(B) Traditional westerns became more prevalent due to filmmakers' rejection of the western myth.

(C) Most revisionist westerns portrayed Native Americans more positively than did most traditional westerns.

(D) The death of John Wayne did not affect the popularity of the western as a cinematic genre.

(E) Some of the most universally acclaimed films of all time are westerns.

7. Which one of the following inferences is most supported by the passage?

(A) The popularity of the western genre experienced similar declines in both the 1930s and the 1960s, when major stars left the industry.

(B) *Little Big Man* was only marginally profitable for the studio that produced it.

(C) Science fiction is now the most profitable cinematic genre in the United States.

(D) Movies that portray certain kinds of mythic stories have proven to be popular with U.S. audiences over several decades.

(E) If traditional westerns were still being made, they would continue to attract large audiences.

GO ON TO THE NEXT PAGE.

8. Given the information in the passage, which one of the following films would most closely exemplify the revisionist western?

(A) a film set in the nineteenth-century American West in which a cowboy successfully defends his ranch against savage Native-American raiders

(B) a film set in the American West during the 1960s in which a group of Native Americans is portrayed as struggling for better treatment from the U.S. government

(C) a movie made in 1951 and staring John Wayne as a nineteenth-century U.S. soldier who reconsiders his previously held assumptions about Native Americans

(D) a film that depicts a morally idealized victory by a group of nineteenth-century Native Americans who defeat an American army unit

(E) a movie that portrays a nineteenth-century cowboy who fights Native Americans in the American West as a racist who achieves his goals by morally questionable means

9. Which one of the following most accurately describes the author's attitude toward most westerns made before 1960?

(A) disapproving of their attempts to discredit the western myth

(B) appreciative of the artistic and commercial success that they attained

(C) critical of how they idealized certain values

(D) surprised that they were able to be so popular for so long

(E) nostalgic for the films of a bygone era

10. The critics mentioned in the passage's second paragraph would be most likely to agree to which one of the following statements?

(A) The growth of the science fiction genre can be linked to the decline of the western.

(B) John Ford played a role in bringing vitality to a genre of film.

(C) The myths portrayed in most westerns made before 1960 are what attracted most of the people who attended the movies.

(D) John Wayne was an actor of questionable talent and limited range.

(E) The screenwriters, directors, and producers who made traditional westerns did so in order to raise significant moral questions.

GO ON TO THE NEXT PAGE.

For years, evolutionary biologists have been bewildered by questions pertaining to how cetaceans—the most immense mammals to ever live—evolved from land-based mammals into their present aquatic
(5) forms of whales, dolphins, and porpoises. Attempts to answer questions about the evolutionary rise of cetaceans led to two primary but conflicting views. The first states that cetaceans evolved from mesonychids, an order of carnivores that became extinct
(10) approximately 30 million years ago. The second theorizes that cetaceans descended from an ancestor belonging to the artiodactyl order, the same mammalian order to which modern pigs, cows, and giraffes belong.

(15) Supporters of the mesonychid hypothesis predominantly used morphological evidence and fossil records to support their claim. These scientists cited the similarities between the unusual triangular-shaped teeth indicative of the mesonychid order and the shape of the
(20) teeth possessed by cetaceans such as orcas and sperm whales as evidence linking the extinct carnivores with modern cetaceans. Supporters of the mesonychid hypothesis suspected that the cetaceans' evolutionary line descended from mesonychids to early cetaceans
(25) via the pakicetids, an extinct family of animals thought to be mesonychids. However, this idea could not be confirmed due a dearth of complete pakicetid fossil specimens.

Supporters of the artiodactyl hypothesis of cetacean
(30) evolution cited molecular and genetic evidence to support their theory. By studying the genes of cetaceans and non-cetaceans, scientists discovered that the hippopotamus, an artiodactyl, is the closest living relative to cetaceans. These scientists also found
(35) similarities between the amino acid structures possessed by hippopotamuses and those possessed by cetaceans.

The debate between supporters of the mesonychid hypothesis and the artiodactyl hypothesis raged within
(40) paleontological circles until the recent unearthing of complete pakicetid fossil specimens in Pakistan. These new specimens cemented the connection between pakicetids and early cetaceans that had long been suspected by supporters of the mesonychid hypothesis.
(45) However, by studying the pakicetid specimens scientists also discovered that pakicetid ankle bones were adapted for running and were connected in a way that allowed for great flexibility, two features of artiodactyl ankle bones that are not present in the bones
(50) of mesonychids. The artiodactyl-like features seen in the pakicetid ankle bones led scientists to conclude that pakicetids were a kind of artiodactyl and not, as previously believed, a kind of mesonychid. This conclusion, along with the newly solidified connection
(55) between pakicetids and early cetaceans, offered solid morphological evidence for an ancestral connection between artiodactyls and cetaceans. When coupled with the established genetic and molecular data, this evidence discredited the hypothesis that cetaceans are
(60) descended from mesonychids, and it is now generally accepted that cetaceans are descended from artiodactyls.

11. Based on the passage, the scientists mentioned in the second paragraph would have been most likely to agree with which one of the following statements before the discovery of the complete pakicetid fossil specimens?

(A) The examination of fossilized specimens can be a reliable way to determine an animal's ancestry.

(B) Most marine mammals descended from mesonychids.

(C) It is doubtful any modern mammals evolved from artiodactyls.

(D) It is highly likely that hippopotamuses are the closest non-cetacean relative to dolphins.

(E) It is likely that complete pakicetid specimens will reveal that cetaceans did not evolve from mesonychids.

12. The information in the passage LEAST supports which one of the following statements regarding cetaceans and hippopotamuses?

(A) They are both mammals.

(B) They are both descended from pakicetids.

(C) They share a common ancestor.

(D) They possess amino acid structures that are somewhat similar.

(E) Neither cetaceans nor hippopotamuses are descended from mesonychids.

GO ON TO THE NEXT PAGE.

13. With which one of the following statements would the author of the passage be most likely to agree?

(A) Scientists in the future will likely be able to determine which hypothesis of cetacean evolution is correct.

(B) The hypothesis that cetaceans evolved from a member of the mesonychid order was baseless.

(C) Enhanced understanding of the pakicetids was important in furthering scientific inquiry into the evolution of cetaceans.

(D) Genetic evidence is usually a better indicator of a species' evolutionary origin than is the fossil record or morphological evidence.

(E) The fact that sperm whales possess teeth similar to those possessed by long-extinct members of the mesonychid order proved to be nothing more than coincidental.

14. The passage supports each of the following inferences EXCEPT:

(A) Scientists do not currently think cetaceans evolved from a member of the mesonychid order.

(B) An ancestor of the orca was an artiodactyl.

(C) Porpoises and giraffes are distantly related.

(D) Hippopotamuses are genetically more closely related to dolphins than they are to pigs.

(E) Sperm whales have triangular teeth.

15. Given the information in the passage, which one of the following most closely represents current scientific understanding of cetacean evolution?

(A) Cetaceans descended from pakicetids, which descended from mesonychids.

(B) Modern cetaceans descended from pakicetids, an extinct family of artiodactyl.

(C) Modern whales, dolphins, and porpoises evolved from pakicetids, a family of mammals that evolved from early cetaceans.

(D) The cetaceans that now live in the ocean descended from pakicetids, the same mammalian family from which modern hippopotamuses descended.

(E) Modern cetaceans evolved after an extinct species of artiodactyl moved into the open waters of the earth's oceans.

STOP

IF YOU FINISH BEFORE TIME IS CALLED, YOU MAY CHECK YOUR WORK ON THIS EXAM ONLY. DO NOT WORK ON ANY OTHER EXAM IN THE BOOK.

Answers

1. A
2. D
3. E
4. E
5. C
6. C
7. D
8. E
9. C
10. B
11. A
12. B
13. C
14. D
15. B

IN-CLASS EXAM ICE LECTURE 4

EXAMINATION

LECTURE 4 EXAM

Time—25 minutes

15 Questions

<u>Directions:</u> Each passage in this section is followed by a group of questions to be answered on the basis of what is <u>stated</u> or <u>implied</u> in the passage. For some of the questions, more than one of the choices could conceivably answer the question. However, you are to choose the <u>best</u> answer; that is, the response that most accurately and completely answers the question, and circle the corresponding answer choice.

The practice of advertising prescription drugs on television, on radio, and in other direct-to-consumer formats has become increasingly prevalent in the United States, even though such advertising has been
(5)   banned in all other countries except New Zealand. The pharmaceutical industry justifies direct-to-consumer advertising by claiming that increased profits, which are directly linked to the increased use of the practice, have provided valuable sources of funding that can
(10) drive new medical research. The industry also claims that direct marketing provides consumers greater control over their health care by educating them about common ailments and the latest treatment options for those maladies.
(15)   However, some consumer advocates argue that the marketing of prescription medication directly to consumers is inherently problematic. Because the primary purpose of advertising is to maximize sales and not to educate, the information the public gleans
(20) from the prescription drug advertisements will be intrinsically biased in favor of the pharmaceutical product, the advocates say. The advertisements mislead consumers by only vaguely mentioning side effects and suggesting that there exist no viable treatment options
(25) outside those they are promoting, these critics claim. Various consumer groups also contend that drug companies do not have the consumer's economic benefit in mind when they utilize such advertisements, as they promote their high-priced brand-name drugs
(30) over the equally effective and much less expensive generic versions of the same drugs. These groups say the amounts pharmaceutical companies spend on direct-to-consumer advertising—$4.65 billion in 2005 alone—have driven up the price of older medications
(35) that were profitable before the direct-to-consumer advertising trend began, thereby making them less affordable to the consumers who are reliant on them.
      Many physicians complain that because many patients only hear the promises made by the
(40) prescription drug advertisements, the marketing campaigns foster unreasonable patient expectations regarding the effectiveness of the drugs. Furthermore, because the direct-to-consumer marketing campaigns focus on symptoms instead of diagnosis, patients can
(45) become convinced they are suffering from one ailment when, in fact, they are suffering from a completely different and unrelated condition. These ill-informed patients may then pressure their doctors to prescribe a particular drug, and the doctors may yield to this
(50) pressure, according to some physician groups. Even more jeopardous, say health care practitioners, is the

intentional expansion of the definition of illnesses in order to grow markets, leading healthy consumers to believe they are ill. For example, sleep problems are
(55) most frequently due to transient life events that are more effectively and safely treated by stress management or psychotherapy than by medication, which doctors say should be used only under extreme circumstances. However, direct-to-consumer
(60) advertisements present even mild insomnia as an appropriate target for medications that may cause serious side effects or mask the underlying condition that caused the insomnia in the first place.

1. Which one of the following statements most accurately summarizes the passage's main point?

   (A)   Although it has brought financial benefits to companies in the pharmaceutical industry, some consumer advocates and a number of health care professionals think the marketing of prescription drugs directly to consumers can be harmful.

   (B)   The United States and New Zealand are the only two countries in the world that allow pharmaceutical companies to market directly to consumers through radio and television advertising.

   (C)   Sleep problems are most frequently due to temporary events and are best treated by stress management or psychotherapy, but prescription medication may also be helpful in alleviating the symptoms.

   (D)   Consumer advocates have argued that direct-to-consumer advertising of prescription drugs is inherently problematic, but many health care practitioners groups find the practice beneficial.

   (E)   Marketing prescription drugs directly to consumers should be allowed to continue in the United States, despite the objections of consumer advocates, who find the practice to be inherently problematic, and health care professionals, who find the practice dangerous.

GO ON TO THE NEXT PAGE.

2. Which one of the following, if true, would most call into question the arguments used by the pharmaceutical industry to justify direct-to-consumer advertising?

(A) The pharmaceutical industry has seen unprecedented revenue growth since it began to market prescription drugs directly to consumers.

(B) Since the prescription drug industry began marketing directly to consumers, all additional revenues earned by prescription pharmaceutical companies have gone directly to shareholders.

(C) In surveys, the majority of American consumers admit that most of the information they get about prescription drugs comes from television and radio advertising.

(D) Prescription drug prices have risen, on average, 120 percent since pharmaceutical companies began marketing prescription drugs directly to consumers.

(E) Pharmaceutical companies do everything in their power to provide the most accurate information about their products to consumers.

3. Based on the passage, with which one of the following statements would the advocates mentioned in line 15 be most likely to agree?

(A) Increased knowledge of common ailments and their latest treatment options allows consumers to exercise greater control over their health care.

(B) It is rare that patients become convinced they are suffering from one malady when they are suffering from a completely unrelated condition.

(C) Pharmaceutical companies attempt to lead healthy consumers to believe they are ill in order to grow markets and expand the list of conditions that should be treated with medication.

(D) Despite the fact that pharmaceutical advertisements may contain a substantial amount of information about a drug, many consumers attain from them an inaccurate understanding.

(E) New sources of funding have driven increased medical research and led to the discovery of many new drugs that were unavailable to consumers only a few years ago.

4. Which one of the following hypothetical circumstances most closely parallels the problems with direct-to-consumer marketing of prescription drugs cited by the physician groups mentioned in line 50?

(A) A public service campaign regarding a potentially dangerous and highly contagious illness causes many people to become too afraid to leave their own houses.

(B) A propaganda campaign leads many to unfairly scapegoat a group of people for a social problem rather than blame the groups who actually caused the problem.

(C) An advertising campaign causes people to believe that a certain food product is good for their health when, in fact, the product is unhealthy.

(D) A fashion trend leads many people to buy and constantly wear a certain style of clothing, a style that many others see as ridiculous.

(E) A marketing campaign for a motion picture portrays the film as being highly respected among movie critics when, in fact, most critics had a completely different opinion on the film.

5. Which one of the following, if true, would strengthen the argument advanced by the practitioners mentioned in line 51?

(A) Most cases of insomnia can successfully be treated with certain prescription drugs with limited side effects.

(B) A glass of wine before bed has also been found to be an effective and healthy treatment for insomnia.

(C) Certain drugs that are used to treat insomnia have been known to cause severe and sometimes fatal respiratory problems in rare cases.

(D) Only two percent of those with sleeping problems report that those problems were made better after receiving stress management and psychotherapy treatment.

(E) Hypochondriacs are especially likely to believe they suffer from whatever ailment advertised prescription drugs are purported to treat.

GO ON TO THE NEXT PAGE.

The debate over mandatory sentencing intensified in the United States with the passage of proposition 184 in California in 1994. The law, which was upheld by the Supreme Court in several rulings, mandated a
(5) minimum sentence of 25 years upon the conviction of a third felony, which earned it the nickname "the three strikes law." Soon after the California law was overwhelmingly approved by voters, 25 other states established similar mandatory sentencing laws.
(10) Proponents of mandatory sentencing managed to successfully frame the debate in terms of the anti-crime rationales of incapacitation and deterrence. Recently, statistical evidence has begun to show flaws in the arguments supporting the laws. Additionally, new
(15) challenges to the laws have emerged, as opponents, who originally argued against proposition 184 on moral grounds, have now turned to more practical rationales, particularly the costs of increased incarceration.

One of the main arguments by proponents of
(20) mandatory sentences is that the public is served by the incapacitation of repeat offenders. Prior criminal activity is one of the best predictors of future criminal activity, and advocates argue that locking up repeat offenders for extended sentences is in the public
(25) interest because it removes from the streets those most likely to commit serious crimes. However, critics argue that there is a danger of false positives— cases in which someone who would not have committed future crimes is incarcerated under a mandatory sentence.
(30) These false positives place an economic and moral burden on the penal system. Critics also argue that most crimes are committed by young people, indicating that with maturity comes restraint.

Proponents of mandatory sentencing often tout the
(35) deterrent effect of severe sentencing. In some cases, it is argued, would-be offenders are daunted when they consider the severity of sentences. However, this kind of deterrence has been a focus of debate, as many consider the commission of a crime an irrational act in
(40) the first place. A potential criminal would have to weigh the consequences of the act beforehand for deterrence to take effect. The converse of the deterrence argument is that mandatory sentencing may actually increase the severity of certain crimes.
(45) Criminals, knowing they will be severely punished regardless of the crime they commit, might commit more serious crimes than they otherwise would have. Once incarcerated, there is no incentive for criminals to rehabilitate, as their sentence is fixed.
(50) Some opponents who call for the end of mandatory sentencing have marshaled their attacks behind the consideration of the cost-effectiveness of incarceration. A cost-benefit analysis by one think tank found that money spent on crime prevention programs
(55) such as parent training programs, cash incentives for high school graduation, and assistance for families with children at risk is nearly three times as effective in preventing crime as money spent on longer sentences. Recent polling shows that California voters are
(60) increasingly inclined to consider alternatives and to

consider the repeal of proposition 184. Similar polling results have been seen in other states as well.

6. The situation discussed in lines 42–47 is most analogous to which one of the following?

(A) After the state dropped the speed limit from 75 to 55 miles per hour in an effort to curb the number of fatal automobile accidents, the number of traffic accidents in the state actually rose.

(B) By politely asking a talkative group of teenagers to be quiet, the movie theater usher only instigated the rowdy youths to make louder noises.

(C) When told by his doctor that any additional smoking would cause irreparable damage to his health, the addicted smoker began to vastly exceed his previous self-imposed daily limit of cigarettes.

(D) After being informed on Wednesday that she was going to be fired on Friday because she frequently argued with her coworkers, the employee decided not to go to work on Thursday.

(E) When the principal began punishing truant students with a mandatory five days of detention instead of one, truancy rates at the school dropped dramatically.

GO ON TO THE NEXT PAGE.

7. Which one of the following, if true, would most seriously challenge the position of the proponents mentioned in line 10?

(A) Although the vast majority of minor misdemeanors are committed by repeat offenders, roughly 74 percent of all serious felonies are committed by first-time offenders.

(B) People who live in urban areas are ten times more likely to be convicted of three felonies during their lifetime than are those who live in rural areas.

(C) Since 1994 the number of incarcerated individuals in California has risen by 41 percent, and the penal system's budget has risen 67 percent.

(D) Most people given long-term sentences under "three strikes" laws committed at least one of their three felonies before they turned 20 years of age.

(E) Violent crime rates in California dropped dramatically between 1994 and 2001.

8. Given the information in the passage, the evolution of California voters' opinion of proposition 184 between 1994 and today is most analogous to which one of the following?

(A) the popularity of a governor who took office in a very close election but won reelection four years later by a large margin

(B) the public opinion regarding a music group that was very popular twenty years ago, receded to relative anonymity 10 years ago, and reemerged as a popular group five years ago

(C) the critical perception of a movie that was lauded by critics when first released, but that is now less enthusiastically received by critics

(D) the public perception of a restaurant that was very popular when first opened, but, after several food poisoning incidents, was forced by health inspectors to close.

(E) the popularity of a law that was passed overwhelmingly by voters but was later repealed when a court found it to be unconstitutional

9. Which one of the following could most logically be appended to the end of the final paragraph?

(A) Therefore, it would come as little surprise if many mandatory sentencing laws were abolished in some states within the next ten years.

(B) However, it is likely that states will have to live with their mandatory sentencing laws for many years to come.

(C) Thus, it is likely that mandatory sentencing laws will be created in the few states that do not yet have them.

(D) Due to this negative perception, it is certain that within the next ten years mandatory sentencing laws will be completely removed from the American criminal law system.

(E) Although the future of mandatory-minimum sentencing laws is uncertain, it is clear that prisoners will continue to suffer due to the overbearing nature of the laws.

10. Which one of the following is a principle upon which opponents mentioned in the fourth paragraph base their argument?

(A) Taxpayer funds should be spent in the manner in which taxpayers want them spent.

(B) Moral considerations should be taken into account by policymakers.

(C) Economic considerations should take precedent over moral considerations.

(D) When presented with multiple options, the government should spend funds in the most efficient manner.

(E) An action designed to prevent a certain kind of behavior often encourages a more severe manifestation of that very behavior.

GO ON TO THE NEXT PAGE.

For the majority of the twentieth century, the Clovis theory dominated archeological studies pertaining to the initial peopling of the Americas. The theory states people belonging to the Clovis culture—
(5) so named because the culture's hallmark spear points were first discovered in 1932 near Clovis, New Mexico—were the first Americans. According to the Clovis theory, people first set foot in North America around 11,500 years ago after following game across
(10) the Bering land bridge, which connected Siberia and Alaska at the height of the last Ice Age. According to the theory, these Eurasian hunters passed quickly through present-day western Canada via an ice-free corridor and then proceeded to populate the remainder
(15) of North and South America.

Cracks in the Clovis theory first began to appear in the 1970s, when discoveries at the Meadowcroft Rockshelter in Pennsylvania produced contentious artifacts that supporters claimed predated Clovis
(20) colonization by 7,000 years. Some years later, the Clovis theory was further undermined when evidence from the Monte Verde dig in southern Chile produced evidence of human settlement in southern South America 1,000 years before the Clovis people
(25) supposedly first set foot in Alaska. Recent genetic studies also indicate that American and Asian populations separated from each other 20,000 years ago, some 8,500 years earlier than what the Clovis theory postulates. These discoveries have forced many
(30) in the field of paleoamerican archeology to abandon the Clovis theory and seek out new theories regarding the first Americans.

The coastal migration theory states that people first arrived in the Americas from Siberia several thousand
(35) years before the Clovis culture flourished. The first Americans traveled not by land but by sea, skirting the Pacific coast and sustaining themselves on fish and fauna from an ice-free coastal ribbon situated between the sea and interior glaciers, coastal migration theorists
(40) claim. Although genetic evidence bolsters the proposed timeline of the coastal migration theory, artifactual evidence in support of this theory is lacking.

The Solutrean hypothesis postulates the Americas were first peopled by migrants who used Inuit-like
(45) survival techniques to cross over a North Atlantic ice pack that connected west Eurasia and North America. Proponents of this theory point to the similarity between stone tools found in Virginia and tools used 16,000 years ago by the Solutrean people in modern-
(50) day France. However, genetic evidence indicates that the first Americans came from east Eurasia as opposed to west Eurasia.

Although many archeologists support either the Solutrean hypothesis or the coastal migration theory,
(55) some still cling to the Clovis theory, accusing challengers to this archaeological dogma of planting artifacts or misinterpreting evidence. Thus, the field of paleoamerican archeology presently lacks a dominant theory regarding initial peopling of the Americas, as all
(60) current hypotheses have significant evidentiary problems.

11. According to the passage, the major problem that has prevented the coastal migration theory from gaining wider acceptance is most closely analogous to which one of the following?

(A)   the inability to find a murder weapon during a homicide investigation

(B)   the presence of conflicting genetic evidence in an assault investigation

(C)   the discovery that a prime suspect in a robbery investigation has a credible alibi

(D)   the presentation by a group of UFO enthusiasts of a metal rod as evidence strengthening a theory that extraterrestrials visited Earth

(E)   the existence of tools of unknown age as the sole evidence supporting a theory about the initial peopling of the Australian continent

12. Which one of the following, if true, would most weaken the theory discussed in lines 43–50?

(A)   New genetic studies have shown that Native Americans and the Basque people of southern France and northern Spain are more closely related than previously believed.

(B)   Scientists have concluded that North America and Europe have not been linked by ice in the Atlantic for over 80,000 years.

(C)   Recently discovered settlements off the western coast of North America have been dated to exactly 20,000 years ago.

(D)   It has been discovered that no ice-free corridor existed in what is now western Canada 11,500 years ago.

(E)   Stone tools found in Virginia also resemble stone tools discovered near Clovis, New Mexico.

GO ON TO THE NEXT PAGE.

13. According to the passage, scholarship regarding the initial peopling of the Americas between 1932 and the present is most analogous to which one of the following?

   (A) scholarship regarding the Egyptian pyramids in which a single prevailing theory of the structures' origin is constantly being challenged by new theories

   (B) the soup industry, which is now highly competitive due to several newer brands that took market share from a brand that dominated the industry for decades

   (C) cosmology, a field that is constantly refining and changing its theories on the origin of the universe

   (D) scholarship regarding the extinction of the dinosaurs, a field in which recent developments have allowed a widely accepted theory to emerge

   (E) the carbonated beverage industry, which has been dominated by two competing companies for most of the twentieth century

14. Based on the information in the passage, which one of the following, if demonstrated to be valid, would most seriously challenge the Clovis theory?

   (A) the revelation that stone tools purported to have been found in Virginia were planted there by unethical European researchers

   (B) test results that definitively date the oldest human artifacts found at Pennsylvania's Meadowcroft Rockshelter to 10,500 years ago

   (C) artifactual evidence indicating humans migrated through western Canada 11,500 years ago

   (D) the discovery of 13,000-year-old spear points in Siberia that are similar to the Clovis spear points

   (E) evidence that shows no game animals ever crossed over the Bering land bridge

15. Which one of the following, if true, would lend the most credence to the coastal migration theory?

   (A) Recently, Clovis spear points were discovered that date from around 20,000 years ago.

   (B) The Pacific coast of South America was populated well before the Atlantic coast of North America, but it was not populated as early as the Great Lakes region of North America.

   (C) During the last Ice Age, a period lasting from approximately 70,000 years ago until 10,000 years ago, the glaciers that covered a large portion of North America never extended all the way to the Pacific Ocean.

   (D) Archeologists have recently shown that similarities between 16,000-year-old stone tools found in France and stone tools unearthed in Virginia are not as great as was first thought by scholars.

   (E) Recent evidence shows that an ice-free corridor existed in western Canada for a first time approximately 20,000 years ago, and for a second time approximately 11,500 years ago.

STOP

IF YOU FINISH BEFORE TIME IS CALLED, YOU MAY CHECK YOUR WORK ON THIS EXAM ONLY.
DO NOT WORK ON ANY OTHER EXAM IN THE BOOK.

Answers

1. A
2. B
3. D
4. B
5. E
6. C
7. A
8. C
9. A
10. D
11. A
12. B
13. B
14. E
15. C

IN-CLASS EXAM **ICE** LECTURE **5**

EXAMINATION

LECTURE 5 EXAM

Time—25 minutes

15 Questions

<u>Directions</u>: Each passage in this section is followed by a group of questions to be answered on the basis of what is <u>stated</u> or <u>implied</u> in the passage. For some of the questions, more than one of the choices could conceivably answer the question. However, you are to choose the <u>best</u> answer; that is, the response that most accurately and completely answers the question, and circle the corresponding answer choice.

The following passages refer to MMORPGs, or Massively Multiplayer Online Role-Playing Games.

Passage A

MMORPGs are more harmful that conventional computer games because they are significantly more addictive. A full account of the addictive nature of these games must analyze the two ways in which they
(5) differ from conventional games: first, that they take much longer to complete, and second, that they are played communally by thousands of players at the same time.

Many experts contend that MMORPG addiction is
(10) induced primarily by what psychologists call a scheduled reward system. Almost all games use a version of this system, of which the dominant paradigm is the introduction of meaningful goals for players and the presentation of a timetable by which that goal can
(15) be achieved. Once a player achieves a goal, he or she reaches an elevated mental state and is informed of the next goal and when its corresponding high can be attained. Unlike most other games, which have somewhere between 40 and 100 hours of play-life,
(20) MMORPGs are designed to involve hundreds of hours of play, some claiming to provide limitless content.

This explanation does not fully account for why playing MMORPGs is more addictive than playing a succession of conventional games. A promising
(25) explanation is that MMORPGs uniquely channel the hierarchical instincts of people. Humans naturally have an impulse to dominate the social hierarchies in which they are willingly involved. The quest to achieve ever greater status is played through a person's avatar—his
(30) or her in-game persona—which represents placement in the hierarchy of the MMORPG's community. The most popular MMORPGs encourage direct competition between players through competitive mechanisms such as simulated combat. Other, subtler forms of
(35) competition for status also arise due to the special powers or items that players can earn for their avatars.

Passage B

Since MMORPGs are addictive, some pundits are advocating a ban on these games. Yet on balance, MMORPGs are worthwhile to society because of their
(40) unique ability to be used as a tool for the collection of research data. A tremendous amount of information about human behavior is recorded daily on the computers that facilitate these games, and, with the cooperation of the games' producers, researchers are
(45) beginning to tap into this quick and inexpensive

laboratory for experimentation.

Part of most MMORPGs is a virtual economy complete with a currency and thriving market for goods and services. Economist Edward Castronova
(50) demonstrated that the laws of supply and demand apply to these game economies and investigated how the competitive aspect of these games impacts their market stability. He also specified the conditions under which these economies can interact with the real-world
(55) economy. This research impacts the study of international economic policy, as well as the growing understanding of the interaction between real and virtual commodities and personal utility.

Psychologists and sociologists have also found
(60) several popular MMORPGs useful in their work. Psychologist Sherry Turkle explores the way in which players of these games use the avatars they create to assume a variety of roles, including different professions, social classes, and genders. She uses a
(65) combination of personal interviews, player surveys, and transcripts of chats from gaming sessions to track the effect of role-playing on players. Her results indicate a possible positive impact of MMORPGs apart from pure research, showing that these games might be
(70) useful in treating patients suffering from a number of anti-empathic conditions.

1. The relationship between which one of the following pairs of documents is most analogous to the relationship between passage A and passage B?

   (A) a philosophical discourse arguing for the ban of stem cell research; another investigating the possible applications of stem cells

   (B) a research report on the history of psychological disorders; another related to research methods involving those disorders

   (C) an account of the two events that led to a major battle; propaganda from one of the involved countries calling for citizens to join the fight

   (D) an analyst's report on two factors considered by those who raise interest rates; an editorial listing social implications of such decisions

   (E) a biologist's investigation of how chemical fertilizers damage waterways; a report extolling the benefits of contemporary methods of farming

GO ON TO THE NEXT PAGE.

2. With which one of the following statements would the authors of both passages be most likely to agree?

(A) MMORPGs allow players the satisfaction of mastering difficult rules systems.

(B) The social interactions between players in MMORPGs are real, even though the environment in which they act is not.

(C) The market interactions between players brokering special items are hampered by competition for greater status in social hierarchies.

(D) MMORPGs are the most addictive of all massively multiplayer online games because they utilize the ability of role-playing games to draw a player into a scheduled reward system.

(E) The popularity of fantasy-themed MMORPGs is due solely to a desire for players to dominate the intense class structure of an imaginary society.

3. Which one of the following most accurately describes a way in which the two passages are related to each other?

(A) Passage A advocates the ban of a social endeavor, while passage B details its benefits.

(B) Passage A relates an account of a phenomenon, while passage B disputes that account.

(C) Passage A argues for a particular understanding of a condition associated with a phenomenon, while passage B argues for positive externalities of the phenomenon.

(D) If the assertions made in passage A are true, then at least some of the assertions made in passage B are false.

(E) The assertions in passage B, if true, lend support to the main argument made in passage A.

4. Which one of the following best exemplifies a consequence of what Castronova calls the "competitive aspect" (line 52) of MMORPGs, as it is discussed in passage A?

(A) a decreasing empathic concern by players for others because of the desire to advance in a social hierarchy

(B) the increasing price of in-game goods as players attempt to surpass others in the social hierarchy of the game community

(C) the decreasing price of in-game goods as players attempt to sell commodities to simplify the complexity of game play

(D) the acceptance by players of economic incentives to produce goods as cheaply and quickly as possible

(E) the eagerness of players to beat others to the next achievable in-game high

5. If the author of passage B were to read passage A, he or she would be LEAST likely to draw which one of the following conclusions regarding matters addressed in passage A?

(A) The harms of MMORPGs are outweighed by the other benefits that society gains through them.

(B) The amount of content and playing time inherent in MMORPGs has a significant impact on their productivity as research tools.

(C) Further social research on MMORPGs might allow more evidence to prove the claims in passage A.

(D) There is no significant social aspect involved in an account of the addictive properties of these games.

(E) Popular MMORPGs do not generate useful research because their addictiveness eliminates social role-playing interactions.

GO ON TO THE NEXT PAGE.

Passage A

Since parents are required by law to entrust schools with the care and development of their children, schools are afforded special authority over students.
(5) Safety is a vital part of this development, and schools are thus justified in violating the civil liberties of students in order to achieve safety.

Some object to any violation of the rights of students, arguing that students need guarantees of their civil liberties in order to fully develop as citizens.
(10) Psychologist Abraham Maslow argues to the contrary, asserting that safety is the most fundamental human need with regards to development. While safety is not more valuable in itself than any other need, it must take priority because it is the prerequisite to the expression
(15) of all higher aims.

The U.S. Supreme Court took this view into account in *Hazelwood School District v. Kuhlmeier* when the Court asserted that the rights of students in public schools "are not automatically coextensive with
(20) the rights of adults in other settings," and must be applied in light of the special characteristics and needs of the school environment. With the aim of fostering students' development, schools have a strong interest in assuring student safety and, in the Court's opinion,
(25) have the authority to limit students' rights.

In the 1985 case of *New Jersey v. T.L.O.*, the U.S. Supreme Court held that a school may permissibly search the lockers and other personal spaces of students while they are on its campus. Preventing students from
(30) bringing weapons and other harmful materials to school represents a more significant interest than the protection of a student's right to privacy. Sociologists have demonstrated that this diminished expectation of privacy restricts students' capacity for personal acts of
(35) expression but is necessary to ensure increased safety and the development of their other abilities.

Passage B

Limitations to the authority of schools are important in the evolution of the legal perception of the status of children. Safety for students is of course one
(40) of our paramount values, but concern for safety ought to be balanced against the other needs of students. While schools are tasked with preserving order, it is vital that they accomplish this in the right ways and for the right reasons. This requires weighing our concern
(45) for safety against respect for the autonomy of students.

An important component of autonomy is the freedom of students to express their political views. The U.S. Supreme Court determined in 1942 that students cannot be forced to salute the American flag,
(50) and more recently, the Court found that students who publish political speech against schools on the Internet are entitled to first-amendment protections. The Court rejected claims that these forms of public political expression harm the mission of schools enough to
(55) justify punishing students and limiting their civil liberties. It found that students should enjoy freedom of political expression similar to that of adults, including the limitation that such freedom should only be

restricted when a student presents a convincing threat
(60) of harm.

Fulfilling our duty to promote the development of students' autonomy requires that we allow students the ability to question authority. Some claim that by allowing students to question the authority of schools,
(65) we create disorder and put students in danger. If an institution's stability is threatened by questioning, then that institution deserves to be thoroughly examined and changed. Remaining vigilant against the abuse of authority is vital to the healthy functioning of a
(70) democracy and is a value that we should ensure is inculcated in our students.

6. Which one of the following is identified in passage A but not in passage B as a consideration to be weighed against the need to create a safe educational environment?

   (A) the right of students to critique school practices
   (B) the ability of students to express themselves politically
   (C) students' right to privacy in their personal spaces on campus
   (D) the convincing threat of harm presented by published speech against schools
   (E) the inculcation of the values of democracy in students

7. With which one of the following statements would the author of passage A be most likely to agree regarding the Supreme Court rulings cited in passage B?

   (A) The rulings do not subvert the primacy of safety considerations because they acknowledge exceptions in cases in which a student presents a convincing threat of harm.
   (B) The rulings directly contradict other Supreme Court judgments such as *New Jersey v. T.L.O.* and must therefore be rejected.
   (C) The rulings are not relevant to the argument presented in passage A because they were reached by justices who no longer serve on the Court.
   (D) No evidence from Supreme Court cases is pertinent to the issue of limiting students' civil liberties because the Court has not been asked to consider the vital consideration of safety.
   (E) The rulings establish that the concern for safety must be duly weighed against respect for the autonomy of students.

GO ON TO THE NEXT PAGE.

8. It can be inferred from the passages that the authors would disagree about which one of the following?

(A) Allowing free expression of political aims leads to greater disorder in schools.

(B) Schools must be devoid of any danger before other developmental aims can be achieved.

(C) Ensuring a safe school environment takes precedence over fostering a child's capacity for personal acts of expression.

(D) Restricting privacy harms students' self-expression.

(E) Schools should not be concerned with preparing students to be vigilant against abuses of authority.

9. Which one of the following most accurately describes the way in which the two passages are related to each other?

(A) Passage A draws its conclusion based on psychological principles, while passage B relies on a purely rhetorical appeal to reach an unrelated conclusion.

(B) Passage A relies on legal precedent to justify its claims and passage B cites inconsistencies among those precedents to reach an opposing conclusion.

(C) Passage A relies on anecdotal evidence, while passage B appeals to the authority of longstanding tradition to reach an opposing conclusion.

(D) The passages cite different bodies of evidence from the same legal source to reach opposing conclusions.

(E) The passages cite different psychological principles but the same legal cases, and both reach the same conclusion.

10. With which one of the following statements would the author of passage B be most likely to agree regarding the "special characteristics and needs of the school environment" (lines 21-22)?

(A) Because it depends on an unreasonable expectation of privacy, the ability to question the authority of a school does not represent a vital interest for students.

(B) These needs are no longer a concern because the precedent in *Hazelwood School District v. Kuhlmeier* has been overturned by subsequent rulings.

(C) The elimination of subversive materials on school property is a more significant need than that of personal expression.

(D) While personal autonomy is not more valuable in itself than other needs, it must take priority because it is the prerequisite to an environment of safety.

(E) The needs of schools include both safety and a respect for the rights of students and thus must be balanced to reflect both.

GO ON TO THE NEXT PAGE.

Passage A

It is clear that the framers of the United States constitution believed that a legally recognized right to revolution was essential to democracy. The constitution directly establishes this right through the second
(5) amendment, whose authors believed that the "inalienable" natural right to protect one's self-interest should be codified into law. Despite this tradition, recognition of a legal right to revolution is unnecessary in a modern democracy.

(10) In the current environment, the exercise of the legal right to revolution would result in a failure to achieve redress for a wrong committed by the government. When the American democracy was still an experiment, it might have made sense to the framers to
(15) give citizens the ability to arm themselves in resistance to bad governance. In those times, there was a chance that revolutionary resistance would have met with success. Given the power of modern law enforcement and the military, contemporary attempts to revolt by
(20) force would inevitably result in great harm to the revolutionary.

There should be no legal right to revolution in an effective democratic government because the institutions of such a government allow for the
(25) rectification of injustice without the subversion of the government or the risk of harm to others. Citizens do not need to bear arms to achieve their political aims, even when their aims are severely antiestablishment. For example, civil disobedients break laws and then
(30) willingly accept their punishments to demonstrate the injustice of those laws. American history shows that this sort of peaceful resistance to unjust laws can be tremendously successful, as demonstrated by many prominent examples from the Civil Rights movement.

Passage B

(35) A legal right is a just claim to governmental redress. There has never been a legal right to revolution as such because a government's recognition of such a limit to its own sovereignty would be absurd. Despite this, there is natural right to revolution—an
(40) incontrovertible personal authority to resist forces hostile to one's personhood, an authority derived from the natural right to liberty. Society is a mutual undertaking for the rational self-interest of all involved, and if society foolishly deviates from its founding
(45) purpose, then no matter the other circumstances, people are naturally free to exit the confines of their social arrangement.

The natural right to revolution does not relate specifically to the question of efficacy but rather to the
(50) value placed on liberty. The most important aspect of liberty is that people are free to judge how best to pursue their own self-interest. People are never obligated to do anything with their lives that they do not at least implicitly want. The existence of the natural
(55) right to violently defy threats to one's liberty is unchanged even when circumstances render such defiance ineffective or unnecessary.

Some incorrectly claim that acknowledging the natural right to revolution would lead to continual
(60) abuse or the debasement of the rule of law. They erroneously presume that no one would ever follow the law if people were free to break the law whenever it conflicted with their self-interest. While people may be innately entitled to break any law, they choose not to in
(65) the vast majority of cases because participating in the structure of society is usually more useful than maintaining self-interest on a particular issue. A rational person would only enact revolutionary force if the government committed a particularly grievous
(70) offense or continued in a pattern of smaller abuses.

11. Which one of the following most accurately expresses the main point of passage B?

(A) People have the inviolate right to exit social agreements that stray from their purpose.
(B) Democratic methods are insufficient as a means of correcting faulty governance.
(C) The power of modern militaries makes the expression of the right to revolution dangerous.
(D) The natural right to revolution derives its force of appeal from its codification in founding legal doctrines.
(E) Respecting the natural right to revolution does not unduly harm the rule of law.

12. Which one of the following most accurately describes the relationship between the argument made in passage A and the argument made in passage B?

(A) Both passages address a single issue from directly opposing viewpoints.
(B) Both passages address a single issue from essentially the same viewpoint.
(C) Both passages address slightly different concerns and hold different conclusions regarding the aspects they share in common.
(D) Both passages address slightly different concerns and hold essentially the same view regarding those concerns.
(E) Both passages address entirely different ideas, and neither passage contradicts the other in its presentation.

GO ON TO THE NEXT PAGE.

13. Passage A differs from passage B in that passage A displays an attitude that is more

   (A) apprehensive
   (B) dispassionate
   (C) speculative
   (D) abstract
   (E) disparaging

14. Which one of the following is the issue over which the two authors would be most likely to disagree?

   (A) If people felt legally empowered to break the law whenever it presented them with inconvenience, no one would ever obey the law.
   (B) The extreme difference in power between the military and citizens makes it impossible for an attempt at violent revolution to succeed.
   (C) The most important quality of liberty is a respect for the self-determination of individuals.
   (D) Civil disobedience is the most effective manner in which citizens can affect laws they see as unjust.
   (E) The framers of the U.S. constitution intended the second amendment to give citizens the legal right to revolution.

15. The author of passage B would be most likely to respond in which one of the following ways to the observation cited in passage A concerning the likely result of an attempted armed revolt (lines 18-21)?

   (A) Such a response by the military and law enforcement would be unjustified given citizens' legal right to revolution.
   (B) The unavoidable failure of the revolutionary force in such a case does not impinge on citizens' natural right to revolution.
   (C) Law enforcement and the military would only respond in such a way in order to avert widespread disrespect for the rule of law.
   (D) Because the exercise of the legal right to revolution would result in a failure to achieve redress, that right should be eliminated.
   (E) The situation underscores the superiority of the natural right to revolution over the legal right to revolution.

STOP

IF YOU FINISH BEFORE TIME IS CALLED, YOU MAY CHECK YOUR WORK ON THIS EXAM ONLY.
DO NOT WORK ON ANY OTHER EXAM IN THE BOOK.

Answers

1. E
2. B
3. C
4. B
5. E
6. C
7. A
8. C
9. D
10. E
11. A
12. C
13. B
14. E
15. B

IN-CLASS EXAM ICE LECTURE 6

EXAMINATION

LECTURE 6 EXAM

Time—25 minutes

15 Questions

Directions: Each passage in this section is followed by a group of questions to be answered on the basis of what is <u>stated</u> or <u>implied</u> in the passage. For some of the questions, more than one of the choices could conceivably answer the question. However, you are to choose the <u>best</u> answer; that is, the response that most accurately and completely answers the question, and circle the corresponding answer choice.

The Treaty of Waitangi is considered by many to be New Zealand's founding document, but its legal status in modern New Zealand remains questionable. It has been cited in many contemporary claims against
(5) the state by the Maori, and the state has accepted the treaty-based claims in several major settlements with these native New Zealanders. Though this seems to secure the document's legitimacy, considerable debate continues to surround the discrepancies said to exist
(10) between the English-language and Maori versions.

The English version of the treaty, which was used for many years as a blueprint for relations between the Maori and the British monarchy, states that the signatory chiefs gave up their sovereign rights to the
(15) Queen of England in exchange for the rights, privileges, and protections of full British subjects. In addition, this version stipulated that the chiefs were required to sell their land to the Crown at a negotiated price if they wished to vacate it.

(20) The Maori version of the treaty, however, continues to provoke debate among legal scholars and citizens. Many native New Zealanders claim that the Maori document has a different meaning from the English one and does not cede sovereignty to the British
(25) government. In addition, many argue that the Maori version does not give the Crown sole rights to native property, but rather gives it the right to bid higher than other private concerns when purchasing the land. Several words in the text, notably *kawanatanga* and
(30) *rangatiratanga*, were created specifically for the text, presumably to match text in the English version, and were not present in the Maori lexicon prior to the signing of the treaty. The suffix *–tanga* was an extant Maori suffix functioning in the same way that *–ship* or
(35) *–dom* does in English. So the two words could be said to mean governorship and chieftainship, respectively, but whether one title establishes the right to rule over the other is a matter of interpretation. The meaning of these two words is at the heart of the crisis surrounding
(40) the document, which continues to play an important role in deciding Maori claims to government-controlled assets, including forests, fisheries, and mineral rights.

Conservative historians argue that the modern debate over the Maori version is moot because it does
(45) not take into account the spirit of the agreement, which was reached over 165 years ago. Maori was traditionally an oral language and historically had no written counterpart—indeed, a standard written version of Maori continues to be developed in the present
(50) day—and these historians suggest that the scrutiny placed upon the exact text of the Maori document is

unwarranted. They contend that the two parties' understanding of the oral agreement was more important, as it would be the part of the agreement that
(55) the Maori of the time accepted as binding. For them, the spirit of this understanding, which is reflected in the historical record of the time, is paramount.

1. Which one of the following most accurately expresses the main point of the passage?

(A) New Zealand's courts have decided several recent claims based on the oral version of the Treaty of Waitangi, which is the part of the agreement that the Maori of the time accepted as binding.

(B) Native New Zealanders have achieved several major settlements regarding forests and fisheries due to the recent deciphering of words such as *kawanatanga* and *rangatiratanga*.

(C) Considering the problems surrounding its framing and subsequent misinterpretations, the Treaty of Waitangi has been given undue influence over the years.

(D) Despite recent agreements that bolster the Treaty of Waitangi's legal legitimacy, significant debate exists over how to reconcile conflicting versions of the document.

(E) The Treaty of Waitangi merits reexamination in light of modern improvements to written Maori and recent changes to legal interpretations.

GO ON TO THE NEXT PAGE.

2. Which one of the following best describes how the last paragraph functions in the context of the passage?

(A) It introduces an alternative basis upon which to interpret the treaty.

(B) It explains the origins of the controversy from a historical perspective.

(C) It points out a flaw in an argument presented in an earlier paragraph.

(D) It suggests that efforts to better understand the treaty are unimportant.

(E) It summarizes the different viewpoints discussed earlier in the passage.

3. Based on the passage, the historians mentioned in the fourth paragraph would be most likely to agree with which one of the following statements?

(A) Laws must be interpreted according to the standards of the community in which they apply.

(B) The intent of the signers of a contract must be considered along with the language used in the contract.

(C) Since the intentions of past lawmakers cannot be known, they cannot be considered by modern courts.

(D) Historical records concerning the functioning of a treaty are invalid when interpreting contemporary laws.

(E) A treaty is valid only if it is codified in a language with an established and standardized written form.

4. Each of the following is mentioned by the passage as a point at issue caused by differences between the two versions of the treaty EXCEPT:

(A) the surrender of sovereign rights by the signatory chiefs

(B) the Crown's right to purchase land from Maori people

(C) the control of forests, fisheries, and mineral rights

(D) the implications of the words *kawanatanga* and *rangatiratanga*

(E) the right of British citizens to own land in New Zealand

5. The passage suggests which one of the following about the creation of the Maori version of the Treaty of Waitangi?

(A) It was designed to deceive the signatory chiefs into giving up concessions of land and sovereignty.

(B) Any substantive discrepancies were a result of poor translation due to a misunderstanding of the English version of the treaty.

(C) Its drafters were obliged to create new terms out of extant suffixes in an attempt to faithfully translate the English version.

(D) Since the oral contract and spirit of understanding between the British and Maori was paramount, little attention was paid to the details of the written version.

(E) The treaty was created primarily to govern Maori claims to British-controlled assets such as forests, fisheries, and mineral rights.

GO ON TO THE NEXT PAGE.

Lecture 6 Examination

By examining human mitochondrial DNA, paleogeneticists have deduced that sometime during the late Pleistocene era, between 100,000 and 50,000 years ago, humans were brought to the precipice of extinction
(5) when the total population of our species was reduced to thousands of individuals. This population bottleneck acted as a catalyst for evolutionary change and enabled the rapid differentiation of our species. Because biologists know that the human species first appeared
(10) about one million years ago, the initial rise of our species could not account for a population bottleneck as recent as the late Pleistocene era, and other theories proposed by paleogeneticists as to what acted as the causal mechanism for the bottleneck have not been
(15) completely successful. However, in the late 1990s a new theory about the bottleneck was developed by anthropologist Stanley Ambrose, who turned to the geologic record and began exploring the probable ramifications on our primordial ancestry of the Toba
(20) event, the largest volcanic eruption in the last two million years.

Under Ambrose's Toba catastrophe theory, the cause of the population bottleneck and its subsequent impact on human diversification was the eruption of
(25) Sumatra's Toba caldera 71,000 years ago. This event ejected a massive amount of magma and pyroclastic material into the earth's atmosphere, causing enormous and long-lasting impacts on the earth's climate by dropping global temperatures enough to induce a
(30) millennium-long ice age. Ice sheets never enveloped the continent of Africa, to which Earth's entire human population was limited at the time, but the continent did see an extended period of drought, and its human inhabitants experienced severe famine. Reduced to
(35) thousands of individuals, the human race lost much of its genetic diversity. When the earth's environment became more hospitable for humans, our ancestors began to spread out of Africa, and the homogeneous population rapidly differentiated as founding
(40) populations moved into diverse ecosystems and climates. For example, populations that moved into areas with less intense sunshine than Africa, such as central Asia and Europe, evolved skin cells that produced little melanin and consequently became
(45) lighter-skinned, while those that moved to areas such as Australia with intense sunshine evolved skin cells that produced significant amounts of melanin.

Critics of Ambrose's theory point out that an exact correlation between the dates of the Toba event and the
(50) late Pleistocene genetic bottleneck has not been established. Until such an exact correlation can be established, the Toba catastrophe theory cannot gain general scientific acceptance as the proper paradigm for explaining why the earth's human population became
(55) critically endangered during the late Pleistocene era. However, if such a firm temporal connection is made, it is likely that Ambrose's theory will be accepted, just as scientists accepted the theory that the Cretaceous-Tertiary extinction event of 65.5 million years ago was
(60) caused by a large extraterrestrial object striking the earth.

6. The author's primary purpose in the passage is to

   (A)   present a hypothesis that attempts to explain how a volcanic eruption caused a population bottleneck that affected human evolution

   (B)   describe the mechanism by which the eruption of the Toba caldera caused significant drops in global temperatures and induced a millennium-long ice age

   (C)   explain a theory regarding the effects of a very large comet on the genetic diversity of prehistoric human populations

   (D)   argue against a scientific theory that details the effects of a catastrophic volcanic eruption on the human species during the late Pleistocene era

   (E)   provide evidence to establish a correlation between the dates of the Toba event and the late Pleistocene genetic bottleneck

7. Which one of the following statements most accurately describes the function of the final paragraph?

   (A)   It illustrates a significant flaw in the Toba catastrophe theory.

   (B)   It explains why the Toba catastrophe theory is not universally accepted by the scientific community and suggests what kind of evidence might lead to its acceptance.

   (C)   It argues against the Toba catastrophe theory by pointing out a vital piece of evidence that contradicts the theory's implications.

   (D)   It contrasts the Toba catastrophe theory with a theory explaining the Cretaceous-Tertiary extinction event of 65.5 million years ago.

   (E)   It concludes the passage by predicting that the Toba catastrophe theory will eventually be accepted by all scientists.

GO ON TO THE NEXT PAGE.

8. Which one of the following, if true, would most weaken Ambrose's theory?

   (A) Studies have shown that a small population of humans in South America also survived through the volcanic winter caused by the Toba event.

   (B) New geological evidence shows that it was not Toba but Tambora, another large volcano in what is now Indonesia, that erupted during the period in question.

   (C) Mitochondrial evidence indicates that the evolutionary bottleneck that struck humans in the Pleistocene occurred 10,000 years before the Toba event.

   (D) New DNA evidence shows that total human populations shrunk to only about 200 individuals shortly after the Toba event.

   (E) Research indicates that numerous extraterrestrial objects struck the Earth throughout the late Pleistocene era.

9. Which one of the following does the passage mention as being the earliest result of the eruption of the Toba caldera?

   (A) the reduction of the human species to thousands of individuals

   (B) the extinction of hundreds of species of plants and birds

   (C) the near total destruction of all life on Sumatra

   (D) the reduction of temperatures around the globe

   (E) an evolutionary bottleneck that sped the differentiation of the human species

10. Given the information in the passage, Ambrose would be most likely to agree with which one of the following statements?

    (A) The effects of the Toba event can still be seen in modern times.

    (B) Geologic cataclysms have only once impacted the course of human evolution.

    (C) The Toba event was the most important occurrence in recent natural history.

    (D) Volcanic eruptions have had little effect on the history of the human race.

    (E) There is no need for modern geologists to monitor volcanic activity at the Toba caldera.

GO ON TO THE NEXT PAGE.

Although the term "graphic novel" has in recent years become part of the literary, artistic, and popular nomenclature, there remains considerable debate as to what exactly constitutes a graphic novel and what
(5) separates graphic novels from comic books. Many attempts by artists and critics to discern the fundamental traits of the graphic novel begin with the assumption that the graphic novel is an art form. Some critics contend that graphic novels differ from comic
(10) books due to their length, just as novels differ from novellas. Flaws within this line of reasoning immediately arise when it is used to differentiate between short graphic novels and long comic books. For example, most in the comics field would call a 64-
(15) page work by Daniel Clowes a graphic novel but few would call a 64-page double-sized Superman story a graphic novel. Other critics and artists have postulated that graphic novels differ from comic books in the quality of their content in the same way that literary
(20) novels differ from popular fiction novels. However, standards for determining what constitutes high-quality work in the fields of comic books and graphic novels seems hopelessly subjective in that they will differ from reader to reader and from critic to critic.
(25) Graphic novelist Eddie Campbell rejects both length-based and content-based graphic novel theories—indeed, all form-based graphic novel theories—by rejecting the assumption that graphic novels should be understood as an art form or as a
(30) literary form. Instead Campbell postulates that the graphic novel should be understood as an artistic and literary movement with the aim of raising the form of the comic book to more ambitious and meaningful levels. A graphic novelist, according to Campbell, is
(35) one who shares that aim.
By defining the graphic novel as a movement and the graphic novelist as a participant in that movement, Campbell's theory successfully circumvents the problems that undermine length-based graphic novel
(40) theories. Under Campbell's heuristic, artists who produce 64-page works can rightfully be considered every bit the graphic novelists as artists who produce 400-page works, as long as both authors aim to raise the comic book form to a higher plateau. Campbell's
(45) theory also solves the unavoidable problem of subjectivity that plagues content-based graphic novel theories, since it is the ambition and intent of the artist that lifts stories to the status of the graphic novel, not the critical response to those stories and their story-
(50) telling techniques. It is hard to say whether Campbell's notion of the graphic novel as an artistic and literary movement will end up being the dominant paradigm in scholarship and criticism pertaining to the graphic novel, as these fields are still in their embryonic stages.
(55) But there is little doubt that Campbell has set forth a valuable and important new way of thinking about graphic novels and graphic novelists that, at the very least, appears more compelling than two of the predominant form-based graphic novel theories.

11. Which one of the following most accurately expresses the main point of the passage?

(A) There are several different theories that have been set forth on how to differentiate comic books from graphic novels.

(B) Scholarship pertaining to graphic novels and graphic novel criticism are fields still in their embryonic stages, and it is difficult to determine whether Campbell's theory will become the dominant paradigm in the field.

(C) Campbell's proposal that the defining characteristic of a graphic novel is the intent of its author is more compelling than two popular theories.

(D) Graphic novels cannot successfully be differentiated from comic books based upon their length or content alone.

(E) Graphic novels use the same story-telling techniques as comic books but are often considerably lengthier.

12. Which one of the following most accurately describes the organization of the passage?

(A) A problem is presented. Two theories for solving the problem are explained. Weaknesses in the first theory are illustrated. The second theory is accepted.

(B) A problem is presented. Weaknesses are uncovered in two theories used to resolve the problem. A third theory is presented. The third theory is concluded to be superior to the first two.

(C) Three paradigms for understanding a certain kind of art are presented. Weaknesses in two theories are revealed. The third theory is accepted.

(D) A problem is presented. Two theories for solving the problem are explained. Weaknesses in both of these theories are expounded upon. A third theory is presented. The third theory is shown to possess the same flaws as the first two.

(E) A problem in classifying a type of art is presented. Theories attempting to solve the problem are explained. Weaknesses are examined in two of the theories. Both theories are rejected.

GO ON TO THE NEXT PAGE.

13. According to the passage, Campbell would be most likely to agree with which one of the following statements about graphic novels?

   (A) Graphic novels and comic books differ from each other due, in part, to their relative lengths.
   (B) Graphic novels do not utilize characters commonly found in comic books, such as popular superheroes.
   (C) Subjective decisions made by the reader and critics should determine what is viewed as a graphic novel.
   (D) The artwork and stories found in graphic novels are superior to those found in comic books.
   (E) Subjective decisions made by the artist play an important role in determining what should be viewed as a graphic novel.

14. If each of the following works employs the same story-telling techniques as comic books do, which one of the following would be most likely to be called a graphic novel based on the method for differentiating graphic novels from comic books set out in lines 17–20?

   (A) a 300-page superhero story that aims to raise the comic book form to a higher plateau but is dismissed by critics
   (B) a 400-page compilation of unimaginative and clichéd stories about average people
   (C) a 60-page work of poor quality that seeks to take illustrated books to more ambitious and meaningful levels
   (D) a 70-page work that stays firmly within the established form of comic books and wins numerous awards for outstanding quality
   (E) a 150-page book that fails to garner any public interest but seeks to overcome traditional limitations of comic books

15. Based on the passage, the author's attitude toward Campbell's theory can most accurately be described as

   (A) outright disapproval
   (B) uninterested ambivalence
   (C) wholehearted optimism
   (D) tempered support
   (E) hesitant skepticism

STOP

IF YOU FINISH BEFORE TIME IS CALLED, YOU MAY CHECK YOUR WORK ON THIS EXAM ONLY.
DO NOT WORK ON ANY OTHER EXAM IN THE BOOK.

Answers

1. D
2. A
3. B
4. E
5. C
6. A
7. B
8. C
9. D
10. A
11. C
12. B
13. E
14. D
15. D

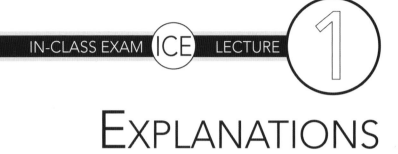

IN-CLASS EXAM ICE LECTURE 1

EXPLANATIONS

Plea Bargaining Passage

Identify

You can identify this as a Thesis passage because it has a one-sentence thesis statement in the first paragraph, and because the rest of the passage is designed to argue in support of that single conclusion.

Analyze

The main point of this passage is: [Legal scholar John Langbein sees this situation as intolerable and believes it to be the direct result of the use of coercive measures that force defendants to give up their constitutional rights, and of a system in which prosecutors are given vastly too much power in deciding who is guilty and how the guilty are punished.] This thesis statement is more specific and certainly more opinionated than the other sentences in the first paragraph.

The purpose of the first paragraph is to introduce the topic and assert Langbein's thesis, which is actually a twofold criticism of the plea bargaining system.

The purpose of the second paragraph is to elaborate upon the first criticism—the idea that plea bargaining is coercive. This is done by comparing it to methods used in medieval Europe.

The purpose of the third paragraph is to explain Langbein's second criticism—the position that the system gives prosecutors too much power. No examples are given, just a short explanation.

The purpose of the fourth paragraph is to show that Langbein acknowledges one advantage of the system but still considers it intolerable.

1. **Choice (D) is the correct answer.**

    This is a Main Point question, as you can tell from the phrase *main point* in the question stem. Look for an answer choice that means the same thing as the thesis statement identified above.

    (A)   Langbein believes that plea bargain agreements place more power in the hands of prosecutors than was intended by the constitutional framers and that all criminal justice systems that use plea bargain agreements are unsound.

    No. The problem here is that the answer choice mentions all criminal justice systems, but the passage discusses Langbein's opinions only of the U.S. criminal justice system. This is **extreme.**

    (B)   According to Langbein, plea bargaining is expedient, and the underuse of the practice leads to constitutional problems parallel to those faced by prosecutors in medieval Europe.

    No. This is an **opposite** distracter, since Langbein thinks the overuse of the practice is problematic, not the underuse.

    (C)   Langbein argues that criminal courts in the U.S. currently place too much emphasis on plea bargaining and calls for more legislative oversight to restrict its use.

    No. The first half of this answer choice is good, but increased legislative oversight is not mentioned in the thesis statement or anywhere else in the passage. This is **out of scope.**

    (D)   Langbein believes that the heavy reliance on plea bargaining in U.S. criminal courts is unjustifiable because the disproportionate influence given to prosecutors compels defendants to surrender their constitutional rights.

    Yes. This uses different words, but it captures all the important ideas, including both major criticisms, found in the passage's thesis statement.

    (E)   According to Langbein, the whole of the U.S. legal system is deeply flawed because defendants, judges, and juries have been stripped of nearly all the power delegated to them by the constitution.

    No. This is **extreme** because the passage conveys Langbein's criticism for a part of the legal system (plea bargaining), not for the entire legal system itself.

2. **Choice (C) is the correct answer.**

    This is a Purpose of a Paragraph question. Look for something that means the same thing as the purpose of the second paragraph as identified above.

    (A)   demonstrate that plea bargaining was a form of torture used in medieval Europe

    No. Langbein *compares* plea bargaining to medieval torture, but doesn't say it was a form of medieval torture. This is **extreme.**

    (B)   suggest that the heavy reliance by U.S. criminal courts on plea bargaining is unconstitutional because it gives prosecutors too much power

    No. This is the **wrong part of the passage.** This choice describes the third paragraph.

    (C)   argue that plea bargaining is unjustly coercive by comparing it to torturous methods used in the past

    Yes. This is a good match for the Prephrased answer, and it captures all the important themes in the second paragraph.

    (D)   concede that plea bargaining can be effective in cases in which defendants are innocent of the levied charges

    No. This **contradicts the passage.** The only good thing that Langbein says about plea bargaining is in the fourth paragraph, where he admits that it can be useful when defendants are guilty, not innocent.

(E)   show that some coercive measures, such as plea bargaining, are acceptable while others, such as torture, are not

No. This **contradicts the passage**. In line 8, you saw that Langbein thinks plea bargaining is intolerable.

3. **Choice (A) is the correct answer.**

This is an Organization question, as you can tell by the word *organization* in the question stem. Look for an answer choice that accurately describes, in the correct order, the purpose of each paragraph as identified in your analysis of the passage.

(A)   Two criticisms are levied against a system; the first is supported with an analogy; the second is reasserted with a brief explanation; a concession of one advantage of the system is made while the overall criticisms are reconfirmed.

Yes. This is a good match for the Prephrased answer. The two criticisms are that plea bargaining is coercive and gives too much power to prosecutors. The analogy is the comparison to medieval torture. The brief explanation is the third paragraph, and the concession is that it's expedient in the case of true guilt, though the fourth paragraph still asserts that plea bargaining is bad.

(B)   Two criticisms are levied against a system; the first is supported with an analogy; the second is reasserted with a brief explanation; a concession is made that the advantages of the system outweigh the disadvantages.

No. This is good up until the end, but Langbein never says the advantages outweigh the disadvantages. This **contradicts the passage.**

(C)   Two criticisms are levied against a system; the first is supported with several examples; the second is restated without support; a third criticism regarding the system is introduced.

No. There are not several examples in the passage, and there is no third criticism introduced at the end of the passage. This is **out of scope.**

(D)   Two criticisms are levied against a system; the first is reasserted with a brief explanation; the second is supported with an extended analogy; a concession of one advantage of the system is made while the overall criticisms are reconfirmed.

No. This is **out of order.** The extended analogy (second paragraph) comes before the brief explanation (third paragraph).

(E)   Two criticisms are levied against a system; the first is supported with an analogy; the second is reasserted with a brief explanation; a third criticism regarding the system is introduced.

No. There is no third criticism. This is **out of scope.**

4. **Choice (E) is the correct answer.**

This is a Purpose of a Phrase question. The stem calls your attention to a particular sentence and asks you *why* the author included it by using the phrase *in order to.* This phrase is found in the paragraph discussing too much power given to prosecutors, and it is a list of powers that should belong to judges and juries but that in realty are exercised by prosecutors. Thus, the phrase acts to show how plea bargaining allows prosecutors to deprive others of their rights.

(A)   strengthen Langbein's argument that the use of plea bargaining is analogous to the practice of torture

No. This describes the **wrong part of the passage.** The analogy to torture is drawn in the second paragraph.

(B)   illustrate how the system of plea bargaining can be expedient in cases in which the defendant is truly guilty

No. Again this is the **wrong part of the passage,** since it describes the fourth paragraph.

(C)   provide a counterexample to weaken Langbein's argument that the system of plea bargaining is unconstitutional

No. This **contradicts the passage.** Nowhere does the passage try to weaken Langbein's argument.

(D)   demonstrate that prosecutors are currently given powers parallel to those afforded to prosecutors in medieval Europe

No. This is the **wrong part of the passage.** Medieval Europe is only discussed in the second paragraph.

(E)   support Langbein's claim that the system of plea bargaining has deprived defendants, judges, and juries of deserved legal rights

Yes. This is a good match for the Prephrased answer.

5. **Choice (B) is the correct answer.**

This is a Purpose of a Passage question. The author spends the entire passage presenting Langbein's argument without any commentary on it. Langbein argues that plea bargaining is intolerable for several reasons but does not go beyond that scope. So the author's purpose it to present this criticism.

(A)   encourage judges to find new ways to limit the use of plea bargain agreements

No. This is the **wrong action.** The author presents no encouragement of any particular course of action.

(B)   call attention to flaws in the U.S. criminal court system, as viewed by one legal scholar

Yes. The author calls out what Langbein sees as the flaws.

(C)   explore the historical roots of one the most prevalent elements of the legal system

No. This is **out of scope**. Although medieval Europe is mentioned, it is presented as part of an analogy, not as the historical roots of plea bargaining. There is no discussion of historical roots.

(D)   articulate one legal expert's theory of how the use of plea bargaining will eventually corrupt prosecutors

No. This is also **out of scope**. No prediction is made about what will eventually happen to prosecutors.

(E)   reveal the unsupported assumptions made by those who compare plea bargaining to torture

No. This is **out of scope**. The author simply presents Langbein's view, but never tries to address any of its assumptions.

Zora Neale Hurston Passage

Identify

You can identify this as a Thesis passage because it has a one-sentence thesis statement in the first paragraph, and because the rest of the passage is designed to argue in support of that single conclusion.

Analyze

The main point of this passage is: [More of an ethnographer than a polemicist, Hurston wrote a unique blend of literature and anthropology that stood outside of the accepted frames of literary and political movements, and her life's work continues to defy such classification.] This thesis statement is more specific and more opinionated than the other sentences in the first paragraph.

The purpose of the first paragraph is to introduce the topic and assert the author's thesis.

The purpose of the second paragraph is to assert that Hurston was foremost an ethnographer—she documented people's lives, in contrast to writers who were concerned with creating political texts. The author does this by contrasting Hurston's training and stated motives with those of Harlem Renaissance writers.

The purpose of the third paragraph is to show how Hurston's work stands outside of the accepted frames of political movements. The author gives two examples of movements that tried to adopt her as a member, then rebuts each one.

The purpose of the fourth paragraph is to continue to show how Hurston transcends other movements. The author does so here by calling attention to one of her works and asserting that it is ignored by movements into which it doesn't fit.

6. **Choice (A) is the correct answer.**
    This is a Main Point question, as you can tell from the phrase *main idea* in the question stem. Look for something that matches the main point identified above.

    (A)   The works of Zora Neale Hurston have been claimed by diverse groups as representative of their own agendas, but the apolitical nature of her writing has belied these assertions.

    Yes. This is well supported by the entire passage.

    (B)   Feminist literary theorists, Harlem Renaissance historians, and libertarian social critics have all found elements of their own philosophies in the writing of Zora Neale Hurston.

    No. This is **incomplete**, because it does not address the author's argument that Hurston's work doesn't belong in any accepted classification.

    (C)   The work of Zora Neale Hurston has been misunderstood for many years and should be reexamined in the context of her political writings, which are opposed to common interpretations of her work.

    No. The author might agree that Hurston's work has been misunderstood, but the author never calls for a reexamination. That goes beyond what the passage supports and so is **extreme**.

    (D)   Although the literary and anthropological works of Zora Neale Hurston are apolitical, the fact that she wrote several political articles has allowed her work to be used by literary critics to make contradictory claims.

    No. This is **incomplete**. The discussion of Hurston's political articles is only one small part of the passage.

    (E)   Zora Neale Hurston had to create meaning through subtext because she was not encouraged to state her views explicitly by the male-dominated literary movements of her lifetime.

    No. This is a mishmash of ideas mentioned in the second half of the third paragraph, but it doesn't add up to the main point.

7. **Choice (D) is the correct answer.**
    This is a Purpose of a Paragraph question. Look for something that means the same thing as the purpose of the second paragraph as identified above.

Lecture 1 Explanations

(A)   argue that Hurston's work has incorrectly been
        classified as unrelated to the Harlem Renaissance

No. This contradicts the passage. The author thinks it would be correct to classify Hurston as unrelated to the Harlem Renaissance.

(B)   reveal the connections between the Harlem
        Renaissance, libertarianism, and feminism

No. Libertarianism and feminism are not mentioned until the third paragraph. Not only is this the wrong part of the passage, it is also out of scope, since the author never tries to connect these movements.

(C)   identify the disparate elements that came together
        to create the Harlem Renaissance

No. This is the wrong action. The second paragraph is about Hurston, not the Harlem Renaissance.

(D)   contrast the work of Hurston with that of the
        defining figures of the Harlem Renaissance

Yes. This is a good match for the Prephrased answer.

(E)   describe the effect of the Harlem Renaissance on
        the work of Hurston

No. This contradicts the passage. The author thinks Hurston was unconnected to that movement.

8. Choice (E) is the correct answer.

This is a Purpose of a Phrase question. The stem calls your attention to a particular part of a paragraph and asks you *why* the author included it by using the phrase *primarily to*. The discussion of this novel is part of the paragraph that shows how she transcends other movements. The phrase in question is an example of one of her works and an assertion that it is ignored by movements into which it doesn't fit.

(A)   demonstrate that she often disagrees with
        more well-known male writers of the Harlem
        Renaissance

No. This is the wrong action. The author says the book lacks overt racial consciousness, but that's not the same as demonstrating disagreement with other writers.

(B)   argue that the attempt to categorize her as a
        feminist writer applies to only some of her
        novels

No. This contradicts the main point of the passage, which is that she does not belong to political movements.

(C)   counter the claim that her works strove to raise
        opposition to government intervention in social
        issues

No. This refers to the wrong part of the passage. Government intervention is referenced in the third paragraph.

(D)   explain why many critics and theorists find
        contradictory views in her work, even though
        such views do not exist

No. This discussion has nothing to do with contradictory views in her work.

(E)   suggest that classifying her as belonging
        to certain literary or political movements
        necessitates disregarding some parts of her work

Yes. This is a good match for the Prephrased answer.

9. Choice (B) is the correct answer.

This is an Organization question, as you can tell by the word *organization* in the question stem. Look for an answer choice that accurately describes, in the correct order, the purpose of each paragraph as identified in your analysis of the passage.

(A)   biographical information about Hurston;
        illustrations of how her work belongs to several
        literary movements; modifications to each of
        those illustrations; an example of her work that
        shows her independence from those movements

No. This contradicts the passage, since the author thinks Hurston's work doesn't belong to any literary movements.

(B)   a presentation of Hurston's approach to
        literature and how it has been received; several
        illustrations of attempts to classify her as
        belonging to a certain movement, each one
        disproved in turn; an example of her work that
        shows her independence from those movements

Yes. This combines the second and third paragraphs, but it is a good match for the presentation of the material.

(C)   an explanation of why Hurston's literature was
        historically ignored; several illustrations of
        attempts by certain movements to revive her
        works; a call for better understanding of the
        universality of her writing and her intentions as
        an author

No. There is no call for better understanding, so this choice is out of scope.

(D)   an argument regarding how Hurston's approach
        to literature should have been received; an
        illustration of attempts to classify her as
        a feminist; counterexamples discrediting
        those attempts; a conclusion that she is best
        regarded as a canonical member of the Harlem
        Renaissance

No. There are several things wrong with this choice, perhaps the most obvious being when it

contradicts the passage by saying she is best regarded as a canonical member of the Harlem Renaissance.

(E)   praise for Hurston's unique blend of literature and anthropology; several examples of how she supported several political and literary movements during her lifetime; a discussion of one of her novels that unites these movements

No. The author thinks she was an ethnographer, not a supporter of political movements. This **contradicts the passage.**

10.   **Choice (C) is the correct answer.**

This is a Purpose of a Passage question. The purpose here is to present the argument found in the thesis statement.

(A)   making the case that it is incorrect to view Hurston as simply a feminist or libertarian, since she also supported the ideals of the Harlem Renaissance

No. This **contradicts the passage.** Rather than saying Hurston is all of the above, the author argues that she is none of the above.

(B)   discussing how some of Hurston's lesser-known novels compare to her journalistic articles

No. Although lesser-known novels and journalistic articles are mentioned, this is at best **incomplete** because it does not mention the author's thesis about classifying Hurston.

(C)   arguing that, despite multiple attempts to classify it, Hurston's work falls outside the boundaries of literary and political movements

Yes. This is a good match for the Prephrased answer.

(D)   dismissing critics who feel that Hurston's unique writing style lacks any overt racial consciousness or strong feminist arguments

No. This **contradicts the passage,** since the author is one of those who feel her writing style lacks overt racial consciousness.

(E)   examining the role that Hurston's work played in revealing connections between several distinct political movements

No. This is **out of scope,** since connections between distinct political movements are never mentioned.

Handicap Principle Passage

Identify

You can identify this as a Thesis passage because it has a one-sentence thesis statement in the first paragraph, and because the rest of the passage is designed to argue in support of that single conclusion.

Analyze

The main point of this passage is: [A recent theory, known as the handicap principle, asserts that stotting and other traits and behaviors that appear to reduce evolutionary fitness and endanger the individual are actually secondary sexual characteristics.] This thesis statement acts as a counterargument to the previous explanation for stotting, which saw it as a warning system to the herd.

The purpose of the first paragraph is to introduce the topic and assert the author's thesis, which is that the handicap principle is correct.

The purpose of the second paragraph is to explain the handicap principle. It explores what a handicap is and how it relates to finding a mate. This is done using the example of the peacock.

The purpose of the third paragraph is to contrast the handicap principle with the previous explanation for stotting (altruism). The author calls the handicap principle "superior" and justifies it using more direct evolutionary principles.

11.   **Choice (D) is the correct answer.**

This is a Main Point question, as you can tell from the phrase *main point* in the question stem. Look for an answer choice that means the same thing as the thesis statement identified above.

(A)   A peacock's tail or a gazelle's stotting encumber the animal with an awkward handicap, but such handicaps are necessary to separate weak members from the group.

No. The author thinks handicaps are used to find a mate, not to separate weak members from the group. This **contradicts the passage.**

(B)   Predators and potential mates benefit equally from honest signaling, while individuals are impaired by inefficient signaling.

No. Saying predators and potential mates benefit equally is not supported by evidence in the passage, and is **extreme.**

(C)   Handicaps, such as a peacock's tail or a gazelle's stotting, are actually signals to prospective mates that the individual with the handicap is both healthy and altruistic.

No. This choice is not bad until it says that a handicap is a signal that an individual is altruistic. That mixes up the separate theories.

(D)   The handicap principle provides an explanation for how the presence of apparently harmful traits and behaviors can coexist with a theory of self-interested individuals.

Yes. This is a good match. Secondary sexual characteristics benefit self-interested individuals, eliminating the need to explain handicaps through altruism.

(E)   A recent theory, the handicap principle, successfully explains how secondary sexual characteristics can also be used by members of a group to warn others of approaching predators.

No. Again this mixes up the two theories, since the author thinks stotting is not a warning to other gazelles.

12. **Choice (B) is the correct answer.**

This is an Organization question, as you can tell by the word *organization* in the question stem. Look for an answer choice that accurately describes, in the correct order, the purpose of each paragraph as you identified it in your analysis of the passage.

(A)   A long-standing problem is identified. Two possible solutions to the problem are posed.

No. This is **incomplete** because it leaves out any mention of the author's preference for one theory over the other.

(B)   A natural phenomenon is explored. One hypothesis to explain the phenomenon is advocated, while another is rejected.

Yes. The handicap principle is advocated, while the warning/altruism theory is rejected.

(C)   Two traits are described. A principle is proposed to account for the two traits. Further exploration of the principle shows it to be flawed.

No. This **contradicts the passage**. There are two theories to explain one trait, not two traits explained by one principle.

(D)   A scientific debate is introduced. Several issues contributing to the debate are summarized.

No. This also is **incomplete** because there is more than summary—the author argues for a particular thesis.

(E)   An unusual behavior is illustrated. A second unusual behavior is shown to have more in common with the first than previously believed.

No. There are no two unusual behaviors. The peacock's tail is a trait, not a behavior.

13. **Choice (C) is the correct answer.**

This is a Purpose of a Passage question. Since this passage is set up as a counterargument, its purpose it to argue for one theory and against another.

(A)   suggest that altruism plays a less significant role in evolution than previously believed

No. This is **incomplete** because it leaves out any mention of the theory the author is arguing for.

(B)   evaluate the relative merits and flaws in two theories regarding the origin of stotting

No. This is **incomplete** because the handicap principle is discussed in relation to more than just stotting, and the author does more than evaluate—he actually makes a choice and argues for one of the theories.

(C)   demonstrate that the handicap principle provides a better justification for certain behaviors than did a previous theory

Yes. This is a good match for the Prephrased answer.

(D)   contrast the phenomenon of honest signaling with that of dishonest signaling, while noting that neither represents altruistic behavior

No. This is **incomplete**. Honest and dishonest signaling is only a small part of the second paragraph.

(E)   argue that handicaps serve mainly to inform potential predators of an individual's health

No. This **contradicts the passage**, which says that the primary function of handicaps is to reveal fitness to potential sexual partners.

14. **Choice (B) is the correct answer.**

This is a Purpose of a Paragraph question. Look for something that means the same thing as the purpose of the second paragraph as identified above.

(A)   provide several examples of honest signaling benefiting a self-interested individual

No. There is only one example of honest signaling, not several.

(B)   explain how a handicap can act as a secondary sexual characteristic

Yes. This is a good match for the Prephrased answer.

(C)   assert that a peacock's tail displays colorations that mimic those of more dangerous species

No. A peacock's tail is honest signaling, while displaying colorations that mimic those of more dangerous species is dishonest signaling. This **contradicts the passage**.

(D)   show that the handicap principle is superior to the theory of altruism

No. This is the **wrong part of the passage**. Altruism is discussed in the third paragraph.

(E)   warn against the dangers of the inefficient display of a handicap

No. This is **incomplete**. It fails to mention the discussion of how a handicap can act as a secondary sexual characteristic.

15. **Choice (A) is the correct answer.**

    This is a Purpose of a Phrase question. The stem calls your attention to a particular sentence and asks you *why* the author included it by using the phrase *main purpose*. The sentence in question explains how the idea of altruism works in the theory the author is arguing against. Why, evolutionarily speaking, would you do something to harm yourself? It helps all your cousins, who have nearly identical genes.

    (A) to explain how altruism was theorized to be able to propagate the genes of even those individuals that died

    Yes. This is a good match for the Prephrased answer.

    (B) to describe why many biologists still believe stotting can be understood as a warning signal to the herd

    No. The passage says the behavior was "previously" explained through altruism, but it never says many biologists still believe this.

    (C) to illustrate how stotting serves as a signal to dissuade predators from expending energy on a chase

    No. This answer relates to the handicap principle, not altruism. This is the wrong part of the passage.

    (D) to defend the theory of altruism by asserting that it explains how information can be communicated on several levels

    No. This is the wrong action. This phrase explains the theory of altruism but doesn't defend it. The author disagrees with it.

    (E) to provide an example of a behavior that the author believes would harm an individual's chances of survival

    No. This is also the wrong action. The phrase in question explains a theory. It doesn't provide an example.

IN-CLASS EXAM **ICE** LECTURE 2

EXPLANATIONS

Lecture 2 Explanations

Memetics Passage

IDENTIFY

You can identify this as an Informational passage because it provides a description of the field of memetics without arguing for a particular viewpoint. The main point of this passage, found in the first paragraph, is not really debatable.

ANALYZE

Main Point

The main point of this passage is: [The field {of memetics} reveals that the manner in which cultural entities change and spread displays some similarities to genetic evolution, as well as some important differences.] This is one of the most general statements in the passage, and all of the paragraphs help to elaborate on this main point.

Purpose of Each Paragraph

The purpose of the first paragraph is to introduce the topic and the main point.

The purpose of the second paragraph is to show some of the parallels between genetics and memetics. This is done with an analogy between an evolving species and the meme complex of Christianity.

The purpose of the third paragraph is to show a difference between memetic and genetic evolution—their different methods of propagation—and to explore several ideas explaining why some memes spread while others disappear.

Major Structural Elements

The biggest structural element is alluded to in the main point: *similarities* and *differences*. This is played out in the organization of the passage: the second paragraph treats similarities, while the third treats differences.

One other structural element shapes the discussion of propagation. The *altruism* mechanism is discussed in lines 39–52, and the *self-spreading* idea is discussed in lines 53–60.

1. **Choice (C) is the correct answer.**

   This is a Definition question since it asks you what the word "mechanism" *means* or *refers to*. As it is used in line 53, the type of mechanism the author is referring to is an *altruism* mechanism. The contextual clues you need are found earlier in the paragraph, in lines 38–40. Altruism "is the driving force" that determines "why some memes spread while others disappear." Look for an answer choice that captures this definition.

(A)   the manner in which memes are replicated

No. The mechanism explains *why* some memes spread, not *how*.

(B)   the type of machine thought to be endangered by the Good Times virus

No. At best, this choice tries to tempt you with the **most common definition** by hoping that you assume a mechanism must be a mechanical device.

(C)   the basis for why only some memes proliferate

Yes. This is a good match for the Prephrased answer.

(D)   the driving force behind the theory of natural selection

No. This is **half wrong**. The *driving force* part is good, but this occurrence of "mechanism" appears in a discussion of memetic propagation, while the answer choice refers to genetic propagation.

(E)   the cause of the frequent mutation of memes

No. Mutation is mentioned in the second paragraph, and this does not match the Prephrased answer.

2. **Choice (C) is the correct answer.**

   This is a Search question since it asks you to determine which answer choices were mentioned in the passage. Before attacking the answer choices, look for some mentions of memes or meme complexes. One list of memes is in lines 14–15; another list of meme complexes is in lines 18–19; a final example is in lines 40–42. Like most Search questions, it's also an EXCEPT question, so you can use the EXCEPT Tool. Put a **Y** next to the choices that did appear in the passage, and an **N** next to the one that did not.

(A)   a song

This was mentioned in line 14. Put a **Y**.

(B)   an image

This was mentioned in line 14. Put a **Y**.

(C)   a rumor

This was not mentioned. Put an **N**.

(D)   a religious doctrine

This was mentioned in lines 18–19. Put a **Y**.

(E)   a hoax

This was mentioned in line 50. Put a **Y**.

Since choice (C) is different from all the rest, pick it.

3. **Choice (C) is the correct answer.**

This is another Search question since you are looking for the question to which the passage *offers* an answer. Unlike question 2, this question stem is much more vague and does not allow you to do any analysis or Prephrasing before you attack the answer choices.

(A) How can the theory of natural selection be used to explain stock market fluctuations?

No. Stock market fluctuations are mentioned in line 3, but there is no answer to this question.

(B) What causes people to combine ideas and habits into meme complexes?

No. A definition of meme complexes appears in lines 17–18, and the third paragraph examines why some spread, but there is no answer as to why people create them in the first place.

(C) Which genetic variations are most likely to proliferate?

Yes. The answer is in lines 33–35: "The genetic variants that proliferate are those that confer an advantage for sexual reproduction."

(D) How did the Good Times virus hoax begin?

No. There is much discussion as to how and why it spread, but none as to how it began.

(E) Why are some widespread ideologies built upon the instruction to spread the ideology?

No. Lines 58–60 mention the existence of such ideologies, but there is no discussion of why people create them that way.

4. **Choice (D) is the correct answer.**

This is a Detail question. It asks you to retrieve a detail about the Good Times virus hoax. The passage provides a few details in the third paragraph, any one of which could be the correct answer. In lines 40–47 you learn that it spread quickly and contained a warning; in line 50 you learn that there was no virus; and in lines 57–58, you learn that the hoax urged people to tell others about the virus.

(A) It no longer exists in its original form, but rather in a variety of regional manifestations.

No. This looks like lines 24–25, which refer to Christianity, not the hoax. This is the **wrong part of the passage.**

(B) It caused widespread fear of the virus, costing companies millions of dollars.

No. There was no mention of the cost of the hoax to companies. This is **out of scope.**

(C) It spread more quickly than any previous meme.

No. You know it spread quickly, but any comparison to other memes was not made and is **out of scope.**

(D) It contained an instruction to disseminate the meme.

Yes. This matches the Prephrased answer and lines 57–58.

(E) Study of the hoax provided a major breakthrough in memetic theory.

No. You know memeticists theorized about the hoax, but there was no mention of a major breakthrough. That's **out of scope.**

5. **Choice (B) is the correct answer.**

This is a Detail question since it asks you to retrieve a specific fact—how memes and genes are analogous—and uses the phrase *according to the author*. In your analysis of the passage, you found that the similarities between the two were discussed in the second paragraph. Specifically, in lines 19–22, the author says that both can change as they are passed on.

(A) physically exist

No. The author never says this, and it's safe to assume that ideas *don't* physically exist.

(B) are informational units capable of evolving

Yes. This is a good match for the Prephrased answer, and the author also uses the term *unit of information* in lines 8–9 to refer to both memes and genes.

(C) are used to explain cultural change

No. The theory of natural selection may be used to explain cultural change, but that's not the same as using genes to explain cultural change. This is a **word trap**.

(D) can be consciously manipulated in order to speed the process of evolution

No. Conscious manipulation is never mentioned in the passage and is **out of scope**.

(E) employ similar methods of propagation

No. This **contradicts the passage**, which says in lines 35–37 that they employ *different* methods of propagation.

Lecture 2 Explanations

Trepanation Passage

IDENTIFY

You can identify this as an Informational passage because it provides a description of trepanation, its history, and its modern uses without arguing for a particular viewpoint. The main point of this passage, found in the first paragraph, is not really debatable.

ANALYZE

Main Point

The main point of this passage is: [An understanding of {trepanation's} long history is useful in examining the relation between medicine and spirituality, since the operation has been used as a cure for a variety of ailments as well as a pathway to spiritual enlightenment.] This is one of the most general statements in the passage, and all of the paragraphs help to elaborate on this main point.

Purpose of Each Paragraph

The purpose of the first paragraph is to introduce the topic, define trepanation, and convey the main point.

The purpose of the second paragraph is to explore the medical uses of trepanation over the years and to show how past "medical" uses also had a spiritual nature.

The purpose of the third paragraph is to show how some incidences of trepanation were associated with rituals rather than therapy.

The purpose of the fourth paragraph is to bring the description of trepanation into the present. Non-therapeutic use is regaining proponents, and it is again tied to spiritual nature.

Major Structural Elements

It's worth noting that the main point gives a preview of the subsequent paragraphs, in which the topics presented concern history, medicine, spirituality, and their connections.

6. **Choice (D) is the correct answer.**

   This is a Detail question, as you can tell from the question stem, which asks you what the passage *states* about a specific use of trepanation. Pre-Columbian use is mentioned in lines 35–41: "Excavations uncovered a ritual use of trepanation, based on the regularity of burr holes in a wide spectrum of the population … The commonality, as well as the incidence of multiple burr holes, suggests a non-therapeutic function…"

   (A)   It was used to allow the elderly to rediscover their infant selves.

No. Infant selves are not mentioned until the fourth paragraph. This is the **wrong part of the passage**.

(B)   It was used to treat epilepsy and mental illness.

No. This is again the **wrong part of the passage**. These ideas were mentioned in line 24.

(C)   The surgery was central to the religious beliefs of most pre-Columbian inhabitants of Peru and Bolivia.

No. Having a ritual use is not the same as being central to religious beliefs. This is **extreme**.

(D)   The surgery was sometimes performed multiple times on a single person.

Yes. This means the same thing as "the incidence of multiple burr holes."

(E)   Historical accounts state that the surgery was performed on children, adults, and the elderly.

No. Although these different segments of the population are mentioned, it was excavations that uncovered the evidence, not historical accounts.

7. **Choice (A) is the correct answer.**

   This Detail question can be simplified to say, "What do you know about modern proponents of spiritual trepanation?" Several answers are found in the fourth paragraph. You know they 1) postulate that patients can rediscover their infant selves and expand their consciousness, 2) argue that this motivation was the reason behind the ancient practice of trepanation, and 3) must perform the surgery themselves.

   (A)   They think that ancient peoples sought to become aware of their infant selves and expand consciousness.

Yes. This is a good match for the Prephrased answer.

(B)   Some have become seriously ill due to infections caused by voluntary trepanation procedures.

No. It's not unreasonable to think this might be true, but the passage never states it.

(C)   They believe that awareness of the infant self can lead to expanded consciousness.

No. These are two separate goals of the practice, and the passage never says that one leads to the other.

(D)   Many of them have undergone surgical procedures that were performed by non-licensed physicians.

No. The passage never says that "many" people have undergone this, and it never mentions non-licensed physicians.

(E)   They share many of Hippocrates's beliefs pertaining to trepanation.

No. Hippocrates advocates trepanation for fracture or contusion of the cranium (lines 19–20), which does not match the information in the fourth paragraph.

8. **Choice (C) is the correct answer.**

This is a Search question. You can try to locate some instances of people who practice trepanation before you look at the answer choices, but since they are introduced throughout the passage, it's just as easy to work from the answer choices and determine whether each one was mentioned. This is also an EXCEPT question, so you can use the EXCEPT Tool. Put a **Y** next to the choices that did appear in the passage, and an **N** next to the one that did not.

(A)   some contemporary rural Kenyans

This was mentioned in lines 45–46. Put a **Y**.

(B)   Europeans of the middle ages

This was mentioned in lines 21–23. Put a **Y**.

(C)   present-day spiritualists of Peru and Bolivia

Peru and Bolivia were mentioned in line 35, but it was in the context of pre-Columbian times, not present day. Put an **N**.

(D)   prehistoric peoples of France

This was mentioned in lines 15–17. Put a **Y**.

(E)   modern medical professionals

This was mentioned in line 6. Put a **Y**.

Since choice (C) is different from all the rest, pick it.

9. **Choice (B) is the correct answer.**

This is a Definition question. The contextual clues that define the term are found in lines 35–36 and in line 44: "a ritual use." The distracters will be things that sound like they might be non-therapeutic, but only the correct answer will match this contextual clue.

(A)   trepanation to relieve pressure on the brain

No. This is a **word trap**, meant to remind you of lines 6–7 or lines 49–50.

(B)   trepanation for ritual purposes

Yes. This matches the Prephrased answer.

(C)   trepanation performed by someone other than a doctor

No. This doesn't match the contextual clues.

(D)   trepanation practiced by a whole society

No. This is never mentioned in the passage. It's out of scope.

(E)   trepanation performed on people without a malady

No. This may sound tempting but it doesn't match the contextual clues stated in the passage.

10. **Choice (D) is the correct answer.**

This is another Search question, and again, because historical uses are found throughout the passage you may want to just move directly to the answer choices. You can again use the EXCEPT Tool. Put a **Y** next to the choices that did appear in the passage, and an **N** next to the one that did not.

(A)   to relieve pressure on the brain caused by skull fracture

This was mentioned in lines 20–21. Put a **Y**.

(B)   to allow blood and fluids to circulate more freely around the brain

This was mentioned in lines 50–51. Put a **Y**.

(C)   to allow evil to escape from the cranium in order to cure migraines

This was mentioned in lines 24–27. Put a **Y**.

(D)   to decrease the dangers associated with infection

Dangers associated with infection are mentioned in lines 58–59, but in the context of something caused by trepanation, not decreased by it. Put an **N**.

(E)   to allow the patient to achieve an expanded consciousness

This was mentioned in line 52. Put a **Y**.

Since choice (D) is different from all the rest, pick it.

Judicial Review Passage

IDENTIFY

You can identify this as an Informational passage because it provides a description of judicial review and a history of how it came about without arguing for a particular viewpoint. The main point of the passage is historical, descriptive, and not really debatable.

ANALYZE

Main Point

The main point of this passage is best expressed by combining statements from the first and last paragraphs: [It was not the Constitution but rather the 1803 interpretation of the Supreme Court's jurisdiction in *Marbury v. Madison* that helped define judicial review, now seen as the primary function of the Supreme Court.] This is a general statement that captures all of the most important information in the passage, and all of the paragraphs help to elaborate on this main point.

Purpose of Each Paragraph

The purpose of the first paragraph is to introduce the topic and the main point.

The purpose of the second paragraph is to give the historical background of the situation that brought about the case.

The purpose of the third paragraph is to explore legal issues and the reasoning of the Court's justices as they reached their decision.

The purpose of the fourth paragraph is to explore some criticisms of the decision and its ramifications, and to reiterate the main point.

Major Structural Elements

There are no particularly important dichotomies, lists, or timelines to take note of in this passage.

11. **Choice (E) is the correct answer.**

    This Detail question asks you what you know about William Marbury. This person was discussed in lines 19–26, in which you learn that he 1) had been given an appointment as a district judge by Adams, 2) was not seated by Jefferson on technical grounds, and 3) petitioned the court to issue a writ compelling the government to recognize his appointment.

    (A)   Marbury was a political ally of John Adams.

    No. Although he was appointed by Adams, the passage never states that he was a political ally. This is **out of scope**.

    (B)   Marbury sought to challenge Section 13 of the Judiciary Act of 1789.

    No. He wanted the court to *obey* Section 13. He didn't want to challenge it.

    (C)   Marbury petitioned the court to issue a writ compelling the government to recognize Jefferson's decision.

    No. Marbury was trying to *fight* Jefferson's decision, not get the government to recognize it. This is a **word trap**.

    (D)   Marbury never had the opportunity to serve as a district judge.

    No. Although he wasn't successful in *Marbury v. Madison*, the passage never tells you the eventual outcome of Marbury's quest to be a judge. This is **out of scope**.

    (E)   Marbury was one of 42 men appointed to district judge positions by President John Adams shortly before he left office.

Yes. This matches the Prephrased answer and lines 19–21.

12. **Choice (B) is the correct answer.**

    This Detail question can be simplified to say, "Why have legal scholars criticized the *Marbury v. Madison* decision?" The answer is found in lines 42–47. They "argue that it implies that justices must try to find some underlying meaning to the Constitution beyond what is expressly stated. They argue that this gives the Court too much power and that justices should abide only by the text of the Constitution."

    (A)   they believe judicial review grants the Supreme Court too much power

    No. Their concern is *that finding some underlying meaning to the Constitution* gives the Court too much power, not that *judicial review* gives it too much power. This is a **word trap**.

    (B)   they think implicit powers should not be derived from the Constitution's text

    Yes. *Implicit* is a good match for *beyond what is expressly stated*, and the scholars indeed believe that justices should not be doing this.

    (C)   they think the Court should have compelled Jefferson to allow Adams's judicial appointments to serve

    No. You're never told what the scholars think about Adams's judicial appointments.

    (D)   they feel judicial review should not be the primary role of the Court

    No. Again, judicial review is not mentioned in these lines. This is **out of scope**.

    (E)   they feel justices should rule according to only the text of the Constitution and legal precedent

    No. Most of this choice is good, but legal precedent is not mentioned and is **out of scope**.

13. **Choice (B) is the correct answer.**

    This is a Definition question. The contextual clues that define what the author means by "irony of the case" are found in lines 14–16: "the law that {the} justices invalidated sought to give the Supreme Court more power." That is indeed ironic. As stated in lines 54–57, "The Court, by unanimously deciding to deny itself the power to issue the writ, consciously claimed for itself a far greater and lasting power."

    (A)   the Supreme Court created its own power of judicial review, which was accepted by Congress

    No. Acceptance by Congress is not mentioned in the contextual clues.

(B)   the Court overturned a law that would have given it extended powers in order to create judicial review

Yes. This is a good match for the Prephrased answer.

(C)   the justices were, in fact, opposed to the Jefferson administration's attempt to withhold the commissions

No. That would be ironic too, but the passage never says this.

(D)   the Court set the precedent of judicial review by denying itself the power to overturn decisions made by the lower courts

No. The denied power had to do with the Court's original jurisdiction, not its review of appellate decisions.

(E)   the history of the Court has been written without a full explanation of the effects of *Marbury v. Madison*

No. This is completely **out of scope**.

14. **Choice (D) is the correct answer.**

This is a Search question, but the question stem is too vague to allow you to do any analysis or Prephrasing before attacking the answer choices. Don't forget to use the EXCEPT Tool.

(A)   the background of the *Marbury v. Madison* case decided by the Supreme Court

This was provided throughout the second paragraph. Put a **Y**.

(B)   the reasoning of the Supreme Court in the *Marbury v. Madison* case

This makes up most of the third paragraph. Put a **Y**.

(C)   the importance of *Marbury v. Madison* in Supreme Court history

Lines 57–60 say this case is the source of the power that is now the Supreme Court's primary function. That tells you the importance. Put a **Y**.

(D)   the political affiliations of Marshall and the other justices

This was never mentioned. Put an **N**.

(E)   the historical importance of the intent of the framers of the Constitution

Lines 47–49 say, "The intent of the framers of the Constitution is often invoked as a rationale in cases on the margins of constitutional language." Put a **Y**.

Since choice (D) is different from all the rest, pick it.

15. **Choice (A) is the correct answer.**

This Detail question can be simplified to say, "What do you know about the Judiciary Act of 1789?" In lines 17–19, you learn that it "granted the Court the power to issue writs compelling government officials to perform their duties if they were negligent." And in lines 50–51, you learn that it "was written concurrently with the Constitution, and by the same individuals."

(A)   was written by the framers of the Constitution

Yes. This matches the Prephrased answer.

(B)   contained several sections that were ruled unconstitutional

No. You know Section 13 was ruled unconstitutional, but the passage says nothing about other sections.

(C)   provided Thomas Jefferson with a reason to deny Marbury his judgeship

No. Jefferson denied Marbury his judgeship "on technical grounds" (line 24).

(D)   granted the Supreme Court the power to issue writs compelling government officials to abstain from performing certain duties

No. This **word trap** distracter looks a lot like lines 17–19 but reverses their meaning.

(E)   granted the Supreme Court the power of judicial review

No. The main point is that the *overturning* of the Judiciary Act created the power of judicial review.

Lecture 2 Explanations

IN-CLASS EXAM ICE LECTURE 3

EXPLANATIONS

Narwhal Passage

IDENTIFY

You can identify this as an Enlightenment passage because it is written to answer the core question, "What is the purpose of the narwhal's tusk?" It also contains several different viewpoints.

ANALYZE

Core Question

The core question in this passage is "What is the purpose of the narwhal's tusk?" The core question is not posed in exactly those terms, but in lines 2–3, the author indicates that there was "curiosity and speculation" about it, and in line 11, you learn that "naturalists were baffled" by it. Finally, in line 14, you learn that scientist were trying to "discern the function" of the tusk.

Various Viewpoints

There are a number of viewpoints in this passage. The first is in lines 3–7, in which the author mentions that people in medieval European courts thought the tusk was magical.

The second paragraph has a list of viewpoints: the tusk is an icebreaker (lines 18–22); the tusk is used for echolocation (lines 22–24); the tusk is used to attract a mate (lines 24–30).

The third paragraph presents Nweeia's viewpoint and also contains some opinionated words to indicate the author's viewpoint. Nweeia thinks the tusk is a hydrodynamic sensory organ, and the author agrees. Some of the author's opinionated words are: "definitive" (line 39); "likely" (line 47); "skillfully" (line 50); "important" (line 52). In lines 57–61, the author speculates about the purpose of tusking.

Purpose of Each Paragraph

The purpose of the first paragraph is to introduce the topic, mention a "supernatural speculation" about the tusk, and foreshadow the fact that scientists now know the true function.

The purpose of the second paragraph is to list early scientific speculation about the tusk and present the support behind some of the theories.

The purpose of the third paragraph is to answer the core question by discussing Nweeia's research in depth and showing the author's viewpoint that Nweeia is correct.

Main Point

The main point is the answer to the core question, found in lines 35–47: [The narwhal's tusk is a unique hydrodynamic sensory organ that allows the narwhal to perceive salinity, navigate, and sense food.]

1. **Choice (A) is the correct answer.**

   This is a Viewpoint question. The author's viewpoint is found in the third paragraph. It's composed of some opinionated words about the validity of Nweeia's research and some speculation about the prospect of determining the purpose of tusking.

   (A) The study of sensory organs in other animals will likely shed little light on why narwhals engage in tusking behavior because the tusks are so unique.

   Yes. This is a close rewording of lines 57–61.

   (B) The prevalence of the hypothesis that narwhal tusks were horns of unicorns delayed the true scientific explanation by decades.

   No. This **contradicts the passage**, specifically lines 47–49. The delay was caused by the uniqueness of the tusk.

   (C) Narwhals are able to navigate the waters of the Arctic using mechanisms similar to those employed by other cetaceans.

   No. This **contradicts the passage**. Lines 47–49 say the tusk and its abilities are unique, and the passage never mentions similar mechanisms.

   (D) Nweeia's contributions to the study of narwhals are relatively insignificant.

   No. This **contradicts the passage**. In line 52 the author calls Nweeia's discovery "important."

   (E) Bull narwhals exhibit the behavior of tusking in order to remove particulates and display dominance to potential mates.

   No. This is a mishmash of unrelated ideas from different viewpoints. Removing things from the tusk is in lines 54–55, particulates are mentioned in line 45, and displaying dominance is in line 25.

2. **Choice (D) is the correct answer.**

   This is a Viewpoint question because it asks what Nweeia would be *most likely to agree with*. Nweeia's viewpoint can be summed up by the main point of the passage: [The narwhal's tusk is a unique hydrodynamic sensory organ that allows the narwhal to perceive salinity, navigate, and sense food.] If this is not specific enough to get the right answer, you can revisit his viewpoint in the passage, found in lines 31–47.

   (A) The narwhal tusk is a sensory organ used for echolocation.

   No. This is the **wrong viewpoint**. The scientists in line 22 believed this, but Nweeia concluded this was "incorrect" (line 33).

   (B) The narwhal tusk assists the animal in breaking through the ice of the Arctic Ocean.

No. Like choice (A), this was believed by scientists in line 22, but judged incorrect by Nweeia.

(C) It is likely science will never find an adequate explanation as to why the narwhal has a tusk.

No. This **contradicts the passage**. Nweeia's research has already answered this question.

(D) The narwhal's tusk assists the animal in its search for squid.

Yes. This matches the Prephrased answer and lines 45–46.

(E) People were foolish to once think the narwhal's tusk was the horn of the unicorn.

No. Although Nweeia clearly doesn't think the tusk is from a unicorn, he never in this passage passes judgment on the people who did. This is **out of scope**.

3. **Choice (E) is the correct answer.**

This is an Inference question since it asks what the passage *suggests*. The second paragraph contains three theories, and lines 31–35 in the third paragraph give a little more information about them. The correct answer will be limited in its scope to the information in these lines.

(A) One of them proved that the tusk was used to establish male dominance and attract a mate.

No. This is a **word trap**. Most of the choice matches lines 25–26, but the theory was never "proved." Nweeia found that it was incorrect.

(B) All of them resorted to supernatural explanations to account for the purpose of the tusk.

No. This **contradicts the passage**. Lines 7–9 say supernatural speculation ceased in the seventeenth century, and the theorists in the second paragraph are scientists.

(C) Some of them were able to correctly identify the nature of the tusk's sensory capabilities, but none could explain tusking behavior.

No. This again **contradicts** line 32–33, which says the hypotheses are incorrect.

(D) None of them came anywhere close to identifying the natural purpose of the narwhal tusk.

No. This is **extreme**. Lines 34–35 say the echolocation hypothesis was "not far off the mark."

(E) At least one of them was lent credence by examinations of narwhal actions in the wild.

Yes. This matches lines 27–30. The narwhal action in the wild was the tusking behavior, and this supported the idea that the bulls used the tusk to display dominance.

4. **Choice (E) is the correct answer.**

This is an Attitude question. In the initial analysis of the passage, you found a number of opinionated words indicating that the author thinks Nweeia's work was *definitive*, *skillful*, and *important*. There aren't any negative words used to temper this attitude.

(A) interest in Nweeia's results but skepticism regarding their accuracy

No. The second half of this choice is bad, as the author never displays any skepticism toward Nweeia.

(B) support for Nweeia's conclusion that the narwhal tusk is used for mating purposes

No. This is a **word trap**. The author does support Nweeia's conclusion, but the choice misrepresents that conclusion—Nweeia does *not* think the tusk is used for mating purposes.

(C) criticism of Nweeia's methods as inhumane

No. This matches nothing in the passage and is **out of scope**.

(D) doubt that Nweeia's research will continue

No. The continuation of the work is also not mentioned and is again **out of scope**.

(E) admiration for Nweeia's results and the manner in which he attained them

Yes. This matches the Prephrased answer and the opinionated words in the passage.

5. **Choice (C) is the correct answer.**

This is an Inference question since it asks for the choice that's *supported by the passage*. The question stem is too vague to allow for a Prephrased answer, so move on to the answer choices.

(A) Nweeia's conclusions have been lauded as a major breakthrough by the majority of the scientific community.

No. This is **extreme**. The author clearly agrees with Nweeia, but praise by a majority of scientists is not mentioned or supported by the passage.

(B) Due to its high concentration of nerve tubules, the tusk is the narwhal's primary sensory organ.

No. This is also **extreme**. Clearly the tusk is important, but it is never compared to the animal's other organs, so the passage doesn't support calling it the *primary* organ.

(C) Electron micrographs have proven to be a useful tool for research on the narwhal.

Yes. This is supported by lines 35–39. The electron micrographs allowed Nweeia to make his "important" discovery.

Lecture 3 Explanations

(D)   The ability to perceive salinity gradients is crucial to the survival of the narwhal.

No. This is **extreme**. You know the animal can perceive salinity gradients, but the passage never calls this ability crucial. Even the ability to sense food (which could reasonably be judged crucial) is related to particulates, not salinity (lines 42–47).

(E)   Female narwhals that lack developed tusks are unable to detect changes in water pressure.

No. Maybe they have other ways of doing so besides a tusk. The passage never says they lack this ability.

Western Passage

IDENTIFY

You can identify this as an Enlightenment passage because it is written to answer the core question, "Why did the western genre decline so drastically in popularity?" It also contains several different viewpoints.

ANALYZE

Core Question

The core question is not presented as a succinct hypothetical question, but throughout the passage, the author writes of the search for an "explanation" for the decline. The core question can be summed up as "Why did the western genre decline so drastically in popularity?"

Various Viewpoints

One viewpoint, attributed to "some critics," is in lines 10–14: the decline was due to the exit of stars and filmmakers.

Another viewpoint, attributed to "other critics," is in lines 21–31: the decline was due to changing attitudes about the western myth.

The author's viewpoint is found throughout. In the second paragraph, she rejects the "exit" viewpoint by saying it "insufficiently" accounts for the decline (line 16). In the third paragraph, she affirms the "attitudes" viewpoint by saying it "correctly" points out some important factors (line 23), and in line 42 she calls the treatment in Native Americans in traditional westerns "unacceptable." The fourth paragraph is entirely the author's viewpoint, in which she goes beyond the "attitudes" viewpoint—she says it "explains" some changes in the industry, but doesn't "sufficiently explain" the complete downfall. She asserts that it was the presence of mythic stories that made westerns popular, and the removal of this feature accounts for their decline.

Purpose of Each Paragraph

The purpose of the first paragraph is to introduce the topic and the mystery of the extinction of the genre.

The purpose of the second paragraph is to introduce and reject the "exit" viewpoint.

The purpose of the third paragraph is to introduce and lend some credence to the "attitudes" viewpoint. There is also a lot of historical fact in the middle and latter parts of the paragraph.

The purpose of the fourth paragraph is to convey the author's answer to the core question.

Main Point

The answer to the core question and the main point is found in the fourth paragraph: [The arrival of revisionist ideas explains the downfall of the traditional western, but the complete downfall of the genre came when the public turned to other cinematic genres to find the mythic stories that had been removed from westerns.]

6. **Choice (C) is the correct answer.**
    The answer to this Viewpoint question will come from the one of the places where the author asserts her viewpoint, as identified in your initial analysis of the passage.

    (A)   Revisionist westerns were better made than the more traditional western films that preceded them.

    No. The author compares the two types of westerns in lines 41–49, but never says which was "better made."

    (B)   Traditional westerns became more prevalent due to filmmakers' rejection of the western myth.

    No. This **contradicts the passage**, which says traditional westerns became *less* prevalent because of the rejection of the western myth.

    (C)   Most revisionist westerns portrayed Native Americans more positively than did most traditional westerns.

    Yes. This is a good match for lines 41–44.

    (D)   The death of John Wayne did not affect the popularity of the western as a cinematic genre.

    No. This is **extreme**. In lines 16–17, the author says that the exit of John Wayne, "insufficiently accounts for" the demise of the genre, but that's not the same as saying it didn't affect the genre's popularity.

    (E)   Some of the most universally acclaimed films of all time are westerns.

    No. This is **out of scope**. The passage never mentions critical reaction to any individual westerns.

Lecture 3 Explanations

7. **Choice (D) is the correct answer.**

This is an Inference question since it asks for the choice that's *supported by the passage*. The question stem is too vague to allow for a Prephrased answer, so move on to the answer choices.

(A)   The popularity of the western genre experienced similar declines in both the 1930s and the 1960s, when major stars left the industry.

No. This **contradicts the passage**. The passage states that the western lost none of its popularity in the 1930s (lines 17–20).

(B)   *Little Big Man* was only marginally profitable for the studio that produced it.

No. This is **out of scope**. Although the passage does say that revisionist westerns as a whole were not popular and that *Little Big Man* is a revisionist western, you cannot infer that *Little Big Man* as an individual film was unpopular and marginally profitable.

(C)   Science fiction is now the most profitable cinematic genre in the United States.

No. This is **extreme**. The passage states that science fiction ascended in popularity around 1965, but it never makes a comparison to *all* other genres or tells you how *profitable* science fiction is today.

(D)   Movies that portray certain kinds of mythic stories have proven to be popular with U.S. audiences over several decades.

Yes. The passage states that westerns were popular for a very long time (lines 1–3) due to the myths they portrayed. The passage also states science fiction films portray mythic stories and also enjoyed popularity (lines 59–63).

(E)   If traditional westerns were still being made, they would continue to attract large audiences.

No. This is **out of scope**. The passage never says whether audiences of today would accept traditional westerns as audiences before the 1960s did.

8. **Choice (E) is the correct answer.**

This is a Match question. It asks for an *example* of a revisionist western. In lines 33–37, you learn that revisionist attitudes "characterized the conquest of the west as the subjugation of a land and a people by an often racist nation through methods wrought with moral ambiguity," and that film-makers began to incorporate these attitudes into their films after 1960. Look for an answer choice that matches this definition

(A)   a film set in the nineteenth-century American West in which a cowboy successfully defends his ranch against savage Native-American raiders

No. This **contradicts** the revisionist viewpoint.

(B)   a film set in the American West during the 1960s in which a group of Native Americans is portrayed as struggling for better treatment from the U.S. government

No. The struggle for better treatment is **out of the scope** of the viewpoint as found in lines 35–38.

(C)   a movie made in 1951 and staring John Wayne as a nineteenth-century U.S. soldier who reconsiders his previously held assumptions about Native Americans

No. Line 33 tells you revisionist westerns were made after 1960, not in 1951.

(D)   a film that depicts a morally idealized victory by a group of nineteenth-century Native Americans who defeat an American army unit

No. Although the definition you're trying to match is supportive of Native Americans, it is about the immorality of their subjugation, not the morality of their military victories.

(E)   a movie that portrays a nineteenth-century cowboy who fights Native Americans in the American West as a racist who achieves his goals by morally questionable means

Yes. This is a good match for lines 35–38.

9. **Choice (C) is the correct answer.**

The opinionated words you need in order to answer this Attitude question are found at the end of the third paragraph: the author thinks the values portrayed by traditional westerns were "unacceptable" (line 42) and "puerile" (line 44).

(A)   disapproving of their attempts to discredit the western myth

No. She disapproves of the western myth, not the effort to discredit it.

(B)   appreciative of the artistic and commercial success that they attained

No. This is a complete **opposite** answer.

(C)   critical of how they idealized certain values

Yes. This is a good match for the Prephrased answer.

(D)   surprised that they were able to be so popular for so long

No. Any mention of surprise is **out of scope**.

(E)   nostalgic for the films of a bygone era

No. Nostalgia is also **out of scope**.

10. **Choice (B) is the correct answer.**

This Viewpoint question asks about those who espouse the "exit" viewpoint. They think "the deaths and retirements of stars {is the} principal cause of the western's decline" because the genre "lost much of its vitality" (lines 10–15). Look for a choice that matches this.

(A)   The growth of the science fiction genre can be linked to the decline of the western.

No. This is the **wrong viewpoint**. The author would agree with this, not these critics.

(B)   John Ford played a role in bringing vitality to a genre of film.

Yes. If the genre lost its vitality without John Ford, then he must have provided some of it.

(C)   The myths portrayed in most westerns made before 1960 are what attracted most of the people who attended the movies.

No. This is the **wrong viewpoint**. The western myth is not mentioned until the third paragraph.

(D)   John Wayne was an actor of questionable talent and limited range.

No. This is the **opposite** of what these critics would likely think, since they feel Wayne brought vitality to the genre.

(E)   The screenwriters, directors, and producers who made traditional westerns did so in order to raise significant moral questions.

No. Raising moral question is not discussed until the third paragraph, and only then in the context of revisionist—not traditional—westerns.

Cetacean Passage

IDENTIFY

You can identify this as an Enlightenment passage because it is written to answer the core question, "How did cetaceans evolve from land-based to aquatic mammals?" It also contains several different viewpoints.

ANALYZE

Core Question

The core question is stated pretty succinctly in the first sentence, which indicates bewilderment about the question, "How did cetaceans evolve from land-based to aquatic mammals?"

Various Viewpoints

With so many scientific names being thrown around in this passage, it's best to find some way to simplify them. You can abbreviate the different species and theories using just their initials, and a simple diagram of each theory can greatly aid you in keeping things straight. This technique can be helpful on a lot of different passages, especially scientific ones.

There are three major viewpoints presented, two of which are introduced in lines 8–14. The mesonychid theory (we'll abbreviate it here as the "MT") is discussed in the second paragraph and basically says this:

$$M \longrightarrow P_{(a\ type\ of\ M)} \longrightarrow C$$

Where **M** means mesonychid, **P** means pakicetid, and **C** means cetacean.

The second viewpoint is the artiodactyl theory ("AT"), presented in the third paragraph. It works like this:

$$A \longrightarrow C$$

Where **A** means artiodactyl.

The third viewpoint is the current understanding ("CU"). It's presented in the last paragraph and works like this:

$$A \longrightarrow P_{(a\ type\ of\ A)} \longrightarrow C$$

In a way, it's somewhat of a combination of the two other theories, but it is presented as a confirmation of a modified version of the **AT**.

Purpose of Each Paragraph

The paragraphs are well organized around the different viewpoints. The purpose of the first paragraph is to introduce the topic and the first two theories.

The purpose of the second paragraph is to explain the **MT**.

The purpose of the third paragraph is to explain the **AT**.

The purpose of the fourth paragraph is to explain how **P** got reclassified from a type of **M** to a type of **A** and to explain how this went on to form the current understanding.

Main Point

The main point is the answer to the core question, which is found in the fourth paragraph as the current understanding of cetacean evolution: [Modern cetaceans evolved from an extinct family of artiodactyls called pakicetids.]

11.   **Choice (A) is the correct answer.**
      This is a Viewpoint question. The scientists in the second paragraph believed the **MT**, so look for something that matches that theory.

      (A)   The examination of fossilized specimens can be a reliable way to determine an animal's ancestry.

      Yes. In lines 15–17 you see that they used fossils to support their claim. They wouldn't have done so if they didn't think fossils were reliable.

      (B)   Most marine mammals descended from mesonychids.

No. The **MT** is only about **C**'s, not *all* or *most* marine mammals. This is **out of scope**.

(C)   It is doubtful any modern mammals evolved from artiodactyls.

No. Lines 12–14 say pigs, cows, and giraffes are all types of **A**'s, and there is nothing in the second paragraph to contradict this.

(D)   It is highly likely that hippopotamuses are the closest non-cetacean relative to dolphins.

No. This is the **wrong viewpoint**. This corresponds to the **AT**.

(E)   It is likely that complete pakicetid specimens will reveal that cetaceans did not evolve from mesonychids.

No. This **contradicts** the **MT**, but you're looking for something that agrees with it.

12.   **Choice (B) is the correct answer.**

This is an Inference question since it concerns which choices are *supported by* information in the passage. The most specific information about **C**'s and hippos is found in lines 31–37, but since both **A**'s and **C**'s are discussed throughout the passage, be open to using information from anywhere in the passage. This is also an EXCEPT question, so you can use the EXCEPT Tool. Put an **S** next to choices supported by the passage, and an **NS** next to the choice with no support.

(A)   They are both mammals.

This is supported by the passage. **C**'s are called mammals in line 3, and **A**'s (of which hippos are a type) are called mammals in line 13. Put an **S**.

(B)   They are both descended from pakicetids.

This is not supported by the passage. **C**'s are now believed to be descended from **P**'s, but all you know about hippos is that they are a type of **A**. Hippos may have been a different type of **A** that did not descend directly from **P**'s. Put an **NS**.

(C)   They share a common ancestor.

This is supported by the passage. In lines 33–34 you learn that they are closely related. From this you can infer that they share a common ancestor. Put an **S**.

(D)   They possess amino acid structures that are somewhat similar.

This is supported by the passage, specifically, lines 34–37. Put an **S**.

(E)   Neither cetaceans nor hippopotamuses are descended from mesonychids.

This is supported by the passage. It matches the current understanding as presented in the fourth paragraph. Put an **S**.

Choice (B) is different from the rest because it has an **NS**. Thus, it's correct.

13.   **Choice (C) is the correct answer.**

This Viewpoint question asks you for something the author would agree with. Since the author endorses the **CU**, the correct answer will likely be close to this.

(A)   Scientists in the future will likely be able to determine which hypothesis of cetacean evolution is correct.

No. The author thinks the answer to this question has already been found and is "generally accepted" (lines 60–61). This **contradicts the passage**.

(B)   The hypothesis that cetaceans evolved from a member of the mesonychid order was baseless.

No. Although the author thinks they were wrong, she says supporters of the **MT** "used morphological evidence and fossil records to support their claim," so the **MT** *was* based on some evidence. This **contradicts the passage**.

(C)   Enhanced understanding of the pakicetids was important in furthering scientific inquiry into the evolution of cetaceans.

Yes. In lines 50–57, the author says that the new evidence that came from the complete **P** skeleton offered solid evidence for the **CU**.

(D)   Genetic evidence is usually a better indicator of a species' evolutionary origin than is the fossil record or morphological evidence.

No. The passage is only concerned with the one case of cetaceans, which can't support a statement about what kind of evidence is "usually" better across all cases. This is **out of scope**.

(E)   The fact that sperm whales possess teeth similar to those possessed by long-extinct members of the mesonychid order proved to be nothing more than coincidental.

No. The author thinks the similarity is not due to an ancestral relationship between the two (that would contradict the **CU**), but she never says there couldn't have been some other reason for the similarity, such as similar food types. This is **out of scope**.

14.   **Choice (D) is the correct answer.**

This is another Inference EXCEPT question. Since the question stem is so vague, move on to the answer choices and use the EXCEPT Tool.

(A)   Scientists do not currently think cetaceans evolved from a member of the mesonychid order.

This is supported by lines 58–60. Put an **S**.

(B)   An ancestor of the orca was an artiodactyl.

This is supported by the passage. Orcas are *C*'s (line 20) and *C*'s are descended from *A*'s (line 61). Put an **S**.

(C)   Porpoises and giraffes are distantly related.

This is supported by the passage. Giraffes are a type of *A*, and porpoises are descended from *A*'s. Put an **S**.

(D)   Hippopotamuses are genetically more closely
            related to dolphins than they are to pigs.

This is not supported by the passage. Lines 33–34 say that *cetaceans'* closest relative is the hippo, but the hippo might be more closely related to something other than a cetacean. Put an **NS**.

(E)   Sperm whales have triangular teeth.

This is supported by lines 18–21. Put an **S**.

Choice (D) is different from all the rest, so pick it.

15. **Choice (B) is the correct answer.**

This Viewpoint question is basically asking you what the *CU* is, which is the answer to the core question: [Modern cetaceans evolved from an extinct family of artiodactyls called pakicetids.]

(A)   Cetaceans descended from pakicetids, which
            descended from mesonychids.

No. This is the **wrong viewpoint**. This is the **MT**.

(B)   Modern cetaceans descended from pakicetids, an
            extinct family of artiodactyl.

Yes. A perfect match for the Prephrased answer.

(C)   Modern whales, dolphins, and porpoises evolved
            from pakicetids, a family of mammals that
            evolved from early cetaceans.

No. This **contradicts the passage**. *C*'s evolved from *P*'s, not the other way around.

(D)   The cetaceans that now live in the ocean
            descended from pakicetids, the same mammalian
            family from which modern hippopotamuses
            descended.

No. Hippos are a type of *A*, but the passage never says they came from *P*'s, which may have been a different kind of *A*. This is **out of scope**.

(E)   Modern cetaceans evolved after an extinct species
            of artiodactyl moved into the open waters of the
            earth's oceans.

No. The passage does not mention at what stage of evolution the ancestors of modern *C*'s took to the water. This is **out of scope**.

IN-CLASS EXAM **ICE** LECTURE **4**

EXPLANATIONS

Drug Advertising Passage

IDENTIFY

You can identify this as Controversy passage because, although there are several viewpoints, the passage is not designed to answer a core question.

ANALYZE

Various Viewpoints

There are three major viewpoints presented in this passage. The pharmaceutical companies' viewpoint is in lines 6–14. The viewpoint of consumer advocacy groups is in lines 15–37. The viewpoint of doctors is in lines 38–63. The author's viewpoint doesn't seem very strongly presented here, although the author dedicates about 85% of the passage to criticisms of the practice of drug advertising and only two sentences to its defense.

Purpose of Each Paragraph

Each paragraph is basically dedicated to a single viewpoint. The purpose of the first paragraph is to introduce the topic and present the pharmaceutical companies' viewpoint.

The purpose of the second paragraph is to present the viewpoint of the consumer advocates. The advocates think that the practice is "problematic" and hurts consumers economically in several ways.

The purpose of the third paragraph is to present the viewpoint of health professionals. They also have a number of complaints, including that the practice leads consumers to seek drugs they don't need or that could actually harm them.

Main Point

There doesn't seem to be any single sentence that sums up the entire passage, so come up with your own main point sentence that captures all the viewpoints and most important ideas. Here's a good one: [Drug companies defend the practice of direct-to-consumer advertising, but consumer advocates think it hurts consumers economically, and physicians think it presents health dangers.]

1. **Choice (A) is the correct answer.**

   This is a Main Point question. Look for something that matches the Prephrased main point above.

   (A)   Although it has brought financial benefits to companies in the pharmaceutical industry, some consumer advocates and a number of health care professionals think the marketing of prescription drugs directly to consumers can be harmful.

   Yes. This is a good match for the Prephrased answer.

   (B)   The United States and New Zealand are the only two countries in the world that allow pharmaceutical companies to market directly to consumers through radio and television advertising.

   No. This is **incomplete**. It only mentions the information in lines 1–5 and ignores the other major topics in the passage.

   (C)   Sleep problems are most frequently due to temporary events and are best treated by stress management or psychotherapy, but prescription medication may also be helpful in alleviating the symptoms.

   No. This seems to **contradict** lines 54–59, and it's also **incomplete** since it doesn't mention the other two major viewpoints.

   (D)   Consumer advocates have argued that direct-to-consumer advertising of prescription drugs is inherently problematic, but many health care practitioners groups find the practice beneficial.

   No. This **contradicts the passage** by misrepresenting the viewpoint of the health care practitioners. They don't like the ads either.

   (E)   Marketing prescription drugs directly to consumers should be allowed to continue in the United States, despite the objections of consumer advocates, who find the practice to be inherently problematic, and health care professionals, who find the practice dangerous.

   No. Most of this choice is good, but the passage never makes a recommendation about whether the marketing should be allowed to continue. That's **out of scope**.

2. **Choice (B) is the correct answer.**

   This is a Weaken question. You found that the industry's viewpoint was presented in the first paragraph, so look there. The two justifications presented are that the ads drive new medical research and provide consumers greater control over their heath care. Look for a choice that weakens either argument by showing that the increased revenues *don't* drive new medical research, or by showing that the education about ailments and treatments *doesn't* provide them with greater control.

   (A)   The pharmaceutical industry has seen unprecedented revenue growth since it began to market prescription drugs directly to consumers.

   No. You already know the industry has enjoyed increased revenue, so this doesn't affect the justifications.

(B)   Since the prescription drug industry began
        marketing directly to consumers, all additional
        revenues earned by prescription pharmaceutical
        companies have gone directly to shareholders.

Yes. This shows that the increased revenues *don't* drive new medical research. The money just makes the shareholders richer.

(C)   In surveys, the majority of American consumers
        admit that most of the information they get about
        prescription drugs comes from television and
        radio advertising.

No. Even if the ads are the primary source of information, that doesn't tell you whether consumers have greater or less control over their health care.

(D)   Prescription drug prices have risen, on average,
        120 percent since pharmaceutical companies
        began marketing prescription drugs directly to
        consumers.

No. Even if this is true, it doesn't tell you anything about whether there is new medical research or whether consumers have greater control.

(E)   Pharmaceutical companies do everything in their
        power to provide the most accurate information
        about their products to consumers.

No. If anything, this is an **opposite** distracter, since if the information were very good, it would be more likely to give people greater control.

3. **Choice (D) is the correct answer.**
    This is a Viewpoint question. The viewpoint of these advocates is found in lines 15–25. They say the ads are "inherently problematic" because the information within them is "intrinsically biased" and can "mislead consumers."

(A)   Increased knowledge of common ailments and
        their latest treatment options allows consumers
        to exercise greater control over their health care.

No. This is the **wrong viewpoint.** This is the industry view of the ads.

(B)   It is rare that patients become convinced they
        are suffering from one malady when they are
        suffering from a completely unrelated condition.

No. This is the opposite of a point made by the doctors in lines 44–47 and has nothing to do with the consumer advocates.

(C)   Pharmaceutical companies attempt to lead healthy
        consumers to believe they are ill in order to grow
        markets and expand the list of conditions that
        should be treated with medication.

No. This is again the **wrong viewpoint.** This has to do with what the doctors were saying in lines 50–63.

(D)   Despite the fact that pharmaceutical
        advertisements may contain a substantial amount
        of information about a drug, many consumers
        attain from them an inaccurate understanding.

Yes. This is a good match for the Prephrased answer.

(E)   New sources of funding have driven increased
        medical research and led to the discovery
        of many new drugs that were unavailable to
        consumers only a few years ago.

No. This is the **wrong viewpoint.** This matches the industry view as expressed on lines 6–10.

4. **Choice (B) is the correct answer.**
    This is an Analogy question since it asks you for a new situation that parallels one in the passage. The major characteristics, in general terms, of the original situation are: *misleading information leads to a problem's misattribution to one cause when there is actually a different cause.*

(A)   A public service campaign regarding a potentially
        dangerous and highly contagious illness causes
        many people to become too afraid to leave their
        own houses.

No. This is missing the idea of the wrong thing being blamed. This is somewhat of a **topic trap**, since it has to do with illness, just like the original situation.

(B)   A propaganda campaign leads many to unfairly
        scapegoat a group of people for a social problem
        rather than blame the groups who actually
        caused the problem.

Yes. The propaganda campaign is the misleading information, and the wrong thing is judged to be the cause of the problem.

(C)   An advertising campaign causes people to believe
        that a certain food product is good for their
        health when, in fact, the product is unhealthy.

No. There is misinformation, but no problem that gets attributed to the wrong cause.

(D)   A fashion trend leads many people to buy and
        constantly wear a certain style of clothing, a
        style that many others see as ridiculous.

No. There is no problem that gets attributed to the wrong cause.

(E)   A marketing campaign for a motion picture portrays the film as being highly respected among movie critics when, in fact, most critics had a completely different opinion on the film.

No. This is like choice (C). There is again misinformation, but no problem gets attributed to the wrong cause.

5. **Choice (E) is the correct answer.**
    This is a Strengthen question. The practitioners' argument is that direct-to-consumer advertisements are "jeopardous" because they can lead healthy consumers to believe they are ill, which in turn would cause them to use medicines (and be exposed to dangerous side effects) when they shouldn't. The only evidence presented to support this claim is an example showing how this *could* come about, but a weakness in the argument is that there is no evidence to say that unnecessary use of medication *actually occurs* as a result of the ads. Look for an answer choice that provides this evidence.

    (A)   Most cases of insomnia can successfully be treated with certain prescription drugs with limited side effects.

    No. This does nothing to show that the ads bring about any danger to patients.

    (B)   A glass of wine before bed has also been found to be an effective and healthy treatment for insomnia.

    No. The healthiness of wine does nothing to prove the danger of the ads. This is **out of scope**.

    (C)   Certain drugs that are used to treat insomnia have been known to cause severe and sometimes fatal respiratory problems in rare cases.

    No. The passage already establishes that some drugs have "serious side effects," so this answer choice adds no new information.

    (D)   Only two percent of those with sleeping problems report that those problems were made better after receiving stress management and psychotherapy treatment.

    No. This casts doubt on the assertion that psychotherapy is a good treatment, but it does nothing to help the argument that the ads are jeopardous.

    (E)   Hypochondriacs are especially likely to believe they suffer from whatever ailment advertised prescription drugs are purported to treat.

    Yes. This provides stronger evidence to say that there are actual occurrences of healthy people believing they need medication, and shows that more advertisements would cause hypochondriacs to believe they suffer from more ailments.

Lecture 4 Explanations

Mandatory Sentencing Passage

IDENTIFY

You can identify this as Controversy passage because, although there are several viewpoints, the passage is not designed to answer a core question.

ANALYZE

Various Viewpoints

The viewpoints in this passage break down roughly between the *proponents* and *opponents* of mandatory sentencing. The first three paragraphs present arguments in favor first, followed by arguments against, and the fourth paragraph is composed completely of opposing arguments. Thus, while the author doesn't present too many opinionated words or sentences not attributed to someone else, the construction of the passage seems to suggest that he agrees with the "against" camp.

Purpose of Each Paragraph

The purpose of the first paragraph is to introduce the topic and the three main points at issue: incapacitation, deterrence, and cost.

The purpose of the second paragraph is to treat the topic of incapacitation. The author presents the proponents' view, then counters it.

The purpose of the third paragraph is to treat the topic of deterrence. Again, the author presents the proponents' view, then counters it.

The purpose of the final paragraph is to treat the topic of cost. Only one view is presented: the opponents' view. The paragraph also mentions that public opinion may be turning.

Main Point

A succinct statement that captures all of the most important ideas from the passage can be synthesized from the material in the end of the first paragraph and the end of the passage: [Mandatory sentencing was accepted by voters on the basis of incapacitation and deterrence, but increased awareness of its cost ineffectiveness and weaknesses in those rationales has begun to shift public opinion.]

6. **Choice (C) is the correct answer.**
    This is an Analogy question. The major components of the original situation, in general terms, are: *knowing that a small transgression will lead to severe consequences causes someone to commit a more serious transgression, since the consequences will be no different.*

(A) After the state dropped the speed limit from 75 to 55 miles per hour in an effort to curb the number of fatal automobile accidents, the number of traffic accidents in the state actually rose.

No. This doesn't have the feature of people making decisions based on knowledge of negative consequences.

(B) By politely asking a talkative group of teenagers to be quiet, the movie theater usher only instigated the rowdy youths to make louder noises.

No. There is no mention of a harsh consequence regardless of the severity of the misbehavior.

(C) When told by his doctor that any additional smoking would cause irreparable damage to his health, the addicted smoker began to vastly exceed his previous self-imposed daily limit of cigarettes.

Yes. A little bit of smoking will lead to severe consequences ("irreparable damage"), so the smoker actually increases the seriousness of his "wrongdoing."

(D) After being informed on Wednesday that she was going to be fired on Friday because she frequently argued with her coworkers, the employee decided not to go to work on Thursday.

No. If her transgression is frequent arguing, then this answer choice is missing any feature where the employee commits a more serious offense than she otherwise would have.

(E) When the principal began punishing truant students with a mandatory five days of detention instead of one, truancy rates at the school dropped dramatically.

No. In this case, the bad behavior decreased rather than increased.

7. **Choice (A) is the correct answer.**

This is a Weaken question. The proponents' argument is that mandatory sentencing removes people from society who would be committing crimes if they were free, and that it discourages people from committing crimes in the first place. Look for a choice that suggests that either of these rationales is untrue.

(A) Although the vast majority of minor misdemeanors are committed by repeat offenders, roughly 74 percent of all serious felonies are committed by first-time offenders.

Yes. If this is true, then it means that the majority of those who commit one felony *don't* commit another—there aren't many repeat offenders. That means locking up those who have committed a

felony is mostly removing people from society who would *not* commit another felony if they were free.

(B) People who live in urban areas are ten times more likely to be convicted of three felonies during their lifetime than are those who live in rural areas.

No. Just because there is a difference between urban and rural populations doesn't mean either of the proponents' rationales is weakened.

(C) Since 1994 the number of incarcerated individuals in California has risen by 41 percent, and the penal system's budget has risen 67 percent.

No. An increased number of people in prison does not necessarily mean that more people are committing crimes; it could simply mean they are staying in prison longer, likely as a result of mandatory sentencing. The other part of this choice has to do with cost, which is not a part of the proponents' argument. Only the opponents mention this.

(D) Most people given long-term sentences under "three strikes" laws committed at least one of their three felonies before they turned 20 years of age.

No. Knowing the age when repeat offenders first went bad has no effect on whether incapacitation or deterrence really works.

(E) Violent crime rates in California dropped dramatically between 1994 and 2001.

No. This is an **opposite** answer, since it would suggest that mandatory sentencing (which came into effect during that time) really worked.

8. **Choice (C) is the correct answer.**

This is an Analogy question. The major components of the original situation, in general terms, are: *general opinion strongly favored something, but counterarguments and new evidence emerged that caused people to begin to reconsider that support.*

(A) the popularity of a governor who took office in a very close election but won reelection four years later by a large margin

No. In the original situation, the public opinion was strongly in favor at first.

(B) the public opinion regarding a music group that was very popular twenty years ago, receded to relative anonymity 10 years ago, and reemerged as a popular group five years ago

No. This has a popularity journey in three parts, whereas the original has only two.

(C) the critical perception of a movie that was lauded by critics when first released, but that is now less enthusiastically received by critics

Yes. Support was enthusiastic at first, but the tide has begun to turn. This is a good match for the Prephrased answer.

(D) the public perception of a restaurant that was very popular when first opened, but, after several food poisoning incidents, was forced by health inspectors to close

No. You're not told what happened to public opinion, and the fact that the restaurant is now closed would be analogous to the laws being repealed, which has not happened.

(E) the popularity of a law that was passed overwhelmingly by voters but was later repealed when a court found it to be unconstitutional

No. This is a **topic trap** because it's about law, but again, the mandatory sentencing laws have not been repealed, so this doesn't match.

9. **Choice (A) is the correct answer.**

This is a Complete question. Look for something that flows logically with the text. In this case, the author has shown that there is new financial evidence against mandatory sentencing and that public opinion is beginning to turn against it. It seems like the author might next make a prediction about such laws being reversed.

(A) Therefore, it would come as little surprise if many mandatory sentencing laws were abolished in some states within the next ten years.

Yes. This is supported by the passage, flows logically with the text, and matches the Prephrased answer.

(B) However, it is likely that states will have to live with their mandatory sentencing laws for many years to come.

No. There is nothing in the passage to suggest that states are stuck with the laws and have no ability to remove them.

(C) Thus, it is likely that mandatory sentencing laws will be created in the few states that do not yet have them.

No. This **does not flow logically** since the preceding sentence says public opinion in other states supports the repeal, not expansion, of such laws.

(D) Due to this negative perception, it is certain that within the next ten years mandatory sentencing laws will be completely removed from the American criminal law system.

No. This is **extreme**. The passage says voters are "inclined to consider alternatives," which is not nearly as strong as "certainty" of their "complete removal."

(E) Although the future of mandatory-minimum sentencing laws is uncertain, it is clear that prisoners will continue to suffer due to the overbearing nature of the laws.

No. This is **out of scope**, since prisoner suffering is not mentioned anywhere in the passage.

10. **Choice (D) is the correct answer.**

This is a Principle question. In the fourth paragraph, the *circumstances* are that mandatory sentencing is less cost effective than prevention programs. The *outcome* is that the opponents call for the end of mandatory sentencing. The correct answer should match these two components.

(A) Taxpayer funds should be spent in the manner in which taxpayers want them spent.

No. The basis for decision should be cost effectiveness, not public opinion.

(B) Moral considerations should be taken into account by policymakers.

No. The proponents argue from a monetary, not moral, angle.

(C) Economic considerations should take precedent over moral considerations.

No. Again, moral considerations are not mentioned in the fourth paragraph.

(D) When presented with multiple options, the government should spend funds in the most efficient manner.

Yes. Picking the most cost efficient option means avoiding the least cost-efficient option. This matches the circumstances and the outcome.

(E) An action designed to prevent a certain kind of behavior often encourages a more severe manifestation of that very behavior.

No. This looks like the argument in the third paragraph, lines 43–47. That's the wrong argument.

Early Americans Passage

Identify

You can identify this as Controversy passage because, although there are several viewpoints, the passage is not designed to answer a core question.

ANALYZE

Various Viewpoints

In addition to the author's viewpoint, there are three major theories presented. The Clovis theory says people came across the Bering land bridge. The coastal migration theory says people came by sea from Siberia. The Solutrean hypothesis says they came over ice pack from Europe. The author thinks all of these theories are problematic.

Purpose of Each Paragraph

The purpose of the first paragraph is to present the Clovis theory in detail and assert that it once enjoyed wide support.

The purpose of the second paragraph is to present the evidence against the Clovis theory, both archaeological and genetic.

The purpose of the third paragraph is to explain the coastal migration theory and point out its shortcoming—a lack of artifactual evidence.

The purpose of the fourth paragraph is to explain the Solutrean hypothesis and point out its shortcoming—contradiction by genetic evidence.

The purpose of the fifth paragraph is to convey the level of disagreement in the field and present the author's viewpoint and main point.

Main Point

The main point is the last sentence in the passage: [The field of paleoamerican archeology presently lacks a dominant theory regarding initial peopling of the Americas, as all current hypotheses have significant evidentiary problems.]

11. **Choice (A) is the correct answer.**

    This is an Analogy question. The problem with the theory, expressed in general terms, is that *a certain kind of evidence is expected but has not been found.*

    (A)   the inability to find a murder weapon during a homicide investigation

    Yes. This is a good match for the Prephrased answer. The murder weapon is the kind of evidence that is expected but has not been found.

    (B)   the presence of conflicting genetic evidence in an assault investigation

    No. The word *genetic* is a **word trap**, but there is no *conflicting* evidence in the original situation.

    (C)   the discovery that a prime suspect in a robbery investigation has a credible alibi

    No. This would discredit some evidence, but that never happened to the coastal migration theory.

    (D)   the presentation by a group of UFO enthusiasts of a metal rod as evidence strengthening a theory that extraterrestrials visited Earth

    No. In this choice, the evidence is present, not missing.

    (E)   the existence of tools of unknown age as the sole evidence supporting a theory about the initial peopling of the Australian continent

    No. This is a **topic trap** since it's about the initial peopling of a continent, but it doesn't match the Prephrased answer.

12. **Choice (B) is the correct answer.**

    This is a Weaken question. The argument in lines 43–50 is the Solutrean hypothesis—it concludes that people crossed from France to North America over ice pack, based on the premise that their tools are similar. Look for an answer choice that suggests that, regardless of the similar tools, people did *not* cross from France to North America over ice pack.

    (A)   New genetic studies have shown that Native Americans and the Basque people of southern France and northern Spain are more closely related than previously believed.

    No. This is an **opposite** answer that would strengthen the Solutrean hypothesis.

    (B)   Scientists have concluded that North America and Europe have not been linked by ice in the Atlantic for over 80,000 years.

    Yes. If there were no ice pack, then crossing the ice pack would be impossible. This definitely weakens the argument.

    (C)   Recently discovered settlements off the western coast of North America have been dated to exactly 20,000 years ago.

    No. The Solutrean hypothesis as described in this passage doesn't mention the date of crossing, so this has no effect on the argument.

    (D)   It has been discovered that no ice-free corridor existed in what is now western Canada 11,500 years ago.

    No. The ice-free corridor is a part of the Clovis theory and is not involved in the Solutrean hypothesis.

    (E)   Stone tools found in Virginia also resemble stone tools discovered near Clovis, New Mexico.

    No. This simply says there was travel between Virginia and New Mexico, which does not affect any theory about how people got to North America in the first place.

13. Choice (B) is the correct answer.

This is an Analogy question. In general terms, the scholarship started out with a single dominant theory, but is now characterized by competition between a number of different theories.

(A)   scholarship regarding the Egyptian pyramids in which a single prevailing theory of the structures' origin is constantly being challenged by new theories

No. This is a **topic trap** as it's also about scholarship, but it doesn't match because there is no "single prevailing theory" in current paleoamerican archaeology.

(B)   the soup industry, which is now highly competitive due to several newer brands that took market share from a brand that dominated the industry for decades

Yes. There was once a dominant player, but there is now a crowded field. This is a good match for the Prephrased answer.

(C)   cosmology, a field that is constantly refining and changing its theories on the origin of the universe

No. This lacks the feature of a once-dominant single theory.

(D)   scholarship regarding the extinction of the dinosaurs, a field in which recent developments have allowed a widely accepted theory to emerge

No. You're looking for a choice in which the "widely accepted theory" declined, not recently emerged.

(E)   the carbonated beverage industry, which has been dominated by two competing companies for most of the twentieth century

No. The passage doesn't mention two dominant players.

14. Choice (E) is the correct answer.

This is a Weaken question. The Clovis theory says people followed game across the Bering land bridge around 11,500 years ago, passed through Canada via an ice-free corridor, then proceeded to populate the remainder of the continent. Look for any answer choice that suggests this was *not* the case.

(A)   the revelation that stone tools purported to have been found in Virginia were planted there by unethical European researchers

No. This would discredit the evidence against Clovis, thereby strengthening the theory. This is an **opposite** distracter.

(B)   test results that definitively date the oldest human artifacts found at Pennsylvania's Meadowcroft Rockshelter to 10,500 years ago

No. This would be consistent with the Clovis timeline and would do nothing to weaken it.

(C)   artifactual evidence indicating humans migrated through western Canada 11,500 years ago

No. This would be consistent with the Clovis theory and would probably strengthen it. This is an **opposite** distracter.

(D)   the discovery of 13,000-year-old spear points in Siberia that are similar to the Clovis spear points

No. This would also strengthen the Clovis hypothesis by showing that the people who supposedly came from Siberia were in the right place just before they are thought to have made that journey.

(E)   evidence that shows no game animals ever crossed over the Bering land bridge

Yes. People can't follow game through a place where game never went.

15. Choice (C) is the correct answer.

This is a Strengthen question. The coastal migration theory states that people first arrived in the Americas from Siberia several thousand years before the Clovis culture flourished, and arrived by sea, skirting the Pacific coast and sustaining themselves on fish and fauna from an ice-free coastal ribbon situated between the sea and interior glaciers. Look for an answer choice that suggests that this was indeed the case.

(A)   Recently, Clovis spear points were discovered that date from around 20,000 years ago.

No. This statement supports a modified Clovis theory, but not necessarily the coastal migration theory as it is presented in the passage.

(B)   The Pacific coast of South America was populated well before the Atlantic coast of North America, but it was not populated as early as the Great Lakes region of North America.

No. This is **out of scope**. The coastal migration theory mentions only the Pacific coast of North America, not any of those other places.

(C)   During the last Ice Age, a period lasting from approximately 70,000 years ago until 10,000 years ago, the glaciers that covered a large portion of North America never extended all the way to the Pacific Ocean.

Yes. This confirms that an ice-free ribbon existed between the Pacific Ocean and North America's glaciers at the right time, a fact that needs to be true for the coastal migration theory to be possible.

(D)   Archeologists have recently shown that similarities between 16,000-year-old stone tools found in France and stone tools unearthed in Virginia are not as great as was first thought by scholars.

No. Although this would weaken the Solutrean hypothesis, it does not specifically strengthen the argument for the coastal migration theory.

(E)   Recent evidence shows that an ice-free corridor existed in western Canada for a first time approximately 20,000 years ago, and for a second time approximately 11,500 years ago.

No. This statement strengthens the Clovis theory or a similar land-migration theory, but it would not strengthen the coastal migration theory at all.

EXPLANATIONS

Lecture 5 Explanations

MMORPG Passage

IDENTIFY

You can identify this as a Comparative Reading set because there are two passages.

ANALYZE

Main Point

The main point of passage A is that [A full account of the addictive nature of these games must analyze the two ways in which they differ from conventional games: first, that they take much longer to complete, and second, that they are played communally by thousands of players at the same time.]

The main point of passage B is that [...on balance, MMORPGs are worthwhile to society because of their unique ability to be used as a tool for the collection of research data.]

Purpose of Each Paragraph

The purpose of the first paragraph in passage A is to introduce the topic and the main point.

The purpose of the second paragraph is to describe scheduled reward systems and how they contribute to MMORPG addiction.

The purpose of the third paragraph is to describe how competitive social hierarchies in games contribute to their addictiveness.

In passage B, the purpose of the first paragraph is to introduce the topic and the main point.

The purpose of the second paragraph is to describe how economists, specifically Castronova, are using MMORPGs in their research.

The purpose of the third paragraph is to demonstrate how MMORPGs can be useful to psychologists by investigating how one psychologist is using them in her work.

Other Components

Passage A functions as a miniature Enlightenment passage, designed to answer the core question, "Why are MMORPGs more addictive than other computer games?" Its structure is organized around the two factors named in the first paragraph.

Passage B functions as a miniature Thesis passage with a single viewpoint. Although other researchers are mentioned, the author simply uses their research to support her main point; they do not present separate arguments or viewpoints.

Relationship Between the Passages

Although they are both concerned with MMORPGs, their scope is somewhat different. Passage A investi-gates the causal mechanism behind *one aspect* of the games (their addictiveness). Passage B asserts that the games *as a whole* are beneficial to society and explores several useful aspects of them. Thus, the passages are not directly concerned with the same topics.

Each Author's Response to the Other

Look for places in which the passages address the same issue. In each of the first paragraphs, the authors address the harmfulness or benefits of the games. Be careful: although author A says the games are more harmful than other computer games, you don't know if he feels they are harmful or beneficial as a whole. Both authors address the exchange of goods, and both authors address social interactions—author A says these factors contribute to the games' addictiveness, and author B says studying these factors can lead to useful results. These viewpoints are not mutually exclusive.

1. **Choice (E) is the correct answer.**

   This is a dual Analogy question because the question stem asks you to find the answer that is most analogous to the relationship between the passages. You determined the first half of the analogy (the relationship between passage A and passage B) in your initial analysis of the passage (and in the correct answer to question 3, if you saved question 1 until after you answered the Relationship question).

   (A)   a philosophical discourse arguing for the ban of stem cell research; another investigating the possible applications of stem cells

   No. The second part of this answer is not bad, because Passage B does look toward possible benefits of MMORPGs, but Passage A never argues for a ban of MMORPGs—it only tries to show why they are addictive. This answer choice **misrepresents a passage.**

   (B)   a research report on the history of psychological disorders; another related to research methods involving those disorders

   No. Neither of these answer choices quite matches either passage. Passage A talks about a psychological condition, but not its history. Passage B is not primarily about a research method—it's more concerned with applications of research. This answer choice **misrepresents both passages.**

   (C)   an account of the two events that led to a major battle; propaganda from one of the involved countries calling for citizens to join the fight

   No. The first part of this answer is okay, as the first passage does try to give a causal account, but the second passage is not disseminating propaganda for MMORPGs or calling for anyone to do anything. This answer **misrepresents a passage.**

(D)   an analyst's report on two factors considered by those who raise interest rates; an editorial listing social implications of such decisions

No. Passage A does discuss two aspects that cause something, and passage B does cover the social implications of something, but this answer goes wrong in how it relates the two arguments. For them to have the same relationship, passage A would talk about the two causes of MMORPG addiction, but passage B would have to talk about the social benefits of the same thing—of MMORPG addiction—which it does not. This answer **misrepresents the relationship**.

(E)   a biologist's investigation of how chemical fertilizers damage waterways; a report extolling the benefits of contemporary methods of farming

Yes. Passage A explores the cause of a certain negative aspect of MMORPGs (their addictiveness), just like the biologist's study explores the cause of a certain negative aspect of modern farming (fertilizers' harm to waterways). Passage B is concerned with the overall benefits of MMORPGs, just like the report is concerned with the overall benefits of modern farming.

2. **Choice (B) is the correct answer.**

This is a dual Viewpoint question because it asks you to infer a viewpoint that the authors share. You can't Prephrase precisely what the correct answer will be, but you can predict that the correct answer will be concerned with something both authors addressed. There were a few topics in common: the harm/benefits of the games, the competition for items, and the social interactions.

(A)   MMORPGs allow players the satisfaction of mastering difficult rules systems.

No. The difficulty of rules systems is not mentioned in either passage. The answer is **out of scope**.

(B)   The social interactions between players in MMORPGs are real, even though the environment in which they act is not.

Yes. Both passages talk about the social interactions between players. The last paragraph in passage A is about the desire to dominate social hierarchies in which players have membership, and the last paragraph of passage B is about Turkle's analysis of the social interactions between players.

(C)   The market interactions between players brokering special items are hampered by competition for greater status in social hierarchies.

No. Passage A never mentions market interactions, and passage B never mentions social hierarchies, so there is not enough support to determine how either author would feel about this statement. This answer is **out of scope**.

(D)   MMORPGs are the most addictive of all massively multiplayer online games because they utilize the ability of role-playing games to draw a player into a scheduled reward system.

No. Passage B never discusses scheduled reward systems. This is **one-sided**.

(E)   The popularity of fantasy-themed MMORPGs is due solely to a desire for players to dominate the intense class structure of an imaginary society.

No. Only passage A mentions anything about the domination of a hierarchy as an explanation for the addictiveness of MMORPGs, but even then it never mentions why MMORPGs are popular. This is part **one-sided**, part **out of scope**.

3. **Choice (C) is the correct answer.**

This is a Relationship question because it asks you to pick the answer that best describes how these two passages are related to each other. You determined this in your initial analysis of the passage.

(A)   Passage A advocates the ban of a social endeavor, while passage B details its benefits.

No. Passage B does establish some benefits of MMORPGs, but as you saw earlier, passage A does not call for a ban of anything. This answer choice **misrepresents a passage**.

(B)   Passage A relates an account of a phenomenon, while passage B disputes that account.

No. Passage B does not attempt to refute passage A's account. This answer choice **misrepresents the relationship**.

(C)   Passage A argues for a particular understanding of a condition associated with a phenomenon, while passage B argues for positive externalities of the phenomenon.

Yes. The "condition" is the addictiveness, and the "phenomenon" is MMORPGs. The "positive externalities" are the research findings that can be applied to other areas of study.

(D)   If the assertions made in passage A are true, then at least some of the assertions made in passage B are false.

No. The point of passage A is unrelated to the claims of passage B. Even if the games are more harmful than other computer games, they could still, as a whole, be a benefit to society. This answer choice **misrepresents the relationship**.

(E) The assertions in passage B, if true, lend support to the main argument made in passage A.

No. Nothing in passage B has anything to do with the causal mechanism of addictiveness. The answer choice **misrepresents the relationship**.

4. **Choice (B) is the correct answer.**

This is a dual Match question because it asks you to match something in one passage against an answer inferred from the other passage. Passage A mentions two competitive aspects of the games in lines 30–36: simulated combat and competition for powers and items, and both are mentioned in the context of the impulse to dominate a social hierarchy. Since you are looking for an example of the competitive aspect that Castronova mentions, and since Castronova is concerned with an economy of goods and services, the correct answer must give an example of competition for powers or items.

(A) a decreasing empathic concern by players for others because of the desire to advance in a social hierarchy

No. Passage B never talks about how empathy in MMORPGs relates to competition.

(B) the increasing price of in-game goods as players attempt to surpass others in the social hierarchy of the game community

Yes. This is a good match for the Prephrased answer.

(C) the decreasing price of in-game goods as players attempt to sell commodities to simplify the complexity of game play

No. Passage B never mentions anything about the complexity of game play as an important factor in MMORPGs.

(D) the acceptance by players of economic incentives to produce goods as cheaply and quickly as possible

No. This doesn't relate to how the exchange of goods is discussed in passage A.

(E) the eagerness of players to beat others to the next achievable in-game high

No. The author of passage B never mentions anything about highs or any animosity between players.

5. **Choice (E) is the correct answer.**

This is a Response question, so the correct answer will fall within the scope of things that both authors discussed, as identified in your initial analysis. Because this question stem asks for the response that author B would be LEAST likely to

have, look for a choice that *contradicts* a claim that author B makes.

(A) The harms of MMORPGs are outweighed by the other benefits that society gains through them.

No. The author of passage B says exactly this in the first paragraph, so this answer fails to contradict the passage.

(B) The amount of content and playing time inherent in MMORPGs has a significant impact on their productivity as research tools.

No. Passage B contains no information about what affects the productivity of MMORPGs. The author could accept a number of explanations that are consistent with the points made. This answer is **out of scope**.

(C) Further social research on MMORPGs might allow more evidence to prove the claims in passage A.

No. Passage B does not mention any response to a claim like the one made in passage A. Based on what is known, it is equally likely that author B would support or reject passage A.

(D) There is no significant social aspect involved in an account of the addictive properties of these games.

No. Passage B does suggest that there is a social aspect to these games, but does not comment on whether this social aspect affects the addictiveness of MMORPGs.

(E) Popular MMORPGs do not generate useful research because their addictiveness eliminates social role-playing interactions.

Yes. Any claim that MMORPGs do not generate useful research directly contradicts the claims in passage B, lines 40–45. It is clear from passage B that the author believes that MMORPGs allow for the generation of useful research, regardless of whether or not they are addictive.

Students' Rights Passage

IDENTIFY

You can identify this as a Comparative Reading set because there are two passages.

ANALYZE

Main Point

The main point of passage A is that [Safety is a vital part of {children's} development, and schools are thus justified in violating the civil liberties of students in order to achieve safety.]

The main point of passage B is that [concern for safety ought to be balanced against the other needs of students.] The needs passage B mentions most are the autonomy of students and their freedom of political expression.

Purpose of Each Paragraph

In passage A, the purpose of the first paragraph is to introduce the topic and main point.

The purpose of the second paragraph is to introduce the argument that safety is a necessary prerequisite for other more important rights.

In the third paragraph, the author's purpose is to show that the school environment has special needs and circumstances that justify violating the civil liberties of students.

The author's purpose in the fourth paragraph is to demonstrate that preventing students from bringing weapons to school or harming other students justifies infringing on their privacy rights, even if that means harming their development.

In passage B, the purpose of the first paragraph is to introduce the main point.

The purpose of the second paragraph is to argue that political expression is important, and thus should only be limited in cases in which a student might harm another with that expression.

The purpose of the third paragraph is to deal with a possible objection to this claim by arguing that even if political expression threatens the stability of a school, it should be allowed in order to bring necessary reform to the school.

Other Components

Passage A functions as a miniature Thesis passage, designed to argue that safety takes priority over guarantees of student civil liberties.

Passage B is also a miniature Thesis passage, designed to argue that safety and student civil liberties ought to be balanced against each other.

Relationship Between the Passages

The two passages are not direct negations of each other, but they are at odds. While passage A argues that safety takes precedence over civil liberties, passage B argues that it *does not* in all cases—there must be a balance between the two.

It's also important to note that both passages cite Supreme Court cases as supporting evidence. So one way in which the passages are related is that they cite evidence from the same source but reach opposing conclusions.

Each Author's Response to the Other

Look for places in which the passages address the same topic. Safety plays an important role in both passages. In passage A, the author says, "While safety is not more valuable in itself than any of our other needs, it must take priority because it is the prerequisite to the expression of all higher aims" (lines 12–15), while in passage B the author says, "Safety for students is of course one of our paramount values, but concern for safety ought to be balanced against the other needs of students" (lines 39–41).

Both passages also talk about students' development. In passage A, the author suggests that by ensuring safety we are doing the right thing, even if we harm development by limiting student civil liberties. In passage B, the author states that we must always balance civil liberties against safety, and that sometimes a little instability is acceptable in order to preserve the liberties that are an important part of students' development.

6. **Choice (C) is the correct answer.**

   This is a dual Search question because it asks you to find something mentioned in one passage but not the other. You can Prephrase an answer to this question. Passage A mentions a few things to be weighed against safety: civil liberties (line 5), the right to privacy (line 32), and the capacity for personal acts of expression (lines 34–35). However, passage B also mentions civil liberties and personal expression (lines 55–57), so the correct answer cannot refer to those and is likely to be about the right to privacy.

   (A)   the right of students to critique school practices

   No. This is mentioned in passage B in line 64.

   (B)   the ability of students to express themselves politically

   No. This is mentioned in passage B in lines 56–57.

   (C)   students' right to privacy in their personal spaces on campus

   Yes. This is mentioned in passage A (lines 29–32) but not in passage B.

   (D)   the convincing threat of harm presented by published speech against schools

   No. This is not specifically mentioned in either passage, although it is a mixed-up conglomeration of ideas mentioned in passage B.

   (E)   the inculcation of the values of democracy in students

   No. This is mentioned in passage B (lines 68–71).

7. **Choice (A) is the right answer.**

This is a Response question. Since author A also cites Supreme Court rulings, he must feel they are relevant, and his response must agree with his overall main point. Author A is most likely to agree with a choice that acknowledges the rulings cited in passage B but that shows how they still allow for his own conclusion to be true.

(A)   The rulings do not subvert the primacy of safety considerations because they acknowledge exceptions in cases in which a student presents a convincing threat of harm.

Yes. This is a good match for the Prephrased answer.

(B)   The rulings directly contradict other Supreme Court judgments such as *New Jersey v. T.L.O.* and must therefore be rejected.

No. There is no direct contradiction between the rulings, and there is no evidence in passage A that its author would reject other evidence.

(C)   The rulings are not relevant to the argument presented in passage A because they were reached by justices who no longer serve on the Court.

No. The justices and whether they still serve on the Court is never mentioned and is **out of scope**.

(D)   No evidence from Supreme Court cases is pertinent to the issue of limiting students' civil liberties because the Court has not been asked to consider the vital consideration of safety.

No. This **contradicts the passage**. Author A clearly thinks evidence from Supreme Court cases is relevant because he cites it himself.

(E)   The rulings establish that the concern for safety must be duly weighed against respect for the autonomy of students.

No. This is the **wrong viewpoint**. It corresponds to author B's thesis as presented in lines 39–41.

8. **Choice (C) is the correct answer.**

This is a dual Viewpoint question because it asks you to find an issue over which the authors disagree. You know both authors disagree on the relative value of safety and on the development of students, so the correct answer probably refers to one of those.

(A)   Allowing free expression of political aims leads to greater disorder in schools.

No. The author of passage A never says anything about disorder in schools, and although it may seem likely for the author to take this view, there is no evidence LSAT that this is definitely the case. This answer choice is **one-sided**.

(B)   Schools must be devoid of any danger before other developmental aims can be achieved.

No. Passage B never mentions anything about the developmental priority of safety, and its author might think that political expression is impossible if students are extremely worried about their safety. This answer choice is **one-sided**.

(C)   Ensuring a safe school environment takes precedence over fostering a child's capacity for personal acts of expression.

Yes. Author A calls this restriction "necessary" (line 35), but author B says these two needs must be "balanced" (line 41).

(D)   Restricting privacy harms students' self-expression.

No. As you saw in your initial analysis, only passage A talks about privacy. Author B could go either way on this answer choice, so it is **one-sided**.

(E)   Schools should not be concerned with preparing students to be vigilant against abuses of authority.

No. Author A never mentions anything about the abuse of authority, and so this answer choice is also **one-sided**.

9. **Choice (D) is the correct answer.**

This is a Relationship question because it asks you to express the relationship between the two passages. You did the necessary work for this question in your initial analysis of the passage.

(A)   Passage A draws its conclusion based on psychological principles, while passage B relies on a purely rhetorical appeal to reach an unrelated conclusion.

No. Passage A employs just one psychological principle (lines 12–15), and passage B makes an argument for its claim using Supreme Court rulings. This answer choice **misrepresents the passages**.

(B)   Passage A relies on legal precedent to justify its claims and passage B cites inconsistencies among those precedents to reach an opposing conclusion.

No. Both passages cite legal precedent and neither passage talks about inconsistencies among those precedents, so this answer choice **misrepresents the passages**.

(C)   Passage A relies on anecdotal evidence, while passage B appeals to the authority of longstanding tradition to reach an opposing conclusion.

No. The evidence used in passage A is legal cases, not anecdotes, and passage B makes no such claim in regard in to tradition. This answer choice **misrepresents the passages**.

(D) The passages cite different bodies of evidence from the same legal source to reach opposing conclusions.

Yes. The same legal source is the Supreme Court, but the authors cite different cases (bodies of evidence) and reach opposing conclusions. This matches the Prephrased answer.

(E) The passages cite different psychological principles but the same legal cases, and both reach the same conclusion.

No. The two passages do not reach the same conclusion. This answer choice **misrepresents the relationship**.

10. **Choice (E) is the correct answer.**

This is a Response question since it asks you to express how author B would respond to something expressed in passage A. Author A thinks those needs are such that safety must take priority over other needs, but author B disagrees. Author B thinks respect for the autonomy of students is equally important.

(A) Because it depends on an unreasonable expectation of privacy, the ability to question the authority of a school does not represent a vital interest for students.

No. This **contradicts** what the author of passage B says in lines 68–71.

(B) These needs are no longer a concern because the precedent in *Hazelwood School District v. Kuhlmeier* has been overturned by subsequent rulings.

No. This answer choice is **out of scope** because neither passage mentions any cases being overturned.

(C) The elimination of subversive materials on school property is a more significant need than that of personal expression.

No. This is the **wrong viewpoint**. This represents what author A says on lines 29–36.

(D) While personal autonomy is not more valuable in itself than other needs, it must take priority because it is the prerequisite to an environment of safety.

No. This answer choice is a direct contradiction of lines 12–15, but it is not supported by anything in passage B.

(E) The needs of schools include both safety and a respect for the rights of students and thus must be balanced to reflect both.

Yes. This answer choice matches the thesis of passage B, and directly responds to the issue of special needs raised in passage A.

Revolution Passage

IDENTIFY

You can identify this as a Comparative Reading set because there are two passages.

ANALYZE

Main Point

Each passage functions as a miniature Thesis passage, with a thesis statement in the first paragraph. The main point of passage A is that [Though the framers of the constitution made the natural right to revolution into a legal right, recognition of a legal right to revolution is unnecessary in a modern democracy.]

The main point of passage B is that [Though there is no such thing as a legal right to revolution, there is a natural right to revolution—an incontrovertible personal authority to resist forces hostile to one's personhood.]

Purpose of Each Paragraph

In passage A, the purpose of the first paragraph is to introduce the topic and convey the main point.

The purpose of the second paragraph is to argue that the legal right to revolution is unnecessary because revolution would be ineffective.

The purpose of the third paragraph is to argue that the legal right to revolution is unnecessary because people's wrongs can be addressed through the system or through otherwise peaceful means.

In passage B, the purpose of the first paragraph is to introduce the topic and convey the main point.

The purpose of the second paragraph is to argue that the natural right to revolution still exists even if it would not be effective.

The purpose of the third paragraph is to argue that the existence of a natural right to revolution is not contrary to the stability of society.

Other Components

The passages act as miniature Thesis passages, so there are no various viewpoints, major structural elements, or core questions to take note of. There are some strongly opinionated words in passage B, such as "absurd" (line 38), "foolishly" (line 44), "incorrectly" (line 58), and "erroneously" (line 61). These give passage B a more confrontational tone.

Relationship Between the Passages

Both passages acknowledge a difference between a *legal* right and a *natural* right, but passage A's main focus is on the legal right to revolution, while passage B's main focus is on the natural right to revolution. Thus, while there are secondary points on which the authors may agree or disagree, the passages are concerned with making arguments about related but different topics.

Each Author's Response to the Other

Look for places where the authors pass judgment about the same topic. Both authors speak of the legal right to revolution and the natural right to revolution. Author B directly contradicts author A in lines 36–38 when she says there was never a legal right to revolution, whereas author A says the legal right to revolution was established by the constitution (lines 3–7).

The other issue addressed by both authors is the effectiveness of trying to start a revolution. In his second paragraph, author A says the impossibility of armed resistance to the government means there should be no legal right to revolution. In her second paragraph, author B says that even if revolution would be ineffective, the natural right to it still exists. These points don't directly contradict each other, but it's important to notice that both authors are addressing the same issue.

11. **Choice (A) is the correct answer.**

    This is a Main Point question that only relates to passage B. Look for something that matches the Prephrased main point from your initial analysis.

    (A) People have the inviolate right to exit social agreements that stray from their purpose.

    Yes. This is a fancy way of saying people have the natural right to revolution.

    (B) Democratic methods are insufficient as a means of correcting faulty governance.

    No. Author A says democratic institutions are sufficient, but author B never contradicts this. She just says it doesn't matter whether there are sufficient legal methods—the natural right to revolution always exists.

    (C) The power of modern militaries makes the expression of the right to revolution dangerous.

    No. Author B never mentions the power of modern militaries. This is **out of scope**.

    (D) The natural right to revolution derives its force of appeal from its codification in founding legal doctrines.

    No. This **contradicts the passage**. Author B says the natural right to revolution comes from the natural right to liberty. She says there is no such thing as a legal right to revolution.

    (E) Respecting the natural right to revolution does not unduly harm the rule of law.

    No. This is **incomplete** since it is an idea mentioned in the third paragraph but is not the main point of the passage.

12. **Choice (C) is the correct answer.**

    This is a Relationship question. In your initial analysis of the passages you found that, while there are secondary points on which the authors may agree or disagree, the passages are concerned with making arguments about related but different topics. Look for an answer choice that matches this.

    (A) Both passages address a single issue from directly opposing viewpoints.

    No. There is more than one issue, and the authors don't directly oppose each other.

    (B) Both passages address a single issue from essentially the same viewpoint.

    No. The authors do not share the same viewpoint.

    (C) Both passages address slightly different concerns and hold different conclusions regarding the aspects they share in common.

    Yes. The slightly different concerns are the legal right to revolution and the natural right to revolution; the aspects they share in common are whether the constitution gives a legal right to revolution and what the ineffectiveness of revolution means regarding the various rights to it.

    (D) Both passages address slightly different concerns and hold essentially the same view regarding those concerns.

    No. The two main points are too different to be called essentially the same.

    (E) Both passages address entirely different ideas, and neither passage contradicts the other in its presentation.

    No. The ideas are related, and there is some minor contradiction that occurs.

13. **Choice (B) is the correct answer.**

    This is a dual Attitude question. In your initial analysis, you saw that the strongly opinionated words in passage B made it more adversarial. Passage A lacks such words and is a little more measured or professional.

    (A) apprehensive

    No. Passage A argues against the need for a legal right to revolution, but it doesn't seem worried about anything.

(B)   dispassionate

Yes. Passage A is indeed less emotional or confrontational.

(C)   speculative

No. Passage A is not based on conjecture or incomplete information.

(D)   abstract

No. Passages A and B deal with equally abstract ideas.

(E)   disparaging

No. This is an **opposite** answer since, if any passage expresses contempt, it's passage B.

14.   **Choice (E) is the correct answer.**

This is a dual Viewpoint question. Because it asks for a point of disagreement, it is basically the same as a Point at Issue question from the Logical Reasoning section of the test. In your initial analysis, you found an explicit disagreement. Author B directly contradicts author A in lines 36–38 when she says there was never a legal right to revolution, whereas author A says the legal right to revolution was established by the constitution (lines 3–7).

(A)   If people felt legally empowered to break the law whenever it presented them with inconvenience, no one would ever obey the law.

No. This is **one-sided**. Author B addresses this topic in lines 60–63, but author A never does.

(B)   The extreme difference in power between the military and citizens makes it impossible for an attempt at violent revolution to succeed.

No. This is also **one-sided**. Author A says this in lines 18–21. Although author B acknowledges that circumstances could render defiance ineffective, she never names those circumstances.

(C)   The most important quality of liberty is a respect for the self-determination of individuals.

No. Author A never mentions liberty or its most important qualities.

(D)   Civil disobedience is the most effective manner in which citizens can affect laws they see as unjust.

No. Author A says civil disobedience can be successful, but he doesn't call it the most effective manner (that's **extreme**), and author B never mentions it at all, so this choice is also **one-sided**.

(E)   The framers of the U.S. constitution intended the second amendment to give citizens the legal right to revolution.

Yes. This matches the explicit disagreement in the Prephrased answer.

15.   **Choice (B) is the correct answer.**

This is a Response question. Author A uses lines 18–21 to show that revolutionary force would not result in success for the unhappy citizen, a point he uses to support the thesis that there should be no legal right to revolution. Author B says in lines 54–57 that the natural right to revolution is unchanged even when it would be ineffective, so author B would respond to these lines by saying that the situation doesn't affect the natural right to revolution.

(A)   Such a response by the military and law enforcement would be unjustified given citizens' legal right to revolution.

No. Author B doesn't believe people have a legal right to revolution.

(B)   The unavoidable failure of the revolutionary force in such a case does not impinge on citizens' natural right to revolution.

Yes. This is a good match for the Prephrased answer.

(C)   Law enforcement and the military would only respond in such a way in order to avert widespread disrespect for the rule of law.

No. Author B never cites anything to indicate what she would have to say about the motives of the military. This is **out of scope**.

(D)   Because the exercise of the legal right to revolution would result in a failure to achieve redress, that right should be eliminated.

No. This is the **wrong viewpoint**. This is author A's main point.

(E)   The situation underscores the superiority of the natural right to revolution over the legal right to revolution.

No. Author B is not concerned with which right is superior, especially since she doesn't feel the legal right to revolution even exists.

IN-CLASS EXAM ICE LECTURE 6

EXPLANATIONS

Treaty of Waitangi Passage

Identify

You can identify this as Controversy passage because, although there are several viewpoints, the passage is not designed to answer a core question.

Analyze

Various Viewpoints

There are a number of viewpoints presented in this passage. The first belongs to those who support the English version of the treaty, presented in lines 11–19. The second belongs to those who are concerned with the Maori version, which is in lines 20–38. The conservative historians present their case in lines 43–58. Finally, the author's viewpoint is present throughout, when he uses opinionated phrases such as "questionable" (line 3), "seems" (line 7), "said to exist" (line 9), "a matter of interpretation" (line 38), and other phrases that indicate that the author is presenting *all* viewpoints in the passage as debatable.

Purpose of Each Paragraph

The purpose of the first paragraph is to introduce the topic and show that there is still debate about the legal status of the treaty.

The purpose of the second paragraph is to convey the viewpoint of those who support the English version of the treaty: the Maori gave up some rights in order to become British subjects.

The purpose of the third paragraph is to convey some of the controversy around the Maori version of the treaty: some parts may be explicitly different from the English version, and some parts' meaning revolves around the interpretation of certain invented words.

The purpose of the fourth paragraph is to present the viewpoint of the conservative historians: the two parties' understanding of the oral agreement at the time is what's truly binding.

Main Point

The author never presents one viewpoint as being the correct one. His purpose is to explore the controversy, not resolve it. You can discern this because all of his opinionated phrases function to present each viewpoint as debatable. Thus, a good main point can be summed up from the material in the first paragraph: [Though its use by national courts seems to secure the Treaty of Waitangi's legitimacy, considerable debate continues to surround the discrepancies said to exist between the English-language and Maori versions.]

1. **Choice (D) is the correct answer.**

   This is a Main Point question. Look for an answer choice that matches the Prephrased main point you put together in your initial analysis of the passage.

   (A) New Zealand's courts have decided several recent claims based on the oral version of the Treaty of Waitangi, which is the part of the agreement that the Maori of the time accepted as binding.

   No. This makes no mention of the debate surrounding the treaty. This is **incomplete**.

   (B) Native New Zealanders have achieved several major settlements regarding forests and fisheries due to the recent deciphering of words such as *kawanatanga* and *rangatiratanga*.

   No. This also makes no mention of the debate surrounding the treaty, which is **incomplete**, and the passage never said those two words were "recently deciphered."

   (C) Considering the problems surrounding its framing and subsequent misinterpretations, the Treaty of Waitangi has been given undue influence over the years.

   No. The author never took a stand regarding how much influence is "due." That's **out of scope**.

   (D) Despite recent agreements that bolster the Treaty of Waitangi's legal legitimacy, significant debate exists over how to reconcile conflicting versions of the document.

   Yes. This is a good match for the Prephrased answer.

   (E) The Treaty of Waitangi merits reexamination in light of modern improvements to written Maori and recent changes to legal interpretations.

   No. This twists the meaning of lines 46–51. The passage doesn't mention "modern improvements to written Maori." It just says it's primarily an oral language.

2. **Choice (A) is the correct answer.**

   This is a Purpose of a Paragraph question. Look for an answer choice that matches what you found to be the purpose of the fourth paragraph in your initial analysis of the passage.

   (A) It introduces an alternative basis upon which to interpret the treaty.

   Yes. That alternative basis is presented by the conservative historians: the two parties' understanding of the oral agreement at the time is what is truly binding, not the text of the various written versions.

   (B) It explains the origins of the controversy from a historical perspective.

No. This is a **word trap** since the word "historical" might remind you of "historians." But the purpose of the fourth paragraph is all about how to interpret the agreement, not about the origins of the controversy.

(C)   It points out a flaw in an argument presented in an earlier paragraph.

No. The fourth paragraph doesn't care about flaws in earlier arguments—it calls those arguments "moot" or irrelevant.

(D)   It suggests that efforts to better understand the treaty are unimportant.

No. This is an **opposite** distracter. The fourth paragraph clearly seeks a way to better understand the treaty.

(E)   It summarizes the different viewpoints discussed earlier in the passage.

No. The fourth paragraph is more than just a summary as it introduces an entirely new viewpoint.

3. **Choice (B) is the correct answer.**
    This is a Viewpoint question. Refresh your memory of what the historians believe by revisiting the fourth paragraph. The historians argue several closely related points, with the oral understanding at the time being paramount.

    (A)   Laws must be interpreted according to the standards of the community in which they apply.

    No. The treaty still applies today, but the historians don't think today's standards are important, only the understanding at the time.

    (B)   The intent of the signers of a contract must be considered along with the language used in the contract.

    Yes. The historians' viewpoint is that "the spirit of the understanding is paramount" (lines 56–57), which matches this answer choice.

    (C)   Since the intentions of past lawmakers cannot be known, they cannot be considered by modern courts.

    No. This **contradicts the passage**. Lines 57–58 say that the spirit of the understanding is "reflected in the historical record of the time."

    (D)   Historical records concerning the functioning of a treaty are invalid when interpreting contemporary laws.

    No. This completely **contradicts the passage**, notably lines 56–57.

(E)   A treaty is valid only if it is codified in a language with an established and standardized written form.

No. This is the **wrong viewpoint**. This is something the supporters of the English version of the treaty might agree with.

4. **Choice (E) is the correct answer.**
    This is a Search question since it asks you to determine which answer choices were mentioned in the passage. Before attacking the answer choices, look for some mention of disagreements caused by the two versions. Several are mentioned in lines 23–28; others are mentioned in lines 38–43. Like most Search questions, it's also an EXCEPT question, so you can use the EXCEPT Tool. Put a **Y** next to the choices that did appear in the passage, and an **N** next to the one that did not.

    (A)   the surrender of sovereign rights by the signatory chiefs

    This was mentioned in lines 23–25. Put a **Y**.

    (B)   the Crown's right to purchase land from Maori people

    This was mentioned in lines 25–28. Put a **Y**.

    (C)   the control of forests, fisheries, and mineral rights

    This was mentioned in lines 41–42. Put a **Y**.

    (D)   the implications of the words *kawanatanga* and *rangatiratanga*

    This was mentioned in lines 35–38. Put a **Y**.

    (E)   the right of British citizens to own land in New Zealand

    This was not mentioned. All discussion about land ownership (lines 17–19 and lines 25–28) had to do with the rights of the British *monarchy*, not British *citizens*. Put an **N**.

    Since choice (E) is different from all the rest, pick it.

5. **Choice (C) is the correct answer.**
    This is an Inference question since it asks what the passage *suggests*. You could try to Prephrase an answer, but since many aspects of the treaty are discussed throughout the passage, it's probably best to just move on and attack the answer choices.

    (A)   It was designed to deceive the signatory chiefs into giving up concessions of land and sovereignty.

    No. There is certainly disagreement, but the passage never mentions intentional deceit. That's **out of scope**.

(B)   Any substantive discrepancies were a result of poor translation due to a misunderstanding of the English version of the treaty.

No. If there was a poor translation into Maori, it would have been due to misunderstanding of the Maori language, not misunderstanding of the English version. After all, it would appear to have been the English who wrote the Maori version, since Maori was historically an oral language.

(C)   Its drafters were obliged to create new terms out of extant suffixes in an attempt to faithfully translate the English version.

Yes. This is a good match for lines 29–33.

(D)   Since the oral contract and spirit of understanding between the British and Maori was paramount, little attention was paid to the details of the written version.

No. This is a **word trap** meant to remind you of lines 55–57, but nothing in the passage supports the idea that "little attention was paid to the details of the written version."

(E)   The treaty was created primarily to govern Maori claims to British-controlled assets such as forests, fisheries and mineral rights.

No. This is **extreme**. Those claims and rights are mentioned in the passage, but nothing says their governance was the primary reason the treaty was created.

Toba Catastrophe Passage

IDENTIFY

You can identify this as an Enlightenment passage because it is written to answer the core question, "What caused the human population bottleneck during the late Pleistocene era?" It also contains several different viewpoints.

ANALYZE

Core Question

The core question in this passage is "What caused the human population bottleneck during the late Pleistocene era?" The core question is posed (in slightly different terms) in lines 13–15, where the author indicates puzzlement over the cause of the bottleneck.

Various Viewpoints

There are a number of viewpoints in this passage. The entire second paragraph is dedicated to Ambrose's viewpoint: the eruption of Sumatra's Toba caldera impacted the climate in such a way as to cause the bottleneck.

Another viewpoint belongs to Ambrose's critics and is presented in the third paragraph: Ambrose's theory is not fully proven because there is a lack of an exact correlation between the relevant dates.

The final viewpoint belongs to the author. In the last sentence, she predicts that if a correlation is established, it is "likely" that the scientific community will accept Ambrose's theory.

Purpose of Each Paragraph

The purpose of the first paragraph is to introduce the topic, show how previous explanations for the bottleneck were not successful, and introduce Ambrose's theory.

The purpose of the second paragraph is to explore the Toba catastrophe theory and to explore how the human population bottleneck had a subsequent impact on human diversification.

The purpose of the third paragraph is to raise some possible objections to the theory (Ambrose's critics) and to allow the author to weigh in with her viewpoint that the objections could be addressed, which would lead to greater acceptance of the theory.

Main Point

The main point is the answer to the core question (lines 22–25) plus the author's viewpoint, found in lines 56–57: [If such a firm temporal connection is made, it is likely that scientists will accept the explanation that the cause of the population bottleneck and its subsequent impact on human diversification was the eruption of Sumatra's Toba caldera 71,000 years ago.]

6. **Choice (A) is the correct answer.**

This is a Purpose of a Passage question. The purpose of this passage (and all other Enlightenment passages) is to explore and try to answer the core question.

(A)   present a hypothesis that attempts to explain how a volcanic eruption caused a population bottleneck that affected human evolution

Yes. This correctly captures the core question, and the passage indeed presents a hypothesis that attempts to explain it.

(B)   describe the mechanism by which the eruption of the Toba caldera caused significant drops in global temperatures and induced a millennium-long ice age

No. This is **incomplete**. It lacks any mention of the human population bottleneck.

(C)   explain a theory regarding the effects of a very large comet on the genetic diversity of prehistoric human populations

No. This is a **word trap** built on lines 60–61, but the extraterrestrial object struck 65.5 million years ago, while the main focus of this passage is the late Pleistocene era, between 100,000 and 50,000 years ago (lines 3–4).

(D)   argue against a scientific theory that details the effects of a catastrophic volcanic eruption on the human species during the late Pleistocene era

No. This is the **wrong action**. The author thinks the theory is likely to be accepted, and she never argues against it.

(E)   provide evidence to establish a correlation between the dates of the Toba event and the late Pleistocene genetic bottleneck

No. This is the **wrong action**. The author in lines 48–55 says there is a need for evidence of a correlation; she does not provide it.

7. **Choice (B) is the correct answer.**
This is a Purpose of a Paragraph question. Look for an answer choice that matches what you found to be the purpose of the third paragraph in your initial analysis of the passage.

(A)   It illustrates a significant flaw in the Toba catastrophe theory.

No. There is some missing evidence in support of the theory, but the author doesn't present this as a "major flaw." She seems to think that evidence could eventually be found. This is **extreme**.

(B)   It explains why the Toba catastrophe theory is not universally accepted by the scientific community and suggests what kind of evidence might lead to its acceptance.

Yes. This is a good match for the Prephrased answer.

(C)   It argues against the Toba catastrophe theory by pointing out a vital piece of evidence that contradicts the theory's implications.

No. The problem with the theory is a lack of certain evidence, not that there is any evidence that contradicts it.

(D)   It contrasts the Toba catastrophe theory with a theory explaining the Cretaceous-Tertiary extinction event of 65.5 million years ago.

No. This is **incomplete**. The other extinction event was mentioned, but the primary purpose of this paragraph is to point out the missing evidence that is needed to support Ambrose's theory.

(E)   It concludes the passage by predicting that the Toba catastrophe theory will eventually be accepted by all scientists.

No. This is **extreme**. In lines 56–57 the author says that if proper evidence is found, "it is likely that Ambrose's theory will be accepted." She doesn't predict that it will definitely be accepted.

8. **Choice (C) is the correct answer.**
This is a Weaken question. The passage already did half your work for you in lines 48–51 when it pointed out the weakness in Ambrose's theory. The volcanic eruption occurred 71,000 years ago (line 25), but the genetic bottleneck occurred between 100,000 and 50,000 years ago (line 3), and there is a lack of an exact correlation between the two events. The correct answer choice is most likely to weaken the theory by showing the eruption occurred *after* the bottleneck, meaning it could not have been the cause.

(A)   Studies have shown that a small population of humans in South America also survived through the volcanic winter caused by the Toba event.

No. By acknowledging a "volcanic winter caused by the Toba event," this choice actually **strengthens** Ambrose's theory.

(B)   New geological evidence shows that it was not Toba but Tambora, another large volcano in what is now Indonesia, that erupted during the period in question.

No. Even if it were a different volcano, everything else in Ambrose's theory could still be valid.

(C)   Mitochondrial evidence indicates that the evolutionary bottleneck that struck humans in the Pleistocene occurred 10,000 years before the Toba event.

Yes. This would make it impossible for the Toba event to have caused the bottleneck.

(D)   New DNA evidence shows that total human populations shrunk to only about 200 individuals shortly after the Toba event.

No. You already know that the population got very small; the exact number doesn't weaken anything.

(E)   Research indicates that numerous extraterrestrial objects struck the earth throughout the late Pleistocene era.

No. This doesn't necessarily weaken the theory because the extraterrestrial objects may not have been large enough to be of any consequence. This is **out of scope**.

9. **Choice (D) is the correct answer.**

This is a Detail question since it asks you to retrieve a fact that the passage specifically *mentions*. Find the place in the passage where the eruption is discussed: it's in lines 25–30. First there's the eruption itself ("a massive amount of magma and pyroclastic material {ejected} into the Earth's atmosphere"). After that the first *result* mentioned is "enormous and long-lasting impacts on the Earth's climate...dropping global temperatures enough to induce a millennium-long ice age." Other subsequent results are mentioned, but since you're looking for the *first*, this is your Prephrased answer.

(A)   the reduction of the human species to thousands of individuals

No. This came after the impact on global temperatures. This is the **wrong part of the passage**.

(B)   the extinction of hundreds of species of plants and birds

No. This was never mentioned and is completely **out of scope**.

(C)   the near total destruction of all life on Sumatra

No. This was never mentioned and is completely **out of scope**.

(D)   the reduction of temperatures around the globe

Yes. This is a good match for the Prephrased answer.

(E)   an evolutionary bottleneck that sped the differentiation of the human species

No. This came after the impact on global temperatures. This is the **wrong part of the passage**.

10. **Choice (A) is the correct answer.**

This is a Viewpoint question since it asks what Ambrose would be *most likely to agree with*. Ambrose's theory takes up the entire second paragraph, so you shouldn't try to Prephrase anything too specific. Just look for something that matches the information presented as part of his viewpoint.

(A)   The effects of the Toba event can still be seen in modern times.

Yes. Ambrose says the event had a "subsequent impact on human diversification," including the diverse skin colors still apparent in modern times and discussed in lines 41–47.

(B)   Geologic cataclysms have only once impacted the course of human evolution.

No. This is **extreme**. Ambrose posits a theory of one cataclysm impacting human evolution, but the passage never says he thinks it's the only one.

(C)   The Toba event was the most important occurrence in recent natural history.

No. This is also **extreme**. Ambrose would likely think the event was important, but you have no evidence that he would consider it the most important.

(D)   Volcanic eruptions have had little effect on the history of the human race.

No. This completely contradicts his theory.

(E)   There is no need for modern geologists to monitor volcanic activity at the Toba caldera.

No. Ambrose never discusses modern geologists in this passage. This is **out of scope**.

Graphic Novel Passage

IDENTIFY

This passage is representative of some of the ambiguity that can arise when you try to identify LSAT passages. Some people say this is an Enlightenment passage designed to answer to core question, "What is a graphic novel?" Others say such a question doesn't really have a proper answer; it's just a matter of opinion, and the author is concerned with presenting his own opinion. Since the passage deals with multiple viewpoints, those people would identify this as a Controversy passage.

In the end, it doesn't matter what you call it. In your analysis you'll **always** look for the various viewpoints, the purpose of each paragraph, and the main point. If you think the passage has a core question, make note if it. If you don't think so, then don't worry—you'll still be well prepared to get the questions right.

ANALYZE

Various Viewpoints

The first viewpoint is the length-based theory, presented in lines 5–11. This is countered by the author's viewpoint in lines 11–17. The second viewpoint is the content-based theory, presented in lines 17–20 (and countered again by the author in lines 20–24).

Eddie Campbell's viewpoint takes up the second paragraph, lines 25–35: the graphic novel should be understood as an artistic and literary movement with the aim of raising the form of the comic book to more ambitious and meaningful levels.

The author continues to present his viewpoint in the third paragraph: he thinks Campbell is right. He uses opinionated words like "successfully" (line 38), "valuable and important" (line 56), and "compelling" (line 58). This praise is only slightly qualified in lines 50–54, where the author says it's hard to say whether people will accept Campbell's theory.

Purpose of Each Paragraph

The purpose of the first paragraph is to introduce the topic, offer several viewpoints, and allow the author to decisively rebut them.

The purpose of the second paragraph is to present Campbell's viewpoint.

The purpose of the third paragraph is to present the author's reaction to Campbell's theory. The author likes it a lot, but acknowledges that it may not become the dominant theory.

Main Point

The main point is best summed up by the first sentence in the third paragraph: [By defining the graphic novel as a movement and the graphic novelist as a participant in that movement, Campbell's theory successfully circumvents the problems that undermine other graphic novel theories.]

11. **Choice (C) is the correct answer.**

    This is a Main Point question. Look for a choice that matches the main point you found in your initial analysis of the passage.

    (A)   There are several different theories that have been set forth on how to differentiate comic books from graphic novels.

    No. This is **incomplete**. It doesn't address the author's judgment about which theories are compelling and which are flawed.

    (B)   Scholarship pertaining to graphic novels and graphic novel criticism are fields still in their embryonic stages, and it is difficult to determine whether Campbell's theory will become the dominant paradigm in the field.

    No. This is **incomplete**. It basically restates lines 50–54, but it doesn't mention the other viewpoints or address the author's strong approval of Campbell's theory.

    (C)   Campbell's proposal that the defining characteristic of a graphic novel is the intent of its author is more compelling than two popular theories.

    Yes. This is a good match for the Prephrased answer.

    (D)   Graphic novels cannot successfully be differentiated from comic books based upon their length or content alone.

    No. This is **incomplete**. It doesn't mention Campbell's alternative theory at all.

    (E)   Graphic novels use the same story-telling techniques as comic books but are often considerably lengthier.

No. This again fails to acknowledge the various viewpoints or the controversy.

12. **Choice (B) is the correct answer.**

    This is an Organization question. In your initial analysis of the passage, you identified the purpose of each paragraph; the correct answer here will convey those purposes accurately and in the correct order.

    (A)   A problem is presented. Two theories for solving the problem are explained. Weaknesses in the first theory are illustrated. The second theory is accepted.

    No. This **contradicts the passage**, since there are at least three answers proposed to determine what a graphic novel really is.

    (B)   A problem is presented. Weaknesses are uncovered in two theories used to resolve the problem. A third theory is presented. The third theory is concluded to be superior to the first two.

    Yes. The problem is how to define a graphic novel. The first two theories are the length-based and content-based theories, which the author rebuts. The third theory is Campbell's. The author uses the final paragraph to conclude that Campbell's theory is superior.

    (C)   Three paradigms for understanding a certain kind of art are presented. Weaknesses in two theories are revealed. The third theory is accepted.

    No. This is **out of order**. The third theory is not presented until after the weaknesses in the first two are revealed.

    (D)   A problem is presented. Two theories for solving the problem are explained. Weaknesses in both of these theories are expounded upon. A third theory is presented. The third theory is shown to possess the same flaws as the first two.

    No. This choice is okay until the end, but then it **contradicts the passage**. The author says that Campbell's theory is "more compelling" than the other two and that it solves the problems inherent in them. He doesn't think it possesses the same flaws.

    (E)   A problem in classifying a type of art is presented. Theories attempting to solve the problem are explained. Weaknesses are examined in two of the theories. Both theories are rejected.

    No. This is **incomplete** because it never mentions a third theory being deemed superior.

13. **Choice (E) is the correct answer.**

This is a Viewpoint question since it asks you what Campbell would *most likely agree with*. Campbell's viewpoint is presented in the second paragraph, so the correct answer will be limited in its scope to the material presented there.

(A)   Graphic novels and comic books differ from each other due, in part, to their relative lengths.

No. This is the **wrong viewpoint.** This matches lines 8–11, but Campbell "rejects" that theory in line 25.

(B)   Graphic novels do not utilize characters commonly found in comic books, such as popular superheroes.

No. This is **out of scope.** In this passage, Campbell never discusses superheroes.

(C)   Subjective decisions made by the reader and critics should determine what is viewed as a graphic novel.

No. This is again the **wrong viewpoint.** This matches lines 17–20, but Campbell "rejects" that theory in line 25.

(D)   The artwork and stories found in graphic novels are superior to those found in comic books.

No. This is **out of scope.** Campbell is not concerned with which form is "superior."

(E)   Subjective decisions made by the artist play an important role in determining what should be viewed as a graphic novel.

Yes. This is a good match for lines 30–35.

14. **Choice (D) is the correct answer.**

This is a Match question. There is a set of criteria given in lines 17–20, and you have to find the example that matches. Lines 17–20 say that "graphic novels differ from comic books in the quality of their content in the same way that literary novels differ from popular fiction novels." Basically, you're looking for the answer choice that gives an example with high-quality content.

(A)   a 300-page superhero story that aims to raise the comic book form to a higher plateau but is dismissed by critics

No. The only information you have here about the quality is that critics dismissed it. That doesn't match the idea of high quality.

(B)   a 400-page compilation of unimaginative and clichéd stories about average people

No. Unimaginative and clichéd is definitely not high quality.

(C)   a 60-page work of poor quality that seeks to take illustrated books to more ambitious and meaningful levels

No. This choice comes right out and says the work is of poor quality.

(D)   a 70-page work that stays firmly within the established form of comic books and wins numerous awards for outstanding quality

Yes. Numerous awards for outstanding quality sounds like what you're looking for.

(E)   a 150-page book that fails to garner any public interest but seeks to overcome traditional limitations of comic books

No. This makes no mention of quality.

15. **Choice (D) is the correct answer.**

This is an Attitude question. In your initial analysis of the passage, you found that the author uses opinionated words like "successfully" (line 38), "valuable and important" (line 56), and "compelling" (line 58) to approve of Campbell's theory. This praise is only slightly qualified in lines 50–54, where the author says it's hard to say whether people will accept Campbell's view.

(A)   outright disapproval

No. This is an **opposite** distracter.

(B)   uninterested ambivalence

No. This is another **opposite** distracter.

(C)   wholehearted optimism

No. This is **extreme** since the author does express some doubt about the theory's future

(D)   tempered support

Yes. This is a good match for the Prephrased answer.

(E)   hesitant skepticism

No. This is also **extreme** since it exaggerates the author's skepticism without mentioning his strong approval.

EXTRA PRACTICE

READING COMPREHENSION
Extra Practice

The following pages contain the full text of Reading Comprehension passages that appeared earlier in this book, including all the questions that accompanied each passage. You have seen some of the questions, but most of them are new. Use these passages for extra practice and reinforcement.

Test 22, Section 1, Questions 22–26

What it means to "explain" something in science often comes down to the application of mathematics. Some thinkers hold that mathematics is a kind of language—a systematic contrivance of signs, the
(5)   criteria for the authority of which are internal coherence, elegance, and depth. The application of such a highly artificial system to the physical world, they claim, results in the creation of a kind of statement about the world. Accordingly, what matters in the
(10)   sciences is finding a mathematical concept that attempts, as other language does, to accurately describe the functioning of some aspect of the world.

At the center of the issue of scientific knowledge can thus be found questions about the relationship
(15)   between language and what it refers to. A discussion about the role played by language in the pursuit of knowledge has been going on among linguists for several decades. The debate centers around whether language corresponds in some essential way to objects
(20)   and behaviors, making knowledge a solid and reliable commodity; or, on the other hand, whether the relationship between language and things is purely a matter of agreed upon conventions, making knowledge tenuous, relative, and inexact.

(25)   Lately the latter theory has been gaining wider acceptance. According to linguists who support this theory, the way language is used varies depending upon changes in accepted practices and theories among those who work in a particular discipline. These
(30)   linguists argue that, in the pursuit of knowledge, a statement is true only when there are no promising alternatives that might lead one to question it. Certainly this characterization would seem to be applicable to the sciences. In science, a mathematical statement may be
(35)   taken to account for every aspect of a phenomenon it is applied to, but, some would argue, there is nothing inherent in mathematical language that guarantees such a correspondence. Under this view, acceptance of a mathematical statement by the scientific community—
(40)   by virtue of the statement's predictive power or methodological efficiency—transforms what is basically an analogy or metaphor into an explanation of the physical process in question, to be held as true until another, more compelling analogy takes its place.

(45)   In pursuing the implications of this theory, linguists have reached the point at which they must ask: If words or sentences do not correspond in an essential way to life or to our ideas about life, then just what are they capable of telling us about the world? In science
(50)   and mathematics, then, it would seem equally necessary to ask: If models of electrolytes or $E = mc^2$, say, do not correspond essentially to the physical

world, then just what functions do they perform in the acquisition of scientific knowledge? But this question
(55)   has yet to be significantly addressed in the sciences.

1. Which one of the following statements most accurately expresses the passage's main point?

(A)   Although scientists must rely on both language and mathematics in their pursuit of scientific knowledge, each is an imperfect tool for perceiving and interpreting aspects of the physical world.

(B)   The acquisition of scientific knowledge depends on an agreement among scientists to accept some mathematical statements as more precise than others while acknowledging that all mathematics is inexact.

(C)   If science is truly to progress, scientists must temporarily abandon the pursuit of new knowledge in favor of a systematic analysis of how the knowledge they already possess came to be accepted as true.

(D)   In order to better understand the acquisition of scientific knowledge, scientists must investigate mathematical statements' relationship to the world just as linguists study language's relationship to the world.

(E)   Without the debates among linguists that preceded them, it is unlikely that scientists would ever have begun to explore the essential role played by mathematics in the acquisition of scientific knowledge.

2. Which one of the following statements, if true, lends the most support to the view that language has an essential correspondence to the things it describes?

(A)   The categories of physical objects employed by one language correspond remarkably to the categories employed by another language that developed independently of the first.

(B)   The categories of physical objects employed by one language correspond remarkably to the categories employed by another language that derives from the first.

(C)   The categories of physical objects employed by speakers of a language correspond remarkably to the categories employed by other speakers of the same language.

(D)   The sentence structures of languages in scientifically sophisticated societies vary little from language to language.

(E)   Native speakers of many languages believe that the categories of physical objects employed by their language correspond to natural categories of objects in the world.

3. According to the passage, mathematics can be considered a language because it

(A)   conveys meaning in the same way that metaphors do

(B)   constitutes a systematic collection of signs

(C)   corresponds exactly to aspects of physical phenomena

(D)   confers explanatory power on scientific theories

(E)   relies on previously agreed upon conventions

4. The primary purpose of the third paragraph is to

(A)   offer support for the view of linguists who believe that language has an essential correspondence to things

(B)   elaborate the position of linguists who believe that truth is merely a matter of convention

(C)   illustrate the differences between the essentialist and conventionalist positions in the linguists' debate

(D)   demonstrate the similarity of the linguists' debate to a current debate among scientists about the nature of explanation

(E)   explain the theory that mathematical statements are a kind of language

5. Based on the passage, linguists who subscribe to the theory described in lines 21–24 would hold that the statement "The ball is red" is true because

(A)   speakers of English have accepted that "The ball is red" applies to the particular physical relationship being described

(B)   speakers of English do not accept that synonyms for "ball" and "red" express these concepts as elegantly

(C)   "The ball is red" corresponds essentially to every aspect of the particular physical relationship being described

(D)   "ball" and "red" actually refer to an entity and a property respectively

(E)   "ball" and "red" are mathematical concepts that attempt to accurately describe some particular physical relationship in the world

Test 23, Section 4, Questions 6–13

Medievalists usually distinguished medieval public law from private law: the former was concerned with government and military affairs and the latter with the family, social status, and land transactions.
(5) Examination of medieval women's lives shows this distinction to be overly simplistic. Although medieval women were legally excluded from roles thus categorized as public, such as soldier, justice, jury member, or professional administrative official,
(10) women's control of land—usually considered a private or domestic phenomenon—had important political implications in the feudal system of thirteenth-century England. Since land equaled wealth and wealth equaled power, certain women exercised influence by
(15) controlling land. Unlike unmarried women (who were legally subject to their guardians) or married women (who had no legal identity separate from their husbands), women who were widows had autonomy with respect to acquiring or disposing of certain
(20) property, suing in court, incurring liability for their own debts, and making wills.

Although feudal lands were normally transferred through primogeniture (the eldest son inheriting all), when no sons survived, the surviving daughters
(25) inherited equal shares under what was known as partible inheritance. In addition to controlling any such land inherited from her parents and any bridal dowry— property a woman brought to the marriage from her own family—a widow was entitled to use of one-third
(30) of her late husband's lands. Called "dower" in England, this grant had greater legal importance under common law than did the bridal dowry; no marriage was legal unless the groom endowed the bride with this property at the wedding ceremony. In 1215 Magna
(35) Carta guaranteed a widow's right to claim her dower without paying a fine; this document also strengthened widows' ability to control land by prohibiting forced remarriage. After 1272 women could also benefit from jointure: the groom could agree to hold part or all of
(40) his lands jointly with the bride, so that if one spouse died, the other received these lands.

Since many widows had inheritances as well as dowers, widows were frequently the financial heads of the family; even though legal theory assumed the
(45) maintenance of the principle of primogeniture, the amount of land the widow controlled could exceed that of her son or of other male heirs. Anyone who held feudal land exercised authority over the people attached to the land—knights, rental tenants, and
(50) peasants—and had to hire estate administrators, oversee accounts, receive rents, protect tenants from outside encroachment, punish tenants for not paying rents, appoint priests to local parishes, and act as guardians of tenants' children and executors of their
(55) wills. Many married women fulfilled these duties as deputies for husbands away at court or at war, but widows could act on their own behalf. Widows' legal independence is suggested by their frequent appearance in thirteenth-century English legal records. Moreover,

(60) the scope of their sway is indicated by the fact that some controlled not merely single estates, but multiple counties.

6. Which one of the following best expresses the main idea of the passage?

(A) The traditional view of medieval women as legally excluded from many public offices fails to consider thirteenth-century women in England who were exempted from such restrictions because of their wealth and social status.

(B) The economic independence of women in thirteenth-century England was primarily determined not by their marital status, but by their status as heirs to their parents' estates.

(C) The laws and customs of the feudal system in thirteenth-century England enabled some women to exercise a certain amount of power despite their legal exclusion from most public roles.

(D) During the thirteenth century in England, widows gained greater autonomy and legal rights to their property than they had had in previous centuries.

(E) Widows in thirteenth-century England were able to acquire and dispose of lands through a number of different legal processes.

7. With which one of the following statements about the views held by the medievalists mentioned in line 1 would the author of the passage most probably agree?

(A) The medieval role of landowner was less affected by thirteenth-century changes in law than these medievalists customarily have recognized.

(B) The realm of law labeled public by these medievalists ultimately had greater political implications than that labeled private.

(C) The amount of wealth controlled by medieval women was greater than these medievalists have recorded.

(D) The distinction made by these medievalists between private law and public law fails to consider some of the actual legal cases of the period.

(E) The distinction made by these medievalists between private and public law fails to address the political importance of control over land in the medieval era.

8. Which one of the following most accurately expresses the meaning of the word "sway" as it is used in line 60 of the passage?

(A) vacillation
(B) dominion
(C) predisposition
(D) inclination
(E) mediation

9. Which one of the following most accurately describes the function of the second paragraph of the passage?

(A) providing examples of specific historical events as support for the conclusion drawn in the third paragraph
(B) narrating a sequence of events whose outcome is discussed in the third paragraph
(C) explaining how circumstances described in the first paragraph could have occurred
(D) describing the effects of an event mentioned in the first paragraph
(E) evaluating the arguments of a group mentioned in the first paragraph

10. According to information in the passage, a widow in early thirteenth-century England could control more land than did her eldest son if

(A) the widow had been granted the customary amount of dower land and the eldest son inherited the rest of the land
(B) the widow had three daughters in addition to her eldest son
(C) the principle of primogeniture had been applied in transferring the lands owned by the widow's late husband
(D) none of the lands held by the widow's late husband had been placed in jointure
(E) the combined amount of land the widow had acquired from her own family and from dower was greater than the amount inherited by her son

11. Which one of the following is mentioned in the passage as a reason why a married woman might have fulfilled certain duties associated with holding feudal land in thirteenth-century England?

(A) the legal statutes set forth by Magna Carta
(B) the rights a woman held over her inheritance during her marriage
(C) the customary division of duties between husbands and wives
(D) the absence of the woman's husband
(E) the terms specified by the woman's jointure agreement

12. The phrase "in England" (lines 30–31) does which one of the following?

(A) It suggests that women in other countries also received grants of their husbands' lands.
(B) It identifies a particular code of law affecting women who were surviving daughters.
(C) It demonstrates that dower had greater legal importance in one European country than in others.
(D) It emphasizes that women in one European country had more means of controlling property than did women in other European countries.
(E) It traces a legal term back to the time at which it entered the language.

13. The primary purpose of the passage is to

(A) explain a legal controversy of the past in light of modern theory
(B) evaluate the economic and legal status of a particular historical group
(C) resolve a scholarly debate about legal history
(D) trace the historical origins of a modern economic situation
(E) provide new evidence about a historical event

Test 23, Section 4, Questions 14–18

The debate over the environmental crisis is not new; anxiety about industry's impact on the environment has existed for over a century. What is new is the extreme polarization of views. Mounting
(5) evidence of humanity's capacity to damage the environment irreversibly coupled with suspicions that government, industry, and even science might be impotent to prevent environmental destruction have provoked accusatory polemics on the part of
(10) environmentalists. In turn, these polemics have elicited a corresponding backlash from industry. The sad effect of this polarization is that it is now even more difficult for industry than it was a hundred years ago to respond appropriately to impact analyses that demand action.

(15) Unlike today's adversaries, earlier ecological reformers shared with advocates of industrial growth a confidence in timely corrective action. George P. Marsh's pioneering conservation tract *Man and Nature* (1864) elicited wide acclaim without embittered
(20) denials. *Man and Nature* castigated Earth's despoilers for heedless greed, declaring that humanity "has brought the face of the Earth to a desolation almost as complete as that of the Moon." But no entrepreneur or industrialist sought to refute Marsh's accusation, to
(25) defend the gutting of forests or the slaughter of wildlife as economically essential, or to dismiss his ecological warnings as hysterical. To the contrary, they generally agreed with him.

Why? Marsh and his followers took environmental
(30) improvement and economic progress as givens; they disputed not the desirability of conquering nature but the bungling way in which the conquest was carried out. Blame was not personalized; Marsh denounced general greed rather than particular entrepreneurs, and
(35) the media did not hound malefactors. Further, corrective measures seemed to entail no sacrifice, to demand no draconian remedies. Self-interest underwrote most prescribed reforms. Marsh's emphasis on future stewardship was then a widely accepted ideal
(40) (if not practice). His ecological admonitions were in keeping with the Enlightenment premise that humanity's mission was to subdue and transform nature.

Not until the 1960s did a gloomier perspective gain
(45) popular ground. Frederic Clements' equilibrium model of ecology, developed in the 1930s, seemed consistent with mounting environmental disasters. In this view, nature was most fruitful when least altered. Left undisturbed, flora and fauna gradually attained
(50) maximum diversity and stability. Despoliation thwarted the culmination or shortened the duration of this beneficent climax; technology did not improve nature but destroyed it.

The equilibrium model became an ecological
(55) mystique: environmental interference was now taboo, wilderness adored. Nature as unfinished fabric perfected by human ingenuity gave way to the image of nature debased and endangered by technology. In contrast to the Enlightenment vision of nature,

(60) according to which rational managers construct an ever more improved environment, twentieth-century reformers' vision of nature calls for a reduction of human interference in order to restore environmental stability.

14. Which one of the following most accurately states the main idea of the passage?

(A) Mounting evidence of humanity's capacity to damage the environment should motivate action to prevent further damage.

(B) The ecological mystique identified with Frederic Clements has become a religious conviction among ecological reformers.

(C) George P. Marsh's ideas about conservation and stewardship have heavily influenced the present debate over the environment.

(D) The views of ecologists and industrial growth advocates concerning the environment have only recently become polarized.

(E) General greed rather than particular individuals or industries should be blamed for the environmental crisis.

15. The author refers to the equilibrium model of ecology as an "ecological mystique" (lines 54–55) most likely in order to do which one of the following?

(A) underscore the fervor with which twentieth-century reformers adhere to the equilibrium model

(B) point out that the equilibrium model of ecology has recently been supported by empirical scientific research

(C) express appreciation for how plants and animals attain maximum diversity and stability when left alone

(D) indicate that the ideas of twentieth-century ecological reformers are often so theoretical as to be difficult to understand

(E) indicate how widespread support is for the equilibrium model of ecology in the scientific community

16. Which one of the following practices is most clearly an application of Frederic Clements' equilibrium model of ecology?

   (A) introducing a species into an environment to which it is not native to help control the spread of another species that no longer has any natural predators

   (B) developing incentives for industries to take corrective measures to protect the environment

   (C) using scientific methods to increase the stability of plants and animals in areas where species are in danger of becoming extinct

   (D) using technology to develop plant and animal resources but balancing that development with stringent restrictions on technology

   (E) setting areas of land aside to be maintained as wilderness from which the use or extraction of natural resources is prohibited

17. The passage suggests that George P. Marsh and today's ecological reformers would be most likely to agree with which one of the following statements?

   (A) Regulating industries in order to protect the environment does not conflict with the self-interest of those industries.

   (B) Solving the environmental crisis does not require drastic and costly remedies.

   (C) Human despoliation of the Earth has caused widespread environmental damage.

   (D) Environmental improvement and economic progress are equally important goals.

   (E) Rather than blaming specific industries, general greed should be denounced as the cause of environmental destruction.

18. The passage is primarily concerned with which one of the following?

   (A) providing examples of possible solutions to a current crisis

   (B) explaining how conflicting viewpoints in a current debate are equally valid

   (C) determining which of two conflicting viewpoints in a current debate is more persuasive

   (D) outlining the background and development of conflicting viewpoints in a current debate

   (E) demonstrating weaknesses in the arguments made by one side in a current debate

Test 24, Section 1, Questions 7–13

In April 1990 representatives of the Pico Korea
Union of electronics workers in Buchon City, South
Korea, traveled to the United States in order to demand
just settlement of their claims from the parent company
(5) of their employer, who upon the formation of the union
had shut down operations without paying the workers.
From the beginning, the union cause was championed
by an unprecedented coalition of Korean American
groups and deeply affected the Korean American
(10) community on several levels.

First, it served as a rallying focus for a diverse
community often divided by generation, class, and
political ideologies. Most notably, the Pico cause
mobilized many young second-generation Korean
(15) Americans, many of whom had never been part of a
political campaign before, let alone one involving
Korean issues. Members of this generation, unlike first-
generation Korean Americans, generally fall within the
more privileged sectors of the Korean American
(20) community and often feel alienated from their Korean
roots. In addition to raising the political consciousness
of young Korean Americans, the Pico struggle sparked
among them new interest in their cultural identity. The
Pico workers also suggested new roles that can be
(25) played by recent immigrants, particularly working-
class immigrants. These immigrants' knowledge of
working conditions overseas can help to globalize the
perspective of their communities and can help to
establish international ties on a more personal level, as
(30) witnessed in the especially warm exchange between the
Pico workers and recent working-class immigrants
from China. In addition to broadening the political base
within the Korean American community, the Pico
struggle also led to new alliances between the Korean
(35) American community and progressive labor and social
justice groups within the larger society—as evidenced
in the support received from the Coalition of Labor
Union Women and leading African American
unionists.
(40) The reasons for these effects lie in the nature of the
cause. The issues raised by the Pico unionists had such
a strong human component that differences within the
community became secondary to larger concerns for
social justice and workers' rights. The workers'
(45) demands for compensation and respect were
unencumbered with strong ideological trappings. The
economic exploitation faced by the Pico workers
underscored the common interests of Korean workers,
Korean Americans, the working class more inclusively,
(50) and a broad spectrum of community leaders.
The Pico workers' campaign thus offers an
important lesson. It demonstrates that ethnic
communities need more than just a knowledge of
history and culture as artifacts of the past in order to
(55) strengthen their ethnic identity. It shows that perhaps
the most effective means of empowerment for many
ethnic communities of immigrant derivation may be an
identification with and participation in current struggles
for economic and social justice in their countries of
(60) origin.

19. Which one of the following best describes the main topic
of the passage?

(A) the contribution of the Korean American
community to improving the working conditions
of Koreans employed by United States
companies
(B) the change brought about in the Korean American
community by contacts with Koreans visiting the
United States
(C) the contribution of recent immigrants from Korea
to strengthening ethnic identity in the Korean
American community
(D) the effects on the Korean American community
of a dispute between Korean union workers and
a United Stated company
(E) the effect of the politicization of second-
generation Korean Americans on the Korean
American community as a whole

20. The passage suggests that which one of the following
was a significant factor in the decision to shut down the
Pico plant in Buchon City?

(A) the decreasing profitability of maintaining
operations in Korea
(B) the failure to resolve long-standing disputes
between the Pico workers and management
(C) the creation of a union by the Pico workers
(D) the withholding of workers' wages by the parent
company
(E) the finding of an alternate site for operations

21. Which one of the following is NOT mentioned in the
passage as a recent development in the Korean American
community?

(A) Young second-generation Korean Americans
have begun to take an interest in their Korean
heritage.
(B) Recent Korean American immigrants of working-
class backgrounds have begun to enter the more
privileged sectors of the Korean American
community.
(C) Korean Americans have developed closer ties
with activist groups from other sectors of the
population.
(D) Previously nonpolitical members of the Korean
American community have become more
politically active.
(E) The Korean American community has been able
to set aside political and generational disparities
in order to support a common cause.

22. It can be inferred that the author of the passage would most likely agree with which one of the following statements about ethnic communities of immigrant derivation?

(A) Such communities can derive important benefits from maintaining ties with their countries of origin.

(B) Such communities should focus primarily on promoting study of the history and culture of their people in order to strengthen their ethnic identity.

(C) Such communities can most successfully mobilize and politicize their young people by addressing the problems of young people of all backgrounds.

(D) The more privileged sectors of such communities are most likely to maintain a sense of closeness to their cultural roots.

(E) The politicization of such a community is unlikely to affect relations with other groups within the larger society.

23. In the second paragraph, the author refers to immigrants from China most probably in order to do which one of the following?

(A) highlight the contrast between working conditions in the United States and in Korea

(B) demonstrate the uniqueness of the problem faced by the Pico workers

(C) offer an example of the type of role that can be played by recent working-class immigrants

(D) provide an analogy for the type of activism displayed by the Korean American community

(E) compare the disparate responses of two immigrant communities to similar problems

24. The primary purpose of the passage is to

(A) describe recent developments in the Korean American community that have strongly affected other ethnic communities of immigrant derivation

(B) describe a situation in the Korean American community that presents a model for the empowerment of ethnic communities of immigrant derivation

(C) detail the problems faced by the Korean need for the empowerment of ethnic communities of immigrant derivation

(D) argue against economic and social injustice in the countries of origin of ethnic communities of immigrant derivation

(E) assess the impact of the unionization movement on ethnic communities of immigrant derivation

25. Which one of the following most accurately states the function of the third paragraph?

(A) It explains why the Pico workers brought their cause to the United States.

(B) It explains how the Pico cause differed from other causes that had previously mobilized the Korean American community.

(C) It explains why the Pico workers were accorded such broad support.

(D) It explains how other ethnic groups of immigrant derivation in the United States have profited from the example of the Pico workers.

(E) It explains why different generations of Korean Americans reacted in different ways to the Pico cause.

Test 24, Section 1, Questions 14–20

In recent years, scholars have begun to use social science tools to analyze court opinions. These scholars have justifiably criticized traditional legal research for its focus on a few cases that may not be representative
(5) and its fascination with arcane matters that do not affect real people with real legal problems. Zirkel and Schoenfeld, for example, have championed the application of social science tools to the analysis of case law surrounding discrimination against women in
(10) higher education employment. Their studies have demonstrated how these social science tools may be used to serve the interests of scholars, lawyers, and prospective plaintiffs as well. However, their enthusiasm for the "outcomes analysis" technique
(15) seems misguided.

Of fundamental concern is the outcomes analysts' assumption that simply counting the number of successful and unsuccessful plaintiffs will be useful to prospective plaintiffs. Although the odds are clearly
(20) against the plaintiff in sex discrimination cases, plaintiffs who believe that their cause is just and that they will prevail are not swayed by such evidence. In addition, because lawsuits are so different in the details of the case, in the quality of the evidence the plaintiff
(25) presents, and in the attitude of the judge toward academic plaintiffs, giving prospective plaintiffs statistics about overall outcomes without analyzing the reason for these outcomes is of marginal assistance. Outcomes analysis, for example, ignores the fact that in
(30) certain academic sex discrimination cases—those involving serious procedural violations or incriminating evidence in the form of written admissions of discriminatory practices—plaintiffs are much more likely to prevail.

(35) Two different approaches offer more useful applications of social science tools in analyzing sex discrimination cases. One is a process called "policy capturing," in which the researcher reads each opinion; identifies variables discussed in the opinion, such as
(40) the regularity of employer evaluations of the plaintiff's performance, training of evaluators, and the kind of evaluation instrument used; and then uses multivariate analysis to determine whether these variables predict the outcome of the lawsuit. The advantage of policy-
(45) capturing research is that it attempts to explain the reason for the outcome, rather than simply reporting the outcome, and identifies factors that contribute to a plaintiff's success or failure. Taking a slightly different approach, other scholars have adopted a technique that
(50) requires reading complete transcripts of all sex discrimination cases litigated during a certain time period to identify variables such as the nature of the allegedly illegal conduct, the consequences for employers, and the nature of the remedy, as well as the
(55) factors that contributed to the verdict and the kind of evidence necessary for the plaintiff to prevail. While the findings of these studies are limited to the period covered, they assist potential plaintiffs and defendants in assessing their cases.

26. Which one of the following best expresses the main idea of the passage?

(A)   The analysis of a limited number of atypical discrimination suits is of little value to potential plaintiffs.

(B)   When the number of factors analyzed in a sex discrimination suit is increased, the validity of the conclusions drawn becomes suspect.

(C)   Scholars who are critical of traditional legal research frequently offer alternative approaches that are also seriously flawed.

(D)   Outcomes analysis has less predictive value in sex discrimination cases than do certain other social science techniques.

(E)   Given adequate information, it is possible to predict with considerable certainty whether a plaintiff will be successful in a discrimination suit.

27. It can be inferred from the author's discussion of traditional legal research that the author is

(A)   frustrated because traditional legal research has not achieved its full potential

(B)   critical because traditional legal research has little relevance to those actually involved in cases

(C)   appreciative of the role traditional legal research played in developing later, more efficient approaches

(D)   derisive because traditional legal research has outlasted its previously significant role

(E)   grateful for the ability of traditional legal research to develop unique types of evidence

28. Which one of the following statements about Zirkel and Schoenfeld can be inferred from the passage?

(A) They were the first scholars to use social science tools in analyzing legal cases.

(B) They confined their studies to the outcomes analysis technique.

(C) They saw no value in the analysis provided by traditional legal research.

(D) They rejected policy capturing as being too limited in scope.

(E) They believed that the information generated by outcomes analysis would be relevant for plaintiffs.

29. The author's characterization of traditional legal research in the first paragraph is intended to

(A) provide background information for the subsequent discussion

(B) summarize an opponent's position

(C) argue against the use of social science tools in the analysis of sex discrimination cases

(D) emphasize the fact that legal researchers act to the detriment of potential plaintiffs

(E) reconcile traditional legal researchers to the use of social science tools

30. The information in the passage suggests that plaintiffs who pursue sex discrimination cases despite the statistics provided by outcomes analysis can best be likened to

(A) athletes who continue to employ training techniques despite their knowledge of statistical evidence indicating that these techniques are unlikely to be effective

(B) lawyers who handle lawsuits for a large number of clients in the hope that some percentage will be successful

(C) candidates for public office who are more interested in making a political statement than in winning an election

(D) supporters of a cause who recruit individuals sympathetic to it in the belief that large numbers of supporters will lend the cause legitimacy

(E) purchasers of a charity's raffle tickets who consider the purchase a contribution because the likelihood of winning is remote

31. The policy-capturing approach differs from the approach described in lines 48–59 in that the latter approach

(A) makes use of detailed information on a greater number of cases

(B) focuses more directly on issues of concern to litigants

(C) analyzes information that is more recent and therefore reflects current trends

(D) allows assessment of aspects of a case that are not specifically mentioned in a judge's opinion

(E) eliminates any distortion due to personal bias on the part of the researcher

32. Which one of the following best describes the organization of the passage?

(A) A technique is introduced, its shortcomings are summarized, and alternatives are described.

(B) A debate is introduced, evidence is presented, and a compromise is reached.

(C) A theory is presented, clarification is provided, and a plan of further evaluation is suggested.

(D) Standards are established, hypothetical examples are analyzed, and the criteria are amended.

(E) A position is challenged, its shortcomings are categorized, and the challenge is revised.

Test 26, Section 4, Questions 6–13

James Porter (1905–1970) was the first scholar to
identify the African influence on visual art in the
Americas, and much of what is known about the
cultural legacy that African-American artists inherited
(5) from their African forebears has come to us by way of
his work. Porter, a painter and art historian, began by
studying African-American crafts of the eighteenth and
nineteenth centuries. This research revealed that many
of the household items created by African-American
(10) men and women—walking sticks, jugs, and textiles—
displayed characteristics that linked them
iconographically to artifacts of West Africa. Porter
then went on to establish clearly the range of the
cultural territory inherited by later African-American
(15) artists.

An example of this aspect of Porter's research
occurs in his essay "Robert S. Duncanson, Midwestern
Romantic-Realist." The work of Duncanson, a
nineteenth-century painter of the Hudson River school,
(20) like that of his predecessor in the movement, Joshua
Johnston, was commonly thought to have been created
by a Euro-American artist. Porter proved definitively
that both Duncanson and Johnston were of African
ancestry. Porter published this finding and thousands of
(25) others in a comprehensive volume tracing the history
of African-American art. At the time of its first printing
in 1943, only two other books devoted exclusively to
the accomplishments of African-American artists
existed. Both of these books were written by Alain
(30) LeRoy Locke, a professor at the university where
Porter also taught. While these earlier studies by Locke
are interesting for being the first to survey the field,
neither addressed the critical issue of African
precursors; Porter's book addressed this issue,
(35) painstakingly integrating the history of African-
American art into the larger history of art in the
Americas without separating it from those qualities that
gave it its unique ties to African artisanship. Porter
may have been especially attuned to these ties because
(40) of his conscious effort to maintain them in his own
paintings, many of which combine the style of the
genre portrait with evidence of an extensive knowledge
of the cultural history of various African peoples.

In his later years, Porter wrote additional chapters
(45) for later editions of his book, constantly revising and
correcting his findings, some of which had been based
of necessity on fragmentary evidence. Among his later
achievements were his definitive reckoning of the birth
year of the painter Patrick Reason, long a point of
(50) scholarly uncertainty, and his identification of an
unmarked grave in San Francisco as that of the sculptor
Edmonia Lewis. At his death, Porter left extensive
notes for an unfinished project aimed at exploring the
influence of African art on the art of the Western world
(55) generally, a body of research whose riches scholars still
have not exhausted.

33. Which one of the following most accurately states the
main idea of the passage?

(A) Because the connections between African-
American art and other art in the Americas had
been established by earlier scholars, Porter's
work focused on showing African-American
art's connections to African artisanship.

(B) In addition to showing the connections between
African-American art and African artisanship,
Porter's most important achievement was
illustrating the links between African-American
art and other art in the Americas.

(C) Despite the fact that his last book remains
unfinished, Porter's work was the first to devote
its attention exclusively to the accomplishments
of African-American artists.

(D) Although showing the connections between
African-American art and African artisanship,
Porter's work concentrated primarily on placing
African-American art in the context of Western
art in general.

(E) While not the first body of scholarship to treat the
subject of African-American art, Porter's work
was the first to show the connections between
African-American art and African artisanship.

34. The discussion of Locke's books is intended primarily to

(A) argue that Porter's book depended upon Locke's
pioneering scholarship

(B) highlight an important way in which Porter's
work differed from previous work in his field

(C) suggest an explanation for why Porter's book was
little known outside academic circles

(D) support the claim that Porter was not the first to
notice African influences in African-American
art

(E) argue that Locke's example was a major influence
on Porter's decision to publish his findings.

35. The passage states which one of the following about the
1943 edition of Porter's book on African-American art?

(A) It received little scholarly attention at first.

(B) It was revised and improved upon in later
editions.

(C) It took issue with several of Locke's conclusions.

(D) It is considered the definitive versions of Porter's
work.

(E) It explored the influence of African art on
Western art in general.

36. Given the information in the passage, Porter's identification of the ancestry of Duncanson and Johnston provides conclusive evidence for which one of the following statements?

(A) Some of the characteristics defining the Hudson River school are iconographically linked to West African artisanship.

(B) Some of the works of Duncanson and Johnston are not in the style of the Hudson River school.

(C) Some of the work of Euro-American painters displays similarities to African-American crafts of the eighteenth and nineteenth centuries.

(D) Some of the works of the Hudson River school were done by African-American painters.

(E) Some of the works of Duncanson and Johnston were influenced by West African artifacts.

37. Which one of the following can most reasonably be inferred from the passage about the study that Porter left unfinished at his death?

(A) If completed, it would have contradicted some of the conclusions contained in his earlier book.

(B) If completed, it would have amended some of the conclusions contained in his earlier book.

(C) If completed, it would have brought up to date the comprehensive history of African-American art begun in his earlier book.

(D) If completed, it would have expanded upon the project of his earlier book by broadening the scope of inquiry found in the earlier book.

(E) If completed, it would have supported some of the theories put forth by Porter's contemporaries since the publication of his earlier book.

38. Which one of the following hypothetical observations is most closely analogous to the discoveries Porter made about African-American crafts of the eighteenth and nineteenth centuries?

(A) Contemporary Haitian social customs have a unique character dependent on but different from both their African and French origins.

(B) Popular music in the United States, some of which is based on African musical traditions, often influences music being composed on the African continent.

(C) Many novels written in Canada by Chinese immigrants exhibit narrative themes very similar to those found in Chinese folktales.

(D) Extensive Indian immigration to England has made traditional Indian foods nearly as popular there as the traditional English foods that had been popular there before Indian immigration.

(E) Some Mexican muralists of the early twentieth century consciously imitated the art of native peoples as a response to the Spanish influences that had predominated in Mexican art.

39. The passage most strongly supports which one of the following inferences about Porter's own paintings?

(A) They often contained figures or images derived from the work of African artisans.

(B) They fueled his interest in pursuing a career in art history.

(C) They were used in Porter's book to show the extent of African influence on African-American art.

(D) They were a deliberate attempt to prove his theories about art history.

(E) They were done after all of his academic work had been completed.

40. Based on the passage, which one of the following, if true, would have been most relevant to the project Porter was working on at the time of his death?

(A) African-American crafts of the eighteenth and nineteenth centuries have certain resemblances to European folk crafts of earlier periods.

(B) The paintings of some twentieth-century European artists prefigured certain stylistic developments in North American graphic art.

(C) The designs of many of the quilts made by African-American women in the nineteenth century reflect designs of European trade goods.

(D) After the movement of large numbers of African Americans to cities, the African influences in the work of many African-American painters increased.

(E) Several portraits by certain twentieth-century European painters were modeled after examples of Central African ceremonial masks.

Test 28, Section 4, Questions 1–5

Some Native American tribes have had difficulty establishing their land claims because the United States government did not recognize their status as tribes; therefore during the 1970's some Native Americans
(5) attempted to obtain such recognition through the medium of U.S. courts. In presenting these suits, Native Americans had to operate within a particular sphere of U.S. government procedure, that of its legal system, and their arguments were necessarily
(10) interpreted by the courts in terms the law could understand: e.g., through application of precedent or review of evidence. This process brought to light some of the differing perceptions and definitions that can exist between cultures whose systems of discourse are
(15) sometimes at variance.

In one instance, the entire legal dispute turned on whether the suing community—a group of Mashpee Wampanoag in the town of Mashpee, Massachusetts—constituted a tribe. The area had long been occupied by
(20) the Mashpee, who continued to have control over land use after the town's incorporation. But in the 1960's, after an influx of non-Mashpee people shifted the balance of political power in the town, the new residents were able to buy Mashpee-controlled land
(25) from the town and develop it for commercial or private use. The Mashpee's 1976 suit claimed that these lands were taken in violation of a statute prohibiting transfers of land from any tribe of Native Americans without federal approval. The town argued that the Mashpee
(30) were not a tribe in the sense intended by the statute and so were outside its protection. As a result, the Mashpee were required to demonstrate their status as a tribe according to a definition contained in an earlier ruling: a body of Native Americans "governing themselves
(35) under one leadership and inhabiting a particular territory."

The town claimed that the Mashpee were not self-governing and that they had no defined territory: the Mashpee could legally be self-governing, the town
(40) argued, only if they could show written documentation of such a system, and could legally inhabit territory only if they had precisely delineated its boundaries and possessed a deed to it. The Mashpee marshaled oral testimony against these claims, arguing that what the
(45) town perceived as a lack of evidence was simply information that an oral culture such as the Mashpee's would not have recorded in writing. In this instance, the disjunction between U.S. legal discourse and Mashpee culture—exemplified in the court's inability
(50) to "understand" the Mashpee's oral testimony as documentary evidence—rendered the suit unsuccessful. Similar claims have recently met with greater success, however, as U.S. courts have begun to acknowledge that the failure to accommodate differences in
(55) discourse between cultures can sometimes stand in the way of guaranteeing the fairness of legal decisions.

41. Which one of the following most completely and accurately expresses the main point of the passage?

(A) Land claim suits such as the Mashpee's establish that such suits must be bolstered by written documentation if they are to succeed in U.S. courts.

(B) Land claim suits such as the Mashpee's underscore the need for U.S. courts to modify their definition of "tribe."

(C) Land claim suits such as the Mashpee's illustrate the complications that can result when cultures with different systems of discourse attempt to resolve disputes.

(D) Land claim suits such the Mashpee's point out discrepancies between what U.S. courts claim they will recognize as evidence and what forms of evidence they actually accept.

(E) Land claim suits such as the Mashpee's bring to light the problems faced by Native American tribes attempting to establish their claims within a legal system governed by the application of precedent.

42. According to the passage, the Mashpee's lawsuit was based on their objection to

(A) the increase in the non-Mashpee population of the town during the 1960s

(B) the repeal of a statute forbidding land transfers without U.S. government approval

(C) the loss of Mashpee control over land use immediately after the town's incorporation

(D) the town's refusal to recognize the Mashpee's deed to the land in dispute

(E) the sale of Mashpee-controlled land to non-Mashpee residents without U.S. government approval

43. The author's attitude toward the court's decision in the Mashpee's lawsuit is most clearly revealed by the author's use of which one of the following phrases?

(A) "operate within a particular sphere" (lines 7–8)
(B) "continued to have control" (line 20)
(C) "required to demonstrate" (line 32)
(D) "precisely delineated its boundaries" (line 42)
(E) "failure to accommodate" (line 54)

44. Based on the passage, which one of the following can most reasonably be said to have occurred in the years since the Mashpee's lawsuit?

(A) The Mashpee have now regained control over the land they inhabit.
(B) Native American tribes have won all of their land claim suits in U.S. courts.
(C) U.S. courts no longer abide by the statute requiring federal approval of certain land transfers.
(D) U.S. courts have become more likely to accept oral testimony as evidence in land claim suits.
(E) U.S. courts have changed their definition of what legally constitutes a tribe.

45. The passage is primarily concerned with

(A) evaluating various approaches to solving a problem
(B) illuminating a general problem by discussing a specific example
(C) reconciling the differences in how two opposing sides approach a problem
(D) critiquing an earlier solution to a problem in light of new information
(E) reinterpreting an earlier analysis and proposing a new solution to the problem

Test 40, Section 4, Questions 6–12

In spite of a shared language, Latin American poetry written in Spanish differs from Spanish poetry in many respects. The Spanish of Latin American poets is more open than that of Spanish poets, more exposed
(5) to outside influences—indigenous, English, French, and other languages. While some literary critics maintain that there is as much linguistic unity in Latin American poetry as there is in Spanish poetry, they base this claim on the fact that Castilian Spanish, the
(10) official and literary version of the Spanish language based largely on the dialect originally spoken in the Castile region of Spain, was transplanted to the Americas when it was already a relatively standardized idiom. Although such unity may have characterized the
(15) earliest Latin American poetry, after centuries in the Americas the language of Latin American poetry cannot help but reveal the influences of its unique cultural history.

Latin American poetry is critical or irreverent in its
(20) attitude toward language, where that of Spanish poets is more accepting. For example, the Spanish-language incarnations of modernism and the avant-garde, two literary movements that used language in innovative and challenging ways, originated with Latin American
(25) poets. By contrast, when these movements later reached Spain, Spanish poets greeted them with reluctance. Spanish poets, even those of the modern era, seem to take their language for granted, rarely using it in radical or experimental ways.

(30) The most distinctive note in Latin American poetry is its enthusiastic response to the modern world, while Spanish poetry displays a kind of cultural conservatism—the desire to return to an ideal culture of the distant past. Because no Spanish-language
(35) culture lies in the equally distant (i.e., pre-Columbian) past of the Americas, but has instead been invented by Latin Americans day by day, Latin American poetry has no such long-standing past to romanticize. Instead, Latin American poetry often displays a curiosity about
(40) the literature of other cultures, an interest in exploring poetic structures beyond those typical of Spanish poetry. For example, the first Spanish-language haiku—a Japanese poetic form—were written by José Juan Tablada, a Mexican. Another of the Latin
(45) American poets' responses to this absence is the search for a world before recorded history—not only that of Spain or the Americas, but in some cases of the planet; the Chilean poet Pablo Neruda's work, for example, is noteworthy for its development of an ahistorical
(50) mythology for the creation of the earth. For Latin American poets there is no such thing as the pristine cultural past affirmed in the poetry of Spain: there is only the fluid interaction of all world cultures, or else the extensive time before cultures began.

46. The discussion in the second paragraph is intended primarily to

(A) argue that Latin American poets originated modernism and the avant-garde
(B) explain how Spanish poetry and Latin American poetry differ in their attitudes toward the Spanish language
(C) demonstrate why Latin American poetry is not well received in Spain
(D) show that the Castilian Spanish employed in Spanish poetry has remained relatively unchanged by the advent of modernism and the avant-garde
(E) illustrate the extent to which Spanish poetry romanticizes Spanish-language culture

47. Given the information in the passage, which one of the following is most analogous to the evolution of Latin American poetry?

(A) A family moves its restaurant to a new town and incorporates local ingredients into its traditional recipes.
(B) A family moves its business to a new town after the business fails in its original location.
(C) A family with a two-hundred-year-old house labors industriously in order to restore the house to its original appearance.
(D) A family does research into its ancestry in order to construct its family tree.
(E) A family eagerly anticipates its annual vacation but never takes photographs or purchases souvenirs to preserve its memories.

48. The passage's claims about Spanish poetry would be most weakened if new evidence indicating which one of the following were discovered?

(A) Spanish linguistic constructs had greater influence on Latin American poets than had previously been thought.
(B) Castilian Spanish was still evolving linguistically at the time of the inception of Latin American poetry.
(C) Spanish poets originated an influential literary movement that used language in radical ways.
(D) Castilian Spanish was influenced during its evolution by other Spanish dialects.
(E) Spanish poets rejected the English and French incarnations of modernism.

49. The passage affirms each of the following EXCEPT:

   (A) The first haiku in the Spanish language were written by a Latin American poet.
   (B) Spanish poetry is rarely innovative or experimental in its use of language.
   (C) Spanish poetry rarely incorporates poetic traditions from other cultures.
   (D) Latin American poetry tends to take the Spanish language for granted.
   (E) Latin American poetry incorporates aspects of various other languages.

50. Which one of the following can most reasonably be inferred from the passage about Latin American poetry's use of poetic structures from other world cultures?

   (A) The use of poetic structures from other world cultures is an attempt by Latin American poets to create a cultural past.
   (B) The use of poetic structures from other world cultures by Latin American poets is a response to their lack of a long-standing Spanish-language cultural past in the Americas.
   (C) The use of poetic structures from other world cultures has led Latin American poets to reconsider their lack of a long-standing Spanish-language cultural past in the Americas.
   (D) Latin American poets who write about a world before recorded history do not use poetic structures from other world cultures.
   (E) Latin American poetry does not borrow poetic structures from other world cultures whose literature exhibits cultural conservatism.

51. Based on the passage, the author most likely holds which one of the following views toward Spanish poetry's relationship to the Spanish cultural past?

   (A) This relationship has inspired Spanish poets to examine their cultural past with a critical eye.
   (B) This relationship forces Spanish poets to write about subjects with which they feel little natural affinity.
   (C) This relationship is itself the central theme of much Spanish poetry.
   (D) This relationship infuses Spanish poetry with a romanticism that is reluctant to embrace the modern era.
   (E) This relationship results in poems that are of little interest to contemporary Spanish readers.

52. Which one of the following inferences is most supported by the passage?

   (A) A tradition of cultural conservatism has allowed the Spanish language to evolve into a stable, reliable form of expression.
   (B) It was only recently that Latin American poetry began to incorporate elements of other languages.
   (C) The cultural conservatism of Spanish poetry is exemplified by the uncritical attitude of Spanish poets toward the Spanish language.
   (D) Latin American poets' interest in other world cultures is illustrated by their use of Japanese words and phrases.
   (E) Spanish poetry is receptive to the influence of some Spanish-language poets outside of Spain.

Test 40, Section 4, Questions 13–19

According to the theory of gravitation, every particle of matter in the universe attracts every other particle with a force that increases as either the mass of the particles increases, or their proximity to one
(5) another increases, or both. Gravitation is believed to shape the structures of stars, galaxies, and the entire universe. But for decades cosmologists (scientists who study the universe) have attempted to account for the finding that at least 90 percent of the universe seems to
(10) be missing: that the total amount of observable matter—stars, dust, and miscellaneous debris—does not contain enough mass to explain why the universe is organized in the shape of galaxies and clusters of galaxies. To account for this discrepancy, cosmologists
(15) hypothesize that something else, which they call "dark matter," provides the gravitational force necessary to make the huge structures cohere.

What is dark matter? Numerous exotic entities have been postulated, but among the more attractive
(20) candidates—because they are known actually to exist—are neutrinos, elementary particles created as a by-product of nuclear fusion, radioactive decay, or catastrophic collisions between other particles. Neutrinos, which come in three types, are by far the
(25) most numerous kind of particle in the universe; however, they have long been assumed to have no mass. If so, that would disqualify them as dark matter. Without mass, matter cannot exert gravitational force; without such force, it cannot induce other matter to
(30) cohere.

But new evidence suggests that a neutrino does have mass. This evidence came by way of research findings supporting the existence of a long-theorized but never observed phenomenon called oscillation,
(35) whereby each of the three neutrino types can change into one of the others as it travels through space. Researchers held that the transformation is possible only if neutrinos also have mass. They obtained experimental confirmation of the theory by generating
(40) one neutrino type and then finding evidence that it had oscillated into the predicted neutrino type. In the process, they were able to estimate the mass of a neutrino at from 0.5 to 5 electron volts.

While slight, even the lowest estimate would yield
(45) a lot of mass given that neutrinos are so numerous, especially considering that neutrinos were previously assumed to have no mass. Still, even at the highest estimate, neutrinos could only account for about 20 percent of the universe's "missing" mass. Nevertheless,
(50) that is enough to alter our picture of the universe even if it does not account for all of dark matter. In fact, some cosmologists claim that this new evidence offers the best theoretical solution yet to the dark matter problem. If the evidence holds up, these cosmologists
(55) believe, it may add to our understanding of the role elementary particles play in holding the universe together.

53. Which one of the following most accurately expresses the main idea of the passage?

(A) Although cosmologists believe that the universe is shaped by gravitation, the total amount of observable matter in the universe is greatly insufficient to account for the gravitation that would be required to cause the universe to be organized into galaxies.

(B) Given their inability to account for more than 20 percent of the universe's "missing" mass, scientists are beginning to speculate that our current understanding of gravity is significantly mistaken.

(C) Indirect evidence suggesting that neutrinos have mass may allow neutrinos to account for up to 20 percent of dark matter, a finding that could someday be extended to a complete solution of the dark matter problem.

(D) After much speculation, researchers have discovered that neutrinos oscillate from one type into another as they travel through space, a phenomenon that proves that neutrinos have mass.

(E) Although it has been established that neutrinos have mass, such mass does not support the speculation of cosmologists that neutrinos constitute a portion of the universe's "missing" mass.

54. Which one of the following titles most completely and accurately expresses the contents of the passage?

(A) "The Existence of Dark Matter: Arguments For and Against"

(B) "Neutrinos and the Dark Matter Problem: A Partial Solution?"

(C) "Too Little, Too Late: Why Neutrinos Do Not Constitute Dark Matter"

(D) "The Role of Gravity: How Dark Matter Shapes Stars"

(E) "The Implications of Oscillation: Do Neutrinos Really Have Mass?"

55. Based on the passage, the author most likely holds which one of the following views?

(A) Observable matter constitutes at least 90 percent of the mass of the universe.
(B) Current theories are incapable of identifying the force that causes all particles in the universe to attract one another.
(C) The key to the problem of dark matter is determining the exact mass of a neutrino.
(D) It is unlikely that any force other than gravitation will be required to account for the organization of the universe into galaxies.
(E) Neutrinos probably account for most of the universe's "missing" mass.

56. As described in the last paragraph of the passage, the cosmologists' approach to solving the dark matter problem is most analogous to which one of the following?

(A) A child seeking information about how to play chess consults a family member and so learns of a book that will instruct her in the game.
(B) A child seeking to earn money by delivering papers is unable to earn enough money for a bicycle and so decides to buy a skateboard instead.
(C) A child hoping to get a dog for his birthday is initially disappointed when his parents bring home a cat but eventually learns to love the animal.
(D) A child seeking money to attend a movie is given some of the money by one of his siblings and so decides to go to each of his other siblings to ask for additional money.
(E) A child enjoys playing sports with the neighborhood children, but her parents insist that she cannot participate until she has completed her household chores.

57. The author's attitude toward oscillation can most accurately be characterized as being

(A) satisfied that it occurs and that it suggests that neutrinos have mass
(B) hopeful that it will be useful in discovering other forms of dark matter
(C) concerned that it is often misinterpreted to mean that neutrinos account for all of dark matter
(D) skeptical that it occurs until further research can be done
(E) convinced that it cannot occur outside an experimental setting

58. Which one of the following phrases could replace the word "cohere" at line 30 without substantively altering the author's meaning?

(A) exert gravitational force
(B) form galactic structures
(C) oscillate into another type of matter
(D) become significantly more massive
(E) fuse to produce new particles

59. The passage states each of the following EXCEPT:

(A) There are more neutrinos in the universe than there are non-neutrinos.
(B) Observable matter cannot exert enough gravitational force to account for the present structure of the universe.
(C) Scientific experiments support the theory of neutrino oscillation.
(D) Neutrinos likely cannot account for all of the universe's "missing" mass.
(E) Dark matter may account for a large portion of the universe's gravitational force.

Test 22, Section 1, Questions 1–8

Painter Frida Kahlo (1910–1954) often used harrowing images derived from her Mexican heritage to express suffering caused by a disabling accident and a stormy marriage. Suggesting much personal and
(5) emotional content, her works—many of them self-portraits—have been exhaustively psychoanalyzed, while their political content has been less studied. Yet Kahlo was an ardent political activist who in her art sought not only to explore her own roots, but also to
(10) champion Mexico's struggle for an independent political and cultural identity.

Kahlo was influenced by Marxism, which appealed to many intellectuals in the 1920s and 1930s, and by Mexican nationalism. Interest in Mexico's culture and
(15) history had revived in the nineteenth century, and by the early 1900s, Mexican *indigenista* tendencies ranged from a violently anti-Spanish idealization of Aztec Mexico to an emphasis on contemporary Mexican Indians as the key to authentic Mexican culture.
(20) Mexican nationalism, reacting against contemporary United States political intervention in labor disputes as well as against past domination by Spain, identified the Aztecs as the last independent rulers of an indigenous political unit. Kahlo's form of *Mexicanidad,* a romantic
(25) nationalism that focused upon traditional art uniting all *indigenistas,* revered the Aztecs as a powerful pre-Columbian society that had united a large area of the Middle Americas and that was thought to have been based on communal labor, the Marxist ideal.
(30) In her paintings, Kahlo repeatedly employed Aztec symbols, such as skeletons or bleeding hearts, that were traditionally related to the emanation of life from death and light from darkness. These images of destruction coupled with creation speak not only to
(35) Kahlo's personal battle for life, but also to the Mexican struggle to emerge as a nation—by implication, to emerge with the political and cultural strength admired in the Aztec civilization. *Self-Portrait on the Border between Mexico and the United States* (1932), for
(40) example, shows Kahlo wearing a bone necklace, holding a Mexican flag, and standing between a highly industrialized United States and an agricultural, preindustrial Mexico. On the United States side are mechanistic and modern images such as smokestacks,
(45) light bulbs, and robots. In contrast, the organic and ancient symbols on the Mexican side—a blood-drenched Sun, lush vegetation, an Aztec sculpture, a pre-Columbian temple, and a skull alluding to those that lined the walls of Aztec temples—emphasize the
(50) interrelation of life, death, the earth, and the cosmos.

Kahlo portrayed Aztec images in the folkloric style of traditional Mexican paintings, thereby heightening the clash between modern materialism and indigenous tradition; similarly, she favored planned economic
(55) development, but not at the expense of cultural identity. Her use of familiar symbols in a readily accessible style also served her goal of being popularly understood; in turn, Kahlo is viewed by some Mexicans as a mythic figure representative of
(60) nationalism itself.

60. Which one of the following best expresses the main point of the passage?

(A) The doctrines of Marxist ideology and Mexican nationalism heavily influenced Mexican painters of Kahlo's generation.

(B) Kahlo's paintings contain numerous references to the Aztecs as an indigenous Mexican people predating European influence.

(C) An important element of Kahlo's work is conveyed by symbols that reflect her advocacy of indigenous Mexican culture and Mexican political autonomy.

(D) The use of Aztec images and symbols in Kahlo's art can be traced to the late nineteenth-century revival of interest in Mexican history and culture.

(E) Kahlo used Aztec imagery in her paintings primarily in order to foster contemporary appreciation for the authentic art of traditional Mexican culture.

61. With which one of the following statements concerning psychoanalytic and political interpretations of Kahlo's work would the author be most likely to agree?

(A) The psychoanalytic interpretations of Kahlo's work tend to challenge the political interpretations.

(B) Political and psychoanalytic interpretations are complementary approaches to Kahlo's work.

(C) Recent political interpretations of Kahlo's work are causing psychoanalytic critics to revise their own interpretations.

(D) Unlike the political interpretations, the psychoanalytic interpretations make use of biographical facts of Kahlo's life.

(E) Kahlo's mythic status among the audience Kahlo most wanted to reach is based upon the psychoanalytic rather than the political content of her work.

62. Which one of the following stances toward the United States does the passage mention as characterizing Mexican nationalists in the early twentieth century?

(A) opposition to United States involvement in internal Mexican affairs
(B) desire to decrease emigration of the Mexican labor force to the United States
(C) desire to improve Mexico's economic competitiveness with the United States
(D) reluctance to imitate the United States model of rapid industrialization
(E) advocacy of a government based upon that of the Marxist Soviet Union rather than that of the United States

63. In the context of the passage, which one of the following phrases could best be substituted for the word "romantic" (line 24) without substantially changing the author's meaning?

(A) dreamy and escapist
(B) nostalgic and idealistic
(C) fanciful and imaginative
(D) transcendental and impractical
(E) overwrought and sentimental

64. The passage mentions each of the following as an Aztec symbol or image found in Kahlo's paintings EXCEPT a

(A) skeleton
(B) sculpture
(C) serpent
(D) skull
(E) bleeding heart

65. Which one of the following best describes the organization of the third paragraph?

(A) contrast of opposing ideas
(B) reconciliation of conflicting concepts
(C) interrelation of complementary themes
(D) explication of a principle's implications
(E) support for a generalization by means of an example

66. The passage implies that Kahlo's attitude toward the economic development of Mexico was

(A) enthusiastic
(B) condemnatory
(C) cautious
(D) noncommittal
(E) uncertain

67. The main purpose of the passage is to

(A) critique an artist's style
(B) evaluate opposing theories
(C) reconcile conflicting arguments
(D) advocate an additional interpretation
(E) reconsider an artist in light of new discoveries

Test 25, Section 1, Questions 14–21

Even in the midst of its resurgence as a vital
tradition, many sociologists have viewed the current
form of the powwow, a ceremonial gathering of native
Americans, as a sign that tribal culture is in decline.
(5) Focusing on the dances and rituals that have recently
come to be shared by most tribes, they suggest that an
intertribal movement is now in ascension and claim the
inevitable outcome of this tendency is the eventual
dissolution of tribes and the complete assimilation of
(10) native Americans into Euroamerican society.
Proponents of this "Pan-Indian" theory point to the
greater frequency of travel and communication
between reservations, the greater urbanization of native
Americans, and, most recently, their increasing
(15) politicization in response to common grievances as the
chief causes of the shift toward intertribalism.
Indeed, the rapid diffusion of dance styles, outfits,
and songs from one reservation to another offers
compelling evidence that intertribalism has been
(20) increasing. However, these sociologists have failed to
note the concurrent revitalization of many traditions
unique to individual tribes. Among the Lakota, for
instance, the Sun Dance was revived, after a forty-year
hiatus, during the 1950's. Similarly, the Black Legging
(25) Society of the Kiowa and the Hethuska Society of the
Ponca—both traditional groups within their respective
tribes—have gained new popularity. Obviously, a more
complex societal shift is taking place than the theory of
Pan-Indianism can account for.
(30)   An examination of the theory's underpinnings may
be critical at this point, especially given that native
Americans themselves chafe most against the Pan-
Indian classification. Like other assimilationist theories
with which it is associated, the Pan-Indian view is
(35) predicted upon an a priori assumption about the nature
of cultural contact: that upon contact minority societies
immediately begin to succumb in every respect—
biologically, linguistically, and culturally—to the
majority society. However, there is no evidence that
(40) this is happening to native American groups.
Yet the fact remains that intertribal activities are a
major facet of native American culture today. Certain
dances at powwows, for instance, are announced as
intertribal, other as traditional. Likewise, speeches
(45) given at the beginnings of powwows are often
delivered in English, while the prayer that follows is
usually spoken in a native language. Cultural
borrowing is, of course, old news. What is important to
note is the conscious distinction native Americans
(50) make between tribal and intertribal tendencies.
Tribalism, although greatly altered by modern
history, remains a potent force among native
Americans: It forms a basis for tribal identity, and
aligns music and dance with other social and cultural
(55) activities important to individual tribes. Intertribal
activities, on the other hand, reinforce native American
identity along a broader front, where this identity is
directly threatened by outside influences.

68. Which one of the following best summarizes the main
idea of the passage?

(A) Despite the fact that sociologists have only
recently begun to understand its importance,
intertribalism has always been an influential
factor in native American culture.

(B) Native Americans are currently struggling with
an identity crisis caused primarily by the two
competing forces of tribalism and intertribalism.

(C) The recent growth of intertribalism is unlikely to
eliminate tribalism because the two forces do not
oppose one another but instead reinforce distinct
elements of native American identity.

(D) The tendency toward intertribalism, although
prevalent within native American culture,
has had a minimal effect on the way native
Americans interact with the broader community
around them.

(E) Despite the recent revival of many native
American tribal traditions, the recent trend
toward intertribalism is likely to erode cultural
differences among the various native American
tribes.

69. The author most likely states that "cultural borrowing is,
of course, old news" (lines 47–48) primarily to

(A) acknowledge that in itself the existence of
intertribal tendencies at powwows is unsurprising

(B) suggest that native Americans' use of English in
powwows should be accepted as unavoidable

(C) argue that the deliberate distinction of
intertribal and traditional dances is not a recent
development

(D) suggest that the recent increase in intertribal
activity is the result of native Americans
borrowing from non-native American cultures

(E) indicate that the powwow itself could have
originated by combining practices drawn from
both native and Non-native American cultures

70. The author of the passage would most likely agree with
which one of the following assertions?

(A) Though some believe the current form of the
powwow signals the decline of tribal culture,
the powwow contains elements that indicate the
continuing strength of tribalism.

(B) The logical outcome of the recent increase in
intertribal activity is the eventual disappearance
of tribal culture.

(C) native Americans who participate in both
tribal and intertribal activities usually base
their identities on intertribal rather than tribal
affiliations.

(D) The conclusions of some sociologists about the
health of native American cultures show that
these sociologists are in fact biased against such
cultures.

(E) Until it is balanced by revitalization of tribal
customs, intertribalism will continue to weaken
the native American sense of identity.

71. The primary function of the third paragraph is to

   (A)   search for evidence to corroborate the basic assumption of the theory of Pan-Indianism

   (B)   demonstrate the incorrectness of the theory of Pan-Indianism by pointing out that native American groups themselves disagree with the theory

   (C)   explain the origin of the theory of Pan-Indianism by showing how it evolved from other assimilationist theories

   (D)   examine several assimilationist theories in order to demonstrate that they rest on a common assumption

   (E)   criticize the theory of Pan-Indianism by pointing out that it rests upon an assumption for which there is no supporting evidence

72. Which one of the following most accurately describes the author's attitude toward the theory of Pan-Indianism?

   (A)   critical of its tendency to attribute political motives to cultural practices

   (B)   discomfort at its negative characterization of cultural borrowing by native Americans

   (C)   hopeful about its chances for preserving tribal culture

   (D)   offended by its claim that assimilation is a desirable consequence of cultural contact

   (E)   skeptical that it is a complete explanation of recent changes in native American society

73. With which one of the following statements would the author of the passage be most likely to agree?

   (A)   The resurgence of the powwow is a sign that native American customs are beginning to have an important influence on Euroamerican society.

   (B)   Although native Americans draw conscious distinctions between tribal and intertribal activities, there is no difference in how the two types of activity actually function within the context of native American society.

   (C)   Without intertribal activities, it would be more difficult for native Americans to maintain the cultural differences between native American and Euroamerican society.

   (D)   The powwow was recently revived, after an extended hiatus, in order to strengthen native Americans' sense of ethnic identity.

   (E)   The degree of urbanization, intertribal communication, and politicization among native Americans has been exaggerated by proponents of the theory of Pan-Indianism.

74. Which one of the following situations most clearly illustrates the phenomenon of intertribalism, as that phenomenon is described in the passage?

   (A)   a native American tribe in which a number of powerful societies attempt to prevent the revival of a traditional dance

   (B)   a native American tribe whose members attempt to learn the native languages of several other tribes

   (C)   a native American tribe whose members attempt to form a political organization in order to redress several grievances important to that tribe

   (D)   a native American tribe in which a significant percentage of the members have forsaken their tribal identity and become assimilated into Euroamerican society

   (E)   a native American tribe whose members often travel to other parts of the reservation in order to visit friends and relatives

75. In the passage, the author is primarily concerned with doing which one of the following?

   (A)   identifying an assumption common to various assimilationist theories and then criticizing these theories by showing this assumption of be false

   (B)   arguing that the recent revival of a number of tribal practices shows sociologists are mistaken in believing intertribalism to be a potent force among native American societies

   (C)   questioning the belief that native American societies will eventually be assimilated into Euroamerican society by arguing that intertribalism helps strengthen native American identity

   (D)   showing how the recent resurgence of tribal activities is a deliberate attempt to counteract the growing influence of intertribalism

   (E)   proposing an explanation of why the ascension of intertribalism could result in the eventual dissolution of tribes and complete assimilation of native Americans into Euroamerican society

Test 25, Section 1, Questions 22–26

Scientists typically advocate the analytic method of studying complex systems: systems are divided into component parts that are investigated separately. But nineteenth-century critics of this method claimed that
(5) when a system's parts are isolated its complexity tends to be lost. To address the perceived weaknesses of the analytic method these critics put forward a concept called organicism, which posited that the whole determines the nature of its parts and that the parts of a
(10) whole are interdependent.

Organicism depended upon the theory of internal relations, which states that relations between entities are possible only within some whole that embraces them, and that entities are altered by the relationships
(15) into which they enter. If an entity stands in a relationship with another entity, it has some property as a consequence. Without this relationship, and hence without the property, the entity would be different— and so would be another entity. Thus, the property is
(20) one of the entity's defining characteristics. Each of an entity's relationships likewise determines a defining characteristic of the entity.

One problem with the theory of internal relations is that not all properties of an entity are defining
(25) characteristics: numerous properties are accompanying characteristics—even if they are always present, their presence does not influence the entity's identity. Thus, even if it is admitted that every relationship into which an entity enters determines some characteristic of the
(30) entity, it is not necessarily true that such characteristics will define the entity; it is possible for the entity to enter into a relationship yet remain essentially unchanged.

The ultimate difficulty with the theory of internal
(35) relations is that it renders the acquisition of knowledge impossible. To truly know an entity, we must know all of its relationships; but because the entity is related to everything in each whole of which it is a part, these wholes must be known completely before the entity
(40) can be known. This seems to be a prerequisite impossible to satisfy.

Organicists' criticism of the analytic method arose from their failure to fully comprehend the method. In rejecting the analytic method, organicists overlooked
(45) the fact that before the proponents of the method analyzed the component parts of a system, they first determined both the laws applicable to the whole system and the initial conditions of the system; proponents of the method thus did not study parts of a
(50) system in full isolation from the system as a whole. Since organicists failed to recognize this, they never advanced any argument to show that laws and initial conditions of complex systems cannot be discovered. Hence, organicists offered no valid reason for rejecting
(55) the analytic method or for adopting organicism as a replacement for it.

76. Which one of the following most completely and accurately summarizes the argument of the passage?

(A) By calling into question the possibility that complex systems can be studied in their entirety, organicists offered an alternative to the analytic method favored by nineteenth-century scientists.

(B) Organicists did not offer a useful method of studying complex systems because they did not acknowledge that there are relationships into which an entity may enter that do not alter the entity's identity.

(C) Organicism is flawed because it relies on a theory that both ignores the fact that not all characteristics of entities are defining and ultimately makes the acquisition of knowledge impossible.

(D) Organicism does not offer a valid challenge to the analytic method both because it relies on faulty theory and because it is based on a misrepresentation of the analytic method.

(E) In criticizing the analytic method, organicists neglected to disprove that scientists who employ the method are able to discover the laws and initial conditions of the systems they study.

77. According to the passage, organicists' chief objection to the analytic method was that the method

(A) oversimplified systems by isolating their components

(B) assumed that a system can be divided into component parts

(C) ignored the laws applicable to the system as a whole

(D) claimed that the parts of a system are more important than the system as a whole

(E) denied the claim that entities enter into relationships

78. The passage offers information to help answer each of the following questions EXCEPT:

(A) Why does the theory of internal relations appear to make the acquisition of knowledge impossible?

(B) Why did the organicists propose replacing the analytic method?

(C) What is the difference between a defining characteristic and an accompanying characteristic?

(D) What did organicists claim are the effects of an entity's entering into a relationship with another entity?

(E) What are some of the advantages of separating out the parts of a system for study?

79. The passage most strongly supports the ascription of which one of the following views to scientists who use the analytic method?

(A) A complex system is best understood by studying its component parts in full isolation from the system as a whole.

(B) The parts of a system should be studied with an awareness of the laws and initial conditions that govern the system.

(C) It is not possible to determine the laws governing a system until the system's parts are separated from one another.

(D) Because the parts of a system are interdependent, they cannot be studied separately without destroying the system's complexity.

(E) Studying the parts of a system individually eliminates the need to determine which characteristics of the parts are defining characteristics.

80. Which one of the following is a principle upon which the author bases an argument against the theory of internal relations?

(A) An adequate theory of complex systems must define the entities of which the system is composed.

(B) An acceptable theory cannot have consequences that contradict its basic purpose.

(C) An adequate method of study of complex systems should reveal the actual complexity of the systems it studies.

(D) An acceptable theory must describe the laws and initial conditions of a complex system.

(E) An acceptable method of studying complex systems should not study parts of the system in isolation from the system as a whole.

Test 27, Section 3, Questions 15–21

Homing pigeons can be taken from their lofts and transported hundreds of kilometers in covered cages to unfamiliar sites and yet, when released, be able to choose fairly accurate homeward bearings within a
(5) minute and fly home. Aside from reading the minds of the experimenters (a possibility that has not escaped investigation), there are two basic explanations for the remarkable ability of pigeons to "home": the birds might keep track of their outward displacement (the
(10) system of many short-range species such as honeybees); or they might have some sense, known as a "map sense," that would permit them to construct an internal image of their environment and then "place" themselves with respect to home on some internalized
(15) coordinate system.

The first alternative seems unlikely. One possible model for such an inertial system might involve an internal magnetic compass to measure the directional leg of each journey. Birds transported to the release site
(20) wearing magnets or otherwise subjected to an artificial magnetic field, however, are only occasionally affected. Alternately, if pigeons measure their displacement by consciously keeping track of the direction and degree of acceleration and deceleration of
(25) the various turns, and timing the individual legs of the journey, simply transporting them in the dark, with constant rotations, or under complete anesthesia ought to impair or eliminate their ability to orient. These treatments, however, have no effect. Unfortunately, no
(30) one has yet performed the crucial experiment of transporting pigeons in total darkness, anesthetized, rotating, and with the magnetic field reversed all at the same time.

The other alternative, that pigeons have a "map
(35) sense," seems more promising, yet the nature of this sense remains mysterious. Papi has posited that the map sense is olfactory: that birds come to associate odors borne on the wind with the direction in which the wind is blowing, and so slowly build up an olfactory
(40) map of their surroundings. When transported to the release site, then, they only have to sniff the air en route and/or at the site to know the direction of home. Papi conducted a series of experiments showing that pigeons whose nostrils have been plugged are poorly
(45) oriented at release and home slowly.

One problem with the hypothesis is that Schmidt-Koenig and Phillips failed to detect any ability in pigeons to distinguish natural air (presumably laden with olfactory map information) from pure, filtered air.
(50) Papi's experimental results, moreover, admit of simpler, nonolfactory explanations. It seems likely that the behavior of nostril-plugged birds results from the distracting and traumatic nature of the experiment. When nasal tubes are used to bypass the olfactory
(55) chamber but allow for comfortable breathing, no disorientation is evident. Likewise, when the olfactory epithelium is sprayed with anesthetic to block smell-detection but not breathing, orientation is normal.

81. Which one of the following best states the main idea of the passage?

(A) The ability of pigeons to locate and return to their homes from distant points is unlike that of any other species.

(B) It is likely that some map sense accounts for the homing ability of pigeons, but the nature of that sense has not been satisfactorily identified.

(C) The majority of experiments on the homing ability of pigeons have been marked by design flaws.

(D) The mechanisms underlying the homing ability of pigeons can best be identified through a combination of laboratory research and field experimentation.

(E) The homing ability of pigeons is most likely based on a system similar to that used by many short-range species.

82. According to the passage, which one of the following is ordinarily true regarding how homing pigeons "home"?

(A) Each time they are released at a specific site they fly home by the same route.

(B) When they are released they take only a short time to orient themselves before selecting their route home.

(C) Each time they are released at a specific site they take a shorter amount of time to orient themselves before flying home.

(D) They travel fairly long distances in seemingly random patterns before finally deciding on a route home.

(E) Upon release they travel briefly in the direction opposite to the one they eventually choose.

83. Which one of the following experiments would best test the "possibility" referred to in line 6?

(A) an experiment in which the handlers who transported, released, and otherwise came into contact with homing pigeons released at an unfamiliar site were unaware of the location of the pigeons' home

(B) an experiment in which the handlers who transported, released, and otherwise came into contact with homing pigeons released at an unfamiliar site were asked not to display any affection toward the pigeons

(C) an experiment in which the handlers who transported, released, and otherwise came into contact with homing pigeons released at an unfamiliar site were asked not to speak to each other throughout the release process

(D) an experiment in which all the homing pigeons released at an unfamiliar site had been raised and fed by individual researchers rather than by teams of handlers

(E) an experiment in which all the homing pigeons released at an unfamiliar site were exposed to a wide variety of unfamiliar sights and sounds

84. Information in the passage supports which one of the following statements regarding the "first alternative" (line 16) for explaining the ability of pigeons to "home"?

(A) It has been conclusively ruled out by the results of numerous experiments.

(B) It seems unlikely because there are no theoretical models that could explain how pigeons track displacement.

(C) It has not, to date, been supported by experimental data, but neither has it been definitively ruled out.

(D) It seems unlikely in theory, but recent experimental results show that it may in fact be correct.

(E) It is not a useful theory because of the difficulty in designing experiments by which it might be tested.

85. The author refers to "the system of many short-range species such as honeybees" (lines 9–11) most probably in order to

(A) emphasize the universality of the ability to home

(B) suggest that a particular explanation of pigeons' homing ability is worthy of consideration

(C) discredit one of the less convincing theories regarding the homing ability of pigeons

(D) criticize the techniques utilized by scientists investigating the nature of pigeons' homing ability

(E) illustrate why a proposed explanation of pigeons' homing ability is correct

86. Which one of the following, if true, would most weaken Papi's theory regarding homing pigeons' homing ability?

(A) Even pigeons that have been raised in several different lofts in a variety of territories can find their way to their current home when released in unfamiliar territory.

(B) Pigeons whose sense of smell has been partially blocked find their way home more slowly than do pigeons whose sense of smell has not been affected.

(C) Even pigeons that have been raised in the same loft frequently take different routes home when released in unfamiliar territory.

(D) Even pigeons that have been transported well beyond the range of the odors detectable in their home territories can find their way home.

(E) Pigeons' sense of smell is no more acute than that of other birds who do not have the ability to "home."

87. Given the information in the passage, it is most likely that Papi and the author of the passage would both agree with which one of the following statements regarding the homing ability of pigeons?

(A) The map sense of pigeons is most probably related to their olfactory sense.

(B) The mechanism regulating the homing ability of pigeons is most probably similar to that utilized by honeybees.

(C) The homing ability of pigeons is most probably based on a map sense.

(D) The experiments conducted by Papi himself have provided the most valuable evidence yet collected regarding the homing ability of pigeons.

(E) The experiments conducted by Schmidt-Koenig and Phillips have not substantially lessened the probability that Papi's own theory is correct.

Test 40, Section 4, Questions 20–27

Leading questions—questions worded in such a
way as to suggest a particular answer—can yield
unreliable testimony either by design, as when a lawyer
tries to trick a witness into affirming a particular
(5) version of the evidence of a case, or by accident, when
a questioner unintentionally prejudices the witness's
response. For this reason, a judge can disallow such
questions in the courtroom interrogation of witnesses.
But their exclusion from the courtroom by no means
(10) eliminates the remote effects of earlier leading
questions on eyewitness testimony. Alarmingly, the
beliefs about an event that a witness brings to the
courtroom may often be adulterated by the effects of
leading questions that were introduced intentionally or
(15) unintentionally by lawyers, police investigators,
reporters, or others with whom the witness has already
interacted.

Recent studies have confirmed the ability of
leading questions to alter the details of our memories
(20) and have led to a better understanding of how this
process occurs and, perhaps, of the conditions that
make for greater risks that an eyewitness's memories
have been tainted by leading questions. These studies
suggest that not all details of our experiences become
(25) clearly or stably stored in memory—only those to
which we give adequate attention. Moreover,
experimental evidence indicates that if subtly
introduced new data involving remembered events do
not actively conflict with our stored memory data, we
(30) tend to process such new data similarly whether they
correspond to details as we remember them, or to gaps
in those details. In the former case, we often retain the
new data as a reinforcement of the corresponding
aspect of the memory, and in the latter case, we often
(35) retain them as a construction to fill the corresponding
gap. An eyewitness who is asked, prior to courtroom
testimony, "How fast was the car going when it passed
the stop sign?" may respond to the query about speed
without addressing the question of the stop sign. But
(40) the "stop sign" datum has now been introduced, and
when later recalled, perhaps during courtroom
testimony, it may be processed as belonging to the
original memory even if the witness actually saw no
stop sign.

(45) The farther removed from the event, the greater the
chance of a vague or incomplete recollection and the
greater the likelihood of newly suggested information
blending with original memories. Since we can be
more easily misled with respect to fainter and more
(50) uncertain memories, tangential details are more apt to
become constructed out of subsequently introduced
information than are more central details. But what is
tangential to a witness's original experience of an event
may nevertheless be crucial to the courtroom issues
(55) that the witness's memories are supposed to resolve.
For example, a perpetrator's shirt color or hairstyle
might be tangential to one's shocked observance of an
armed robbery, but later those factors might be crucial
to establishing the identity of the perpetrator.

88. Which one of the following most accurately expresses
the main point of the passage?

(A) The unreliability of memories about incidental
aspects of observed events makes eyewitness
testimony especially questionable in cases in
which the witness was not directly involved.

(B) Because of the nature of human memory storage
and retrieval, the courtroom testimony of
eyewitnesses may contain crucial inaccuracies
due to leading questions asked prior to the
courtroom appearance.

(C) Researchers are surprised to find that courtroom
testimony is often dependent on suggestion to fill
gaps left by insufficient attention to detail at the
time that the incident in question occurred.

(D) Although judges can disallow leading questions
from the courtroom, it is virtually impossible to
prevent them from being used elsewhere, to the
detriment of many cases.

(E) Stricter regulation should be placed on lawyers
whose leading questions can corrupt witnesses'
testimony by introducing inaccurate data prior to
the witnesses' appearance in the courtroom.

89. It can be reasonably inferred from the passage that which
one of the following, if it were effectively implemented,
would most increase the justice system's ability to
prevent leading questions from causing mistaken court
decisions?

(A) a policy ensuring that witnesses have extra time
to answer questions concerning details that are
tangential to their original experiences of events

(B) thorough revision of the criteria for determining
which kinds of interrogation may be disallowed
in courtroom testimony under the category of
"leading questions"

(C) increased attention to the nuances of all
witnesses' responses to courtroom questions,
even those that are not leading questions

(D) extensive interviewing of witnesses by all lawyers
for both sides of a case prior to those witnesses'
courtroom appearance

(E) availability of accurate transcripts of all
interrogations of witnesses that occurred prior to
those witnesses' appearance in court

90. Which one of the following is mentioned in the passage
as a way in which new data suggested to a witness by a
leading question are sometimes processed?

(A) They are integrated with current memories as
support for those memories.

(B) They are stored tentatively as conjectural data
that fade with time.

(C) They stay more vivid in memory than do
previously stored memory data.

(D) They are reinterpreted so as to be compatible with
the details already stored in memory.

(E) They are retained in memory even when they
conflict with previously stored memory data.

91. In discussing the tangential details of events, the passage contrasts their original significance to witnesses with their possible significance in the courtroom (lines 52–59). That contrast is most closely analogous to which one of the following?

    (A) For purposes of flavor and preservation, salt and vinegar are important additions to cucumbers during the process of pickling, but these purposes could be attained by adding other ingredients instead.

    (B) For the purpose of adding a mild stimulant effect, caffeine is included in some types of carbonated drinks, but for the purposes of appealing to health-conscious consumers, some types of carbonated drinks are advertised as being caffeine-free.

    (C) For purposes of flavor and tenderness, the skins of apples and some other fruits are removed during preparation for drying, but grape skins are an essential part of raisins, and thus grape skins are not removed.

    (D) For purposes of flavor and appearance, wheat germ is not needed in flour and is usually removed during milling, but for purposes of nutrition, the germ is an important part of the grain.

    (E) For purposes of texture and appearance, some fat may be removed from meat when it is ground into sausage, but the removal of fat is also important for purposes of health.

92. Which one of the following questions is most directly answered by information in the passage?

    (A) In witnessing what types of crimes are people especially likely to pay close attention to circumstantial details?

    (B) Which aspects of courtroom interrogation cause witnesses to be especially reluctant to testify in extensive detail?

    (C) Can the stress of having to testify in a courtroom situation affect the accuracy of memory storage and retrieval?

    (D) Do different people tend to possess different capacities for remembering details accurately?

    (E) When is it more likely that a detail of an observed event will be accurately remembered?

93. The second paragraph consists primarily of material that

    (A) corroborates and adds detail to a claim made in the first paragraph

    (B) provides examples illustrating the applications of a theory discussed in the first paragraph

    (C) forms an argument in support of a proposal that is made in the final paragraph

    (D) anticipates and provides grounds for the rejection of a theory alluded to by the author in the final paragraph

    (E) explains how newly obtained data favor one of two traditional theories mentioned elsewhere in the second paragraph

94. It can be most reasonably inferred from the passage that the author holds that the recent studies discussed in the passage

    (A) have produced some unexpected findings regarding the extent of human reliance on external verification of memory details

    (B) shed new light on a long-standing procedural controversy in the law

    (C) may be of theoretical interest despite their tentative nature and inconclusive findings

    (D) provide insights into the origins of several disparate types of logically fallacious reasoning

    (E) should be of more than abstract academic interest to the legal profession

95. Which one of the following can be most reasonably inferred from the information in the passage?

    (A) The tendency of leading questions to cause unreliable courtroom testimony has no correlation with the extent to which witnesses are emotionally affected by the events that they have observed.

    (B) Leading questions asked in the process of a courtroom examination of a witness are more likely to cause inaccurate testimony than are leading questions asked outside the courtroom.

    (C) The memory processes by which newly introduced data tend to reinforce accurately remembered details of events are not relevant to explaining the effects of leading questions.

    (D) The risk of testimony being inaccurate due to certain other factors tends to increase as an eyewitness's susceptibility to giving inaccurate testimony due to the effects of leading questions increases.

    (E) The traditional grounds on which leading questions can be excluded from courtroom interrogation of witnesses have been called into question by the findings of recent studies.

Answers

1.	D	25.	C	49.	D	73.	C
2.	A	26.	D	50.	B	74.	B
3.	B	27.	B	51.	D	75.	C
4.	B	28.	E	52.	C	76.	D
5.	A	29.	A	53.	C	77.	A
6.	C	30.	A	54.	B	78.	E
7.	E	31.	D	55.	D	79.	B
8.	B	32.	A	56.	D	80.	B
9.	C	33.	E	57.	A	81.	B
10.	E	34.	B	58.	B	82.	B
11.	D	35.	B	59.	A	83.	A
12.	A	36.	D	60.	C	84.	C
13.	B	37.	D	61.	B	85.	B
14.	D	38.	C	62.	A	86.	D
15.	A	39.	A	63.	B	87.	C
16.	E	40.	E	64.	C	88.	B
17.	C	41.	C	65.	E	89.	E
18.	D	42.	E	66.	C	90.	A
19.	D	43.	E	67.	D	91.	D
20.	C	44.	D	68.	C	92.	E
21.	B	45.	B	69.	A	93.	A
22.	A	46.	B	70.	A	94.	E
23.	C	47.	A	71.	E	95.	D
24.	B	48.	C	72.	E		

About the Author

David Lynch has been teaching test preparation since 2001. He has scored in the 99th percentile on the LSAT, GMAT, SAT, and GRE, and enjoys turning his abilities into unique and powerful materials that can help others achieve their career goals. He has won several awards for his teaching and has authored all the books in the Examkrackers LSAT series. He currently resides in Philadelphia with his wife.